Young America

Young America
The Flowering of Democracy in New York City

Edward L. Widmer

New York   Oxford
Oxford University Press
1999

Oxford University Press

Oxford   New York

Athens   Auckland   Bangkok   Bogotá   Buenos Aires   Calcutta
Cape Town   Chennai   Dar es Salaam   Delhi   Florence   Hong Kong   Istanbul
Karachi   Kuala Lampur   Madrid   Melbourne   Mexico City   Mumbai
Nairobi   Paris   São Paulo   Singapore   Taipei   Tokyo   Toronto   Warsaw

and associated companies in
Berlin   Ibadan

Copyright © 1999 by Edward L. Widmer

Published by Oxford University Press, Inc.
198 Madison Avenue, New York, New York 10016

Oxford is a registered trademark of Oxford University Press

Library of Congress Cataloging-in-Publication Data

Widmer, Edward L.
Young America : the flowering of democracy in New York City /
Edward L. Widmer.
p.   cm.

Includes bibliographical references and index.
ISBN 0-19-510050-6
1. New York (N.Y.)—Intellectual life. 2. New York (N.Y.)—
Politics and government—to 1898. 3. Democratic review (New York,
N.Y.) 4. United States—Intellectual life—1783–1865. 5. United
States—Politics and government—1815–1861. 6. Youth—United
States—Political activity—History—19th century. 7. American
literature—New York (State)—New York—History and criticism.
8. American literature—19th century—History and criticism.
9. Democracy—United States—History—19th century. I. Title.
F128.44.W58 1998
974.7′104—DC21   97-34744

1 3 5 7 9 8 6 4 2
Printed in the United States of America
on acid-free paper

For Mary

By what perverse magic, I a thousand times think, does such a very autumnal old lady have such a very vernal young soul? When I would remonstrate at times, she spins round on me with, "Oh, don't you grumble, old man (she always calls me old man), it's I, young I, that keep you from stagnating." Well, I suppose it is so. Yea, after all, these things are well ordered.

Melville, "I and My Chimney"

Acknowledgments

A s my long apprenticeship draws to a close, it is a pleasure to declare the intellectual debts I have accumulated. The list of creditors begins with Alan Heimert, whose providential call to the Rhode Island State House launched my effort to become a historian. At his urging, I picked up the trail left by Perry Miller in *The Raven and the Whale* and *The Life of the Mind in America*, an unfinished work that still challenges the reader three decades after it was posthumously published. I hope that I have done justice to their uncompromising high standards.

I cannot express how grateful I am to Leo Marx, who graciously guided me at several moments of Bartlebyesque indecision, though under no obligation to teach a student at a different university. Likewise, Larry Buell always found time to ponder weighty issues like Evert Duyckinck's relationship with William Gilmore Simms, or the intensity with which everyone in this study despised Rufus Wilmot Griswold. When it came time to investigate David Dudley Field, a daunting prospect, I received a great deal of free legal counsel from Morton Horwitz, and I would like to thank Donald Fleming, who first pronounced the name John Louis O'Sullivan to me (I said nothing, wondering why we were discussing a bareknuckle boxer). All these scholars truly went out of their way to improve the thinking expressed in this book.

My financial debts must also be acknowledged. A Mellon Fellowship in the Humanities provided the wherewithal to attend graduate school in the first place. The Committee on the History of American Civilization cheerfully offered summer research money in the early stages. A Mark DeWolfe Howe Fellowship defrayed expenses incurred while researching David Dudley Field. And the Program in History and Literature at Harvard provided an invaluable context for the various texts I was working on between 1987 and 1997. I will always be grateful to the students and teachers I encountered there who provided a real feeling of community, uneasily achieved in this solipsistic profession.

While on the subject of professions, let me make one thing perfectly clear. This book was written well before I left Harvard for the White House, and reflects my own independent views. In fact, its origin dates back to 1989, the year of Beijing and Berlin, when youth and democracy were in the air, and hope renewed its battle against despair. Though the delay was unintended, there is an anniversary logic to the book's appearance in 1998, the sesquicentennial of the revolutions that electrified Young America.

John O'Sullivan, the philosopher of Manifest Destiny, would be delighted to know that his manuscripts have been scattered to the four corners of the North American continent. To the extent I was able to track them down, I depended on the assistance of countless librarians and archivists. I would like to thank the American Antiquarian Society, Boston Athenæum, Columbia County (NY) Historical Society, Historical Society of Pennsylvania, Library of Congress, Maine Historical Society, Massachusetts Historical Society, Metropolitan Museum of Art, Museum of the City of New York, New York Public Library, New-York Historical Society, and the libraries of Brown, Columbia, Duke, Harvard, Princeton, and Yale universities.

Among my own cohort of graduate students, I would like to single out several whose camaraderie made the endless process flow by, if not more quickly, then at least more happily: Robert Allison, Leslie Dunton-Downer, Dirk Killen, David Leviatin, Jessica Marshall, Steve Szaraz, and Sally Wyner. And a large number of people gave advice at various moments: Michael Anesko, Doug Brinkley, Alex Chilton, William Gienapp, Ezra Greenspan, Sheldon Harris, Maybelle Mann, John McGreevy, Michael McLaughlin, Werner Sollors, Richard Slotkin, Alan Trachtenberg, Stephan Thernstrom, and Kevin Van Anglen. More than any scholar, Lou Masur helped me convert a pedantic dissertation into a book. At Oxford, Sheldon Meyer, Thomas LeBien, Susan Ferber, Bob Milks, and many others offered steady guidance. And throughout the experience, Dan Aaron furnished proof that a doctorate in American Civilization means something, and that a thirst for learning is an eternal source of rejuvenation.

Finally, I wish to mention how thankful I am for the unflagging support tendered by my family. If writing about Young America has curiously aged me, I am delighted to find that Old Fogydom brings so much domestic tranquility. I hope my son, Freddy, will someday take pleasure in the fact that this book was gestating during the same period he was. He lets me think there might be hope for Young America after all.

I cannot resist the temptation of closing these remarks with Herman Melville's introduction to the chapter on "Young America in Literature" in *Pierre*:

> Among the various conflicting modes of writing history, there would seem to be two grand practical distinctions, under which all the rest must subordinately range. By the one mode, all contemporaneous circumstances, facts, and events must be set down contemporaneously; by the other, they are only to be set down as the general stream of the narrative shall dictate; for matters which are kindred in time, may be very irrelative in themselves. I elect neither of these, I am careless of either; both are well enough in their way; I write precisely as I please.

With none of Melville's daring nonconformity, but all of his disorganization, I have often suffered a similar confusion, if only because I could not bear to leave out any of the findings I laboriously excavated. I would like to claim the book's expansiveness is justified by an internal Manifest Destiny, but to do so would betray a helpless dependence on the rhetoric of Young America, and require yet another scholarly digression. To conclude immediately is the best way to display the respect I have come to feel for wise territorial limits.

Contents

Young America

Prologue

History Rewritten

All history has to be re-written; political science and the whole scope of all moral truth have to be considered and illustrated in the light of the democratic principle. All old subjects of thought and all new questions arising, connected more or less directly with human existence, have to be taken up again and re-examined.

—John O'Sullivan, October 1837

This modest editorial statement appeared in the first issue of the *Democratic Review*, the most ambitious magazine of antebellum America. And like most renunciations of the past, the rhetorical blast issued by John O'Sullivan fit snugly in a long continuum. Remembering the Declaration of Independence, and anticipating Manifest Destiny (which he would name in 1845), the young editor was intensely aware of history as he denied the influence of previous generations. This was only one of countless contradictions in the career of one of America's great rhetoricians, a career riddled with brilliant triumphs, stunning naïveté, and bitter frustration. Yet for all the melodrama surrounding him and the Young America movement he helped launch, his meandering life offers penetrating insight into the complexity of American nationalism. Despite countless inconsistencies, O'Sullivan succeeded better than most at purveying a flexible mode of thinking that could explain the United States to its people after the long hangover of the Revolution, through the many aftershocks of the Jacksonian era, and into the bumptious 1850s. In more than a few ways, Americans remain intellectually indebted to this shrill voice they know only as a footnote, if at all.

Youth and newness were the mantras of American rhetoric in 1837, a year of intense interest in rejuvenating American culture. Most famously, Emerson commanded the American Scholar to shun the courtly muses of Europe in his oration before the Phi Beta Kappa Society of Harvard College. Working his collegiate audience, he called for books relevant to a new generation of Americans: "Each age, it is found, must write its own books. Or rather, each generation for the next succeeding. The books of an older period will not fit this."[1]

3

But Emerson was far from alone in emphasizing the saving grace of youthfulness. That same year, as Martin Van Buren assumed the presidency from the venerable Andrew Jackson, he boasted, "I belong to a later age." At fifty-five, Van Buren was no spring chicken, but he could honestly claim to be the first president born after the Revolution, still the defining event of the republic. Throughout the United States, public speakers followed his example and invoked the newness of the "spirit of the times," a trite phrase that conjured the nineteenth century's explosive pace, with its railroads, newspapers, and the ubiquity of young Americans aggressively seeking to "get ahead." Eight years later, as James Polk was inaugurated, he drew notice to the fact he was "so much younger" than "the more aged and experienced men" who preceded him.[2]

Much of this was pure bombast, of course. Youth had always provided a convenient store of oratorical metaphors, as it would long after 1837, in the United States and every other nation. Most famously, John F. Kennedy thrilled Americans in 1961 by proclaiming the torch had been passed to "a new generation of Americans, born in this century." Indeed, Kennedy used the word *generation* four times during his short address, a record that was tied by Bill Clinton in his 1993 inaugural. Kennedy triumphantly concluded, "I do not believe that any of us would exchange places with any other people or any other generation."[3]

Many young Americans felt likewise in the 1830s and 1840s, in what we might call the post-Jacksonian period, for lack of a better term (antebellum has always seemed monolithic to me, as if the Civil War was the only event of the period). Across the country, there was the sense of a new generation rising to take the helm from the aging political leadership. One reason was simply demographic—there were a great number of young people in the United States. According to the 1840 census, the median age of Americans was 17.8, and over 12 million of the country's 17 million people were under 30 (about 73 percent). Yet the country's leadership, divided among the triumvirate of Webster, Clay, and Calhoun, had dominated politics for decades, with no sign of relinquishing power.[4]

A few months after Emerson's American Scholar address, a young politician at the nation's periphery expressed the conflicting feelings of this rising generation. In his first major address, Abraham Lincoln wondered aloud how his cohort could replace the irreplaceable founding fathers, "the generation just gone to rest." But he also hinted ominously that young Americans were tired of waiting for their opportunity. For all his filiopiety, Lincoln remarked a temptation to destroy the edifice the fathers had erected, if only to do something new ("nothing left to be done in the way of building up, he would set boldly to the task of pulling down"). Others with less rigid self-control were venting their spleen at the same moment, for various reasons. In November 1837, John Brown stood in the back of a prayer meeting in Hudson, Ohio, and suddenly consecrated his life to the destruction of slavery, by any means necessary.[5]

There were immediate reasons for youthful rhetoric and high drama in 1837. Throughout the spring, just as Martin Van Buren inherited the presidency, a terrible panic gripped the American economy. The price of cotton fell precipitously in the South, while banks suspended specie payments and unemployment climbed in northern cities. The panic severely shook public confidence and galvanized Americans to take sides, defining themselves both politically and in a generational sense. Whigs and Democrats bitterly blamed each other for the disaster. But for many young Americans, the Panic of 1837 exposed the bankruptcy of *all* American politics, and an older generation conducting its affairs selfishly.

Did this cynicism lead them to turn away from politics? Anything but. As the last survivors of the American Revolution died off, the new generation asked, with painful curiosity, what had happened to America's revolutionary heritage. To many, the United States now appeared a crassly commercial nation with no interest in toppling tyranny or righting wrongs around the world. Jackson had warned of "the money power" in his farewell address, and in the aftermath of the Panic, his warning seemed all too prophetic. Especially in northern pockets of urban radicalism, hard hit by the panic, many young Americans felt a new revolution was needed to slay the Anglo-American financial establishment, fantastically described with epithets like "monster" and "Babylonish dragon." The liveliness of the 1840 election has been attributed to electioneering arts, but it was also related to a keen sense that the future of the republic was being decided with more urgency than usual.[6]

Part of the reason for this new generation's dawning consciousness of itself lay in its awareness of similar developments abroad. In Europe, students and young radicals were enlisting in political organizations like Mazzini's Young Italy, which originated in the early 1830s and flowered into Young Europe. In 1837 the young Karl Marx, newly infatuated with the Young Hegelians, wrote his father a momentous letter, mirroring some of Emerson's words, including the call for "a great new poem." "There are moments in life which mark the close of a period like boundary posts and at the same time definitely point in a new direction," Marx wrote with the flourish of epiphany. Throughout Europe, young intellectuals and agitators sensed an exciting struggle ahead, one that would liberate the Old World from its antiquated ways of thinking. Some of these winds blew across the Atlantic, adding to the excitement of the moment and heightening the feeling that the New World would be called on to play an important role in the impending drama. Across the United States, young Americans wondered if there would be a Young America, or if one was necessary in a country that was supposedly young and democratic by definition.[7]

As the European struggles implied, the generational battle lines being drawn in 1837 revealed a strong political shading. In the United States, the least despotic nation on earth, it was not always easy to find reactionary targets for invective. And it was unlikely any would-be Mazzinis would be jailed for their activity. But there was still a palpable political tension in the air, and inevitably the rising generation entered into the partisan debate between the two leading political organizations of the day, the Whigs and the Democrats, who blamed each other for the 1837 crisis and every other problem. Despite reservations about both parties, young Americans had to choose where they stood between two clear options.

For decades, historians have argued various counterintuitive positions concerning Whigs and Democrats: that they resembled each other more than they differed, or that they acted differently at the local level than one might expect from their national platforms. But the fact remains that they presented very different ideological positions to the voters at large. The Whigs, including young Lincoln, stood for careful and prudent management of financial affairs, self-restraint, and moderation in all things. In other words, a polite Christian society governed by consensual rules, "systems" like Henry Clay's plan for a regulated American economy, and managed from above by those best qualified to do so, older leaders with long experience. They were appalled by Jackson's interference with the smooth-running American economy, and his hostile attack on Nicholas Biddle's Bank of the United States. In an address to Princeton in 1835, Biddle warned of rabble-rousing politicians who deliberately incite crowds with appeals to "the people," a term he found vague and meaningless in the hands of demagogues.[8]

Many Democrats, on the other hand, retained a lively interest in the radical message of the Revolution, and a furious contempt for the selfish business leaders whom they thought had precipitated the crisis. In northern cities and other nodes of class friction, they felt Jackson had not gone far enough to smite "the money power." True, Jacksonian Democracy could be a front for aggressive new entrepreneurs, or simple nostalgia for Jefferson's agrarian yeomanry, but its leveling energies propelled important new reforms designed to check the concentration of capital, including enlarged suffrage (as in the Dorr Rebellion of 1842), reduced special privilege, and better conditions for urban laborers. From all different backgrounds, especially after 1837, Democrats called for resistance to the chicanery of Wall Street. Predictably, Whig ideologues demonized Democrats as fanatics who ran through the land screaming "DOWN WITH THE BANKS! DOWN WITH MANUFACTORIES! DOWN WITH CORPORATIONS! DOWN WITH CAPITALISTS!"[9] The battle lines were drawn.

It is not difficult to guess how the most restless young Americans sided in this partisan debate, particularly in the urbanizing North. The more restless they were, the more likely they were to throw their lot in with the Democracy, as the Democratic party was generally known. Walt Whitman, for example, insisted that democracy and capital were at war, and that America's financial interests "were as great an incubus on its young energies, as impure air is to growing youth." He and others like him cloaked themselves under the Democratic mantle as they chased dreams from the "liberation" of Europe to the elimination of class tensions at home. Overwhelmingly, the young Americans in search of Young America found the Democracy far more exciting than the dull, complacent paragons of model citizenship populating Whiggery.[10]

How could it be otherwise? For all its flaws, the Democratic party offered a more inclusive, fraternal social vision, less obsessed with individual profit, and more truly "revolutionary," to use the charged, contradictory word that thrilled the rising generation. Looking backward and forward at the same time, young Democrats peered through history to Jefferson and Paine, and also projected themselves into the future as role models for the rest of humanity. Many admired the French Revolution (hardly a popular sentiment in Whig circles), and distrusted England as the aristocratic enemy. All expressed Talmudic reverence for the Declaration of Independence, the living document that marked "the new order of things," "the dividing point in the history of mankind," "the moment of the political regeneration of the world." Though devoted in their way, few Whigs invested Jefferson's equalizing screed with this much cosmic significance. The Constitution, with its serene sense of order—*that* was the wellspring of happiness, according to Webster, Clay, and their minions.[11]

One of the young Democrats reflecting on America's revolutionary past in 1837 was Nathaniel Hawthorne, still living in Salem, although not quite so young anymore at thirty-two. He was at a watershed moment in his life, having just published his first book, *Twice-Told Tales*, on March 6. The last of these tales, "Dr. Heidegger's Experiment," meditated on age and youth, complaining, "the same ideas and phrases have been in vogue these fifty years," and expressing Americans' longing to feel "like new-created beings, in a new-created universe."[12] Insecure about his literary prospects, Hawthorne was angling for a government job through his many Democratic connections.

In April, just after the Panic, he received a letter from two young editors, John O'Sullivan and Samuel Langtree, who were starting a magazine that would address the rising Democratic generation. Unlike most intellectual journals, this one was based in Washington and emanated an electric political excitement. The *United States Magazine and Democratic Review*, the editors boasted, "will have a vast circulation through the Union," and "will afford to Mr. Hawthorne what he has not had before, a field for the exercise of his pen, and the acquisition of distinction."[13] By coincidence, the letter was dated April 19, the day the American Revolution began in 1775. Although Hawthorne knew little of the editors, he instantly answered the call of the infant magazine. A story of his appeared in the first issue, released in October 1837, which also contained John O'Sullivan's manifesto about the need to rewrite all history. The *Review* was thereafter his favorite place of publication until O'Sullivan departed in 1846.

One could crassly assume Hawthorne was responding to the letter's hint of liberal compensation. But everything in Hawthorne's background suggests a sincere desire to join the cause (the magazine's compensation was nowhere near as liberal as its politics). Despite his habitual reserve and Salem's reputation as a Whig stronghold, Hawthorne's embrace of the *Democratic Review* was carefully considered. Since his youth, he had declared himself a Democrat, and one of the more remarkable stories of his early life is the anecdote recounted by his sister Elizabeth about Andrew Jackson's visit to unfriendly Salem in 1833: "When General Jackson, of whom he professed himself a partisan, visited Salem in 1833, he walked out to the boundary of the town to meet him, not to speak to him—but only to look at him, and found only a few men and boys collected, not enough, without the assistance that he rendered, to welcome the General with a good cheer." As if she herself were amazed by this story, Elizabeth Hawthorne added, "It is hard to fancy him doing such a thing as shouting."[14]

To a degree that has never been sufficiently explored, many other young writers felt exactly the same way. Walt Whitman intercepted Jackson in Brooklyn during the same tour and never forgot the excitement of seeing the "Hero and Sage" in his "big-brimmed white beaver hat," passing through the multitudes that revered him as a savior:

> One sweet fragrant summer morning, when the sun shone brightly, he rode up from the ferry in an open barouche. His weather-beaten face is before us at this moment, as though the scene happened but yesterday—with his snow white hair brushed stiffly up from his forehead, and his piercing eyes quite glancing through his spectacles—as those rapid eyes swept the crowds on each side of the street.[15]

Up the Hudson in Albany, Herman Melville and his brother Gansevoort felt many of the same stirrings. The brothers defied their family's enmity toward Jackson to become ardent young Democrats, and most of Herman's juvenilia was written in the *Democratic Press and Lansingburgh Advertiser*. Gansevoort, ruined by the 1837 Panic, later enjoyed mercurial success as a Democratic orator, baptizing James Polk as "Young Hickory" in the stormy 1844 campaign. Herman denounced "joint-stock companies" as "detestable" in *Moby-Dick*, and spoke from experience when he cited the whale fishery as an asylum for "many romantic, melancholy, and absent-minded young men, disgusted with the carking cares of earth." He immortalized Jackson in one of the book's most frequently quoted passages: "Bear me out in it, thou great democratic God! . . . Thou who didst pick up Andrew Jackson from the pebbles; who didst hurl him upon a war-horse; who didst thunder him higher than a throne!"[16]

There was something powerful in Jackson's irascible persona, and his crotchety contempt for bankers and speculators, that spoke eloquently to the unformed intellects of this rising, vaguely dissatisfied generation. Despite his age, he appealed to this audience because he too hated the intervening generation that had perverted America into what seemed more like a business concern than the light of the world. To resort to family clichés, he struck young Americans as a feisty grandparent, far more interesting than the dull parental types surrounding them. When he finally departed the American scene in 1845, a eulogist wrote, "The spirit of an age sometimes descends to future generations in the form of a man."[17]

Paradoxically, this ancient political warrior, a living embodiment of the democratic principle, struck young Americans as a vivid role model. His war on the Bank allowed them to feel some of the revolutionary fervor missing from their lives, and confirmed their belief that the Revolution remained unconsummated in many aspects. So as the aged president was leaving office in 1837, his reputation was anything but diminished among them, and many were more committed than ever to the Democracy and the war against dandified mediocrity. These post-Jacksonian thinkers would become the backbone of the *Democratic Review*.

As Whitman's account indicates, the cult of Jackson was exceptionally healthy in New York City in 1837, where John O'Sullivan grew up and where the most restless of all young Americans were located. The Democrats found a particular foothold among these precocious partisans, wooing the working-class b'hoy culture along with collegians who believed fervently in the American Revolution and longed for an epochal event to define their generation. Jackson excited juvenile New Yorkers across the class spectrum, although credit must also be given to a charismatic journalist whose name has almost vanished from the history books, save for a cameo appearance in Gore Vidal's *Burr*.

William Leggett, more than any other person, heated the cauldron of New York's "Young Democracy" in the 1830s. With his fiery editorials and caustic invective, he challenged his readers to reenact the excitement of the Revolution and to oppose the power elites of Wall Street and Whiggery. His contempt for the old guard included the entrenched Democrats of Tammany Hall, and he precipitated a serious party crisis in October 1835. Inspired by Leggett's writings in the *New York Evening Post*, thousands of young New Yorkers bolted the party to form their own "ultra-Democratic" party (Bryant's phrase), grudgingly reentering the fold in 1837. They were jocosely called "Locofocos" (after a type of match used to illuminate their first meeting in October 1835, when older party leaders tried to turn out the lights on them). They derided their opponents as "the old hunkers of Tammany Hall, who go up the back stairs."[18]

Leggett's private war had an intellectual dimension as well as a political one. He prided himself on his literary attainments (he wrote several volumes of poetry and tales), and served as a role model for aspiring authors intimidated by the elitist book world of genteel Manhattan. Specifically, he showed the press could distribute ideas to an enormous audience of sympathizers. In 1837 Leggett observed, "The power of the newspaper press in this country, and more particularly of the diurnal press, is prodigious." In the right hands, journalism offered the "glorious opportunity" of "effectually advancing the great interests of mankind." Newspapers were naturally democratic, found "in the mansions of the rich, and the hovels of the indigent." After technical advances in the mid-1830s, cheap papers spread news, entertainment, and claptrap to an insatiable readership. From the Battery to its rapidly expanding northern precincts, the omnivorous city craved information.

It followed that this widespread distribution brought power. The week Van Buren was inaugurated, Leggett argued that journalism could introduce cultural revolution, giving new ideas to people who had not dared to think before: "It communicates knowledge to those who had no means of acquiring it. It calls into exercise minds that before rusted unused." Likewise, the person who could reach these people might evolve into a democratic oracle: "He becomes the *thinker*, in fact, for a vast number of his fellow-beings. His mind tranfuses itself through many bodies. His station renders him, not an individual, but a host; not one, but legion." Leggett concluded emotionally, "Is this a vocation without dignity?"[19]

Leggett's career had an electrifying effect on young New Yorkers. With his acerbic wit and fearless willingness to take on powerful interests, Leggett radiated romantic heroism. His image as a democratic martyr gained luster with his early death in 1839 and the suspicion he had suffered from shabby treatment at the hands of political enemies. Journalism suddenly seemed glamorous, especially if it gave vent to these reform impulses. In a moving eulogy of Leggett, his friend and partner William Cullen Bryant stressed over and over again his appeal to the rising generation: "His most ardent admirers—his peculiar *party*, we may say—were chiefly found among *the young men* of his native city; because it was chiefly to the unsophisticated and uncorrupted mind of generous youth, that his mind addressed itself." According to Bryant, Leggett embodied a "noble impatience" with "the palsying conventionalism" seen everywhere in the 1830s, and his enemies were "the timid, who dread innovation because they cannot foresee all of its consequences, and the friends of whatever is established, who dread innovation because it disturbs their customary ideas." Appropriately, Bryant remarked, a monument to Leggett was being built by the Young Men's Committee of Tammany Hall.[20]

A more important monument might be observed in Leggett's lasting effect on the writers and journalists he inspired. His words resonated deeply with Whitman, who never forgot "the glorious Leggett," and remembered him to the end of his days, speaking of him often to Horace Traubel. Melville likely borrowed a few motifs from Leggett's nautical tales, and O'Sullivan obviously considered him a role model. The *Review* planned to lean on his services from the very beginning, before fate intervened. O'Sullivan felt a "profound impression" at Leggett's early death and eulogized him as "the most ardent, the most unflinching, the most able, and the most successful" political journalist of his day. One of O'Sullivan's friends, Theodore Sedgwick, lovingly edited Leggett's far-flung editorials into a two-volume collection, still the best source a century and a half later. Another, David Dudley Field, reviewed this collection and discovered his mission to reform American law, to "speak to the American people a language they will all understand," offering "new motives, new hopes" in place of "old opinions."[21]

Whitman, O'Sullivan, and Field were not the only young New York Democrats inspired by Leggett and Jackson. In 1836 a group of school friends, eager to become involved in the quest for American literature, formed a group called the Tetractys, all of whose members became journalists and editors. Their leader was a bookish sort named Evert Duyckinck whose family had been publishers and painters for generations. Filled with enthusiasm about the future, this group of friends composed "The Song of the Tetractys," with the diptych: "Shall we not weep when joyous Youth is dying—And broken hopes around us wither'd lying?" Nine years later, with considerably more eloquence, the Tetractys rebaptized themselves Young America, insisting "we form a new generation, for good or evil." Like Hawthorne and Whitman, they too would work for O'Sullivan and the *Democratic Review*.[22]

If youth and democracy were in the air in 1837, there were plenty of other reasons beside Jackson and Leggett. Many ambitious intellects were frustrated by the stranglehold that Whigs seemed to have on American culture, such as it was. The vast majority of libraries, publishers, magazines, and art collections were concentrated in the hands of wealthy Americans who disapproved of Jackson, particularly his war against Biddle and the bank. The two cities dominating the cultural landscape, Boston and Philadelphia (both claiming to be "The Athens of America"), were centers of anti-Democratic feeling and took pride in their exclusionary culture. When Andrew Jackson was granted an honorary degree by Harvard on the same northern tour that inspired Hawthorne and Whitman, the leading citizens of Boston were outraged. John Quincy Adams was apoplectic, refusing to witness his alma mater's "disgrace in conferring her highest literary honors upon a barbarian who could not write a sentence of grammar and hardly could spell his own name."[23]

Adams's pride in his alma mater revealed part of the problem, as thinkers like O'Sullivan saw it. Not only did New England dominate national definitions of culture, but Boston and Harvard in particular did so. These places were hardly on the cutting edge of social and intellectual change. Even the younger New England intellects had trouble slaking off the long tradition of regional filiopiety. Rufus Choate, in an 1833 speech that likely inspired Hawthorne, called for a great literature based on Puritan history, assuming "the grand destinies of New England and North America" were one and the same. And Alexander Everett, one of the most open-minded New Englanders (and friendly with O'Sullivan), told students to maintain "the correct and elevated moral tone" in their literary aspirations, to avoid the "licentiousness" linked to French Revolution, and to always be faithful "to the principles and examples of our fathers." This speech, delivered to "the present generation," was given at Brown University on September 4, 1837, almost the exact moment Emerson and O'Sullivan were promoting their more radical notions of change to America's youth.[24]

To demand a new, more exciting, more inclusive culture was almost by definition a Democratic statement, since it was so often a response to the restrictive standards embodied by Adams, Choate, Everett, and their ilk. It was a protest against New England, and by extension, England, reenacting all the sweet memories of the Revolution. And to an extent, it was an ethnic protest, striving to replace New England's emphasis on Anglo-Saxon and Puritan traditions with a more universal belief in the openness and variety of the American experience.

The new American culture naturally emanated from New York City, already undergoing a stunning metamorphosis. All American cities were growing quickly in the 1830s, but New York was truly different, outstripping all rivals in size and complexity. As it became the great emporium of American commerce, it inevitably emerged as the nation's cultural marketplace as well, attracting a swarm of intellectuals sympathetic to the Democratic party. Jackson's war on the United States Bank in Philadelphia had removed some of the luster from that city's reputation, with New York the immediate beneficiary of the struggle. Martin Van Buren's presidency (1837-1841) brought further spoils to the Empire State. As New York swelled in size and wealth, it exerted a powerful attraction on cultural entrepreneurs like O'Sullivan, who would divert its financial might into the creation of a national art and literature. Artists and writers, and notably, the brokers representing them to the public at large, all flocked to Manhattan to exploit the new mass market for American ideas.

As this transformation was happening, it was abetted by an explosion of journalistic activity. As Leggett had predicted, newspapers were springing up across the landscape. By 1850 New York City alone had 104 publications with an annual circulation of 78,747,600. And the scope of journalism was expanding, bringing ideas about politics and culture into the same discourse, and dominated by brash editors who felt qualified to descant on both. With its exponential population growth, Manhattan struck young Jacksonians as the perfect laboratory to witness the democratic unraveling of history. In an 1846 editorial for the *Brooklyn Eagle*, Whitman celebrated the cultural "revolution" (his term) before it even took place, knowing it had to happen in Manhattan.

> In New York, also, are gathered together a number of men—literary persons and others—who have a strong desire to favor any thing which shall extricate us from the entangled and by no means creditable position we already hold of playing second fiddle to Europe. These persons, most of them young men, enthusiastic, democratic, and liberal in their feelings—are daily acquiring a greater and greater power.[25]

The same word was used by Evert Duyckinck's friend Cornelius Mathews, an ambitious novelist who remarked, "as in all great revolutions, this, the era of broadcast publication, has also been an era of unbounded confusion and uncertainty."

But if this was a "revolution" that in some sense pitted young Democrats against old Whigs, it also reflected simple geography. Closer than Bostonians to the national government and the leaders of the Democracy, New York thinkers were sensitive to the fragility of the national coalition and the need to accommodate the South and West. Appropriately, the national culture they sought to promote was more panoramic than the single-minded vision of New England writ large. As they fantasized about the country's future, New York's Young Americans intuitively comprehended the farthest reaches of American territory (including regions not yet admitted to the Union). Grandiose, ebullient, and ultimately unmappable, these Young American dreams were literally all-encompassing.[26]

I am not arguing every important new intellect of the 1830s and 1840s was an adolescent Locofoco hailing from New York. But to a degree I think unappreciated, a creative movement occurred that partook strongly of these elements. The founding of the *Democratic Review* in 1837 was the first blow in a cultural argument that raged throughout the antebellum era and still flickers quietly today. To state it baldly, it involved taking control of American culture from Boston, from the Whigs, and from old conservatives everywhere. At the heart of this regional, political, and generational argument were basic ideas we now take for granted; namely, that a creative artist does not have to be educated or wealthy to be taken seriously as an intellectual; that a raw teenager can say something as interesting as an older person; and that a successful work ought to speak clearly to the mass of the American people, not just to intellectuals.

It may seem odd to give partial credit for these exciting ideas to the antebellum Democratic party. As historians have argued, it was a retrograde organization in many ways, defending slavery and Jefferson's outmoded concept of an agrarian nation. It is difficult, if not impossible, to think of curmudgeonly politicians like William Marcy or Lewis Cass leading a youth rebellion (in fact, Young America detested these career politicians). But paradoxically, the revolutionary nostalgia felt by many Democrats also contained an intensely futuristic vision of America. Despite its many limitations, the party of Jackson struck a chord with the rising young generation.

Party bosses were not oblivious to this phenomenon, especially in the North. At some point in 1836, the smartest boss of them all, Martin Van Buren, approved secret funding for John O'Sullivan's *Democratic Review*. Van Buren shrewdly reasoned that O'Sullivan would be his spokesman to the new generation. Diverting some of the monies available to him as the incoming president, he agreed to support a new magazine that would appeal to this audience and give the Democrats a voice in the cultural world they had been excluded from. It was a brilliant maneuver, and in 1844 O'Sullivan would receive credit for winning the New York vote, and consequently the entire election, for James Polk.

In other words, a major political party, usually suspected by modern historians of reactionary tendencies and a fear of change, actively supported a magazine that introduced the freshest writing in America, and the newest ideas available in every intellectual discipline. At first glance, these developments are more suggestive of the twentieth century than the nineteenth: A canny politician perceives a demographic trend and uses the media to exploit it, which it does with feisty writing and catchy slogans emphasizing novelty. Is there so vast a gulf between Van Buren's use of O'Sullivan and Bill Clinton's use of MTV in 1992, fielding questions about rock and roll from an audience of teenyboppers?

Yet the *Democratic Review* was no insipid *Tiger Beat* of the 1840s. Far more than the Van Buren administration, it was a resounding success. From 1837 to 1846, O'Sullivan cobbled together a first-rate magazine that was unique in American history, combining political journalism with pathbreaking new fiction. The *Review* published important articles on public policy, including the first editorial to invoke the phrase "Manifest Destiny," and addressed all aspects of American cultural achievement. In particular, it fostered native literature, with the bulk of Hawthorne's stories from 1837 to 1846 (when O'Sullivan left the magazine) and Whitman's earliest major publications. Far from being unknown when he wrote *Leaves of Grass*, Whitman first received national attention when he began writing tales for the magazine in 1842. Indirectly, the *Review* also sponsored the arrival of a writer it announced as "Sherman Melville," the brother of a rising star of the Democracy, whose speeches electrified the new generation.

And relentlessly, incessantly, the *Review* called attention to the newness and youthfulness of its message. With characteristic immodesty, O'Sullivan asserted in his first editorial that "all old subjects of thought" had to be reconsidered by the new generation. The *Review*'s young editors and writers were clever in their hyperactive approach to journalism, setting a new standard of magazine excellence in a quickly evolving market. With its populistic style, its sprightly wit, its unending search for novelty and originality, and even its inane bombast, O'Sullivan's *Review* remains lively reading a century and a half later. More than any other magazine, it signaled the advent of periodical journalism as an important means of communication to the entire nation, rather than to specific readerships. It was freely cited on the floors of Congress by representatives of both parties.[27]

John Louis O'Sullivan personified his generation's hopes and anxieties. He was twenty-three as he launched his new magazine, and it is interesting to contrast his situation with Emerson's in 1837. While their visions of American culture struck some of the same chords, there were important differences. Emerson's address, far more famous, was a dramatic oration with highly original phrasings, but little in the way of an orchestrated approach to the problem of American cultural vacuity. O'Sullivan's cry for a new democratic culture, on the other hand, was truly a call to action, with his magazine the focal point. Unlike Emerson, he had a program that he pursued with whirlwind energy. As the sage of Concord was lecturing on "The American Scholar," O'Sullivan was already in the field, planning his attack on the old forms of thought he saw everywhere arrayed against him. Within months, he would be denouncing his elders with a ferocity that would shock Emerson (ten years older).

Politics also drove a wedge between the two visionaries. While Emerson hoped to inspire self-reliant individuals, O'Sullivan was inviting allies like Hawthorne to join an intellectual crusade with palpable political undertones, one in which the people and their thinkers would be linked together by membership in the same party organization. And of course, Emerson did not possess (nor would he have wanted) the imprimatur of the newly elected president of the United States. If

O'Sullivan could rejuvenate America, it would be through the agency of the Democratic party.

Despite Van Buren's ouster after one term, the young Democrats behind O'Sullivan gained momentum in the 1840s. The *Democratic Review* moved to New York in 1841, where O'Sullivan was joined by a number of like-minded young intellects, including Evert Duyckinck and his Tetractys. Eventually these writers would appropriate the sobriquet "Young America" for themselves, spontaneously claiming the long-awaited term in a burst of patriotism in 1845, a year that renewed Democratic self-confidence for many reasons, including O'Sullivan's ill-fated discovery of "Manifest Destiny." In that year, with Polk newly installed in the White House, there seemed no limits to what a young Democrat could accomplish. O'Sullivan was everywhere, visiting the White House frequently, urging expansion; Duyckinck launched the first publishing series devoted to American literature; other friends were turning the worlds of art and law on their heads, all in the name of democracy. History was indeed being rewritten, as O'Sullivan had predicted in 1837. Young Americanism was a force to be reckoned with, a refreshing blast of fresh air in a stultified world of dull Anglophilia. But like most exciting intellectual movements, it also had a dark side, one that would manifest itself as increasingly unsavory things were done in America's name during the late 1840s and 1850s.

It was tempting to end this study in 1845, with Young Americanism hale and hearty. But that would fail to address one of the most provocative aspects of the story, the metamorphosis of an innocent youth movement into a call for more territory, unleashing tensions over slavery and exposing democracy to ridicule. Clearly, "Young America" was complicated. For a variety of reasons, historians have had a hard time with it. I will clarify the term, never defined very well to begin with. Was it an intellectual circle, a political action committee, or an ambient *Weltanschauung?* Depending on one's perspective, it was all three. Among other problems, it was claimed by several different interest groups with competing agendas. Even the Young Americans themselves were a little fuzzy on the subject. Given O'Sullivan's close association with Young America, it is comical to note that his newspaper, the *New York Morning News*, tried to nip it in the bud after an oration by the writer Cornelius Mathews gave the term wide currency in 1845:

> The term Young America, if introduced, would soon get to be annoying. It would be adopted as a cover for every loose suggestion in religion, politics and literature; a whole army of pretenders would echo it; there would be a hundred disputes as to which was the genuine Young America; there would be a vast increase of noise and a proportionate absence of any genuine work.[28]

Despite this prescient admonition, "Young America" has been abused ever since in exactly the pattern outlined. For my purposes, it applied to two very different groups, albeit with some rhetorical similarities, thanks to O'Sullivan's link to both. The first claimant to the Young American mantle, as I hinted, was the clique of "Tetractys" gathered around Evert Duyckinck, the *Democratic Review*'s literary editor. They were not exactly radicals, but they strongly believed their generation deserved expression in the republic of letters, and they praised "democratic" authors like Paine and Leggett, anathema to the Whig cultural elite. Far more intellectual than political, their activity peaked in the 1840s, although they continued well into the next decade, by which point they had slaked off the Young America label.

As Duyckinck divested himself of the term, a new version of Young America emerged, more political than intellectual, and more juvenile than its predecessor. This group, whom I call Young America II, was chiefly composed of southern and western expansionists, but still worked through the *Democratic Review* in New York, which was now in different hands (although O'Sullivan was nominally attached). It entered the public eye in 1852 with blustery support for Cuban annexation and military intervention against European monarchies. Anyone opposed to these continental infatuations was ridiculed as an incontinent "old fogy." It is true that O'Sullivan adhered to both versions of Young America and that the *Review* was always central to their shifting programs, but that does not imply, as many scholars have assumed, that they were one and the same.[29]

In fact, they were quite different. While all Young Americans cheered the 1848 revolutions in Europe, they divided neatly over the Mexican War, the Wilmot Proviso, and the ultimate test of democracy, slavery. Duyckinck and his literati denounced bondage, but the more "political" Young Americans shouted down any restrictions on expansion whatsoever. This subtle disagreement displayed in microcosm an important tectonic shift in the American intellectual universe, and one with gloomy forebodings, for if exuberant ultranationalists could not agree about America's future, then how could the more fractious regional spokesmen?

It did not bode well for democracy that its most energetic defenders distrusted one another. If Young America I strove for the flowering of democracy, promoting culture and ideas, Young America II stood for its deflowering, misleading people through empty promises and slogans designed to steal land and treat human beings like chattel. Young America's failure to find consensus, even within its own ranks, revealed the fragility of the underpinnings Manifest Destiny rested upon. Its rhetoric was far more robust than its reality.

But if Young America was bifurcated and confused, few scholars have realized it, deceived perhaps by the windstorm of confidence and bravado these professional ideologues generated. For generations, literary and political historians have been oblivious to the distinctions separating Young America's incarnations, and as a result, have frequently confused their agendas. Beginning with an essay Merle Curti wrote in 1926, most historians have identified "Young America" only as the wild-eyed expansionists of the 1850s (Young America II). Literary scholars, generally following Perry Miller's lead in his 1956 study, *The Raven and the Whale*, have focused instead on the more intellectual Duyckinck clique of the 1840s (Young America I). Further, they have almost unanimously oversimplified Duyckinck's participation in the political arena. Some have cited him as an effete snob who nearly ruined his disciple Melville with his prudery, others as a raving locofoco hell-bent on world revolution. The real answer was more complicated.[30]

In this book, I hope to harmonize the historical and literary perspectives on Young America to provide a fuller apprehension of the group's significance and its metamorphosis over time. I would also like to expand the conventional definition of Young America to reflect the deep interest the young New York Democrats felt in art and law, both of which were amply treated in the *Democratic Review.* The Young Americans of both major phases articulated clear philosophies about American culture, and I will discuss many of the ancillary projects they pursued between roughly 1837 and 1855. The latter date struck me as a logical terminus, not only for Whitman's *Leaves of Grass* (in some ways the result of Young American posturing), but for Evert and George Duyckinck's *Cyclopædia of American Literature,* the summary of American literary achievement to that date. It was also the year Melville, tired of all the excitement about youth and revolution, wrote, "Old myself, I take to oldness in things."[31]

Despite the divergences between various Young Americans, their collective story is not only interesting, but important, and helps us to understand the manic psychology of the antebellum period, with its strange combination of progress and retrenchment. For almost twenty years, O'Sullivan and his friends clung to the youthful rhetoric of 1837, and insisted to the point of being tiresome that a new generation was about to take control of American politics and culture. This belief was nearly confirmed at several moments of acute excitement. After the 1837 agitation, another nationalist hiccup occurred in 1845, followed by the explosive paroxysms of 1848.

In that year, the *annus mirabilis* of world liberalism, Young Americans were in a lather of excitement, convinced the European revolutions and the American triumph over Mexico signaled a cosmic shift that marked their ascension to power. With a mystical faith, these secular thinkers awaited some kind of divine vindication of the American political experiment. Whitman expected a "holy millennium of liberty"; Melville hinted "the political Messiah had come." More than just an exercise in geopolitical wanderlust, "Manifest Destiny" expressed the social and intellectual aspirations of a generation who felt poised at the threshold of a new historical era. For a fleeting moment, they dared to think it the culmination of world republicanism. The American Revolution would happen all over again, on a global scale this time. But then, unexpectedly, everything collapsed. The revolutions petered out, the Democracy split over Free Soil, a fat old Whig was elected president, and on the surface, almost nothing changed at all.

Yet deep down, at some subterranean level of the Young American psyche, something inscrutable did happen, and it was not pleasant. Between 1848 and 1851, the ultranationalists of Young America I underwent a crisis of faith and emerged with a chastened sense of America's destiny. Contrary to much academic thinking, many of the original Young Americans were profoundly troubled by the Mexican War and what it represented. After thinking for so long that American democracy would sweep peacefully across the western hemisphere before capturing the world, they were left with the sickening specter of the Compromise of 1850 and the awareness that slavery and corruption were spreading more quickly than "freedom" or similar platitudes. Somehow their ambitious intellectual agenda had been distorted to justify a dubious war against the wrong enemy. Other events happening almost simultaneously in New York (the Astor Place riot) increased the gloom in the Young American camp, and the feeling that democracy was more complicated than they bargained for. Almost overnight, their innocent Democratic universe imploded, contracting even more quickly than Poe's astronomical fantasy in *Eureka* (1848).

In other words, within a few short years, the early adherents of Young America plummeted from an ecstasy of expectation into an agony of despair, a despair made all the more galling by the rise of the inferior second Young America aping their position without understanding its nuances. In the early 1850s, following the disappointing revolutions and compromises, the rhetoric that had seemed so meaningful to Young Americans sounded hollow. Of course, they were bitterly disappointed, and despite occasional renewals of the call to fulfill their youthful promise, many of the so-called Young Americans would end their careers prematurely, permanently dejected. A few unfortunates like O'Sullivan lived out long lives filled with reflection on their extraordinary youth, which stood in melancholy counterpoint to their futile old age.

The same trajectory of optimism followed by despair and cynicism can be observed in many of the writers who accompanied Young America on its journey toward a future that never happened. Almost all showed the same pattern of early infatuation followed by disappointment around 1848–1851. Hawthorne, the self-titled "Locofoco Surveyor," eagerly participated in O'Sullivan's and Duyckinck's schemes in the mid-1840s, even while gently mocking their excesses in stories like "Old Esther Dudley" and "A Select Party." His personal crisis occurred when he was removed from the Salem Custom House in 1849, and both of the novels that followed, *The Scarlet Letter* (1850) and *The House of The Seven Gables* (1851), contain strong statements of his disgust with the world of politics.

Whitman, younger and more removed, was no less committed to the Democracy and the *Review*, where his first important stories were published, and where he shamelessly reviewed *Leaves of Grass* in September 1855 ("An American bard at last!"). But even he underwent a crisis of faith, as we can divine from his poetry of the early 1850s and its rarely remarked undercurrent of gloom. The preface to *Leaves of Grass* warned that the nation's largeness could become "monstrous" without a corresponding largeness of spirit. And before that, many of his editorials showed the same tortured combination of optimism and nervousness that was endemic to Young America. In 1846 he betrayed a secret fear when he wondered if the "holy millennium of liberty" might not come to pass: "If it should fail! O, dark were the hour and dreary beyond description the horror of such a failure—which we anticipate not at all!" To fully understand *Leaves of Grass*, we need to consider the anxiety Whitman overcame.[32]

More than any writer, Herman Melville registered an acute disappointment with the failure of Young America, a psychic wound that coincided with his thrust at greatness. Not only did he grow disillusioned with Duyckinck's literary clique, but he perceived at the same time the larger and more disturbing collapse of America's moral purpose. Although uninvolved in the early machinations of O'Sullivan and Duyckinck, he and Young America I had embraced each other when he entered the literary profession in 1845. But by a quirk of fate he might have appreciated, had he written the script, he was struck by Young America's shortcomings at his greatest creative moment, and right after a desperate attempt to rejuvenate his own belief in cultural nationalism. The black pessimism of *Moby-Dick* and *Pierre* fell hard on the heels of his extraordinary essay "Hawthorne and His Mosses," which tried too hard to convince an imaginary reader (perhaps Duyckinck, for whom it was written) that the fervor of the 1840s was still intact. Like the essay, *Moby-Dick* veered precariously between a fraternal feeling of democratic *agape* and a cynical renunciation of the possibilities of politics. By a savage irony, its most vicious review appeared in the *Democratic Review*, now housing Young America II, and ill disposed toward the ambitious literature it had once championed. Its new editors must not have liked the question he posed to braggarts who measure achievement by size: "Why then do you try to 'enlarge' your mind? Subtilize it."

Following the rude shocks of the early 1850s, young Melville aged quickly, and almost always described himself, like the narrator of Bartleby, as "a rather elderly man." Like O'Sullivan, he too was destined to outlive most of his fellow Young Americans, lingering in New York for decades before expiring in 1891. Introspective to the end, he never forgot the fury of the 1840s, its excitement and its failure to make good its promise. He concluded his poem "Apathy and Enthusiasm," from *Battle-Pieces*, with the haunting line: "Grief to every graybeard / when young Indians lead the war."[33]

As Americans search for a national purpose in the waning years of the millennium, it is profitable to glance at the triumphs and failures of these early nationalists. Like us, they placed a high premium on youth, and tried valiantly to enlarge the definition of American culture, to bring it into consonance with the nation's democratic ideals. But these rhetorical goals lost their meaning as the nation's political and financial leaders, pursuing reckless economic and geographic expansion, lost sight of their moral compass. Most of the idealistic nationalists of Young America I emerged scarred and cynical from their brush with political reality.

In some respects, the problem is familiar. Americans today are still struggling to come to terms with the crushing despair that followed the idealism of the 1950s and 1960s. Assassinations and scandals permanently tarnished the notion that government could exercise a positive influence, or that a better democracy was attainable. Today, it is difficult for many Americans to reclaim even a fraction of the national pride they once felt unquestioningly. This is a tragedy, not just for the present generation of young Americans, but for the next, who like all past generations have to build upon what is bequeathed to them, even while denying the influence of the past.

I do not propose for a moment to resurrect Vietnam and Watergate in this book. But I do think we can gain psychological insight into our present condition by examining a different crisis of faith, when a generation of hopeful idealists forged a definition of the American identity that still has some resonance today. In so doing, I hope to show the deep reciprocal influence culture and politics can exert on each other under the right circumstances. By a helpful coincidence, many of the idealists who underwent this crisis were extraordinary creative thinkers capable of translating their anxiety into art.

A close examination of the *Review* restores a sense of political immediacy to the literature of the 1840s. The Young American network rewarded writers with proven party credentials, distributing political and literary plums to Hawthorne, Whitman, and Melville, among many others. A pattern of cultural-political symbiosis arose in which a writer like Hawthorne could expect certain favors from the party (i.e., patronage positions, publishing opportunities) in return for placing articles in the *Democratic Review*. Even if many of these artists expressed a measure of cynicism toward Young America after it ran its course, they curried its favor when it stood at the nexus of political and literary empowerment. They wrote on issues dear to O'Sullivan, they supported Duyckinck's publishing ventures, and they tried, in different ways, to promote the Democratic party at election time. For all their naïveté, the early Young Americans achieved a meaningful synthesis of political rhetoric and cultural productivity.

Am I suggesting that three of our most individualistic writers marched in lockstep with obscure magazine editors and politicians? Hardly. No one would dare suggest the writers in the *Review* stable supported all the tenets cherished by O'Sullivan and Duyckinck. In fact, they often criticized them, despite the many favors they received at their hands. Melville parodied Duyckinck in *Pierre*, and Hawthorne probably re-created O'Sullivan, less harshly, as Holgrave in *The House of the Seven Gables*. Thoreau, anything but a Young American, was allowed to attack Young America's premises in an essay published in its house organ. All developed a keen distrust of statesmanlike rhetoric and eventually renounced the idea that the 1848 generation was in any way unique. But the fact this great writing occurred in Young America's penumbra requires that fuller attention be paid to the group than the scattershot references it has received to date.

In this book I would like to tell the story of this angry, hopeful generation, or at least some of its more interesting leaders and creative thinkers. In so doing, I will focus on the group that gathered around the *Democratic Review*, which I find fascinating for the shrillness of its youthful rhetoric, and also for its rhetorical confusion in the aftermath of the Mexican War. My chapters overlap somewhat, but in essence they will follow the same pattern, treating the successes of the 1840s and the failures of the 1850s within each discrete section. I will begin with O'Sullivan's background and the early history of the *Review*, then move into specific cultural areas. Chapters on the *Review*'s writers and Evert Duyckinck will discuss the Young American philosophy of literature. I will follow with chapters on art and law, where friends of the Young Americans hoped to introduce new "American" principles into what were considered European domains. I will then retell the story of Young America II, emphasizing its tragic remove from Young America I. Finally, I will conclude with a discussion of O'Sullivan's later career, coupled with a brief meditation on the message his generation holds for future Young Americans.

One of the surprising aspects of this story is how quickly it unfolded. By 1855, the year of Whitman's apotheosis, all Young Americans had aged dramatically. By that time, Young America had become a slangy nickname for the spirit of restless expansionism and ugly greed that characterized the decade. In other words, a movement that originated with a reaction against an older generation's acquisitiveness became a synonym for a new and different kind of selfishness, even more damaging. In 1859 Lincoln would again rise to denounce what he had always felt to be a puerile outlook on the world: "We have all heard of Young America. He is the most *current* youth of the age. Some think him conceited, and arrogant; but has he not reason to entertain a rather extensive opinion of himself? Is he not the inventor and owner of the *present*, and sole hope of the *future?*"[34]

Two years later, with the outbreak of hostilities, the hyperbole of Young Americanism was irrelevant and embarrassing. Those few who looked back on 1848 were at a loss to explain the dementia that had seized them, and in some cases, this improved hindsight brought sadder, wiser reappraisal. In 1858 Whitman reflected on the 1840s and incredulously recalled the naïveté of the *Democratic Review* crowd, all of whom so earnestly believed in a "good time coming." It never came.[35]

But even if we admit what Lincoln diagnosed as Young America's immaturity (always present, to some extent, when youthful rhetoric is invoked), the story of John O'Sullivan and his cohorts is a compelling one. Historians have long granted him an asterisk as the namer of Manifest Destiny, but have never delved deeply into his extraordinary life, which brought him to dizzying peaks of influence and bottomless precipices of futility. As the presiding genius behind the *Review*, and the one man who really united the disparate fragments of the Young American persuasion, he deserves a better fate.

I would like to argue for his continuing interest, both as an early shaper of young voters' opinions, and as a brilliant cultural impresario, bringing new ideas of literature and art to the masses when most thinkers, like Emerson, were bewailing American timidity in an abstract language indecipherable to most. Unlike the majority of intellectuals in this utopian era, O'Sullivan had a real program, or so it seemed for a while, until 1848 exposed its unattainability. I am curious about many questions raised by this program, both from historical and literary perspectives. As a historian, I am intrigued by the shrewd use O'Sullivan made of young writers for political purposes, sweetening the message of the *Democratic Review* with smart articles describing the modern American culture exploding into being, and winning new voters in the process. And as a student of literature, I am eager to ascertain the effect these political maneuvers had on the young writers in question, and the degree to which their literature was complicated by the need to think in concrete political terms.

Obviously, these are not easy questions to answer, even under optimal circumstances, and the dearth of manuscript material relating to O'Sullivan has made my task even more difficult. But at the very least, I would like to address some riddles that have begged attention for a long time. For example, how did the eloquent rhetoric of Young America I (ca. 1845) turn into the flummery of Young America II (ca. 1852)? Why did many Young Americans feel ambivalent about the Mexican War they helped to bring about? Why were some (though not all) of the Young Americans blind to slavery while ranting of liberty? How do we get from Manifest Destiny to individual thinkers, what Whitman called, "the unknown want, the destiny of me"?[36] And can an intellectual revolution be said to happen when the political one it is based on fails to arrive?

It is impossible to answer these questions to unanimous satisfaction, but if I can begin the inquiry, I believe it will shed important light on a period that remains opaque despite our continuing obsession with it. It has always seemed peculiar to me that so many Americans were exuberant about the American future as the republic plunged headlong into the darkest crisis in its history. I hope this work will help explain that paradox, and even suggest a relationship between exaggerated nationalism and a sense of impending national doom.

There are many other paradoxes I intend to investigate. For example, why were so many of these rabid young Democrats from patrician families whose status had slipped during the market revolution? Why did they feel such rage against "these plodding, careful, hankering money-getters," to cite Mathews, or as Hawthorne alliterated, the "gouty old goblin of a capitalist." Was their campaign for a fresh new culture actually a smokescreen for a secret conservatism, designed to put new-monied Whigs in their place? I was startled to discover that O'Sullivan, the legal reformer David Dudley Field, and the Rhode Island radical Thomas Wilson Dorr were old friends dating back to early summer vacations together in the wealthy Democratic enclave of Stockbridge, Massachusetts. To quote Hawthorne on Phoebe Pyncheon, "It was a fair parallel between new Plebeianism and old Gentility!" Whitman, who badly wanted to be included in Young America's early adventures, hinted at this snobbery in a reminiscence about Duyckinck and his brother:

> I was left out. Why not? It was not surprising: I am not even today accepted in New York by the great bogums—much less then. I met these brothers: they were both "gentlemenly men"—and by the way I don't know any description it would have pleased them better to hear: both very clerical looking—thin—wanting in body: men of truly proper style, God help 'em![37]

O'Sullivan was vulnerable to similar critiques. For all his rabble-rousing, he had trouble working with subterranean politicians like Mike Walsh, the robust champion of New York's Spartans, and hero to the b'hoys. Around the time of the Dorr Rebellion (which O'Sullivan vigorously championed), Walsh poked fun at his physical delicacy in a speech:

> I find men that are very willing to have their names placarded around the street, at the head of a list—very willing to have their names at the head of an editorial article, . . . willing to make speeches, draft resolutions, go on committees, and talk about laying their bones to bleach on the soil of Rhode Island, when a shoemaker could strap 'em through the street without their making the slightest show of resistance. [Loud cheers and roars of laughter.][38]

Another paradox is that these superpatriots were strangely cosmopolitan. In their antagonism toward English culture, the Young Americans closely followed parallel developments among the young liberals of Europe. As New Yorkers, they read the new French literature of urban realism with fascination, and admired German theories about "folk" culture and its unifying effects on a divided people. With European events of the 1840s indicating progress in a democratic direction, excitement consumed the nationalists, who were innocently convinced this represented an "Americanization" of the world. They followed every movement of Mazzini's Young Italy and O'Connell's Young Ireland, envying their political use of national culture. But perversely, these prophets of America's cultural destiny seemed blind to the antinomies dividing their own nation and rendering all talk of unilateral American culture an absurdity. Even more ironically, O'Sullivan's invocation of a "Manifest Destiny" to expand the democratic principle westward across the continent acted as the spark that ignited the powder keg of the slavery question. It could be argued his unbridled nationalism actually caused the collapse of the Union.

And yet the overused word *ironically* is misleading, because surely the apparent paradox originated in an awareness that divisive problems existed. The attempt to call forth great American works as the extension of democracy was not simply naive escapism, but represented an effort to bind bickering Americans to a united purpose. In 1840 the *Democratic Review* stated clearly why culture was important to Americans, stressing literature as "ligament":

> The literature of a nation is its common property, and one of the strongest bonds of common feeling. More particularly does it become so, when the subject is domestic. The fame of an author who is universally admired is part of the inheritance of every individual citizen of his country. He adds another ligament to the ties which bind a people together; and in so doing, although the immediate object of his effort may have been, to amuse his readers, he becomes the benefactor of his country.[39]

In other words, nationalistic literature had a political use, a centripetal power at an increasingly centrifugal point in American history. The same year, Evert Duyckinck revealed something of the complexity of his patriotism. Rather than ranting stupidly of American superiority, he hoped that a great literature would instill a common purpose into a society edging toward the "chaos" of sectional and class conflict:

> much that now lies hid would be discovered, to do honor to the national character—much to rescue elements essentially good, from the chaos of frivolity and uproar in which they are now lost—many genial qualities brought to light, now not often recognized, but inseparable from the heart of man; something thereby to gain the love of other people abroad, to endear us to one another, as warm-hearted, kindly-affectioned brethren at home.[40]

Other Young Americans expressed similar hopes for unification. In a book called *Young America in Wall Street*, a New York businessman named George Train wrote in 1857, "Let us be Americans—not Northerners or Southerners—but simply Americans."[41] Yet another New Yorker, David Dudley Field, hoped his plan for legal codification would bring contentious Americans together. Praising the Allegheny Mountains as the embodiment of national strength, he admired the forceful way the mountain range "binds the country together, as with a band of iron." William Gilmore Simms, Young America's man in South Carolina, wrote Duyckinck that a strong national literature "will equally please and pacify."[42]

Herman Melville echoed this sentiment in his seminal 1850 review of Hawthorne, praising in weirdly sexual language the sectional union promoted by a great national writer: "He expands and deepens down, the more I contemplate him; and further, and further, shoots his strong New-England roots into the hot soil of my Southern soul." Unsurprisingly, the historic meeting of Melville and Hawthorne took place in the house of one Young American (Field), at the instigation of another (Duyckinck). It was anything but a chance encounter; as Melville might have written, the entire chapter was "predestinated." Like the other Young Americans, Melville demanded a national masterpiece, an "American Shiloh," insisting it was for "the nation's sake," and not merely for its authors. He obviously hoped the book he was writing, *Moby-Dick*, would perform this nationalistic office.[43]

Of course, he failed, as did all the Young Americans in one sense or another. But I find their failure as interesting as their success might have been. Despite all their energy and accomplishments, they were complex beings with inconsistent aspirations, and did not always understand one another. Erratic, often confused, they changed their ideologies as they worked them out, and as they aged. O'Sullivan followed his ultranationalism by supporting the Confederacy. His chief lieutenant in the literary campaign, Evert Duyckinck, provided Melville with many of the ideas necessary to write *Moby-Dick*, and then rejected the book when it was presented to him, although it fulfilled both of their quests. David Dudley Field became the very model of the mercenary lawyer he had long campaigned to reform. Ultimately, Young America was jejune, and all-too-painfully human.

History often recounts the great stories of successful battles against adversity, or irresistible social forces tending toward some culminating event. In this case it is rather the opposite. The tapestry of rhetoric and idealism woven by the young journalists was utterly unraveled by the confusing, defeating events of the 1850s, and by the disuniting tendencies even within their own movement. Indeed, we might even look at Young America, with its confusing costume changes and contradictions, as the exemplification of the moral entropy undercutting America's furious expansion. Melville's war poem, "The Conflict of Convictions," penetrated the paradox of an intense nationalism subverted by nagging doubts about the validity of the experiment: "I know a wind in purpose strong— / It spins *against* the way it drives." That remains, perhaps, the most fitting eulogy for hydra-headed Young America, spinning against itself, gaining intensity as the very Union whose glories it promised to sing crumbled into nothingness.[44]

In the end, I will be satisfied if four objectives, all related, are met by this study. First, I intend to argue that generational tension should be added to our understanding of the problems facing antebellum Americans. As part of this approach, I will try to show how important the American Revolution was to the generation of 1848, allowing restless Americans to fantasize about rebellion and revere their elders simultaneously. Young Americans knelt at the shrine of 1776, using the world "revolution" liberally to describe the progress they sought for themselves. This bond was transgenerational, for at the same time they venerated their grandparents, they repudiated their parents' generation for its flaccid conformity and bourgeois materialism. Interestingly, almost all the principal Young Americans were fatherless from childhood, and correspondingly obsessive about proving their own mettle. As a restless generation came of age, they tried to redefine every intellectual discipline to fit their needs, fully expecting the rest of the world to pay attention.

Second, I think a close study of Young America requires us to amend the frequently drawn conclusion that the Democratic party was backward, the party of fear rather than hope, in Marvin Meyers's memorable formulation. Despite their revolutionary reverence, the Young Americans were tenacious in their pursuit of change. No one embodied the concept of hope more fully than O'Sullivan, whose chief vulnerability was that his quixotic plans for American culture were too grandiose ever to be realized. True, he was reluctant to denounce slavery, which casts a terrible pall over his ideology today. But few Americans ever looked forward as searchingly as the writer who equated the United States with the concept of "futurity."

A third argument concerns New York City. The Young American struggles for recognition touched on regional as well as political tensions. It could hardly be otherwise. New York simply could not be contained. The city Leggett warmed in the 1830s spontaneously combusted in the 1840s. Growing at breakneck speed, antebellum New York contained in microcosm almost all of the pressures affecting the nation as a whole, as well as a host of new ones never seen before. The work of Sean Wilentz, Christine Stansell, Thomas Bender, Charles Sellers, and David Reynolds, among others, has shown how complex a world it was, presenting unprecedented social problems and market opportunities at the same time. Extreme wealth stood alongside poverty, a steady stream of immigration continually upset the status quo, technology revolutionized industry, labor began to find its voice, and a system of information- dissemination emerged that gave journalists great influence over the affairs of the nation. Well before the Civil War, which permanently altered the social mores of the rest of the country, New York underwent changes we normally ascribe to late-nineteenth-century America. The *Democratic Review* vividly described this modern place just before transplanting its operations there: "All was open, bold, and genuinely, radically democratic."[45] Ann Douglas recently gave an enthralling portrait of New York as a city bursting at the seams and defining the twentieth century during the 1920s. But the intense cultural battles of the 1840s served as distant prelude to her drama. New Yorkers had very different ideas than Bostonians about the coming intellectual revolution, as Melville made clear in his denunciation of "this Bostonian leaven of literary flunkeyism towards England." Bostonians noticed this New York style, and were irritated by it. Even Hawthorne, in some respects the archetypal New England writer, was a part of New York's efflorescence, as was South Carolina's William Gilmore Simms.[46]

Finally, I hope a better definition of Young America will expand the dialogue between historians and literary scholars. Quite frankly, it is impossible to fully understand Young America without a dialogue of this kind. More than most intellectual movements, it comprehended political *and* literary action. The ugly adjective "politico-literary" was used by both Emerson and Longfellow to describe Young America's hybrid intellectual program, which disturbed them for its wallowing in the gutters of Locofocoism.

In many ways, this is a study of the unsteady relationship between language and action. O'Sullivan was an inspired wordsmith, and Young America I succeeded in painting a compelling portrait of the future. But their ideas were appropriated by others with less generosity. By the end of Young America's journey, what began as a sincere desire to spread the best hopes of democracy had disintegrated into a host of ugly threats toward neighboring countries. In the 1950s, Soviet ideologues cited Young America II as proof that American ideology was always self-serving, and that behind every ode to liberty was another politician ready to plant the stars and stripes on someone else's land. The accusation was unfair, of course. Young America's early intentions were good. But they lost control of the rhetorical juggernaut they created.

Throughout the writing of this book, I have been aware of the difficulty of writing about history and literature simultaneously. It would have been easier to confine myself to O'Sullivan, or a ward-by-ward breakdown of the 1844 election, but I did not think the full story of Young America could be conveyed without an attempt to render the intense intellectual ferment behind the scenes. If at times it seems that I am considering too many topics, it is only because the Young Americans themselves thought everything on earth relevant to their quest. While some purists will object that this omnivorous approach sacrifices something in organic whole-ness, I hope others will find the breadth of the study challenging.

The student of Young America comes away impressed by the elaborate set of "ligaments" connecting political and literary endeavors in the period. In the pages of the *Democratic Review*, culture and politics enjoyed a tempestuous but happy marriage. The magazine's ligaments not only tied together writers like Melville and Hawthorne well before they met, but also yoked literary production to related cul-tural projects like so many fast-fish. In 1845, the year of Jackson's demise and Young America's debut, Manifest Destiny served as an umbrella for Duyckinck's Library of American Books, the American Art Union, David Dudley Field's campaign for le-gal codification, and the appearance of young "Sherman" Melville. All signaled a desire for new thinking—expansive as the continent, compassionate toward the un-lettered, and contemptuous of precedent.

The so-called New Historicism often labors to draw parallels between historical and literary production; here they are already tied together seamlessly. Many New Historicists have already written about issues like Manifest Destiny and its relation to Melville or Whitman, but I usually find their treatment patchy, especially from the historical side. Certain points are made well, while other questions are ne-glected, especially those beginning with the word "why." Too many of these schol-ars dwell on "ideology" as a monolithic entity, little perceiving that any ideology is the sum of its inconsistent human parts, changing with time and circumstances. Few of the New Historicists writing on Melville, Whitman, or Hawthorne have ac-knowledged what I consider crucial points: that O'Sullivan was more complex than the raving expansionist he is routinely branded as; that Young America had a broad program touching many different areas of culture; and that for all of these writers, flawed Democratic politics still held more promise than a Whiggery that cared more about the present than the future, and more about the self than society.

Some scholars have begun to delve cautiously into the politics of American lit-erature, but there remains a considerable distance yet to travel. Michael Rogin, Larry Reynolds, Betsy Erkkila, and Wynn Thomas have all added to our under-standing of Melville's and Whitman's interest in politics, but they have stopped short of providing the full national and international context, without which the hope and despair of the period are difficult to comprehend. It is not always easy to tease out a writer's politics—Hawthorne and Melville, especially, were always coy about expressing their position. But they, like Whitman, were indisputably allied to the cultural revolution emanating from New York. As Melville wrote, "great ge-niuses are parts of the times; they themselves are the times; and possess a correspon-dent coloring."[47]

F. O. Matthiessen said all five of the writers he examined in *American Renais-sance* were devoted to the "possibilities" of democracy, as indeed he was. But Whit-man, Hawthorne, and Melville were far closer than the transcendentalists to the real workings of the American political world, with all its double dealing, and like Matthiessen, they sustained a ruder shock from it than most of their contempo-raries. In the preface to *American Renaissance*, Matthiessen drew an outline for a book he never wrote, detailing the response of his canonical writers to "the economic and social forces of the time," and "the rise of the common man." This book is not exactly that book, but it owes something to the excitement Matthiessen felt for the political interpretation of literature.[48]

I hope to reassert something that was obvious to Melville, Hawthorne, and Whitman: They lived in a hyperpolitical time, when every question was probed for its relevance to the great party struggle taking place, and America's precarious position as the world's only large-scale democracy. Too little has been done to convey the cultural sense of politics in these years, the feeling of belonging to and believing in a party, of sharing a creed (a word little used or understood anymore). Hawthorne used it to describe the Democracy, adding "Methinks no scanty share of such faith is essential" for its members. Melville partisans may question the extent to which I am placing the iconoclastic novelist in a political school of thought. But to my mind, it is impossible to fully appreciate his later pessimism without comprehending how deeply he believed, with his fellow Young Americans, in the unfulfilled revolutionary potential of America.[49]

Americans were simply obsessed with politics, following events and crises with the excitement we reserve for popular culture today. No decade, in my opinion, saw a more intense interest than the 1840s, when by a common agreement on all sides, the very principles of the Revolution seemed to be at stake in a way they never had previously. When looked at individually, events like the Dorr Rebellion, the Mexican War, the Wilmot Proviso debate, and the Astor Place riot have a circumscribed significance. But considered together, as part of America's restless struggle to consummate the political and social revolution begun seven decades earlier, they assume a cosmic meaning that helps to explain the frenzy of Young America, and the ennui felt after its course was run.

But the disappointing dénouement of Young American nationalism should not obscure the service it rendered, almost in spite of itself, to the cause of promoting a vital American culture. Men like O'Sullivan and Duyckinck were easily caricatured for the hyperbolic zeal they brought to their sclerotic profession, but their incessant bleating did foreshadow (if it did not exactly cause) the most important creative burst in American literary history. Duyckinck knew both meanings of the word *culture*, and devoted his life to the agricultural principle that American creativity had to be tended, like a garden, before its harvest could be gleaned. So Duyckinck implied with his definition of the critic's role he was forging in 1845: "The critic's business now is to build up the national literature. If the materials are too scanty to construct the edifice, he is, at least, to bring such [as] are ready together, and see that they are of the right kind and quality for future use."[50]

If the Young Americans overshot their short-term goal of using culture to promote a sense of nationhood, they succeeded in this more remote objective, providing future observers with plenty of material to reflect upon. In 1852 the eternally youthful *Democratic Review*, incapable of understanding the need to look backward, predicted that no historical researcher would take any interest in the magazine after a few generations had passed. Furthermore, this imaginary scholar was lampooned as a dreary "Dryasdust," or worse, a "future fogy." While challenging the first prediction, I will try to avoid the stigma of the second.[51]

1

The Politics of Culture

O'Sullivan and the Democratic Review

Measures are now in active progress to furnish the democratic party throughout the United States with what they have never yet had—a magazine, literary as well as political, of their own. The importance of such an assistant to the great cause of the people cannot be too highly estimated, especially as their adversaries have assumed the credit of an entire monopoly of learning, talent, wit, argument, and LITERATURE, par excellence. The democratic party has not merely to fight its battle by the ballot-box and the vote. It must attack the enemy with his own weapons.

—*Washington Globe*, March 4, 1837

Modestia Victrix

In May 1823 U.S. authorities at Buenos Aires seized the brig *Dick* "on suspicion of her being engaged in piratical pursuits." The *Dick*'s captain was an American merchant of noble Irish extraction, John Thomas O'Sullivan. A year later he drowned in a shipwreck off South America, still trying to recover his confiscated fortune. An ancient family title, the count of Bearhaven, ultimately descended to his second son after an elder brother also perished at sea. Unfortunately, the papers proving the title were also lost in the shipwreck.[1]

Is this the plot of a Cooper novel, deservedly undiscovered until now? No, the story is real enough. Even better, these incidents, reeking of high-seas romance and international intrigue, gave birth to a magazine that cut a piratical swath across antebellum America: the *Democratic Review*. Appropriately, its founder, John Louis O'Sullivan, became one of the most swashbuckling journalists of the period, every bit as quixotic as his unfortunate father. Completing the circle of unlikelihoods, the last count of Bearhaven was possibly the most energetic spokesman for democracy America has ever seen.

In 1836, during the final summer of Andrew Jackson's presidency, the U.S. government agreed to compensate Captain O'Sullivan's widow for its seizure of the *Dick*'s cargo thirteen years earlier. But this was no ordinary squaring of accounts. A great deal of money was involved, and Jackson was not known for his kindly disposition in these matters (especially since O'Sullivan may well have been guilty). An invisible hand was almost certainly guiding the progress of the overdue payment. It could only belong to Martin Van Buren, looking ahead to his interests as well as those of the fatherless family. In a twist of fate Cooper would not have dared inflict on his readers, the aristocratic O'Sullivans were enriched in return for their promise of fealty to the mighty Democratic party and its rising new leader.

The wily Van Buren was no stranger to the O'Sullivans. He had known them at least since 1829, when he identified the fifteen-year-old John Louis O'Sullivan as a promising youth who merited his protection. Two letters to C. C. Cambreleng that year indicate Van Buren felt a "real solicitude" for the teenager and arranged a job for him with the governor of New York. This intervention must have impressed young O'Sullivan, for as late as 1845, he was still writing filial letters to Van Buren and traveling to his home at Kinderhook for career advice.[2]

The inheritor of Jackson's mantle in 1836, Van Buren was powerfully positioned to steer spoils to his supporters. The O'Sullivan claim was shepherded through the Senate he presided over as vice president, and it would have been uncharacteristic of Jackson to approve a large payment if there were not strong political incentives. In the summer of 1836, these incentives were everywhere. Van Buren, waging a difficult presidential campaign, needed all the allies he could find, especially if they offered unique advantages. Young O'Sullivan was not only precocious, but showed promise as a political journalist, and probably confided to Van Buren his dream of starting a national magazine with Democratic leanings. A year later, with the O'Sullivan claim realized, the *Democratic Review* became a reality.

As I argued in the prologue, everything felt different in 1837. The watershed year marked the end of Jackson's reign, Van Buren's accession, and the panic attending the transfer of power. Oliver Wendell Holmes later dubbed it the year of our literary Declaration of Independence, referring to Emerson's American Scholar address, but his words applied just as well to young O'Sullivan, newly enriched by the settlement. At almost precisely the moment of Emerson's talk (August 31), he and his brother-in-law, Samuel Langtree, were in Washington, frantically preparing the first issue of the new magazine, which they were sure would reshape the journalistic landscape. There is no evidence they were especially moved by Emerson's address, but in effect they were soldiers in the same nationalistic campaign. Indeed, they went beyond Emerson in many respects.

O'Sullivan and Langtree intended to combine the newsiness of a monthly magazine with the intellectual snuff of a quarterly review. Hence the portentous name with which they baptized their creation: *The United States Magazine and Democratic Review*. This wording instantly signaled ambitions of nationwide circulation and an unmistakable partisan affiliation. They wanted their magazine to be definitively "American" and "Democratic," and soon it was known across the land simply as the *Democratic Review*. The editors solemnly announced their goals in a prospectus released during the last week of Jackson's administration: "As the United States Magazine is founded on the broadest basis which the means and influence of the Democratic Party in the United States can present, it is intended to render it in every respect a thoroughly NATIONAL WORK, not merely designated for ephemeral interest and attraction, but to continue of permanent historical value."[3]

Unlike most pronouncements of this sort, their braggadocio was more or less fulfilled. The first issue was released in October 1837 and arrived at an opportune moment. In the short term, the beleaguered new administration of Martin Van Buren, reeling from the financial panic of the spring, needed all the popular support it could get. And from a wider historical perspective, O'Sullivan picked a timely occasion to remedy an imbalance in American cultural politics.

Specifically, he noted that almost all of America's influential literary periodicals issued from the camps of the enemy: Whiggery. Van Buren could count on daily newspapers like Bryant's *New York Evening Post* or Francis Blair's *Washington Globe* to serve as party organs, but there was nothing in the way of a respectable national magazine with Jacksonian leanings. Unlike the newspaper, the magazine was still the domain of well-educated minds with a conservative bent and little interest in disrupting the status quo. The *Democratic Review* did not displace these magazines over its long tenure, but it brought a fresh voice and a measure of equilibrium to the publishing world of antebellum America.

Hence the exuberance shown by O'Sullivan and Langtree as they commenced their undertaking. As O'Sullivan reflected in 1842, they were "very young, very sanguine, and very democratic." Their goal was nothing less than "to strike the hitherto silent string of the democratic genius of the age and country as the proper principle of the literature of both." Democracy was the engine that drove both O'Sullivan and his magazine. It was an ill-defined concept, to be sure, but one that could be depended upon to excite American readers, whether embracing the specific doctrines of the partisan Democracy, or the larger set of meanings yoked to the lower case "d." Either way, the editor saw the American political experiment as the beginning of a worldwide revolution that would soon spread to other domains of the mind. With proper tending, an entire intellectual system of great art, literature, and philosophy ought to spring from the same impulse that had declared all men created equal. For O'Sullivan, politics and culture were indissolubly linked, and his advocacy of Democratic authors went hand-in-hand with his support of the Van Buren administration.[4]

Well before his arrival on the literary scene, the founder of the *Democratic Review* had been groomed to the task. Yet it is remarkable how little is known today of John Louis O'Sullivan. He was unusually intimate with eminent writers and politicians, yet there exist almost no likenesses of him, nor any substantial manuscript collections. Impressions of him varied wildly, from the close friendship of fellow travelers to the sharp hostility he provoked among political rivals.

Nathaniel Hawthorne's son Julian judged him "one of the most charming companions in the world," a character whose absurd optimism was straight out of *Martin Chuzzlewit*. Hawthorne found O'Sullivan "impossible to resist": "the most courteous and affectionate of men, with the most yielding and self-effacing manners, he had the spirit of a paladin, and was afraid of nothing." Furthermore, he was gifted with "a low, melodious, exquisitely modulated voice," a "sparkle in his soft eyes," and a "lock of hair that fell gracefully over his forehead only a trifle disordered." Walt Whitman recalled, "I knew him well—a handsome, generous fellow. He treated me well." Catharine Maria Sedgwick called the O'Sullivan family "these most picturesque of all the moderns." Half a century after the *Democratic Review* folded, Julia Ward Howe wrote the following upon meeting William Butler Yeats: "He is a man of fiery temperament, with a slight, boyish figure: has deep-set blue eyes and dark hair, reminds me of John O'Sullivan in his temperament."[5]

His political credentials were no less impressive. Writing Van Buren in 1839, Benjamin F. Butler claimed, "As a political writer, no man in the country, of his age, surpasses O'Sullivan" and called the *Review* "a beacon of light in the darkest hours." Van Buren himself wrote George Bancroft, "Your feelings, warm and generous towards O'Sullivan as I know them to be, are scarcely equal to my own." In 1857 an American diplomat stationed in London recorded a favorable impression in his diary: "A plain, unprepossessing slight made man of light complexion, about 5 ft. 8, thin face, light moustache, about 43 years of age, quick spoken and altogether decidedly a man of mark such as one would notice in a crowd."[6]

Longfellow, on the other hand, whose feathers he ruffled on several occasions, described him to a friend as "a young man, with weak eyes, and green spectacles, who looks like you, and is a *Humbug* nevertheless and notwithstanding." In a fit of pique (which he later recanted), Poe called him "that ass O'Sullivan." Thoreau dismissed him as "rather puny-looking," though grudgingly admitted him to be one of the "not-bad." Hawthorne knew him as well as anyone, and was always frustrated by his friend's erratic behavior, particularly "his defects in everything that concerns pecuniary matters." He pitied him as "a wanderer, a man of vicissitudes, as if his native waves were all the time tossing beneath him." Yet he liked him immensely, claiming "the Devil has a smaller share in O'Sullivan than in other bipeds who wear breeches." As he cryptically put it, "He is miraculously pure and true, considering what his outward life has been."[7]

Like most editors, he was a chameleon of sorts, responsible not only for editorials, but also "the windings of fictitious narrative, the distinctions of a critique, statistical calculations, political argument and enlightened legislation." Despite his personal vagaries, the fact of his influence remains indisputable. In his heyday, O'Sullivan enjoyed great power as a shaper of public opinion, and consequently of both political policy and literary taste. Respected by players in both spheres, he was especially intimate with the unlikely triumvirate of Martin Van Buren, Nathaniel Hawthorne, and the young Samuel Tilden. He was also very close to the Rhode Island radical Thomas Wilson Dorr and the Cuban revolutionary Narciso Lopez. Clearly, he was drawn to other fiery temperaments.[8]

But despite this prominence, his career is difficult to read. As these comments show, O'Sullivan was a strange bundle of paradoxes. One of the most nationalistic of Americans in an already nationalistic era, he sided with the Confederacy in the Civil War, although he never lived in the South and had prominently supported the Free Soil campaign of 1848. Closely connected with power brokers and financiers, he spent much of his life with little or no money, though he always lived in high style. Inspired by a messianic vision of democracy with palpably religious undertones, he was critical of organized religion (the "rubbish" of a "theocracy of priests") and became embroiled in a vituperative debate with clergymen over the death penalty in the early 1840s. Passionately devoted to popular sovereignty, and descended from recent immigrant stock, he was equally proud of his quasi-aristo-cratic heritage and devoted inordinate time to bizarre personal plots to overthrow foreign governments. Yet he was not simply a sloganeering Yankee imperialist, but a cosmopolitan scholar who respected foreign traditions and differences.[9]

The contradictions continue. Like most Democrats, O'Sullivan supported the doctrine of states' rights and limited government, but his rampant nationalism al-lowed him to encourage federal construction of a canal across the Isthmus of Darien and the underwriting of his own magazine. He was a reformer of sorts; friendly with kindred spirits like Julia Ward Howe, Orestes Brownson, and Catharine Maria Sedgwick, and devoted to the abolition of capital punishment, the improvement of prisons, the creation of a "Congress of Nations," and the cause of worldwide peace. Hawthorne wrote in "The Hall of Fantasy," "no philanthropist need blush to stand on the same footing with O'Sullivan." Yet this pacifist was also cool toward abolitionism, urged American military intervention in any country where the spark of liberty was in danger of being snuffed out, and screamed for the forceful acquisition of additional territory. The act for which he is remembered, if at all, is his coining of the term "Manifest Destiny," and of this he seems to have been oblivious. Almost every history of the Jacksonian period contains a one-sen-tence summation of O'Sullivan as the author of the phrase, but he never claimed his territorial rights to it, despite his self-aggrandizing personality.[10]

He has also been oversimplified by historians. Though intrigued, Arthur Schlesinger, Jr., dismissed him as "a clever and charming Irishman" whose maga-zine "dealt in the immediacies of action and enjoyment, caring little for the swirling depths of theory." Frederick Merk, along with many others, saw his promo-tion of Manifest Destiny as an attempt to extend Anglo-Saxon hegemony across the continent, when in fact he preferred a panethnic extension of American democracy and was more or less indifferent to the march of Protestantism (most of his family was Catholic). In fact, he spent surprising time in the company of Latin Americans, seeing their liberation from Spain as yet another part of Manifest Destiny.[11]

No doubt he added to this confusion by his own contradictory actions, often difficult to interpret. In 1845, while composing some of the most bellicose editorials in American history, he wrote George Bancroft, then secretary of the navy, that his "peace principles" led him to regret "our present warlike attitude" toward Mexico. A more blatant and disturbing paradox is that he never showed much interest in slavery, even while ranting of liberty in every other context. These vicissitudes char-acterized his entire life and occlude our vision of him, but they do not diminish his relevance to antebellum culture. Nor did his life begin and end in 1845, as most his-tories assume. Almost no one has considered the interesting later phase of O'Sulli-van's career, as if his personal destiny ceased to exist after giving expression to the nation's with an unusually memorable turn of phrase.[12]

Thankfully, historians no longer investigate the genealogy of their subjects, but in O'Sullivan's case, there were interesting correlations between his pedigree and his sense of fate. The O'Sullivan family motto was *Modestia Victrix*, which trans-lates as "Victory through Moderation." This is amusing in retrospect, for few fami-lies ever saw so little of either ("Defeat through Excess" would have been more appropriate). A glance at O'Sullivan's bizarre lineage establishes several traits the different Young Americans held in common and identifies important sources of their shared radicalism. Descended from a long line of Irish patriots fighting against English imperialism, O'Sullivan inherited a strong dislike of hegemonic Anglo-Saxon culture. This ideology was oddly intensified in his mind as his family's status slipped during the early nineteenth century. Like Evert Duyckinck, David Dudley Field, and a host of other Young Americans (including, broadly speaking, Melville and Hawthorne), a combination of inherited elitism and precarious class standing resulted in a fiercely democratic cosmogony.[13]

From their first appearance on the page of history, the O'Sullivan family had been devoted to political intrigue and complicated foreign liaisons. A distant ancestor, Donal O'Sullivan, a Cork County chieftain during the Elizabethan age, tenaciously resisted English incursions into Ireland and entertained close relations with shadowy Spaniards. After the accession of James I, he fled to Spain in 1604 where he was harbored by Philip III and honored as a Grandee of Spain and Earl of Bearhaven. The latter place, in Ireland, was outside Philip's realm, but no one seems to have objected. His descendant later took great pride in these specious titles, and Hawthorne humorously addressed him as "the Count," or in his preface to "Rappacini's Daughter," as "le comte de Bearhaven." Strange as it may sound, O'Sullivan, who spent most of his life denouncing antique privileges, was recognized by some of Europe's titled aristocracy as one of their own.[14]

Almost all of the family's achievements had been spectacular disasters. O'Sullivan's great-grandfather, also named John O'Sullivan, was an officer in the French army who joined Bonnie Prince Charlie's campaign and conceived the plan for the catastrophic battle of Culloden in 1745. His son, equally ill-starred, was forced to leave the French army after a violent altercation with John Paul Jones, then allied with France as the American naval commander. In the aftermath of this incident, he prudently removed to New York, where he became an officer with the occupying British (O'Sullivans always chose the wrong sides), married a local girl, and brought her back to Ireland.[15]

Their son John Thomas O'Sullivan ran off to sea, and like his father resurfaced in New York, where he met the Venezuelan patriot Francisco Miranda around 1806, planning an expedition to free his country from Spain. O'Sullivan fell in with the plotters, commanding the schooner *Bacchus* in their tiny armada, but needless to say, it proved unsuccessful. He spent a year in prison at Cartagena, then escaped and returned to New York, resuming his career as a mariner-merchant and marrying Mary Rowly, a genteel Englishwoman. Years later Julian Hawthorne would recall her as "a type of the fine-grained, gently-bred aristocrat."[16]

Somehow the young couple wended their way to the Barbary Coast where, according to tradition, John Louis O'Sullivan was born aboard a British warship off Gibraltar on November 15, 1813. This is singular, since a state of war existed between the United States and England, but the subject of nationality was always slippery with the ultranationalistic O'Sullivan. Nathaniel Hawthorne elaborated,

> O'Sullivan was born on shipboard, on the coast of Spain, and claims three nationalities—those of Spain, England, and the United States—his father being a native

of Great Britain, a naturalized citizen of the United States, and having registered his birth and baptism in a Catholic church of Gibraltar, which gives him Spanish privileges. He has hereditary claims to a Spanish countship. His infancy was spent in Barbary, and his lips first lisped in Arabic. There has been an unsettled and wandering character in his whole life.[17]

Despite his dubious citizenship, the elder O'Sullivan was appointed the U.S. consul to Mogador (February 1817) and Tenerife (July 1818). He wasted little time stirring up controversy, causing a rift with a British official and losing his appointment in the process. He returned to private commerce by purchasing the brig *Dick* and sending her to South America, where, as already recounted, a U.S. agent impounded the boat on suspicion of piracy and sold its cargo of hides at a loss. The charges were never proven, but the affair was disastrous for O'Sullivan. A year later, in 1824, trying vainly to repossess his treasure, he perished in a shipwreck on a return voyage to South America.[18]

At the time young O'Sullivan was continuing the family tradition of Catholic education in France. Following news of her husband's demise, Mary O'Sullivan united her children in London, and in the fall of 1827 they moved *en masse* to New York. The eldest son, William, joined the Navy, and like his father disappeared in a shipwreck. John, gifted in languages, was sent to Columbia College at the tender age of fourteen, despite deteriorating finances. Leaping to the top of his class by the end of the year, he received two prestigious scholarships and taught younger students in the Columbia Grammar School (including, probably, the Duyckinck and Melville brothers). Excused from the formality of taking classes, he easily took his degree in 1831 and received a Master of Arts in 1834, after teaching freshmen mathematics and classics (again, including Evert Duyckinck). He appears also to have passed the bar around 1835, but never showed more than a perfunctory interest in his legal career.[19]

Even at this early date, his real ambitions probably lay elsewhere, in the exciting world of print journalism transforming New York. Writer-reformers like Bryant and Leggett were effecting social change through their control of the *Evening Post*, and the latter thrilled aspiring journalists with his scabrous editorials against entrenched power. In May 1831, a local intellectual named John Francis gave a speech at Columbia calling attention to the new technologies of printing and the increased power of written culture to sway the masses. He also singled out the "beardless" youth of Paris for their role in the recent revolution of 1830. The two messages, implicitly related, must have affected the promising graduate, who had been schooled in France and cherished the strange revolutionary lineage bequeathed to him by his ancestors.[20]

Despite these academic successes, the O'Sullivan family had little income and many expenses. It may well have been that the combination of family pride and poverty in these lean years provoked O'Sullivan's reverse class consciousness, an acute antisnobbery proceeding from his own confused sense of status. If so, he would hardly have been the only Young American to suffer this disruption. In these same years, Hawthorne and Melville were living off the charity of family relations as their mothers' fortunes plummeted.

Ultimately, Mary O'Sullivan decided to press a claim against the U.S government over the 1823 incident in which her husband's cargo had been seized. Accordingly she entered a petition to the House of Representatives for over $100,000 in retribution. Ludicrous as this sum may seem, she slowly made progress toward compensation. In 1835 she moved the family to Georgetown to facilitate her lobbying efforts. Young O'Sullivan was deeply involved in the process. In July 1836 an abridged claim was finally approved by Congress and signed by President Jackson, following which Mary O'Sullivan was awarded $20,210. With this windfall, O'Sullivan and his brother-in-law suddenly possessed the wherewithal to consummate their journalistic ambitions. It is fitting the outgoing president signed the document that did so much to perpetuate his ideological legacy.[21]

Launching the *Democratic Review*

The success of the claim brought financial stability to the family, and O'Sullivan quickly took steps to begin his new career. O'Sullivan's sister Mary had recently married Langtree, a young doctor who immigrated from Ireland in 1832. Despite his medical training, Langtree plunged headlong into magazine work almost immediately on arrival. O'Sullivan later recalled, his tastes "were decidedly literary, and adverse from his profession." After a brief stint at the *New York Commercial Advertiser*, he edited the fledgling *Knickerbocker* magazine from March 1833 to April 1834. In that month he surrendered the reins to Lewis Gaylord Clark, who would direct it for three decades.[22]

In retrospect, it is ironic that the *Knickerbocker*, which was to evolve into the pride of New York Whiggery, owed its origin in part to Dr. Langtree, who was not only an Irish immigrant, but a staunch Jacksonian. In its early days, under Langtree's stewardship, the magazine was devoted to the literary nationalism Clark would later belittle in the same pages. The July 1833 number fulminated, "When the Knickerbacker [sic] shall be purely American, . . . then, and not till then, will its destiny be complete; and our object and our wishes be fulfilled, in giving to America a native Magazine." With a prophetic voice, Langtree called forth "the genius of this young America." Appropriately, he also published one of William Leggett's few magazine pieces, a story about his early life at sea. Summarizing the year in December 1833, he wrote what might have been a blueprint for his and O'Sullivan's progress: "The horizon of society has been enlarged. Where we might a few years back have looked for a civic patronage with local objects and illustrations—we must now look for a National—where the sphere was narrow before it has become vast,—from a circumscribed we have arisen to a grander destiny."[23]

Probably through Langtree, O'Sullivan was seduced by the hurly-burly world of magazine work. In the summer of 1835 the brothers-in-law joined forces to buy the *Georgetown Metropolitan*, a struggling semiweekly they hoped to inject with new life. With improved writing and ardent support for the cause of liberty in Europe (an O'Sullivan trademark), they succeeded in boosting the size and frequency of circulation. On other issues they were characteristically Democratic, supporting striking shoe workers in New York, Texan independence, and the general reluctance to discuss slavery. They also showed an eye for literary talent, publishing reprints of Poe along with regular book reviews and "Literary Intelligence." According to a self-puffing editorial of March 3, 1837, "The literary character of the Metropolitan is much higher than aimed at, or professed by the usual newspaper press." This was probably true, although it was not much of a claim at the time.[24]

Despite early success, the paper stalled in 1836, doubtless because the editors were distracted by higher ambition. Their prospects had dramatically improved with the O'Sullivan claim and Van Buren's election. Feeling flush, O'Sullivan and Langtree decided to broaden their compass beyond the District of Columbia and launch a national magazine. Why not take on the entire country? The first mention of the *Review* ran in the *Metropolitan* of February 27, 1837, clearly displaying the new administration's interest:

> It is the contemplation of the proprietors of this journal to commence, with Mr. Van Buren's administration, the publication of a political and literary Magazine of the first class in the city of Washington, which in the former department will be devoted to the advocacy of democratic principles, and in the latter will be rendered, as far as a liberal use of means and the co-operation of some of the best writers in the country can effect it, creditable to the United States. . . . It is believed that the proposed Magazine can be made to a great extent a means of concentrating, and if we might use the word, of popularizing this description of talent.[25]

The word *popularizing* was a relative neologism (the *Review* boasted five years later, "Why should we be afraid of introducing new words into the language which it is our mission to spread over a new world?"). More important, it was a new idea, promising to open American cultural politics as the new state constitutions of the 1820s had enlarged suffrage. The article was reprinted in the *Washington Globe*, along with a promise that the magazine would be "thoroughly democratic in its price" (five dollars a year). The *Globe* expounded on its historic significance, crowing that the Democrats could finally "attack the enemy with his own weapons."[26]

What did this belligerent taunt mean? Quite simply that the Democrats were tired of Whig claims to superiority in literature and fine art, which if not exactly "weapons," were useful tools of persuasion in a volatile period of political and cultural contest. What O'Sullivan called the enemy's "monopoly," recalling Leggett's rhetoric, consisted of the well-heeled magazines reflecting cultured opinion in Boston, New York, and Philadelphia, exemplified by the crusty *North American Review*. Regional magazines like the *Southern Literary Messenger* and the *Western Monthly Review* tried to make inroads, but made slow progress against "the North American Quarterly Hum Drum" (Poe's term). The *Democratic Review* would fare better, combining politics and literature in a concerted attack.

Since the *Review* was closely connected with the incoming president, and could not have been launched without his protection and tacit support, it possessed a crucial advantage from the outset. The illusion of aloofness was maintained, but Washington insiders knew the magazine was a pet interest of Van Buren's, and that he had been shrewdly nurturing O'Sullivan's ambitions for such a purpose. A rival magazine complained the *Review* was "born at Washington, in the very vestibule of the palace—suckled and papped in the grand official nursery of government patronage." In 1840 Hugh Garland, the clerk of the House of Representatives, wrote

Van Buren, "On the first establishment of the Democratic Review, I understood it was under the auspices of the Administration, and that its Editors were your personal friends." Francis Blair's *Washington Globe*, Jackson's official organ, irritated Van Buren with its inconsistency and lack of polish, and many northern Democrats agreed a new Democratic mouthpiece was necessary. Apparently, O'Sullivan and Langtree were given an informal "compact" from the administration promising them the *Globe*'s lucrative government printing business, although this did not turn out to be the case. A disappointed O'Sullivan later wrote Benjamin F. Butler that the *Review* emanated from "a design calculated more for the promotion of your and the President's general personal interests than for our own."[27]

Butler, the attorney general under Jackson, and Van Buren's law partner since 1817, was especially supportive of the plan and acted as its chief sponsor within the Van Buren circle. As O'Sullivan wrote, "More than any other individual, Mr. B. F. Butler, an intimate personal as well as political friend, sympathized with the views which animated us, and united with us in the counsels which resulted in our determination." Beyond acting as a mentor and liaison with the White House, Butler subsidized the undertaking with a thousand-dollar investment.[28]

Butler had almost certainly met O'Sullivan earlier. His son William Allen Butler introduced his father to a number of promising young New York intellectuals, including Evert Duyckinck, the nucleus of the Young American literati. Butler himself nurtured a pet interest in literature. He and Henry D. Gilpin, Van Buren's attorney general, both dilettante writers, contributed small pieces once the *Review* was underway. The two attorneys general frequently met to advise the young staff, and Butler attempted to raise twenty-five thousand dollars for the *Review* by selling bonds to Democratic well-wishers. A letter he wrote to George Bancroft promoted the politico-literary connection, arguing the *Review* furnished Democrats with "a literature unalloyed with adverse political views."[29]

Butler also asked Andrew Jackson to lend his magical name to the enterprise, as revealed by a manuscript fragment left by the general, complete with Jacksonian syntax:

> My name to the original work of OSulivan [sic] and Langly [sic], was asked by my friend B. F. Butler, to head the subscription, for the work, not as a subscriber for the Book, but to recommend it to the public. he [sic] was told by me that I had subscribed to no work, to give it my pecuniary aid.
>
> A.J.[30]

Despite the rejoinder, political principles triumphed, for a euphoric (and grammatical) letter, allegedly penned by Old Hickory to the editors, was unveiled in the *Washington Globe* of March 13, 1837: "I have just received your note of the 4th instant, enclosing the prospectus of the [sic] 'The United States Magazine and Democratic Review.' I have received the prospectus with much interest, as I have long thought such a work in the great city of the Union was much wanted; and as an evidence of approbation of the work, you will find me one of your subscribers."[31]

O'Sullivan was perfectly happy to believe this fiction, and years later he nostalgically reminisced, "Old General Jackson took a great deal of interest in it, and was its first subscriber." Beside Jackson's laying-on of hands, the *Globe* printed the magazine's prospectus:

> In the mighty struggle of antagonist principles which is now going on in society, the Democratic Party of the United States stands committed to the world as the depository and exemplar of those cardinal doctrines of political faith with which the cause of the People in every age and country is identified. Chiefly from the want of a convenient means of concentrating the intellectual energy of its disciples, this party has hitherto been almost wholly unrepresented in the republic of letters, while the views and policy of its opposing creeds are daily advocated, by the ablest and most commanding efforts of genius and learning.[32]

The secretary of the treasury, Levi Woodbury, mailed the prospectus out to postmasters around the country, asking Democrats to subscribe, and thereby lending the official imprint of government support to what was ostensibly a private undertaking. O'Sullivan and Langtree immediately set about recruiting as many of the country's top intellects as they could. To maintain the appearance of bipartisan objectivity, the young editors approached the venerable John Quincy Adams, urging him to contribute. He recorded the event in his journal: "Long evening visit from Mr. Langtree—a fulsome flatterer. He urged me to write for his Democratic Review and Magazine; but I told him literature was, and its nature must always be, aristocratic; that democracy of numbers and literature were self-contradictory."[33]

The account of this meeting, brief as it must have been, contained in a nutshell what was important about the new magazine. Like most well-educated Americans, Adams felt an abstract devotion to democratic idealism, but doubted the yeomanry could actually give voice to their ideas in literature. His conception of American *belles lettres* fit his understanding of the political world: Those who were best suited to participate had proper schooling, taste, and a reverence for tradition. For all their correctness of demeanor, young Irish Locofocos did not fall into this category.

In the months before the magazine was ready, O'Sullivan busied himself writing would-be contributors, outlining his plan for the enterprise and how its glory would redound to all associated with the project. Hawthorne was one of many summoned to join "the finest writers of the country'" with the promise that compensation "will be on so liberal a scale as to command the best and most polished exertions of their minds." Langtree wrote George Bancroft, imploring him to lend his talents with the grand injunction, "The republic hath need of your services." Langtree also hinted at Van Buren's background role: "It is of vital importance to the success of this hazardous plan, and the mighty interests involved in it, that such a pen as yours, should be perpetually involved." Distracted by his own mighty interests, Bancroft did not become a steady contributor, though he did write occasional historical pieces.[34]

O'Sullivan often described the aborning magazine in terms that would appeal to the would-be contributor. In a letter to Orestes Brownson, he wrote the *Review* would "be democratic, in the broad and historical signification of the word," adding, however, that "to every measure of a political and extended political party, it would be impossible to pledge such a work." This legalistic phrasing, well suited to Brownson, meant that O'Sullivan would toe the Democratic party line, but not in a lapdog fashion.[35]

At the same time, O'Sullivan tried to allay Longfellow's Whiggish suspicions by admitting "its politics to be democratic, and of course supporting (the) present dominant party," but adding "its literary department will be however quite independent of the political." Therefore, O'Sullivan concluded, "the bias of your political or party opinions I neither know nor consider at all material. Our anxiety is to make a magazine of a higher order than those that the country now possesses." These words told the truth somewhat slant, as did many of O'Sullivan's communiqués, for almost anyone might have perceived the importance of politics to the larger plan of the *Review*, including its literature. Longfellow himself must have seen this plainly, for he wrote caustically two years later: "The *Loco-focos* are organizing a new politico-literary system. They shout Hosannas to every *loco-foco* authorling, and speak coolly of, if they do not abuse, every other. They puff *Bryant* loud and long; likewise my good friend *Hawthorne* of '*Twice-Told Tales*'"; also a Mr. O'Sullivan, once editor of the "Democratic Review."[36]

In other words, the *Review* favored authors with Democratic leanings. Transcending Van Buren's short-term political goals, the magazine offered an aggressive new vision of American culture, a vision that shared little with the genteel guardians of the American literary establishment. Imitating Jackson and the generation of '76, O'Sullivan challenged the stuffy Anglophiles of the literary world as if they were the latest form of Tory. For O'Sullivan, the cause of worldwide democracy simply demanded that the United States, its most enlightened practitioner, sponsor a fresh body of writing to render the old European classics as vestigial as their aristocracies.

O'Sullivan's zeal for American letters burned with a whiter heat than the more tempered optimism of the established magazines. From the distance of a century and a half, it is difficult to discern differences between various American voices demanding essentially the same thing. Certainly there were many Whigs who advocated new and vigorous works of imagination. But by and large, these appeals were intended to uphold tradition, and to ensure that previous definitions of good taste would prevail. Rufus Griswold, one of Young America's rivals, defined poetry as "moral purity," and insisted that ordinary people had no business judging literature for themselves: "There is no more pernicious error than that the whole people should be instructed alike."[37]

O'Sullivan never would have written that, nor Evert Duyckinck (at least, not in his early phase). They wanted American literature in the present tense, not the past, written by the people and for the people. A close reading indicates a different tenor, a politicized urgency, on the part of the critics located in the Democratic part of the spectrum, particularly the New Yorkers. Although Timothy Flint, editor of the *Western Monthly Review*, was zealously in favor of American literature, he felt "the phrenzy of political excitement" was distracting Americans from more elevated pursuits. This "phrenzy" constituted the very thrust of O'Sullivan's appeal.[38]

Emerson and his followers were put off by the *Democratic Review*'s nearness to vulgar politicians. But O'Sullivan cared not a whit, sensing an intangible link be-

tween real democracy, with its sweaty speeches and squalid promises, and the literature of the new generation. Possessed by a crude, proto-Marxist certainty, he believed the system by which a people ruled themselves would inevitably manifest itself in their cultural creations, with the rest of the world slowly following the best
example set for them. In politics, this meant enlarged suffrage, with minimal government interference in private life; in literature, original works treating commonplace themes with forcefulness, directness, and dignity. In O'Sullivan's conceit,
great works would spring naturally from an unencumbered people, describing
things with no precedent in the tired world of courtly romances and Waverleyesque
imbroglios, but rather new things, American things, incomparable things said in-
comparably well.

Washington (1837–1840): Blustery Beginnings

The *Review*'s first issue, assembled frantically after several writers failed to turn in
anything, was released October 15, 1837. O'Sullivan and Langtree worked day and
night for a fortnight, and O'Sullivan finally produced the leading articles "under
much bad health, and literally by inches." Like everything he did, this inaugural effort emanated a pleasantly manic quality. The politico-literary calculus received immediate articulation in the opening essay. One of O'Sullivan's better efforts, this absurdly ambitious manifesto revealed all of the new generation's expansiveness. It
began with a call "for the advocacy of that high and holy DEMOCRATIC PRIN-
CIPLE which was designed to be the fundamental element of the new social and
political system created by the 'American experiment.'" O'Sullivan's religious language was appropriate for the crusade he was undertaking, and he calmly described
his creation as the "ark of democratic truth."[39]

With breathless excitement, O'Sullivan spelled out his political and literary
principles from the outset. The *Review* claimed "abiding confidence in the virtue,
intelligence and full capacity for self-government, of the great mass of our people—
our industrious, honest, manly, intelligent millions of freemen." Accordingly, it opposed "all self-styled 'wholesome restraints'" on public opinion and believed,
in theory at least, "all government is evil." Hence the Jeffersonian slogan of the
magazine, which was inscribed under a portrait of Washington on the title page:
"The best government is that which governs least." Paying homage to Southerners,
O'Sullivan suggested that majorities ought to be sympathetic to minority rights to
avoid "a house divided against itself" (like Lincoln, he knew his Bible). And he opposed "all precipitate radical changes in social institutions," a reference to abolitionism requiring no translation.[40]

Despite this unsavory opinion, shared by most Democrats in 1837, O'Sullivan's
social philosophy generally embraced the reforms of the day, particularly those that
reduced government intrusiveness. In some respects, his libertarian outlook meshes
with the antigovernmental conservatism of the late twentieth century. But in 1837,
the fight against government meddling signaled a dislike of the economic elite promoting tariffs and monopolies, and a desire to return power to "the people" in the
Leggett tradition. It was not a conservatism the modern Republican party would

have understood. In many ways O'Sullivan's rhetoric was downright radical, attacking the entrenched lords of commerce, and arguing for better treatment of the poor and disenfranchised.

Of course, it was also a selective radicalism, offering little comfort to African-Americans or Native Americans. But it excited thousands of young readers who saw no reason to glare at its internal contradictions. The antebellum Democratic party is often dismissed as reactionary or simplistic—true enough in many parts of the country, especially where it defended the peculiar institution. But we should not overlook the aggressive, reformist zeal felt by many northern Democrats who entertained millennial notions about the future of the country and their destiny within it. Citing the "gigantic boldness" of the American Revolution, and insisting "the eye of man looks naturally forward," O'Sullivan displayed this energetic, futuristic philosophy of democracy better than anyone, save perhaps Whitman. More than most Whigs, or southern Democrats for that matter, he could barely wait for the next chapter in America's evolving experiment.[41]

The enthusiastic tone adopted by O'Sullivan in this manifesto revealed more than a little of the perplexing secular religiosity of the early French Revolution. Despite their skepticism toward religion, these young Democrats felt their creed to be spiritually and intellectually valid, in a deeper sense than mere politics gave expression to, and occasionally O'Sullivan, for all his bombast, was able to grope toward its articulation. Lauding the "democratic principle," which he also called "the voluntary principle," he wrote:

> It is borrowed from the example of the perfect self-government of the physical universe, being written in letters of light on every page of the great bible of Nature. It contains the idea of full and fearless faith in the providence of the Creator. It is essentially involved in Christianity, of which it has been well said that its pervading spirit of democratic equality among men is its highest fact, and one of its most radiant internal evidences of the divinity of its origin.[42]

O'Sullivan's conception of democracy as a "creed" not only lent it a spiritual hue, but more specifically, invested it with a collective sense of philanthropy, a disinterested benevolence toward all humankind, in contrast to the Whig philosophy of individual self-betterment. O'Sullivan often wrote in the first person plural, imploring his fellow Democrats as a preacher might his flock, although his millennium was all sweetness and light, with none of the usual fire and brimstone: "For Democracy is the cause of humanity. It has faith in human nature. It believes in its essential equality and fundamental goodness. . . . It is, moreover, a cheerful creed, a creed of high hope and universal love, noble and ennobling; while all others, which imply a distrust of mankind . . . are . . . gloomy and selfish."[43]

Later issues of the *Review* maintained this secular religiosity, arguing "the source of the democratic principle is essential love and essential truth." More tellingly, "it is not, therefore, *man* in which the democracy puts their trust, for this does aristocracy, but in God, whom it, aristocracy, virtually renounces." In 1839 Parke Godwin came right out and said what O'Sullivan was hinting, "Christianity and Democracy are one." For a bunch of freethinkers, the *Review* writers were oddly dependent on the vocabulary of evangelical piety. Though wary of New England, O'Sullivan even suggested "the reminiscence of Puritanism was the most powerful element of that spirit which produced the Revolution."[44]

Following his epiphany of spiritualized democracy, O'Sullivan spoke out no less vehemently for democracy applied to literature. He was troubled by the nagging suspicion that cultured Americans were "educated" into conservative political thinking simply because higher learning and the press were controlled by the urban "mercantile classes." To his mind, this was anathema. If America was "to carry forward the noble mission entrusted to her, of going before the nations of the world as the representative of the democratic principle and the constant living exemplar of its results," then it ought to be with a spirit of exuberance instilled into every American from his earliest schooling. Not only should the democratic cause "engage the whole mind of the American nation," but it "ought peculiarly to commend itself to the generosity of youth."[45]

With his usual bluntness, O'Sullivan insisted, "the spirit of Literature and the spirit of Democracy are one." This would be meaningless if third-rate politicos had written for his magazine, but throughout his tenure as editor, the *Democratic Review* consistently attracted the finest writing of any American periodical of its day. Literature and fine arts had always seemed imbued with unspoken conservative qualities by virtue of the elitism of European culture. Langtree had expressed a few of these thoughts during his tenure as editor of the *Knickerbocker*, but without the shrillness O'Sullivan now brought to the task. In all his pronouncements, he violently rejected the elitist assumptions Adams had betrayed in his refusal to write for the *Review*, and praised all those allied with him. He described George Bancroft not merely as a successful historian, but "the most democratic historian of modern times," for they were laboring toward a common goal: the intellectual vindication of the American political experiment.[46]

Like the early-twentieth-century critics who rebelled against the genteel tradition, O'Sullivan and his sympathizers celebrated a ruder, more participatory vision of American letters. The rubric of "America" was loosely constructed, and they encouraged literary exploration of pre-Columbian America, the Revolution, the unexplored West, Canada, and even South America (a literary expansionism prefiguring Manifest Destiny). Of kindred importance was the portrayal of the realistic elements of daily life, especially the new realism of urban America. Many French authors such as Balzac, Pierre Jean de Béranger, Eugène Sue, and Victor Cousin, generally ahead of their English peers on this score, found unusual acceptance among *Review* readers for their candid treatment of menial and modern character types in their fiction. The prevalence of French authors and articles on the French Revolution also betrayed nostalgia for the egalitarian intellectual traditions earlier American democrats such as Jefferson and Joel Barlow had admired. German thinkers, too, were featured prominently, although more for their theories of nationalism and folk culture than for the misty philosophical tenets cherished by New England transcendentalists.

When treated at all in histories of the Jacksonian period, the *Democratic Review* has usually been described as a magazine of above-average quality that advanced the political interests of its party through persuasive articles on policy. This is accurate enough, but it neglects the depth of the magazine's commitment to

American literature. The *Review* saw no disjuncture between the struggles to advance partisan interests and foster a new style of writing. The two causes, part and parcel of the umbrella concept of the "democratic principle," were seen to be in perfect harmony. The phrase was applied indiscriminately to both, describing a Hawthorne tale in one use and, say, the insurrection of Thomas Dorr in the next. Following Bancroft, O'Sullivan regarded all history as "the progress of the democratic principle," from Pericles through Cicero, William Tell, Cromwell, Mirabeau, and Simon Bolivar to the present.[47]

Like many nationalists before and since, O'Sullivan expected the democratic principle to culminate soon around the world. Benighted foreign lands needed to learn democracy, which might be taught through a great American literature. Likewise, American literature, in order to become great, needed to express the innate essence of American society, which of course was democracy. This circular thinking, albeit syllogistic, formed the core of O'Sullivan's manifesto, including the extraordinary paragraph cited at the outset:

> The vital principle of an American national literature must be democracy. Our mind is enslaved to the past and present literature of England. . . . We have a principle—an informing soul—our own, our democracy, though we allow it to languish uncultivated; this must be the animating spirit of our literature, if indeed, we would have a national American literature. There is an immense field open to us, if we would but enter it boldly and cultivate it as our own. All history has to be re-written; political science and the whole scope of all moral truth have to be considered and illustrated in the light of the democratic principle. All old subjects of thought and all new questions arising, connected more or less directly with human existence, have to be taken up again and re-examined in this point of view.[48]

In the first number, following O'Sullivan's garrulous introduction, the magazine established the basic format it would follow for the next decade. Poems by Bryant and Whittier were offered, alongside a political portrait of Thomas Hart Benton, and a short piece by Nathaniel Hawthorne entitled "The Toll-Gatherer's Day." Cogent articles were also offered on topics ranging from Mexico to Tocqueville and democracy's potential in Europe. The presence of Bryant and Hawthorne, both Democrats, indicated a political agenda within the literature department as well as without. Whittier was acceptable for his labor sympathy and other quirky reforms.

All in all, the first number of the *Review* was an impressive success. O'Sullivan understood the arts of publicity, and some sources rated circulation as high as five thousand. This was an obvious exaggeration (later estimates by O'Sullivan placed the circulation around two or three thousand), but the magazine certainly earned a wide fame early. From the outset, the *Review* upholstered the party's tarnished image in the wake of the 1837 crisis, with lengthy articles blaming the residual ill effects caused by the Bank of the United States. According to O'Sullivan's characteristically self-flattering assessment, "The testimony of friends and foes was pretty general that these labors were very influential on public opinion."[49]

Orestes Brownson, reviewing the first issue in his *Boston Quarterly Review*, instantly noticed its twofold purpose, both political and literary:

It is to be devoted to the interests of the Democratic party, and will explain and defend its doctrines and measures. But it also proposes to itself a higher, and, in our-judgement, a far more praiseworthy aim. It avows its design to give, as far as it may be able, a democratic tone and character to American literature. . . . A literature cannot be a national one, unless it be the exponent of the national life, informed with the national soul. . . . The national soul of America is democracy, the equal rights and worth of every man, as man. This is the American Idea.[50]

Successive issues repeated the politico-literary formula of the first (which had gone through three editions). Hawthorne frequently contributed, and even Butler wrote sonnets, an impressive burst of intellectual energy for an entrenched politician. O'Sullivan was already hinting at America's soon-to-be-manifest destiny with leading articles on South America and Canada, and betrayed a persistent obsession with novelty and youth. Like a *sans-culotte*, he felt the entire calendar should be redefined to reflect "that Past which was terminated when the American experiment first dawned upon the world as the commencement of a new era." He added, "We can see no reason why, at some future day, our 'experiment' should not be in successful operation over the whole North American continent, from the isthmus to the pole."[51]

The O'Sullivan creed received what was perhaps its most succinct articulation in a short article entitled "The Great Nation of Futurity" in November 1839. In the course of four and a half pages the editor again trumpeted his program, but in more measured cadences than usual. By virtue of its political program, America was unique, occupying "a disconnected position as regards any other nation." Again he insisted, "Our national birth was the beginning of a new history." The blessings of the Godhead were invoked to shore up this position as O'Sullivan waxed metaphysical about time and space, defining an "America" that transcended any normal definition of nationhood, an idea more than a place:

The expansive future is our arena, and for our history. We are entering on its untrodden space, with the truths of God in our minds, beneficent objects in our hearts, and with a clear conscience unsullied by the past. We are the nation of human progress, and who will, what can, set limits to our onward march? . . . The far-reaching, the boundless future will be the era of American greatness. In its magnificent domain of space and time, the nation of many nations is destined to manifest to mankind the excellence of divine principles; to establish on earth the noblest temple ever dedicated to the worship of the Most High—the Sacred and the True. Its floor shall be a hemisphere—its roof the firmament of the star-studded heavens, and its congregation an Union of many Republics.[52]

Naturally, the vehemence with which the *Review* expressed its opinions created problems for it on occasion. Literary journals were aghast at the vulgar idea of combining "the cause of polite literature with the cause of loco-focoism," and the *American Monthly* magazine denounced party leaders who tried to order the faithful to admire certain writers and disregard others. Not only were Whigs suspicious, but many dissenting Democrats as well. Under Van Buren, the *Review* was perceived as an administration organ, which, though desirable from many points of view, also alienated some readers. An 1839 article attacking William Marcy and his clique of old-guard Democrats produced a small crisis in party circles, and Marcy blamed Van Buren. O'Sullivan was admonished from all sides.[53]

A similar incident ruffled Boston literary society, confirming how closed and Whiggish it truly was. In September 1840, Charles Sumner's brother George, the consul at Rome, wrote an article entitled "The Present Condition of Greece" for the *Review*. To his chagrin, he learned from his brother that his fellow Bostonians considered the article and its author politically suspect simply because the *Review* had published it. As O'Sullivan wrote, many Americans, "in quarters where better might have been expected, have not hesitated to denounce us in advance," expecting the *Review* inevitably to promote "the deeds of Marat, Robespierre, and Danton."[54]

Sumner wrote an indignant response from Europe, outraged at Boston's narrow-mindedness:

> Will you believe, that because that article on Greece appeared in the Democratic Review, the only review we have which goes to foreign capitals, the review which champions in a moderate way those principles upon which our Government is founded, the only review published at Washington, therefore the most fitting to receive an article written abroad, and discussing the movements in a foreign nation, the review which Advaros (Min. of Pub. Ins. in Russ.) hailed as a publication which gave a tone to America abroad, and enabled her to appear with a review not a poor repetition of the poor matter of English reviews—because that article appeared in the Democratic Review, it is trodden under foot, and I am denounced as "an Administration man." . . . God damn them all!![55]

Sumner was especially incensed that the article aroused opprobrium not only among Boston's politicians, but even worse, its intellectuals, who exemplified the cultural-political hegemony O'Sullivan bewailed in his manifesto. Charles Sumner had written his brother of the censure the article received from Boston's professors and journalists, who liked the "striking article" but were "sorry to see it in such company" and refused to reprint it. Even Charles urged his brother, "think of abandoning your leaky craft."[56]

At the same time, the leaky craft was barely avoiding the shoals of financial ruin. In the heady early days of the *Review*, O'Sullivan had been led to believe the Van Buren administration would supply the *Review* with lucrative government printing contracts. Like most political promises, this "compact" was never fully realized. Van Buren refused to remove the printing from Francis Blair's influential *Washington Globe*, a long-term Democratic mouthpiece, and the *Review* editors had to make do with occasional small printing jobs and the printing of the James Madison papers, a plum given them in 1839. In other words, O'Sullivan was politically crucified, as hinted by Attorney General Gilpin, who wrote of his "manly and honorable spirit equal in every respect to what you would expect of Jesus preparing himself for the result." The editor was less Christlike in his anguished letters to Butler, complaining of ruin and likening himself to a martyr, while the president sat idle on his "throne." Butler in turn passed on these sentiments to Van Buren, but to no avail. In a letter to his wife, Butler complained the affairs of O'Sullivan and Langtree were "weighing me down like a millstone."[57]

O'Sullivan withdrew in the spring of 1839 as coeditor, ostensibly because of bad health, and spent the summer in Stockbridge, Massachusetts, doubtless still angry with Van Buren. Langtree continued the enterprise, with occasional help from his sulking kinsman. O'Sullivan had spent previous time in this strangely heterodox community, where he formed lifelong friendships with Thomas Wilson Dorr and several Stockbridge natives, including the lawyer David Dudley Field and members of the Sedgwick clan (see chapter 5).[58]

To make money, O'Sullivan started a law practice on Wall Street, but like Bartleby, found the work uncongenial to his temperament, especially taking money from indigent clients. He referred to his fellow lawyers as "useless, if not pernicious leeches upon the body social." Another financial setback for the *Review* occurred on April 11, 1840, when a fire consumed its Washington offices and bindery, leaving fifteen to eighteen thousand dollars of damage with only six thousand dollars of insurance. O'Sullivan's exchequer was reduced to such a low ebb that even the perennially underpaid Hawthorne, who had loaned him money, told him to postpone his payments. This was the nadir of the *Democratic Review*'s early existence.[59]

New York (1840–1847): Destiny Manifested

The election of 1840 forced a rapprochement between O'Sullivan and Van Buren, who realized a closing of the ranks was crucial in the campaign against William Henry Harrison. O'Sullivan not only promoted the national platform, but ran as a local candidate for the New York legislature. Unlike Van Buren, O'Sullivan was elected, and immediately undertook a personal crusade of reform, entering the lists against every relic of Whiggery and feudalism he could find, from Governor Seward's title "His Excellency" to the state's outdated legal system, which he and his friend David Dudley Field were beginning to scrutinize. He also promoted the peace movement (yet another "unfolding of the democratic principle") and confessed to Van Buren a "monomania" for an interoceanic canal across Central America.[60]

Most important, O'Sullivan attacked the death penalty. This issue historically appealed to Democratic lawmakers, for Edward Livingston had broached it in Louisiana as early as 1822, and Robert Rantoul proposed abolition for Massachusetts in 1837. O'Sullivan wrote Bancroft from Albany that this was the "sole motive which has brought me up here." Although ultimately unsuccessful, he enlarged his sphere of influence considerably, supported by an unlikely coalition of old guard Jacksonians and New England moralists. Auguste Davezac, Livingston's brother-in-law and Jackson's personal aide at the Battle of New Orleans, rendered much assistance. O'Sullivan also wrote Van Buren to enlist his support, but the Old Fox of Kinderhook was typically Van Burenish (to use the prevailing adjective) and refused to commit himself. Yet William Lloyd Garrison, whom one would hardly link to Young America, applauded his efforts, and Lydia Maria Child privately paid to circulate one of O'Sullivan's speeches. O'Sullivan was also assisted by the *Review* writers, including Whittier, Lowell, and Whitman, all of whom introduced elements of the issue into their creative work.[61]

O'Sullivan was again elected in 1841, but only narrowly, as nativist opponents mounted an anti-Catholic campaign against him (he was in fact Episcopalian, although he later converted to his ancestral Catholicism). Actually, O'Sullivan disliked all organized religion, as he revealed in a long report on the death penalty he released through the *Review's* printer in 1841. O'Sullivan not only questioned the legal authority of Moses, he offered a classic locofoco formulation of Christ, whose "radically democratic spirit" was suffused with an "inevitable tendency to level in the dust every political or social institution at variance with that spirit." His campaign against the death penalty and the Protestant establishment culminated in early 1843, when he publicly debated the issue against George Cheever, a Presbyterian minister with a literary bent. Their debates attracted much interest among the public, and O'Sullivan continued the campaign in the *Review*, offending a number of clergymen in the process with the antireligious tone of his rejection of the Mosaic Code.[62]

By this time O'Sullivan had decided to move the *Review* permanently to Manhattan to accommodate his rising sphere of influence there. In late 1840 he purchased his brother-in-law's interest and assumed total control of the enterprise. Instead of depending on sporadic printing income, O'Sullivan dropped his sideline entirely and arranged for the Democratic publishers J. and H. G. Langley to issue the *Review*, leaving him free to concentrate on editorial duties. Liberated from the encumbrances of Washington, the editor and his creation were free to embark on the happiest period of their history. Suddenly, the *Review* was an independent magazine, still Democratic to be sure, but free to pursue a multiplicity of interests in a cosmopolitan setting.[63]

New York in the 1840s was the most exciting place in America for an aggressive young thinker like O'Sullivan. The completion of the Erie Canal and rapid immigration had swelled its wealth and numbers beyond comprehension. From a population of 152,056 in 1820, the city quadrupled in three decades, reaching 391,114 in 1840 and 696,115 at midcentury. The *Review* was inevitably drawn there, especially after the accession of a hostile administration in Washington. Not only was the thriving publishing business centered in New York, but the Democratic party considered it a vital stronghold, despite internecine tensions lingering from the Locofoco period. Indeed, Locofocoism was on O'Sullivan's mind as he explained the move. The city appealed to him for its class tensions and because it harbored some of the most aggressive Democratic thinkers in the country, worthy heirs to Leggett, with fresh memories of the ravages causes by the 1837 Panic. The difficult social conditions New York experienced during this growth almost demanded that its intellectuals reflect on the larger issues of social justice, particularly as the state clamored for a new constitution (which it received in 1846). As O'Sullivan wrote,

> All was open, bold, and genuinely, radically democratic. The city had been gradually prepared, by a long process of deep agitation on fundamental principles during four or five years past, for the reception of this strong regimen of 'radical' opinions. It was there that had commenced the movement which has now swept over the whole land, north, east, south, and west. It was there that first appeared the incipient fermentation of that purifying leaven of 'Locofocoism' which is now fast leavening the whole lump.[64]

New York appealed to literary nationalists because it exerted a powerful attraction on writers from all over the country, including Westerners, Southerners, and New Englanders. It was far more representative of the pan-American literary identity O'Sullivan was eager to mine than Boston, Concord, or Philadelphia. In the boom years of the early 1840s, as the publishing business leapt forward, new books were everywhere in Manhattan. The rejuvenated *Review* rejoiced: "The prevailing activity and spirit which has begun to pervade almost all departments of commercial industry has not failed to extend itself to the book business: printers, binders, stationers, and all parties concerned with the purveyors of literary productions, being as fully occupied as they can be."[65]

The *Review* resumed publishing in July 1841 and expanded its literary format with new features on recent books and "Monthly Literary Intelligence." Despite the distraction of another term in the state legislature in 1842, O'Sullivan's editorial skills were improving. With an eclectic mix of articles, the magazine displayed increasingly intellectual ambitions, reflective of New York's distance from Washington. Its panoramic scope included drama, music, art, and all the other amenities softening the great city's rapid transformation, along with the usual dose of Locofoco politics. Notes from the New-York Historical Society began appearing in the November 1843 number, adding to the magazine's metropolitan feel.

In this period Hawthorne wrote some of his most famous stories for the *Review*, and a young Brooklynite named Walter Whitman published his earliest works. Rival periodicals were effusive in their praise. The *Standard* called it "the best periodical in the country," and the *Boston Post* opined, "No review in the country is conducted with more ability." Likewise, *Brother Jonathan* declared no American magazine "has ever presented a prouder array of talent." Even Horace Greeley's Whiggish *New York Tribune* admitted "it is quite equal to any thing in the Magazine line extant." Judging from circulation lists occasionally published, its subscribers ranged across the entire nation. From Maine to Texas, Americans wished to sample Manhattan's cultural vivacity.[66]

Boosted by growing subscriptions, the *Review* enjoyed renewed vigor in the early 1840s. Its talented writers defined a robust Americanism in cultural categories ranging from Edwin Forrest's proletarian theater to genre painting to the urban novels esteemed by Evert Duyckinck's circle. Needless to say, it continued to address political issues, supporting the rising tide of liberalism in Europe, American resistance to English foreign policy, and Thomas Dorr's militant attempt to extend suffrage in Rhode Island in 1842. O'Sullivan led a cacophonous campaign to support his old friend Dorr, and even tried to drum up military support among New York Democrats, foreshadowing the militarism that would later bedevil this self-described pacifist. Another future problem surfaced in O'Sullivan's reluctance to let black Rhode Islanders share the suffrage he wanted to give the working class. Horace Greeley lambasted O'Sullivan's two-faced stance, rightly criticizing the racial hypocrisy of the "Progressive Democracy." But in 1842, racial hypocrisy was acceptable to most Americans; indeed, it was indispensable to a successful political career.[67]

As the *Review*'s prestige mounted, O'Sullivan was able to delegate authority and spend more time hobnobbing with Democratic heavyweights. Soon he found

himself accepted in the party's inner sanctum, both because of the *Review*'s efficiency at marshaling public opinion, and the rising awareness that New York was a
crucial swing state for the election of 1844. The summer of 1844 was extremely
volatile in the political realm, with the first temblors presaging the earthquake to
follow in the next decade. A strong portent was the discord within the Democratic
party at the Baltimore convention to nominate a presidential candidate. Van Buren,
smarting from his defeat in 1840, but still a political force, wished to be renomi-
nated for another chance to win the presidency from the weakened Whigs. But
there were signs that divisions within the Democratic party would prevent his accession. The most formidable of the anti-Van Buren factions was clustered around
John Calhoun. As early as 1843, O'Sullivan had foreseen the impending North-
South split in the party, writing Van Buren, "I shall, I cannot but confess, tremble
for the consequences."[68]

The fierce struggle came to a head at the Baltimore nominating convention in
May 1844. O'Sullivan attended the convention with his press credentials, but he
was secretly reporting on the proceedings in a series of letters to Van Buren in
Kinderhook. A bitter sarcasm pervaded them, as if O'Sullivan knew the outcome of
the schism before it happened. He observed, "The very atmosphere is burthened
with the putrid odor of the corruption so rotten and rife in men's hearts." As he predicted, the Calhoun circle ("the world of traitordom"), abetted by Michigan's Lewis
Cass, effectively blocked Van Buren's plan.[69]

In the end, James Polk was nominated as a compromise candidate, but the
New York delegation was left unsatisfied. Even thirty-five years later, O'Sullivan
could not reminisce about this campaign without bitterness, calling Polk "the com-
paratively second-rate man." A friend recorded O'Sullivan's private account of his
faction's crushing defeat at Baltimore, with Benjamin Butler so overwrought that
"he lay upon the bed and cried like a child." But despite their disappointment,
northern Democrats resolved to hold their noses and work for the party despite the
stench attached to it (although as late as October 28, O'Sullivan was writing Van
Buren with farfetched ideas how he might be elected). O'Sullivan praised the appropriate Democrats in the *Review*, while privately writing Van Buren that publishing a profile of the two-faced Cass was akin to taking poison.[70]

This digression into political history helps account for the sudden emergence
of the Young America cultural alliance around 1845. In my opinion, the tension felt
by New Yorkers following the disappointment at Baltimore in 1844 set the stage for
the explosion of nationalist culture that followed immediately afterward. Not only
were the young nationalists disheartened by the older generation's failed politics,
but they were likely terrified as well. Having glimpsed the specter of a schism between the North and South (and few saw it more closely than O'Sullivan in 1844),
the Young Democracy poured all of its energy into allaying tensions with appeals to
Americanism. Despite his ambivalence, O'Sullivan exerted himself heroically, and
may have singlehandedly won the election for Polk.

All eyes were focused on New York as a crucial swing state, and O'Sullivan was
encouraged to start a daily newspaper in the metropolis with Samuel Tilden. On
June 20, John Bigelow, then a young *Review* writer, noted in his diary: "O'Sullivan

told me yesterday of a design of his to start a new daily paper." The first issue of the *New York Morning News* was released upon the city August 21, 1844, displaying all the hallmarks of the O'Sullivan style, and representing the "Young Hickory" school of New York Democrats. Ebullient editorials reminded readers of the high cause of democracy, and American literature was loudly trumpeted throughout. The front page not only advertised "Young Hickory Tobacco" in blatant promotion of James Polk's nickname (guaranteed to "act like a charm on the Whigs"), but also featured Nathaniel Hawthorne's tale, "A Select Party."[71]

This story, which also ran in the July 1844 *Review*, is not one of his most famous, but its mock-sardonic call for the "Master Genius" of American literature worked well alongside O'Sullivan's literary nationalism. This was quality fare for a political newspaper, again showing the politico-literary conflation (in one editorial O'Sullivan even called John Milton a "barnburner"). From its inception, O'Sullivan announced, "It is intended in the Morning News to give a special attention to the department of literary criticism and the noticing of all the new publications of the day." Toward that end he enlisted the able support of Evert Duyckinck, whom he announced as "one of the most accomplished scholars and elegant writers of the country," along with his circle of literary nationalists.[72]

Duyckinck was well known to O'Sullivan through several channels. They had attended Columbia together, Duyckinck graduating four years after O'Sullivan in 1835, and O'Sullivan probably acted as a tutor to him while studying toward his master's degree, if not even earlier, when Duyckinck was in high school. They served together on a committee to secure an observatory for their alma mater in 1845 and were fellow members of the New-York Historical Society. More important, Duyckinck had already distinguished himself in the campaign for a democratic literature.[73]

He and his associates (see chapter 3) were less overtly political than O'Sullivan, but still loyal Democrats. Besides offering loud support for his crusade against capital punishment, they echoed his intellectual patriotism in their writings for various periodicals. Returning the favor, O'Sullivan warmly praised "that excellent magazine, Arcturus," edited by Duyckinck, and solicited articles from Duyckinck's friends for the *Review*, especially following the demise of *Arcturus* in 1842. In his diary, John Bigelow recorded with great excitement being seated at the same table as O'Sullivan and Duyckinck at a New-York Historical Society banquet in 1844. He knew that these two men were central to the project of rejuvenating American culture.[74]

The short-term goal of the paper was realized with Polk's narrow triumph in New York and consequent election. The *Richmond Enquirer* considered "*there was no single individual* to whom the Union was more indebted" than O'Sullivan. The paper continued for two years, hotly tracing the same issues on the *Review*'s agenda, from Young Ireland to Texas to the war against Whiggish literature. Giving in to the new format, O'Sullivan composed many incendiary editorials for the *News* that he withheld from the more dignified *Review*, including some of his most fervent calls for Manifest Destiny in 1845.[75]

A word should be inserted about this phrase, O'Sullivan's most tangible legacy, and possibly his most confusing one. I agree he authored the phrase, as Julius Pratt argued long ago. But I think several misrepresentations need to be cleared up about his role. To begin, he never conceived Manifest Destiny in a vacuum. O'Sullivan was one of dozens of journalists calling for something similar (it was a popular position in New York in 1845). At the same time, James Gordon Bennett was feverishly promoting America's "ultimate destiny" in the *New York Herald*. Unluckily, his term was less catchy.[76]

More interestingly, no historian has ever probed the paradox that Manifest Destiny, a term synonymous with Yankee imperialism, was coined by a man with a profound personal attachment to Latin America. Few journalists knew more about the geography and politics of the region than O'Sullivan. In its early years, the *Democratic Review* lavished attentions on the Latin American republics, praising them for their rebellion against Spain (whose aristocracy he was nominally attached to). These articles disappeared with the Mexican tensions of the mid-1840s.[77]

O'Sullivan also had extensive personal connections south of the border. His father fought for Venezuelan independence before his South American shipwreck, and other family members lived in Central America and the Caribbean. The very year of Manifest Destiny, O'Sullivan's sister married a Cuban planter, and a year later O'Sullivan himself honeymooned there. Clearly, Latin America occupied a vital place in his worldview, and there were complex psychological reasons for his obsession. When he later became a Cuban filibuster, he expressed a bizarre combination of democratic longing and megalomania, expecting a Cuban Revolution to free the people and enrich him simultaneously. Doubtless O'Sullivan believed in Manifest Destiny, but beneath his assertive voice there were problems that few historians have recognized.[78]

This background may help to explain the singular fact that O'Sullivan expressed reserve about his increasingly frenzied tone in 1845. Most historians have assumed his jingoism knew no limits, but he expressed doubts about his own actions. In January, he wrote Silas Wright that his editorials were only to satisfy "mass feeling," but this was perhaps to appease Wright's own ambivalence on the issue. Even more strangely, he urged George Bancroft, the secretary of the navy, to avoid war in August 1845, the very month Manifest Destiny was coined in a *Review* editorial. He elaborated, "My peace principles make me greatly regret our present warlike attitude. I devoutly pray that you may not be placed in a position of necessity to let fly the thunderbolts placed officially in your hands." O'Sullivan was beginning to betray the quirkiness that would mar his later career.[79]

The problem lay in O'Sullivan's temporary adherence to the movement for international peace in the early 1840s, and his lingering hope that Manifest Destiny unfold naturally, without anyone's feelings getting hurt. He never lost his desire for expansion, penning countless editorials on the same theme before and after the one authoring the famous catchwords. But sometime in the mid-1840s, a significant change took place in his attitude toward war. As the pacifistic *Review* grew obsessed with new territory for the expansion of democracy, it dropped its objection to hostilities. The excitement of the 1844 campaign and the stirring of his familial interest in Latin America awakened an ugly new belligerent tone in 1845–46. He briefly disapproved of the war when it erupted, but reversed himself shortly afterward. Despite the contradiction of demanding Oregon and California while championing the right to self-determination elsewhere, O'Sullivan forged ahead with characteristic energy.[80]

There were foreshadowings of O'Sullivan's celebrated coining of Manifest Destiny prior to its large-scale adoption in the mid-1840s. Both "manifest" and "destiny" were cherished words in his vocabulary, and it was inevitable they would be coupled to advance a concept neither manifest nor destined until, by dint of constant repetition, the phrase became enacted as reality. Surprisingly, he wrote in 1839 that it was the "manifest common interest" of Canada and the United States to stay separate.[81]

In November 1838, O'Sullivan wrote, "It is manifest that the reaction now apparent over the whole length and breadth of the land is a great national movement that must go on" (this article used the word *manifest* no fewer than four times). A year later, in "The Great Nation of Futurity," he announced America would "manifest" its "glorious destiny" in "the far-reaching, the boundless future," in a place with no boundaries. Beginning in 1845, he stepped up the campaign with increasingly aggressive editorials. On February 7 the *News* fairly screamed, "Yes, more, more, more! . . . till our national destiny is fulfilled . . . and the whole boundless continent is ours." On February 28, the *News* said the feeling of expansion was "manifest." The *Review* finally coined the phrase in its July-August number, but it went unnoticed until December 27, when the *News* claimed "the right of our manifest destiny to overspread and to possess the whole of the continent." It entered the national lexicon a week later following a speech in the House of Representatives by Robert C. Winthrop. Fourteen years later, Lincoln would identify "Young America" as "the unquestioned inventor of Manifest Destiny."[82]

It is chiefly through this coining, and the subsequent researches of Julius Pratt, Frederick Merk, and Albert K. Weinberg, that anyone has heard of O'Sullivan at all. But a misconception has arisen over O'Sullivan's expansionism. Some scholars assert that his theory was always rooted in a race-based attitude that vaunted Anglo-Saxon supremacy as the origin of the legal right to occupy the West. This overstates the case somewhat, judging from a *News* editorial of August 13, 1845, in which the editor assailed this prevalent mode of thinking. For O'Sullivan, the key to the American right of expansion lay mainly in the superiority of its political system. It was democracy, not Anglo-Saxonism, that he wished to spread across the continent and around the world. Earlier *Review* editorials had taken pains to criticize the militarism of "the Anglo-Saxon race" while promoting O'Sullivan's pet interest in pacifism. In fact, some of his most strident editorials were directed against England's aggression, arguing for more territory as a way to check the gluttonous monarchs of Europe (an early version of containment). When one considers his Irish heritage and his latent Catholicism, for which he had been unjustly persecuted in his campaign for the state legislature, his complicated (and not always consistent) position becomes clearer.[83]

But if this correction makes O'Sullivan seem more appealing to a modern readership, there is no way to overlook his blindness on the race issue. As generous as "Manifest Destiny" was in almost every category of national life, it held no place for African- Americans. O'Sullivan never approved of slavery, but he never thought very hard about how to end it, other than to postulate its "natural" and "inevitable" disappearance as Americans expanded westward. True, he hoped the new territory would hasten slavery's demise, draining it toward the southwest "by the same unvarying law that bids water descend the slope that invites it." This hardly turned out to be the case. It was precisely the question of slavery's expansion into the west that led to the implosion of the two-party system, and the proponents of Manifest Destiny as a providential solution to America's problems could not have been more naive about the future. For all his brilliance, O'Sullivan, like most Americans, refused to confront the slavery issue, and it ultimately proved his undoing.[84]

But 1861 was still a world away in 1845. The Manifest Destiny editorials for which O'Sullivan is remembered form only a tiny fragment of the opinions he rendered on an immense constellation of contemporary issues. From 1844 to 1846 O'Sullivan was in charge of both an important daily newspaper in the nation's metropolis and one of the country's foremost magazines. Throughout this period he was in constant communication not only with Van Buren and his faction, but also with Polk in the White House, often acting as an intermediary between the two. A fellow writer bemusedly wondered how the overtaxed O'Sullivan could come up with opinions on "politics, news, city gossip, theatrical criticism, notices of new books . . . museums, music, merchandize, mechanic's institutes" and other "motley topics."[85]

Beside Texas and Oregon, O'Sullivan continued to report frequently on the activities of Young Europe, and he began to display the proprietary interest in Cuba that would emerge in the scandal of the ill-fated Lopez expedition in 1851 (see chapter 6). The literary side of the *Review* was capably directed by Duyckinck and his nationalistic friends, and the magazine also took a strong position in favor of the actor Edwin Forrest during his travails with English audiences, foreshadowing the Astor Place riots of 1849. George Bancroft once told him he was "wasting [his] mind in a New York newspaper," but O'Sullivan countered this suggestion credibly, writing back, "The times seem to me only too pregnant with reason for satisfaction in the possession of an instrument of influence on the public mind, at once so powerful and so honorable." Even more nakedly, he wrote, "Give me the making of the newspapers of a nation, and I will make its minds."[86]

Indeed, there was much justification for this statement. At the age of thirty-one, O'Sullivan had the entire nation's ear. The *New York Mirror* praised him as "a scholar, an ambitious politician, and something of a revolutionist," and predicted he was "very likely destined to fill some higher mission than bearer of despatches from Washington to St. James." But in retrospect, this period would prove to be the apogee of O'Sullivan's career, although he always felt bigger and better things were on his way.[87]

Financial trouble had plagued him since the windfall from his mother's settlement, and as he moved more and more freely in the company of nabobs, he paid less attention to the daily operations of his periodicals. In September 1844, a *Review* writer had noted, "The Editor, in most cases, has too much work put upon him." In July 1845 he attempted without success to persuade the trusted Duyckinck to purchase a half-interest in the *Review*. Duyckinck declined, writing a friend, "Its pecuniary affairs have been so loosely conducted that it has become the means of unpleasantness to any one closely connected with it, by its spurious non-paying relations with authors." Two months later O'Sullivan hired John Bigelow to take over the political section of the magazine, and one of its publishers pleaded with him to replace O'Sullivan as editor. Bigelow had complained in his diary of O'Sullivan's rascality toward authors, adding, "If he were not a good fellow, I would see him toasted."[88]

Among other distractions, the editor was tempted with diplomatic prospects, including a job in the State Department under James Buchanan and a nomination to become chargé to Austria. He also thought about starting a new newspaper to represent the northern Democracy at Washington, writing Samuel Tilden that "Polk's knees would knock together" at the thought. At the end of 1845 he went to England to pursue a business scheme investing in dry docks with other Democratic leaders. A few months later he was appointed a regent of the University of the State of New York, apparently as a political favor, a post he retained until 1854. He was also distracted by the wedding of his sister, Langtree's widow, to a wealthy Cuban and his own impending nuptials to the daughter of a New York doctor, Susan Kearny Rodgers. Thomas Dorr teased him mercilessly when he discovered her politics: "Are you the captive of a *Whig* lady?"[89]

Thus ensnared by the opposition, he allowed the *News* to die a relatively painless death in 1846, just as Manifest Destiny was reaching fruition in hostilities toward Mexico. Its business manager wrote Tilden, "The long agony is over—the *Morning News* is dead." The *Democratic Review*, though apparently successful, was reduced in price and length in late 1845 in a gambit to win more subscribers. The following spring, he sold his pride and joy to Henry Wikoff, a maverick like O'Sullivan, for a price between five and six thousand dollars. O'Sullivan maintained a nominal association with the *Review*, but it was never the same under anyone else's stewardship. Its fortunes declined along with the cause of nationalism it served, and despite an intense burst of popularity in 1852 (see chapter 6), it folded in 1859, with its founder far away in Europe, and the Democracy in a shambles.[90]

Young America

In his preface to *History of a Literary Radical*, Van Wyck Brooks described Randolph Bourne in words that apply equally to O'Sullivan: "As we look over his writings today, we find them a sort of corpus, a text full of secret ciphers, and packed with meaning between the lines, of all the most intimate questions and difficulties and turns of thought and feeling that make up the soul of young America."[91]

So far I have concentrated on the *Democratic Review* without delineating the wider concept of "Young America" that became attached to it. There is little doubt the *Review* was a successful venture, both for O'Sullivan and the Democratic party at large. The politicians who invested in the magazine were pleased to see the party's image refurbished, and the young thinkers swarming New York in the 1840s were delighted to have such a lively, eclectic periodical in their midst. George Parsons Lathrop reckoned the *Review* "the most brilliant periodical of the time."[92]

Perhaps the highest compliment is that the Whig party saw fit to create a rival to the *Democratic Review*, also based in New York, called the *American Review: A*

Whig Journal of Politics, Literature, Art and Science. This magazine, which ran from 1845 to the Whig collapse in 1852, mimicked the *Democratic Review*'s formula, but its fiction was of a lower caliber, and its editorials could not match the sense of engagement and adventure offered by O'Sullivan. His readers were thrilled or outraged by his invective, but rarely bored.

The relative success of the *Review* is not hard to explain. First, it presented its information in a pyrotechnic style that starkly contrasted with its staid competition. O'Sullivan's adolescent infatuation with revolution and the future appealed to a wide spectrum of disgruntled readers, many of whom, of course, were also young. Whether discussing Cromwell, the Glorious Revolution, Culloden, or the American and French revolutions, he effectively conveyed a sense that history was malleable and each generation endowed with the ability to shape its own destiny. This was a very effective political message after the disenchantment of 1837.

In some ways the *Review* was more like a newspaper than a magazine. Every event was given increased significance through a few neat rhetorical tricks, always emphasizing newness and boldness. Accordingly, the Declaration of Independence was no mere document, but "a tremendous act of revolution," and "our national birth was the beginning of a new history." When the Supreme Court membership was altered, it inaugurated a "new era," and O'Sullivan solemnly wrote, "We are in the midst of a revolution." The Bank Crisis was "the Second War of the Revolution," and the 1837 crisis "the Revolution of 1837." On the passage of the subtreasury reform, "this event will stamp the year eighteen hundred and forty as one of the leading epochs of our history." The Whigs and Democrats were locked in "a holy war," although American progress would soon bring "a great awakening." A good book by William Prescott signaled "the new era is approaching." The ebullient editor might have been describing himself when he wrote of the nation's Democratic press that despite their inferior numbers, "they are full of energy, boldness, confidence, earnestness, argument and eloquence," in contrast to the "specious sophisms" of Whiggery.[93]

O'Sullivan leavened his discussion of these portentous issues with a quick wit and vivacious style. Discussing the merit of articles mocking Whigs in a letter to Benjamin Butler, he wrote, "They appear to be very useful. . . . They diversify and lighten—and making our friends laugh, have the best effect of inspiring confidence and good spirit." As he advised Orestes Brownson, a good editor should strive for "the greatest entertainment of the greatest number." His editorials and his correspondence often railed hilariously at the slow-witted opposition, capturing brilliantly the mocking tone of Young American nationalism. This was an effective selling point in the new mass market for journalism, and many young readers were captivated by his élan. A short story he published by Joseph Neal, "The Newsboy," captured his philosophy: "Without sauciness, what is a newsboy? what is an editor? what are revolutions? what are people? Sauce is power, sauce is spirit, independence, victory, everything. It is, in fact,—this sauce, or 'sass,' as the vulgar have it— steam to the great locomotive of affairs."[94]

Another reason for the *Review*'s importance is more specific, simply that it paid more attention to continental news and literature than other periodicals. O'Sullivan's linguistic ability and international background helped him here. Most Ameri-

can magazines of the day were obsessed with English affairs, paying far less attention to the rest of Europe. Who could better lead the campaign to discredit slavish
Anglophilia than two Irish-American journalists? Their success was measured by a
comment in *Blackwood's Edinburgh Magazine* in 1848: "The *Democratic Review*
. . . has a habit of predicting twice or thrice a year that England is on the point of
exploding utterly, and going off into absolute chaos."[95]

The fact that O'Sullivan was partly Irish (and Langtree entirely so) has rarely
been discussed by historians, but surely it helps to explain the *Review's* difference
from other periodicals. Ethnic tension was increasingly prevalent in the United
States, and certainly played into politics, with the Whig party composed largely of
Anglo-Saxon Protestants and the Democrats a hodgepodge of different elements.
Lee Benson argued that the New York Democratic party depended heavily on a
loose alliance of Dutch and "Old British" New Yorkers with Irish, German, and
French immigrants. The *Review* circle mirrored Benson's formulation, and many of
its leading lights must have derived some of their Anglophobia from the human fact
of their ancestry. Duyckinck was from an old Dutch family (as were Whitman and
Melville through their mothers), Auguste Davezac was French, and besides O'Sullivan, Langtree and Butler were proudly Irish. Van Buren shrewdly ascribed this
heritage to Jackson as well, recounting to Gansevoort Melville that the general's
family was "driven from ill-fated Ireland and its oppressions."[96]

Despite his monomaniacal patriotism, O'Sullivan was no isolationist. In fact,
one of his many minor claims to distinction is that he issued an early American call
for a "Congress of Nations" to adjudicate matters of international law and diplomacy, and in so doing, "to republicanize the world." For all its ultra-Americanism,
the *Review* covered the non-English world with surprising thoroughness. Its inaugural issue left no doubts about its international outlook, calling for "the voice of
America" to speak out to a prostrate Europe, as it would in the twentieth century.[97]

If anything, O'Sullivan's tone grew more impassioned with time. In May 1840
he wrote, eight years early, "We incline strongly to the belief, that a republic not less
free than our own might be reconstituted in France to-morrow." Two months later
he foresaw the "impending commotion" in France and Germany, which he translated as the tension between Europe's "ancient feudalism and the principles of
American freedom," thus wrapping the European republicans in a mantle they
probably would have cast off. Like many before and since, he was convinced that
"the eyes of the world are fixed upon the citizens of this young republic." He also
felt America's "mission" conferred the right to interfere in other national struggles against "the tyranny of kings, hierarchs and oligarchs," either by "example,"
or if necessary, by action. Toward the bizarre end of its term, after O'Sullivan had
sold his interest but remained a contributor, the *Review* earned dubious distinction as the first forum to advocate American military intervention in Europe (see
chapter 6).[98]

Beyond the ethnicity of the contributors, the *Review's* French focus suggested
an extension of the alliance between democrats and France dating back to the first
party struggles of the 1790s. Lewis Cass wrote a lengthy series of articles on France
in 1840 while serving as the American ambassador, and many more were written
around 1848. The magazine fawned over Tocqueville and Guizot, and French fic-

tion was often featured, especially when it treated themes of poverty and government insensitivity (Balzac and Hugo were particular favorites). Even Louis Napoleon, the future villain of 1848, was the subject of several glowing articles when in
prison.[99]

Yet another reason for the *Review*'s significance was its interest in the lower
classes of readership. This is not to say it pandered to proletarian interests, although
the accusation might have been leveled in the upper echelons of Whiggery. Rather,
it demonstrated a constant concern for the underprivileged in consonance with
its perception of the Jacksonian legacy. O'Sullivan saw the "Barnburners" (New
York's radical Democrats) as only the most recent in a long chain of popular cham-
pions dating back to the Jacobins and Roundheads. Beyond its affiliation with
Brownson, the *Review* announced its support for any measures that would improve
the laborer's lot, and outspokenly praised Albert Brisbane and William Ellery
Channing.[100]

Finally, the central hallmark of the *Review* was its unrelenting emphasis on
youth. From the moment it was founded until well into the 1850s, the magazine
sounded this theme, exciting young Americans about their role in the country's
"destiny," a word that naturally appeals to immaturity. Young people of all nations
were praised for their instinctive liberalism, while the monarchies of Europe were
always described with adjectives of senescence and decrepitude. O'Sullivan bluntly
asserted, "We have no interest in the scenes of antiquity, only as lessons of avoid-
ance of nearly all their examples." Around the world, he expected democracy soon
to replace "the old system, the old yokes, the old burdens."[101]

America, on the other hand, was invested with all the virtues of playful innocence. Like many other writers of the period, O'Sullivan often depicted America
as a sinewy manchild, barely conscious of his strength. The value of youth might
be transferred to any concept O'Sullivan advocated, and anything else dismissed
as an "old barbarism." Of course, the Democrats represented "the true genius
and spirit of America and the American destiny," while the Whigs were "the party
of the old ideas, the old things." This dualism could also be applied to intellectual efforts, as one of Evert Duyckinck's original Young Americans argued. In a
piece titled "The Early Maturity of Genius," W. A. Jones defined the best time
for artistic genius as "the period of mature adolescence, from twenty-four to
thirty." Jones added that many great thinkers discover their abilities "while in their
teens," but almost nobody who begins an intellectual career after thirty can sustain it very long. His words would come back to haunt him, when an even crueler version of Young America would lambaste him for his "Old Fogydom" (see
chapter 6).[102]

O'Sullivan's distrust of the older generation crept into his criticism of Orestes
Brownson, whose early enthusiasm he admired but whose articles for the *Review*
fell far short of the mark. The editor revealed a complex discomfort with aging as he
dismissed Brownson's mature views: "The general current and direction of his Article look very suspiciously like the usual process by which, after passing the grand
climacteric of life, the young Liberal so often becomes metamorphosed into the
old Conservative." Fearing that conservatism may increase "as flake after flake of
the snow of years shall begin to streak our head with its whiteness," O'Sullivan

vowed he would surrender the editorship "on the appearance of our first grey hair."[103]

In his provocative study of the age, George Forgie suggested that a generational Oedipal complex afflicted the players of the post-Jacksonian period, all of whom felt a desire to equal the revolutionary achievement of the founding fathers but were unable to specify how this might be done. O'Sullivan and Langtree were not the only Americans who were, in O'Sullivan's words, "very young, very sanguine and very democratic." They also gathered into their camp a host of fresh writers, equally obsessed with the patricidal precedent of the Revolution. O'Sullivan (b. 1813), Theodore Sedgwick III (b. 1811), Evert Duyckinck (b. 1816), John Bigelow (b. 1817), and Parke Godwin (b. 1816) all cut their teeth on New York journalism at an early age and felt an instinctive alliance with the party that seemed to speak to their concerns, especially in the wake of William Leggett and Locofocoism. The novelist Cornelius Mathews (b. 1817) spoke for many of them in the 1845 speech claiming the name Young America: "Here, in New York, is the seat and strong-hold of this young power: but, all over the land, day by day, new men are emerging into activity, who partake of these desires, who scorn and despise the past pettiness of the country, and who are ready to sustain any movement toward a better and nobler condition."[104]

The psycho-historical approach is especially interesting when one considers the strange insurgent lineage of the O'Sullivan pedigree, and the fact that so many Young Americans grew up with conservative fathers, many of whom died young. It is almost as if by attacking the party of privilege, they were establishing their own in-dependence from domineering patrimonies, just as Hawthorne's Robin did in "My Kinsman, Major Molineux." Specifically addressing "The Young American" in 1844, Emerson orated, "I call upon you, young men, to obey your heart and be the nobility of this land."[105]

The youthfulness of the *Democratic Review* clique was well captured by a private diary kept by John Bigelow, an early associate of O'Sullivan's. Like countless others, Bigelow gravitated to New York from the upstate outlands, ready to pursue both his literary interests and his career as a lawyer. He soon fell in with O'Sullivan's crowd of young Democrats, becoming friends with Samuel Tilden, studying law with the Sedgwicks, and joining the overworked staff at the *Democratic Review*.[106]

Bigelow's impressions revealed the *Review* set as a fast-moving crowd of ambitious and hard-working young men, not far removed from college, trading books and ideas freely, and eager to take on all comers. They met frequently to socialize in hurly-burly New York and contemplated everything under the sun. O'Sullivan attended concerts and plays at Niblo's Theater, invited chess players to his house, and threw dinner parties for luminaries such as Robert Dale Owen, Alexander Everett, and his closer friends the Sedgwicks and David Dudley Field. When Bigelow needed a favor, such as election to the New-York Historical Society, or appointment to be inspector of Sing Sing prison, O'Sullivan was happy to assist him. Bigelow also recorded passing "a very pleasant time" on several occasions with O'Sullivan's friends the literary nationalists: Duyckinck, Cornelius Mathews, "and others of that ilk." In his *Retrospections*, he recalled contributors frequently wrote for the *Morning News* without pay, simply because they were bubbling over with exuberance "for the cause."[107]

The functions of social reform and socializing frequently intermingled. To look at one example, some of the leading lights of the New York Democracy (including O'Sullivan, Theodore Sedgwick III, and Benjamin F. Butler) came together as the New York Prison Association to improve the lot of the state's incarcerees. Not to be excluded, a number of their female friends formed The Ladies of the New York Prison Association, among them Caroline Kirkland, Catharine Sedgwick, and O'Sullivan's sister Mary Langtree. O'Sullivan particularly encouraged female participation, although it is hard to call him a feminist. He engaged a "corps de réserve of young female friends" to help with editorial duties and obviously enjoyed the company of women. Now and then, he even argued for something like equal rights. The May 1844 *Review* attacked "The Legal Wrongs of Women" in a long essay to which O'Sullivan added a postcript of agreement. The same issue promoted female novelists and excerpted several different novels and poems by women authors.[108]

Over half a century later, the dowager Julia Ward Howe still recalled the brilliancy of the young New York set and the vivacity of their social routine ("a series of balls, concerts and dinners," to say nothing of "dancing parties" which "usually broke up soon after one o'clock"). During this festive period of her life, she saw many "literary people," the first of whom she recalled was "John L. O'Sullivan, the accomplished editor of the Democratic Review."[109]

It was inevitable, given his youthful radicalism, that O'Sullivan and his cohorts would cheer on the European republican movements known variously as Young Italy, Young Germany, Young France, Young Poland, Young Ireland, or collectively as Young Europe. All these movements shared a certain common dynamic: enmity toward the standing order, disaffection with the older power structure, and a literary interest in nurturing the folk traditions and popular culture of the country as a subtle form of political protest. Furthermore, their attempts to unify their countries through cultural cohesion precisely mirrored O'Sullivan's hopes of preserving the fragile Democratic coalition through appeals to vaguely American traditions.

Young Italy was the earliest of the movements, gathering around Giuseppe Mazzini in 1831, and trying to use the bond of common Italian culture to unite the hopelessly dispersed Italian states. The *Review* found this group fascinating, not in the least because of its belief that "without union there is in truth no nationality." O'Sullivan devoted a close study to *Giovine Italia* in his September 1841 number, which pleased Mazzini immensely. Uncoincidentally, a New York branch of Young Italy had formed that very year, led by E. F. Foresti, an exile whom the Sedgwicks had established at Stockbridge before he moved to New York and began teaching at Columbia. O'Sullivan and Catharine Sedgwick tried to help him by publishing his work in the *Review*.[110]

Young Germany was more of an intellectual phenomenon, but sufficiently irksome to the government that the phrase was interdicted in 1835. In England, Benjamin Disraeli's group in Parliament assumed the name Young England, albeit somewhat misleadingly, for their nationalism was reactionary and antidemocratic, characterized by Disraeli's *Coningsby; or, the New Generation* (1844). Reviewing the latter, William Gilmore Simms wrote disgustedly that Young England's "talent seems to have been utterly wasted on ultra-conservatism." Yet despite its odd politics, Young England also believed in the regenerative power of juvenility, as exemplified by Coningsby's declaration, "It is a holy thing to see a State saved by its youth."[111]

More widely known was the Young Ireland group, formed in 1840 when Daniel O'Connell organized the Repeal Association to protest the Act of Union. The deeds of Young Ireland drew wide attention in America, especially from the Democratic press and O'Sullivan. Not only did he rejoice in the stirrings of Irish nationalism for ancestral reasons, but he saw similarities between his own situation and the O'Connellites. Abetted by young journalists invoking "the great end of Nationality . . . a Nationality which may come to be stamped upon our manners, our literature and our deeds," they agitated against English cultural dominance in favor of indigenous literature, art, and libraries. O'Sullivan poured lavish attentions on Young Ireland throughout the 1840s. As with Young Italy, there was an Americanist appeal in Daniel O'Connell's attempt to give Ireland the "strength of union." New York's growing immigrant population strongly supported these movements, and in 1843 a "mammoth Repeal Convention" met for three days there to support Irish republicanism.[112]

It should thus come as no surprise that the sobriquet Young America grew to be loosely associated with O'Sullivan. There is some accuracy in this, but the term needs to be clarified, for it was claimed by several groups simultaneously, and "Young America," as interpreted today, is almost universally oversimplified. Several writers flirted with the phrase before it was adopted. I have noted that Samuel Langtree proclaimed the genius of a lower-case "young America" as early as 1833. Three years later, Cornelius Mathews published some early poems by "a young American." In *Home as Found* (1838), Cooper wrote, "If there is *la jeune France*, there is also *la jeune Amérique*."[113]

More Americans found the phrase congenial in the early 1840s. In January 1840 Orestes Brownson noted, "Young America pronounces with ever increasing enthusiasm the name of Jefferson." The trend was contagious: During the excitement of the 1842 constitutional crisis in Rhode Island, a young *citoyen* proclaimed that as France was called "Young France" after 1830, so Rhode Island would now be known as "Young Rhode Island." Even more regional was a pamphlet writer who signed his name, "Young Narragansett." Likewise, "Young Carolina" emerged as a radical political group opposed to old-guard banking interests in Charleston.[114]

The trend crystallized in 1844 and 1845, when "Young America" was suddenly on everyone's lips, even people very different from one another. The radical Anglo-American labor leader George Evans used it in his campaign for free western land, as did the German socialist Hermann Kriege. After Evans combined his newspaper, *The Workingman's Advocate*, with Mike Walsh's *The Subterranean*, they called the combined version *Young America*, repeating the term enthusiastically in articles guaranteed to inflame New York's lower classes of readership. Despite a common infatuation with 1830s Locofocoism, O'Sullivan kept a respectful distance from Walsh and never showed any interest in Evans's extreme land reforms, insulting his Agrarianism as "the greatest humbug of all." But they were all deeply interested in the activities of "Young Europe," and it may have been a series of articles in the

Review that galvanized Evans to his new slogan. Ironically, a Nativist incarnation of Young America in the 1850s would attack the immigrant constituency represented by Evans, Walsh, and to some extent O'Sullivan.[115]

The *Review* group added to the phrase's currency in several ways, besides its constant reporting on Young Europe. In February 1844 an article claimed industrial poverty could never affect "young America." That same month, Emerson delivered his address on "The Young American," interesting for its word choice but rather tepid by O'Sullivan's standards. In June, the *Review* writer John Bigelow, who recorded reading *Coningsby* in his diary, jumped on the bandwagon. Lamenting his poverty, he confided, "The young American ought not to grieve at an oppression which seems to be shutting him out from the whole world of art and beauty when it is the process of by which he is being educated to a higher and better destiny. . . . If it is in the Young American, then I ask is there anything in our institutions to keep him down." Finally, Alexander Everett, the former editor of the *North American Review*, displayed a true nose for spotting trends when he donated a short poem entitled "The Young American" to the *Democratic Review* in May 1845. This achievement was all the more remarkable for the fact Everett, a former Whig, was fifty-five years old at the time.[116]

The phrase "Young America" could hardly continue to float around the journalistic vernacular without someone laying claim to it, and it finally happened on June 30, 1845, when the novelist Cornelius Mathews delivered the valedictory address of Evert Duyckinck's literary clique. Duyckinck and Mathews had been increasingly contributing to the *Review* in the 1840s, and for Mathews, all the simmering nationalism came to a boil with this speech, delivered before the Eucleian Society of New York University (his alma mater). Declaring "We are a new generation, for good or evil," Mathews moved to the heart of the speech:

> Whatever that past generation of statesmen, law-givers and writers was capable of, we know. What they attained, what they failed to attain, we also know. Our duty and our destiny is another from theirs. Liking not at all its borrowed sound; we are yet (there is no better way to name it,) the Young America of this people: a new generation; and it is for us now to inquire, what we may have it in our power to accomplish, and on what objects the world may reasonably ask that we should fix our regards.[117]

At almost the precise moment O'Sullivan coined the term Manifest Destiny (in the July–August 1845 *Review*), Mathews insisted America has "an intellectual as well as a physical destiny to accomplish," disdaining a republicanism that seeks only the expansion of territory. Instead, he cried out what he called the "manifest demand of the country," the quest for American literature (along with art, drama, and music). Indulging O'Sullivan's interest in world revolution, he linked the themes together: "I therefore, in behalf of this young America of ours, insist on nationality and true Americanism in the books this country furnishes to itself and to the world. . . . It is a literature of this kind that the world (revolutionizing slowly under the influence of our example,) asks at our hands."[118]

Mathews's speech gave wide currency to the phrase, although others were still using it on their own. Another *Review* contributor, Parke Godwin, advertised it in several speeches and magazine projects. In December 1845, an obscure address given by Edwin DeLeon in South Carolina repeated some of these intellectual aspirations. Beside the Duyckinck clique, another very different group would call themselves Young America around 1852. Primarily western and southern politicians, equally nationalistic but less literary, they favored European intervention, the annexation of Cuba, and the absorption of any other territory America could get its hands on (see chapter 6). This group entered the limelight in 1852 behind the abortive presidential campaign of Stephen Douglas and denounced all who would oppose them as "Old Fogies," but held little appeal for Duyckinck and his friends. Despite their common nationalism, literary Young America (Young America I) was almost to a man against the expansion of slavery and had misgivings about the Mexican War. For their part, political Young America (Young America II) had little interest in obscure matters of copyright and book publishing.[119]

O'Sullivan was the one man who joined both major Young Americas, thereby ensuring his own permanent identification with the term (though as I noted earlier, his newspaper first reacted negatively to it: "With respect to the term Young America, we have no relish for it after its use in Europe — Young France, Young England, Young Germany. It looks too much like the foreign caricatures)." Indeed, it was probably his connection with each that has led modern scholars to conflate the two groups unthinkingly. O'Sullivan acted as the linchpin between the political and literary worlds and allowed the use of the *Democratic Review* as a mouthpiece for both causes. But as I will argue, there were profound, even tragic differences between Young America I and Young America II.[120]

No one could foresee O'Sullivan's dark destiny in the glory years of the *Review*. As revealed through the pages of this remarkable magazine, the Democratic personality was active and aggressive, eager to expand in both politics and literature. This contrasts with much of what we have been taught by historians, many of whom see the Jacksonian alliance as a retrograde group cowed by rapid change into nostalgia for the preindustrial past. Marvin Meyers loosely differentiated the two parties in this fashion, arguing "the Whig party spoke to the explicit hopes of Americans as Jacksonians addressed their diffuse fears and resentments." Lawrence Frederick Kohl similarly posited that Democrats found progress threatening, and that their accommodation to modernity was "reluctant and painful." For the most part, he saw them yearning naively for "a simpler, arcadian past," as if to escape the improvements championed by Whigs. In other words, recent generations of scholars have overturned the earlier belief (exemplified by Schlesinger's *Age of Jackson*) that the Democrats had an optimistic, forward-looking program that was doing all it could to deal with the complexities of modernity. The revised version would hold the Jacksonian persuasion as either backwards or so local as to be devoid of meaningful national aspiration.[121]

This seems an oversimplification. Judging by the influential coterie of northern Democrats around the *Democratic Review*, change was constantly, passionately yearned for, and those who resisted it were bitterly denounced, be they Whigs or old Hunker Democrats like William Marcy. When the *Democratic Review* did dwell on the past, it was to commemorate America's revolutionary heritage and laud the courage of Founding Fathers who flew in the face of standing tradition.

This is hardly the same thing as nostalgia for America's agricultural heritage or the "simplicity" of the eighteenth century.

It would be difficult to find an American in the 1840s who was as excited about the future and America's role in it as John O'Sullivan. Through his writing and his actions he displayed a passionate devotion to change and improvement, and warned against the fallacy of dwelling on the "thoughts and things of the past." Nor was his progressive philosophy divorced from his politics; they were intimately connected in his worldview. Rather than a nation of yeomen farmers existing in the Virgilian past, this democrat saw America as it was, a hodgepodge of disparate types, including urban immigrants, evolving rapidly into "the great nation of futurity."[122]

It is also wrong to assume reform was exclusively pursued by Whigs, or at least centered around those with a stereotypical New England intellectual pedigree. Parke Godwin was strongly antislavery, as were most of the early Young Americans, but he ridiculed New England reformers for the smallness of their dreams for America: "If the Deity should consult New England about making a new world, they would advise that it should be made of the size of Massachusetts, have no city but Boston and insist in making an occasional donation to a charitable institution and uttering shallow anti-slavery sentiments."[123]

The crowd who associated with O'Sullivan and the *Review* displayed a catholicity of religion, upbringing, and professional expertise, but they were united in their youthful ardor for reform and their distance from the Whig party. As Orestes Brownson wrote in 1839, "The idea of the Whig party is of yesterday, not of to-day, far less of to-morrow. The party is the anti-progress party." For a wide variety of reasons, from slipping economic status to missing fathers to literary ambition to a genuine desire to help people, the Young Americans located the world of tomorrow within the Democracy.[124]

Before closing this chapter, I would like to throw out several other observations. Historians should explore the northern Democratic promotion of an alternative cultural universe to the monistic, self-centered "individualism" that Tocqueville dwelled on until his neologism entered the language. Almost every general history of the period cites this term, coupled perhaps with a nod to Emerson's philosophy of self-reliance. But northern Democrats believed in a populistic vision of citizens pulling together, sharing responsibility, and refusing the special privileges attached to extreme individualism. Under Leggett's influence, and the memory of the Locofoco rhetoric of "Equal Rights," the unifying principle of the young Democrats clustered around the *Review* was their shared hope of communal betterment, their *collective* view of the social universe. Unlike Emerson, who called it "the age of the first person singular," O'Sullivan loved the first person *plural*, promising the Democracy, "We cannot fail in such a cause!" An 1842 article on Fourierism decried those "common-place minds" steeped in society's "individualism, and its selfish precepts for individual conduct." A year later, Thoreau wrote Emerson of his distaste for O'Sullivan's emphasis on the "collective we."[125]

Scholars should also expand their definition of antebellum New York to comprehend a larger cultural region: the rough triangle between New York, Albany, and Stockbridge. The area not only contributed a president and attorney general in Van Buren and Butler, the chief sponsors of the *Review*, but legions of reformers and writers from the Sedgwicks to Bryant to David Dudley Field. Their reform interests tended to cluster around class issues and democratic precepts rather than moral causes such as abolitionism, but these New York and western Massachusetts Democrats were no less committed to the betterment of society than the New Englanders operating concurrently within the radius of Boston's influence. The improvement of New York's prisons during this period, for example, earned international repute for the state, and particularly for this group. This enlarged regional definition helps to place Herman Melville in a better perspective.

Finally, as my last point hints, it is fallacious to assume the creative minds of the period worked their magic in an intellectual vacuum, removed from the daily pressures of the marketplace and its politics. The *Democratic Review* succeeded because its peculiar and serendipitous mixture of politics and culture struck a sensitive nerve with an American public predisposed to think along politico-literary lines by fiery fourth of July orations and Bancroft's delineation of the democratic principle in his history. The two had certainly been combined in previous magazines, but never in so dramatic a fashion, with so public a manifesto, such ardent energy, and such a clear intention of presenting literature and politics as part and parcel of the same idea. Sometimes it was done clumsily (for example, a "Sonnet to Martin Van Buren"); at other times, as with Hawthorne, "the Locofoco surveyor," political opportunism and publishing came together to forge a meaningful partnership. For a people consumed by political passions, it was inevitable that their emerging literature would reveal, in some degree, the obsession with democracy.

The *Review*'s prominence as a literary organ was not coincidental or unintentional, but reflected the universal American interest in local and national government, and it came closer to articulating the folk culture of the growing nation than magazines that rigidly adhered to older standards of didactic articles for the elite. An important index of the magazine's originality is the degree to which it succeeded abroad. As noted earlier, the czar's minister of public instruction called the *Review* "a publication which gave a tone to America abroad, . . . not a poor repetition of the poor matter of English reviews." At the very heart of the Russian Empire, they knew that Americanism is never so convincing as when it is expressed with a barbaric yawp.[126]

The writers and artists who joined their fate to the *Democratic Review* did so because something about its outlook appealed to them, and they did not do this without reflection about the political issues of the day. Many writers specifically submitted material to the *Review* because of its heartening promotion of collective endeavor uniting democratic thinkers. Anne Lynch, a Rhode Island poet, offered to work for free "because I like the company I meet there." Despite O'Sullivan's claim to the contrary in his attempt to woo Longfellow, the politics and the writing *were* connected. For this reason, Longfellow denounced the magazine while Hawthorne donated his best short stories. There was no enmity involved, as we can judge from the fact that Longfellow and Hawthorne remained close friends throughout their lives, but the politics of literature were important to both men, and to almost every other writer of the era. A close study of the *Review*'s relationship with prominent authors, along with the literary circle most closely linked to it, will amplify this point further.[127]

2

Democracy and Literature

> Altogether, in his culture and want of culture, in his crude, wild, and misty philosophy, and the practical experience that counteracted some of its tendencies; in his magnanimous zeal for man's welfare, and his recklessness of whatever the ages had established in man's behalf; in his faith, and in his infidelity; in what he had, and in what he lacked—the artist might fitly enough stand forth as the representative of many compeers in his native land.
>
> —Nathaniel Hawthorne, *The House of the Seven Gables*

A Politico-Literary System

There is no proof that Hawthorne's description of Holgrave was intended to conjure John O'Sullivan. Yet the accuracy of the description and the intimacy of the two men suggests more than coincidental resemblance. To this day, extraordinarily, Hawthorne retains the image of the political naïf, unfamiliar with the real world, and more comfortable with antiquarian legends than the political currents pulsing through O'Sullivan. But like most writers of the period, even a sentimental versifier like Longfellow, he had shrewd insight into the politics of literature. By his own choice, Hawthorne became the centerpiece of what Longfellow diagnosed as O'Sullivan's "politico-literary system."

In 1845, the year Young America and Manifest Destiny sprang on the world, Hawthorne could not have been more deeply immersed in the Democratic milieu. He wrote constantly for the *Review* and *News*, and received crucial help from O'Sullivan and Duyckinck in his campaign for employment from the newly elected Polk administration. The story that most excited Herman Melville when he discovered Hawthorne, "A Select Party," was written just before this burst of Young Americanism. Struggling with his own complicated feelings toward democratic culture, Melville felt a profound shock of recognition when he chanced upon it in 1850.

Having considered O'Sullivan's aspirations and his philosophy of the "democratic principle," I will now examine the *Review*'s relations with prominent writers of the day, and the extent to which they toed the party line. Besides assembling an impressive stable of contributors, O'Sullivan often interacted with these writers, and his "crude, wild and misty philosophy" resurfaced in their fiction, either parodied or at face value. He influenced Whitman directly (who wrote frequent editorials supporting O'Sullivan's projects), and likely Melville as well, albeit less immediately. More than anyone, Hawthorne enjoyed a close relationship with him that began with them almost killing each other and ended with the catastrophe of the Civil War. In addressing Hawthorne's literary treatment of O'Sullivan, I hope to reassert the complexity and richness of his attention to political nuance.

In the prospectus of the *Democratic Review* unveiled before publication, the editors disavowed any intention to bring the strife of party warfare into the ethereal realm of literature: "In this department, the exclusiveness of party, which is inseparable from the political department, will have no place. Here we all stand on a neutral ground of equality and reciprocity, where those universal principles of taste to which we are all alike subject will alone be recognized as the common law." No one believed this for a second. Despite the disclaimer, a general attitude toward literature prevailed within the *Review* that distinguished it from most of its competitors and revealed that antagonistic political stances might well result in divergent "principles of taste." As William A. Jones, a *Review* critic, admitted, "The situation of parties, the bias of partizan feeling, can hardly fail to influence even literary criticism, though they fall into this sin to a much less extent in this country than in England."[1]

I have already outlined the *Review*'s formula for success: high-quality articles by authors with Democratic leanings, deep sympathy with popular movements around the world, antipathy toward elitism and exclusionary culture, an eclectic mix of political and literary articles, and overblown editorials calling attention to the importance of it all. An article entitled "Democracy and Literature" in August 1842 condensed this philosophy to a nutshell: "Literature is not only the natural ally of freedom, political or religious; but it also affords the firmest bulwark the wit of man has yet devised, to protect the interests of freedom. It not only breathes a similar spirit, — it is imbued with the same spirit."[2]

Despite these generous sentiments, O'Sullivan also regarded literature with the jealous eye of a publicity seeker. His obsession with Democratic intellectual stature led to many immodest claims about the writers enlisted in "the cause." Boasting his party's intellectual preeminence, O'Sullivan crowed, "Hardly with one exception, our writers of the first class, Bancroft, Channing, Hawthorne, &c., have not only spoken out freely their belief in the stability and integrity of the Republic, but have also expressed themselves plainly in the terms of the democratic creed." Four years later, after helping Hawthorne secure appointment in the Salem Custom House, O'Sullivan claimed for the Democracy "the first Poet, the first Historian, the first Novelist, and the first Tragedian, our country has produced. How do the Whigs explain this 'singular coincidence'?" As Benjamin Butler reminded Van Buren, the simple appearance of these names under the Democratic banner held real political significance. During the Panic of 1837, Butler remembered:

> In the midst of all the untoward circumstances by which we were surrounded it
> was seen that a fair proportion of the literary talent of the country was enlisted in

the defense of yr. admn.; when its support was given through an organ combining elegance with argument, and taking the very first place among our periodicals; . . . this is the great service rendered by the Review.[3]

Reading O'Sullivan's self-puffery, one is often tempted to disbelieve him. But almost everything he claimed in the literary arena was true. The *Review* lined up an extraordinary coterie of writers to drive home the politico-literary link. Until O'Sullivan severed his connection with the magazine in 1846, Hawthorne and Whittier were steady contributors during their most fecund period. Bryant and Cooper were less prolific, but donated the strength of their reputations. More important, O'Sullivan encouraged and published a number of young reformist writers, including Whitman, and surprisingly, Thoreau and Lowell as well, eager to expand beyond Concord and Cambridge. Dozens, if not hundreds of other writers, many with little experience, found the *Review* a friendly proving ground.

The mercurial O'Sullivan was always drawn to those with quicksilver interests, and inevitably this pattern crept into the magazine's literary policy. O'Sullivan published writers not only for their writing ability, but for their general empathy with his aggressive worldview and disdain for the past. These writers reacted in different ways to O'Sullivan, but many of them repeated his insistence that a "new" literature needed to be written to validate the American mission. No one knew exactly what this democratic literature would look like, and some attempts were embarrassing (i.e., a clunky sonnet to Andrew Jackson in May 1839). But a pattern of O'Sullivan's favorite story themes emerged, and the *Review*'s fiction often treated familiar issues like the urban poor, westward expansion, and the horror of capital punishment.

And despite his blustery patriotism, O'Sullivan offered good editorial advice to writers, inspiring them with his sense that a different generation was on the scene, with no obligation to follow the formulaic style of its predecessors. He warned James Russell Lowell to discipline his literary excesses and avoid sentimentality, since "magazine writing is very apt to lead to bad habits in this way." He particularly disliked overemotional poetry, "in this age when we are sonneted to death." Likewise, he counseled Charles Sumner to inject a current of political excitement into an article on sculpture he was writing: "I will only hint that if you should feel prompted by the occasion to discourse a few [sic] about the connexion between Liberty and Art, on the level of ancient Greece, etc. and the remarkable indications this country has already afforded of a genius for this particular art of sculpture — there will be no harm done."[4]

The cultivation of the *Review*'s network began with O'Sullivan's ties to New York journalism. No writer had more experience than William Cullen Bryant, whom O'Sullivan knew well. Even if Bryant was moderate and middle-aged by comparison, he was a crucial ally. They fought numerous political battles together and Bryant's *Evening Post* heaped praise on the *Review* during its shaky early period. Bryant also helped the *Review* establish itself by lending his poetic talents on occasion (including "The Battlefield" in the first issue, a spirited defense of his politics). Out of the ten poems he published from 1837 to 1841, nine originally appeared in the *Review*, and the only one that did not was printed anyway to keep the record perfect. One of them honored William Leggett, and he also wrote Leggett's eulogy for the *Review*. Even more directly linked to the magazine was Bryant's son-in-law Parke Godwin, closer in age and spirit to the Young American crowd, and a frequent contributor.[5]

The magazine reciprocated Bryant's help with glowing praise: "His poems are strictly American. . . . They breathe the spirit of that new order of things in which we are cast." But to say they were "American" was not enough, for by an alchemy only O'Sullivan could understand, these verses became America itself, expanding westward toward Manifest Destiny (faster than Bryant probably wanted):

> They are fresh, like a young people unwarped by the superstitions and prejudices of age, free, like a nation scorning the thought of bondage, generous, like a society whose only protection is mutual sympathy, and bold and vigorous like a land pressing onward to a future state of glorious enlargement. The holy instincts of democracy guides [sic] every expression and prompt and animate every strand.[6]

Another talent O'Sullivan recruited from the milieu of New York Democracy was Catharine Maria Sedgwick. He may have known her from his early visits to Stockbridge, or through Bryant, or simply as the aunt of his friend Theodore Sedgwick III. In any event, he enlisted her before the magazine started, and she continued writing for it into the 1840s. The *Review* praised her just as O'Sullivan was moving to Stockbridge in 1839, calling her work "thoroughly *American* and *Democratic*—words that we regard as altogether synonymous." William Leggett praised her in the same terms in his *Plaindealer*. Today it seems unlikely that her work would have been politically controversial, but the conservative *New York Review* denounced her for "a tinge of Radicalism" and a "quiet taking-for-granted that ultrademocratic sentiments are the only philanthropic ones." One piece, "The Irish Girl," attacked anti-Irish prejudice, and Sedgwick shared O'Sullivan's ardor for European liberalism.[7]

O'Sullivan also looked to New England for talent, although rarely to the established constellation of Bostonians who wrote for the quarterlies. Despite the *Review's* cool stance toward abolitionism, John Greenleaf Whittier became an enormously prolific contributor, authoring twenty poems and two prose works during O'Sullivan's tenure as editor. Indeed, the sheer number of his contributions forces reevaluation of his oft-perceived status as an insular Yankee poet. The two men found enough common ground to overlook their disagreements. O'Sullivan did not mind that Whittier was writing antiexpansion verse elsewhere, and Whittier submitted proletarian poems that lent themselves perfectly to the democratic tenor of the magazine. In return, the *Review* praised him, as it had Hawthorne, for his "manly firmness," and for being a "true poet, true man, true American, true democrat, true Christian."[8]

Whittier was never an active Democrat, despite a lifelong friendship with the Massachusetts statesman Robert Rantoul. He was ardently anti-Jacksonian in his early career, but ambivalent toward the Whigs as well (he sympathized with the Liberty party in 1844, and the Free Soilers and Republicans thereafter). The paramount issue for him was the abolition of slavery, but he also felt deep sympathy for the cause of labor reform, where he and O'Sullivan were in agreement. In addition, he wrote editorials for the *Middlesex Standard* on many of the latter's pet interests: Young Ireland, the peace movement, William Leggett, and Thomas Dorr.[9]

For these reasons, Whittier considered the *Review* a worthy vehicle for his muse. O'Sullivan may have convinced him he was more of an abolitionist than he was. A letter he wrote to Whittier in 1838 asked that one of the latter's papers be sent to him at Washington, with O'Sullivan joking he would take "the risk of the Lynching," and proudly pointing out an anti-Calhoun comment he had made in a *Review* article. In December 1841 Whittier published "Democracy," which celebrated a Jacksonesque spirit "unawed by pomp or power," but also disclaimed allegiance to the Whigs or Democrats, preferring to be a "Party worshipper" in the old Christian sense. Several poems displayed him in perfect consonance with O'Sullivan on the capital punishment issue. "The Human Sacrifice" attacked the clergy as "the Hangman's ghostly ally" and ghoulishly detailed the convict's "fingers of ghastly skin and tone / Working and writhing on the stone." Another poem attacked the death penalty as the residue of the tyrannical "kingcraft" O'Sullivan scorned.[10]

Yet another major theme for Whittier emerged in his "Songs of Labor," which were issued primarily in the *Review* from 1845 to 1846. The poems displayed a deep reverence for the dignity of working-class occupations, attacking the "foplings" O'Sullivan wished to rescue American letters from. As he wrote a friend, "My 'Songs of Labor' are written for the working, *acting*, rather than *thinking* people. I wish to invest labor with some degree of beauty." The poems were not his most sophisticated, but one strongly suspects them of exerting an influence on the burgeoning poetic consciousness of Walter Whitman, whose work was appearing in the very same issues.[11]

O'Sullivan knew most of the other prominent New England writers as well. Emerson immediately sensed O'Sullivan's peculiar mix of literary and political interests, although it was not much to his liking. For all his eloquence concerning the common man, Emerson was unnerved by O'Sullivan's closeness to the world of real politics. During a visit to New York in early 1843, he wrote to Margaret Fuller, using the same hybrid adjective Longfellow had used to describe O'Sullivan: "Today I dined with Mr O'Sullivan at Mr Field's, but the man is politico-literary and has too close an eye to immediate objects. *Washington* is supposed in every line of the 'Demo. Review.'" Yet Emerson qualified this interesting objection by adding quizzically, "Or do I mistake him altogether." They were clearly wary of each other.[12]

Emerson also socialized with O'Sullivan's set, as indicated by a successive letter to Fuller, "I see O Sullivan & his handsome sister Mrs Langtree & Bryant & the Sedgwicks & Park Godwin & Eames and many more." He even wrote a piece of criticism for the September 1843 *Review* entitled "Mr. Channing's Poems," privately complaining to Thoreau it was so "interpolated with sentences and extracts, to make it long, by the editor" that he recognized "little beyond the first page." Emerson's complicated attitude toward contemporary politics was made even murkier by his exposure to O'Sullivan's vagaries. A journal entry from this New York trip praised the fight against capital punishment, but also contained Emerson's pithy remark, later used in "Politics," that "Whigs have the best men, Democrats the best cause." Emerson was distressed by the New York Democracy, thinking them "destructive, not constructive."[13]

About four years later, during the agitation over the Mexican War (and surely mindful of O'Sullivan's role in it), Emerson huffily confided to his journal his disapproval of editors manipulating public opinion: "Democracy becomes a government of bullies tempered by editors. The editors standing in the privilege of being last devoured. Captain Rhynders tempered by Father Ritchie and O'Sullivan." Yet at the same time Emerson confided passages to the journal that might easily have sprung from the editorial desk of the *Review*. In one outburst, the philosopher of self-reliance recapitulated every thought in O'Sullivan's head: "The office of America is to liberate, to abolish kingcraft, priestcraft, caste, monopoly, to pull down the gallows, to burn up the bloody statute-book, to take in the immigrant, to open the doors of the sea and the fields of the earth,—to extemporize government in Texas, in California, in Oregon,—to make provisional law where statute law is not ready."[14]

Thoreau, too, was perplexed by O'Sullivan, dismissing him curtly as "a rather puny-looking man," but also admitting, "he is at any rate one of the not-bad." They met through Hawthorne during a trip O'Sullivan paid to Concord in 1843. Thoreau wrote tersely to Emerson, "We had nothing to say to another, and therefore said a great deal. He, however, made a point of asking to write for his Review, which I shall be glad to do." That same year, Thoreau moved to Staten Island to become a tutor to William Emerson's family and make his writings familiar to the larger New York literary market. His only New York pieces were a pair of articles in the *Review*. In October 1843 he issued a small piece entitled "The Landlord," which Thoreau did not think "worth fifty cents." In November appeared his more famous review of J. A. Etzler's *The Paradise Within the Reach of All Men*, entitled more simply "Paradise (to be) Regained." O'Sullivan apparently initiated the idea of the review, after rejecting another Thoreau manuscript. He wrote Thoreau asking for "some of those extracts from your journal, reporting some of your private interviews with nature, with which I have before been so much pleased," then amplified his query: "That book of Etzler's I had for some time had my mind upon to review. If you have got it, I should be very much obliged to you for a sight of it, and if you would not object I think it very likely that some addition & modification made with your concurrence would put your review of it into the shape to suit my peculiar notion of the subject."[15]

The resulting piece was a harsh critique of the windy utopian schemes men like O'Sullivan held dear to the hearts, but O'Sullivan published it nevertheless. Like Emerson, Thoreau complained privately about O'Sullivan's inclination to tinker with articles to make sure they were sufficiently "Democratic." He wrote his mentor, "O'Sullivan wrote me that articles of this kind have to be referred to the circle, who, it seems, are represented by this journal, and said something about 'collective we' and 'homogeneity.'" One can still hear the derision in Thoreau's voice. He claimed the sticking point for O'Sullivan was "my want of sympathy with the Communities."[16]

But no matter who initiated the article or how much of it was edited, it represented an important early statement of Thoreau's beliefs before a national audience. For all his suspicion of O'Sullivan, Thoreau seems to have regarded him as the most sympathetic editor in New York, and like Hawthorne gave him material despite inferior pay. He wrote his mother, "The Democratic Review is poor, and can only afford half or quarter pay—which it *will* do—and they say there is a Ldy's [sic] Companion that pays—but I could not write anything companionable."[17]

James Russell Lowell, in his early years something of a firebrand, united with O'Sullivan and Whittier against the death penalty. In May 1842 he composed six sonnets in protest against Wordsworth's stand in favor of capital punishment: "A poet cannot strive for despotism / His harp falls shattered." O'Sullivan nudged Lowell toward more political stands, and counseled him not to write too much of "the fugitive verse with which we are so surfeited." In his next *Review* poem, Lowell rhapsodized over the idea of the innate dignity of "men rude and rough," and he contributed several more poems which would embarrass him in later life, including "Prometheus" (August 1843), which he admitted was "overrunning with true radicalism," and "The Fatherland" (October 1843), an interventionist poem calling upon liberal-minded men around the world to help one another in their struggles. He jokingly described "Prometheus" as "the first reformer and locofoco of the Greek mythology."[18]

Like Thoreau, Poe expressed his feelings about the editor unabashedly, calling him "that ass O'Sullivan" at one point, but also thanking him profusely for helping him through difficulties. His mixed feelings may have stemmed from the fact O'Sullivan rejected several of his manuscripts before publishing his "Marginalia" pieces in the mid-1840s. Poe's poem "The Haunted Palace," from "The Fall of the House of Usher," was turned down in 1839 because O'Sullivan "found it impossible to comprehend it." This hardly comes as a surprise, given the poem's lugubrious, European, and decidedly nondemocratic cast. Poe was also dismayed that "The Landscape Garden" was rejected in 1842, and once disturbed the Langleys (the magazine's publishers) by drunkenly barging into their establishment after a few too many mint juleps.[19]

Despite this miscue, Poe published four of his "Marginalia" installments, an essay ("The Power of Words"), and a "Literati" piece under the auspices of the *Review*. In return, Poe labeled O'Sullivan "a man of fine matter-of-fact talents, and a good political writer, though not a brilliant one." He also praised the *Review* in what were for him lavish terms: "Were it not for its ultraism in politics, we should regard the Democratic Review as the most valuable journal of the day." Many references in his correspondence indicate he considered the *Morning News* to be one of the more enlightened newspapers in New York, probably because of his respect for Evert Duyckinck, its literary editor. Judging from a letter to Duyckinck seeking information about O'Sullivan, he was preparing to write about him for his "Literati" series, but the article never appeared.[20]

The *Democratic Review* publicly defended Poe during his bitter wars with rival editors in the mid-1840s, praising his courage in attacking the Longfellow clique with typically Jacksonian phrasing: "It is for the interest of literature that every man who writes should show his honesty and not bring letters into contempt. If in doing this he should happen to fall on the other side of harshness or rudeness . . . let him be pardoned, for it is better both for the cause of truth and virtue that this should be the case than that a man should always be dull and complaisant." Poe remembered a good turn done to him as keenly as an insult and publicly thanked "the O'Sullivans—the Duyckincks" in the *Broadway Journal* of March 8, 1845, "the choice and magnanimous few who spoke promptly in my praise" at this critical moment in his career, "and who have since taken my hand with a more cordial and more impressive grasp than ever."[21]

James Fenimore Cooper, a peculiar sort of Democrat, also wrote for the *Review*. In 1842 he authored two anonymous articles defending his *History of the Navy of the United States* from a poor review in the *Edinburgh Review*. Even Longfellow, who represented the apotheosis of the Whig-Bostonian cultural matrix loathed by O'Sullivan and the Young Americans, managed to write a small poem, "God's Acre," for the *Review* in December 1841.[22]

In keeping with his nationalistic outlook and his hope the "United States Magazine" would live up to its name, O'Sullivan also solicited southern and western writers. Langtree wrote William Gilmore Simms in 1840 requesting articles, and his patriotic sonnets appeared throughout the 1840s, despite the author's worries concerning "indifference on the part of O'Sullivan." Perhaps his problem was overproduction: A humorous magazine announced sarcastically in 1846 that "Mr. Simms, after an incredible labor, has produced another sonnet. It will appear in the next number of the Democratic Review." Although this joke was at his expense, O'Sullivan shared the sentiment. Writing Duyckinck, his liaison to Simms, about the "queer sonnets you have sent me," he labeled them a "mongrel breed between prose and poetry, worse than either . . . of course this note is not for Mr. Simms' eye."[23]

Despite the sarcasm, O'Sullivan was intent on publishing pieces from beyond the northeastern seaboard, including countless ruminations on prairie life and other western features obviously meant to whet the public appetite for more land. Foreshadowing similar comments from Melville and Whitman, the *Review* wrote,

> The American poet is not in our view to be born in New-England, but in a broader and more genial region, where nature is less restricted. The great men of this country are to appear beside the mighty rivers and amidst the fruitful fields to the west. Thence too will come to us the poets of immortal name; great world-embracing souls, who shall weave all things into their strains.[24]

Simms wrote political pieces as well as sonnets, including biographies of southern Democrats. Like most contributors, he admired O'Sullivan's aggressive stance on the death penalty, and he joined the Young America bandwagon as a full-fledged member of Duyckinck's clique in the mid-1840s. With him on board, the *Review* had a national coalition of writers mirroring the party's regional balance.[25]

Hawthorne

Before this expansive network was established, even before the *Review* published its first issue, O'Sullivan scored the greatest editorial coup of his career by persuading Nathaniel Hawthorne to join the cause. Nathaniel Hawthorne wrote no fewer than twenty-four short stories for the magazine during a relatively brief period, from 1837 to 1845. Among them were many of his most celebrated works today, such as "The Celestial Railroad," "Rappacini's Daughter," and the Province House sketches, along with quite a few that have drifted into obscurity. Almost the entire stock of *Mosses from an Old Manse* found its way into the *Review* in one way or another.[26]

Over the course of their long, mutually beneficial relationship, O'Sullivan and Hawthorne developed a deep friendship that went far beyond the usual camaraderie of editors and writers. They were an odd pair; O'Sullivan always intriguing, near the center of things, and Hawthorne, as he wrote in his first story for the *Review*, more content "to pore over the current of life, than to plunge into its tumultuous waves." Of course, this claim was more than slightly disingenuous.[27]

On the surface, the two men shared several similarities. Both of their fathers, sea captains of a sort, had disappeared off South America during their childhood, and both had developed early fixations with Andrew Jackson. They probably met sometime in 1837, a pivotal year for both, when O'Sullivan was trying to round up contributors to his first number, and Hawthorne was bringing out his first book, *Twice-Told Tales*. O'Sullivan was alerted to Hawthorne's existence by Jonathan Cilley, a Democratic congressman from New Hampshire who had been one of Hawthorne's close friends at Bowdoin, along with Franklin Pierce and Horatio Bridge. The quartet had shared Jacksonian sympathies since 1824, when they joined the Athenean Society in support of Old Hickory (Longfellow, needless to say, joined the Adamsite Peucinian Society). When writing a letter to recommend Hawthorne for a government appointment in 1843, O'Sullivan recollected, "It was he [Cilley] who first interested me in him—who was himself earnestly desirous to obtain some such suitable provision for him."[28]

In other words, politics preceded and made possible their long literary relations. At precisely the moment Cilley and O'Sullivan were discussing him, Hawthorne was already seeking to enter the fray of party journalism. Franklin Pierce, just elected senator from New Hampshire, was trying to procure work for him with the *Washington Globe*, the Democratic paper that printed the prospectus of the *Review* in early 1837. Hawthorne also tried to get appointed historian to the Wilkes South Seas Expedition, an appointment that might have changed the course of American literature, but he was unable to secure either position.[29]

Given the state of his finances and his new interest in party intrigue, the letter he received from O'Sullivan on April 19, 1837, must have seemed a godsend. Furthermore, he was experiencing a new interest in writing about modern social issues, rather than the legends of New England antiquity. As he wrote Longfellow on June 4, 1837, "Sometimes, through a peep-hole, I have caught a glimpse of the real world; and the two or three articles, in which I have portrayed such glimpses, please me better than the others."[30]

The letter O'Sullivan sent promised the high salary of five dollars a page. The editor was not one to mince words, and stoked the fires of Hawthorne's ambition:

> The editors of the "United States Magazine and Democratic Review," a new literary and political periodical about to be commenced at Washington City, knowing and highly appreciating Mr. Hawthorne's style of writing (as shown in a few sketches and tales that have met their eye, such as "David Snow," Fancy's Show-Box," etc.), would be happy to receive frequent contributions from him. . . . As this magazine will have a vast circulation through the Union, and as it will occupy so elevated a literary rank, it will afford to Mr. Hawthorne what he has not had be-

fore, a field for the exercise of his pen, and the acquisition of distinction worthy of the high promise which the editors of the "United States Magazine" see in what he has already written.[31]

Following his letter in person, O'Sullivan visited Salem in the fall of 1837 and found himself in a real-life contretemps with Hawthorne's blend of comedy and tragedy. Both men were flattered by the attentions of Mary Silsbee, a senator's daughter with a reputation for eccentric behavior. She persuaded Hawthorne that O'Sullivan had compromised her, and the shy writer took umbrage on her behalf, journeying to Washington to challenge him to a duel. Shocked, O'Sullivan gallantly claimed she was out of her mind, and they narrowly averted a contest that, no matter how it turned out, would have spelt doom for the infant magazine. Hawthorne returned to Salem chagrined, and in the words of his filial biographer, "crushed her." Interestingly, Elizabeth Peabody later recollected that Mary Silsbee would have married Hawthorne but for his poverty. Years after, when he learned of her subsequent betrothal to another, he wrote O'Sullivan, "She is to be married, I believe, this week—an event which, I am almost sorry to say, will cause a throb in neither of our bosoms."[32]

The story would be merely incidental had it ended here. But shortly afterward, Jonathan Cilley received a contrived challenge from William Graves, a Whig representative from Kentucky. Feeling compelled to imitate Hawthorne's chivalrous example, Cilley accepted the trumped-up challenge and was killed. The entire country mourned him, and antidueling sentiment lasted for years. Hawthorne was inconsolable. His son claimed, "He felt as if he were almost as much responsible for his friend's death as was the man who shot him." Julian Hawthorne also postulated that much of Hawthorne's obsession with the nature of sin and differing degrees of guilt could be traced to this episode.[33]

The sequel to this strange story is that O'Sullivan asked Hawthorne to write the memoir of Cilley for the *Review* (it appeared in the September 1838 issue). He responded with a scathing attack on dueling and the partisan circumstances of Cilley's death, an essay that should be referred to by any who doubt the liveliness of Hawthorne's attention to politics. His verdict of the whole affair was that "a challenge was never given on a more shadowy pretext," and that Graves and Wise, the Southerners responsible, had "overstepped the imaginary distinction which, on their own principles, separates manslaughter from murder." He also denounced the Whigs by praising Cilley in the same populistic language O'Sullivan routinely used. Cilley had little "fastidious polish"; instead, he "loved the people, and respected them, and was prouder of nothing than of his brotherhood with those who had intrusted their public interests to his care." O'Sullivan added a piece on the affair, "The Martyrdom of Cilley," which appeared in the March 1838 issue.[34]

That the episode deeply affected Hawthorne and O'Sullivan is beyond doubt. In a letter O'Sullivan wrote in 1843 to secure political appointment for Hawthorne, he alluded to it obliquely. Writing the influential Virginia congressman Henry A. Wise, who had delivered the challenge to Cilley, O'Sullivan concluded the letter with an emotional peroration:

One of Hawthorne's few intimates & fast friends was *Cilley*, who had been a college companion. It was he who first interested me in him—who was himself earnestly desirous to obtain some such suitable position for him, and specifically this very appointment—who would have done it had he not fallen, so unhappily for us all, and most of all, I doubt not, my dear Sir, for you—and from whom it has always since rested on my mind as a bequeathed duty to be performed for him and in his name.[35]

Despite these dismal circumstances connecting their early lives, O'Sullivan and Hawthorne salvaged a lifelong friendship from the affair. Although Hawthorne ridiculed O'Sullivan's financial and political excesses, the two men reciprocated deep affection. They corresponded frequently, and Hawthorne asked O'Sullivan to be the godfather to his daughter, Una. Julian Hawthorne recalled him with obvious pleasure as "Uncle John" and fawned over him in his memoirs (perhaps because, as he admitted, he fell in love with O'Sullivan's wife in his youth). O'Sullivan reminded the Hawthornes of "a beautiful, innocent, brilliant child, grown up," a rather good description of the Young American personality. In a letter to a Boston publisher, the writer described O'Sullivan as "an intimate personal friend." Sophia went further; he was his "perhaps most highly valued friend," and she was equally infatuated: "I was struck with his gentleness & earnestness, his humanity & fine inward honour, which I felt to be as pure as diamond & as hard to destroy."[36]

This intimacy is not that surprising when one considers Hawthorne met his wife-to-be through the *Review*, at least indirectly. As Elizabeth Peabody recalled decades later, in November 1837 she invited Hawthorne and his sisters to her house, hoping to find out how to get published in the new magazine, and here Hawthorne encountered Sophia Peabody. During the 1850s, when Hawthorne and O'Sullivan were both representing the Pierce administration abroad (in Liverpool and Lisbon, respectively), they exchanged frequent letters and visits. Indeed, it is chiefly through Nathaniel and Julian Hawthorne that we get any glance at O'Sullivan's personal side, for most other allusions are merely through the business of the *Review*. The younger Hawthorne's affection for him reverberated throughout his father's biography. Laughing at his "grand and world-embracing schemes," he also found it "difficult to resist the contagion of his eloquent infatuation."[37]

After Hawthorne contributed "The Toll-Gatherer's Day" to the first number of the *Review* in October 1837, it became his chief vehicle for the next decade. Richard Brodhead gave the credit for this arrangement to Evert Duyckinck, but it is clear that O'Sullivan himself won over Hawthorne, for Duyckinck did not become literary editor of the *Review* until 1845 (although he too met Hawthorne very early in his career). Despite grandiose promises, O'Sullivan was unable to maintain the high salary he had promised Hawthorne, as indicated by a letter from Sophia Hawthorne lamenting that "the *Democratic Review* is so poor now that it can only offer $20 for an article of what length soever, so that Mr. Hawthorne cannot well afford to give any but short stories to it; and besides it is sadly dilatory about payment." Nevertheless, Hawthorne faithfully tendered articles to his friend. He had two great creative periods with the magazine, from 1837 to 1840, and from 1843 to 1845, following his retreat to Concord.[38]

But Hawthorne's importance to the *Review* cannot be gauged by simply counting stories. By lending his name issue after issue, Hawthorne sent a strong signal throughout the New England literary world that he was not merely prolific and talented, but independent as well. In addition, Hawthorne facilitated the hiring of other important writers. I mentioned earlier that O'Sullivan recruited Thoreau over tea at Hawthorne's during a visit to Concord in 1843. Hawthorne also puffed the *Review* in Boston newspapers. Sophia Hawthorne noted that he felt a special kinship with the editor and the message of the magazine: "The last paper he sent to it was a real gift, as it was more than four pages; but he thought its character better suited to the grave *Democrat* than for *Graham's*."[39]

O'Sullivan returned this devotion in several ways, one of which was an attempt to improve Hawthorne's system of distributing work to the public. Hawthorne felt ill used by the publishing profession, considering the Devil "a member of the 'Trade.'" Using his publishing connections and his awareness of new printing technology, O'Sullivan helped the author to improve his publishing arrangements. When in 1842 he visited Albany, where O'Sullivan was pursuing his brief career as a legislator, Hawthorne wrote, "I have much to talk of with O'Sullivan," and he hardly would have gone that distance to discuss a few short stories.[40]

In fact, O'Sullivan was helping Hawthorne to rethink his entire publishing strategy to take advantage of New York's booming market. He wrote his wife on March 16, 1843, "I intend to adhere to my former plan, of writing one of two mythological story books, to be published under O'Sullivan's auspices in New-York— which is the only place where books can be published, with a chance of profit." Hawthorne was doubtless recoiling from the disappointing sales of his second (1842) edition of *Twice-Told Tales*, six hundred copies of which were still languishing in custody of the Boston publisher, James Munroe. An 1844 letter from O'Sullivan to Munroe tried to extricate the author from financial embarrassment, urging the books be sold to Henry Langley, the New York publisher of the *Review*, and reissued there with all the éclat of a new edition. O'Sullivan himself offered to buy the remnant of the *Twice-Told Tales*, if it could be

> furbished anew into a fresh Edition with some additions, so as to be sold off through the superior facilities of our New York publishing houses. In this way, even if nothing may perhaps be made upon it, all parties will get smoothly out of the scrape, the Edition sold off, and the market will no longer be blocked up against the issue of another enlarged one, in a form better adapted to the new system of publication which has grown up since the date of the present one.[41]

The "new system" alluded to by O'Sullivan reflected the cheaper and larger-scale approach being taken by New York firms (as opposed to the Boston stodginess exemplified by Munroe), a phenomenon O'Sullivan had plenty of opportunity to witness firsthand. In the mid-1840s, New York was not only ahead of Boston in technological development (stereotyping, electrotyping, bookbinding, papermaking, etc.), but in every category of commercial development, including advertising and distribution to the hinterland. Hawthorne's correspondence indicated his deep interest in the scheme and his hope "that Mr. Langley's proposal should be carried into effect between him and Munroe." But for all O'Sullivan's good intentions, none of these grandiose plans came off, and Hawthorne's subsequent letters of the mid-1840s were filled with frequent references to his pecuniary embarrassment and frustration at these confusing "tricks of trade."[42]

Beyond the literary relationship, Hawthorne and O'Sullivan performed numerous small favors for one another that bespoke a strong bond. O'Sullivan obligingly inserted articles by friends of Hawthorne's (Elizabeth Peabody, Horatio Bridge) into the *Review* at his request. He also ordered favorable articles written about Hawthorne when he needed government work. During a push to secure the Salem Custom House position, O'Sullivan had Evert Duyckinck compose a puff arguing "authors are the immediate ornaments of the State," and therefore should be found employment within the government as a sort of "Literary Pension Fund." To bolster the case, Duyckinck padded the shy writer with manly Jacksonian virtues, arguing his sensitive nature was buttressed by "a rugged frame of body" and "a physical hardihood to tempt all extremes of weather and suffer no annoyance as a plough-man in the heat of midsummer, or an amateur traveller breasting the storm for mere pleasurable excitement." Ridiculously, Duyckinck likened Hawthorne to "the rough hairy rind of the cocoa-nut enclosing its sweet whiteness."[43]

Most writers would have found it difficult to continue. But Duyckinck loyally pressed on, describing Hawthorne's prose as the very simulacrum of America's melting pot: "Many costly ingredients, many rude ones, like rings and crucifixes tumbled in with masses of ore in the casting of some old church bell, have been melted down and purified before there is music in the heart." To further promote his credibility, O'Sullivan almost inserted Hawthorne's stoic likeness in the magazine (probably as one of the Democratic "portraits" usually reserved for politicians). He explained, "I want you to consent to sit for a daguerreotype, that I may take your head off in it. . . . By manufacturing you thus into a Personage, I want to raise your mark higher in Polk's appreciation." Hawthorne wrote Duyckinck, "Our friend O'Sullivan is moving Heaven and Earth to get me an office."[44]

O'Sullivan's efforts to find Hawthorne a patronage position went far beyond *Review* articles. He lobbied ferociously for the writer, using his political leverage to pull strings from Washington to Boston. George Bancroft, secretary of the navy under Polk, was particularly besieged by the editor. O'Sullivan recommended all different offices, from Charleston to China, adding melodramatically that "Hawthorne is dying of starvation" and that "some place of independent position, and no great amount of clerical drudgery, somewhere near Boston, is what he ought to have." When Bancroft proposed an office at Santa Rosa island, O'Sullivan insolently complained he could not read the salary amount the historian had scribbled, and that Hawthorne would dislike the "Robinson Crusoe solitude" of the post. Throughout the exchange O'Sullivan saw the appointment of the writer as the natural duty of the Democratic administration, fearing it would be "little creditable to our party, that nothing suitable and worthy should be done for such a man as Hawthorne." Bancroft's slowness in arriving at the same conclusion earned him the permanent dislike of Hawthorne and his wife, who called him "the Blatant Beast" after Spenser. Sophia even wrote, "Mr. Bancroft is not a man but a Gnome. I should never wish to be within three feet of him."[45]

Ultimately, Hawthorne was awarded a position in his native town, as all readers of the "Custom House" preface know. He was commissioned surveyor of the Port of Salem on April 3, 1846, where he served until his dramatic removal on June 7, 1849. In the flap attending Hawthorne's defenestration, O'Sullivan was outspoken in his

defense of the writer. It does not seem implausible that the residue of guilt and confusion Hawthorne felt over his firing entered into the portrait he would soon write
of the sensitive Dimmesdale, likewise crucified in public. Two of the Whigs calling
for Hawthorne's dismissal were Mary Silsbee's father and brother, senator from
Massachusetts and mayor of Salem, respectively. The latter accused Hawthorne of
"general locofoco corruption," and doubtless led him to reflect yet again on his
near-duel with O'Sullivan in 1837.[46]

A list of Hawthorne's political friends and enemies might continue indefinitely,
but a more pressing literary question inevitably arises. To what extent was his writing affected by O'Sullivan and the Democratic milieu he embraced? There are several ways to address this difficult query. At the microscopic level, it is not difficult to
locate occasional fictive references to his partisan employer. In fact, Hawthorne delighted in inserting teasing references to O'Sullivan in his prose. In the preface to
"Rappacini's Daughter," he waxed at length about the "Comte de Bearhaven,"
whom he identified further as the editor of "La Revue Anti-Aristocratique." In "P's
Correspondence" the imaginary letter-writer inquired of the narrator, "still scrib-
bling for the Democratic?" The original version of "The Hall of Fantasy," written
for James Russell Lowell's *Pioneer* in February 1843, included O'Sullivan, then distracted by his anti-capital punishment campaign, with the other inhabitants of that
idealistic domain (including such luminaries as Emerson, Bronson Alcott, and Father Miller): "There was a dear friend of mine among them, who has striven with
all his might to wash away the blood-stain from the statute book; and whether he
may finally succeed or fail, no philanthropist need blush to stand on the same footing with O'Sullivan."[47]

There were many less explicit references elsewhere, some affectionate, and
others offering a more serious critique of O'Sullivan's exuberance. "A Select Party,"
mentioned earlier, mimicked his rhetoric as it described the "Master Genius" of
American literature, "this child of a mighty destiny." "Earth's Holocaust" repeated
both sides of the debate O'Sullivan held with George Cheever over capital punishment, with the O'Sullivan character shouting, "Onward, onward!" Discussing his
visitors in "The Old Manse," Hawthorne spoke wistfully of one "who had thrown
his ardent heart from earliest youth into the strife of politics, and now, perchance,
began to suspect that one lifetime is too brief for the accomplishment of any lofty
aim." More ominously, "The Procession of Life" described a scholar "diffusing
depth and accuracy of literature throughout his country" who had accidentally
been "drawn into the arena of political tumult, there to contend at disadvantage,
whether front to front, or side to side, with the brawny giants of actual life." Another
Review tale, "The Intelligence Office," described a man who had spent his life in
futile quest of "Tomorrow." And the John Hancock character in "Old Esther Dudley" bore an unmistakable resemblance to O'Sullivan as he delivered a youth-in-
flected speech at the end of the tale:

> Your life has been prolonged until the world has changed around you. You have
> treasured up all that time has rendered worthless—the principles, feelings, man-
> ners, modes of being and acting, which another generation has flung aside—and
> you are a symbol of the past. And I, and these around me—we represent a new
> race of men, living no longer in the past, scarcely in the present—but projecting

our lives forward into the future. Ceasing to mold ourselves on ancestral supersti-
tions, it is our faith and principle to press onward, onward![48]

And in my opinion, the elements of O'Sullivan's personality were broken down
and reconstituted in the optimistic Holgrave in *The House of the Seven Gables*.
Constantly dilating on the "beautiful spirit of youth," disgusted by "the moss-grown
and rotten Past," Holgrave represented all that was right and wrong about Young
America. Like O'Sullivan, he complained the past "lies upon the Present . . . just
as if a young giant were compelled to waste all his strength in carrying about the
corpse of the old giant, his grandfather, who died a long while ago." Furthermore,
he wrote for the magazines and possessed a keen "faith in man's brightening destiny," a destiny almost made manifest by the shy writer. Just as O'Sullivan had proclaimed "all history has to be re-written," so Holgrave felt there were "harbingers
abroad of a golden era," with everything "to begin anew." Their reading, too, was
similar, varying from the "mystic language" of O'Sullivan's spiritualism to the political "babble of the multitude." Suggestively, Holgrave had traveled in Italy,
France, and Germany, the three chief countries of the 1848 revolutions.[49]

Beyond the fleeting resemblances between O'Sullivan and Hawthorne's characters, it is intriguing to note the occasional flashes of political excitement that
color the tales Hawthorne gave the *Review*. In his far subtler way, Hawthorne shared
many of O'Sullivan's impulses, and even as he restrained himself, he expressed
contempt for the older generation, a particular dislike for speculators (eternally
linked to the Panic of 1837), and a desire for the elimination of capital punishment.
"The New Adam and Eve," a more comprehensive tale than usually acknowledged,
addressed many of these issues. It began by introducing characters "with no knowledge of their predecessors nor of the diseased circumstances that had become
encrusted around them." It then attacked the conventional Democratic targets.
Speculators and other "mighty capitalists," masters of "the most intricate and artifi-
cial of sciences," were dismissed for their selfishness, and locofoco sentiments
mumbled throughout ("one portion of the earth's lost inhabitants was rolling in lux-
ury, while the multitude was toiling for scanty food"). Upon seeing a gallows, Eve
gasps, "There seems to be no more sky!—no more sunshine!" And the story con-
cludes with an O'Sullivanesque appeal for new literature, uncharacteristic for
Hawthorne:

> Should he fall short of good, as even as far as we did, he has at least the freedom—
> no worthless one—to make errors for himself. And his literature, when the progress
> of centuries shall create it, will be no interminably repeated echo of our own po-
> etry, and reproduction of the images that were moulded by our great fathers of
> song and fiction, but a melody never yet heard on earth, and intellectual forms un-
> breathed upon by our conceptions. Therefore let the dust of ages gather upon the
> volumes of the library, and, in due season, the roof of the edifice crumble down
> upon the whole.[50]

Other tales presented similar encoded messages for the *Review*'s audience.
"The Procession of Life" showed the crookedness of a "distinguished financier,"
while daydreaming about the disappearance of "conventional distinctions of society," and a world in which "silk-gowned professors of languages" might give their

arm to "the sturdy blacksmith, and be honored by the conjunction" (an aside to Longfellow, perhaps). The tale betrayed a strong empathy for the urban poor throughout, admiring "those lowly laborers and handicraftsmen, who have pined, as with a dying thirst, after the unattainable fountains of knowledge." It also touched on the intellectuals "who think the thought in one generation that is to revolutionize society in the next."[51]

More than any other tale, "A Select Party" revealed the effect of O'Sullivan. It appeared in the *Review* and the first issue of the *New York Morning News*. Appropriately, it poked fun at Henry Clay, the Whig candidate, describing "a rude, carelessly dressed, harum-scarum sort of elderly fellow, known by the nickname of Old Harry," but preferring to be called "Venerable Henry." Old Harry consorts with another man, the so-called "Oldest Inhabitant," and they are both puzzled by ways of "young folks." Another character, "The Wandering Jew," departs "on a ramble toward Oregon," hardly an accidental destination in July 1844. Finally, Hawthorne mimics O'Sullivan, Duyckinck, and the other cultural nationalists with a description of "the Master Genius" of American literature, "a young man in poor attire," "this child of a mighty destiny." Six years later, this description would send Melville into paroxysms of joy when he, too, was feeling contradictory emotions toward Young American nationalism:

> And who was he? Who, but the Master Genius, for whom our country is looking anxiously into the mist of time, as destined to fulfill the great mission of creating an American literature, hewing it, as it were, out of the unwrought granite of our intellectual quarries. From him, whether moulded in the form of an epic poem, or assuming a guise altogether new, as the spirit itself may determine, we are to receive our first great original work, which shall do all that remains to be achieved for our glory among the nations.[52]

Many other tales might be cited, of course, but these three are richer than most for the contemporary observation I am suggesting in Hawthorne's prose. By addressing these themes, Hawthorne stayed current with the *Review*'s policy, even when he was gently chiding O'Sullivan for his excesses, which he did increasingly over time, particularly as Manifest Destiny loomed. "The Christmas Banquet" (January 1844) recorded the confusion of a gentleman who "had prided himself on his consistent adherence to one political party, but, in the confusion of these latter days, had got bewildered, and knew not whereabouts his party was." "The Intelligence Office" (March 1844) described a political newspaper hiring the devil to scribble "party paragraphs," but wondering "as to his sufficiency of venom."[53]

By the time he wrote *The House of the Seven Gables* (1851) with its critique of party machinations, these feelings were out in the open. The central premise of the novel, that ill-acquired real estate damages the acquisitor, certainly applied to Manifest Destiny and O'Sullivan's new obsession with Cuba in 1851. Hawthorne's middle-aged reflections on Holgrave probably applied to O'Sullivan as well:

> His error lay, in supposing that this age, more than any past or future one, is destined to see the tattered garments of Antiquity exchanged for a new suit, instead of gradually renewing themselves by patchwork; in applying his own little life-span as the measure of an interminable achievement; and, more than all, in fancying that

it mattered anything to the great end in view, whether he himself should contend for it or against it.

Continuing more darkly, he wrote that brilliant young men in search of "the world's prizes" often fail at an early age: "The effervescence of youth and passion, and the fresh gloss of the intellect and imagination, endow them with a false brilliancy, which makes fools of themselves and other people." Melville would mark this passage when he read the book in 1851.[54]

As this quotation would indicate, Hawthorne's political stance is difficult to pinpoint, partly because of his inherent opacity, and also because of vacillations within his lifetime. And yet the problems of democracy were far more important to Hawthorne than we might assume from his meek disclaimers about the artist's removal from everyday life. Understandably, he exaggerated his loyalty to the party when seeking the spoils of office, and minimized it when threatened with removal.

When he was hired for the Salem job, he was praised as a "pure and primitive Democrat," and his detractors later removed him for his "offensive partisanship." The *Boston Atlas* charged he had received his appointment "solely on account of his Locofocoism." Yet after the removal, he indignantly professed the dormancy of his political convictions, writing his Whig friend George Hillard, "I never in my life walked in a torch-light procession, and—I am almost tempted to say—would hardly have done anything so little in accordance with my tastes and character, had the result of the Presidential electorate depended on it." Hillard himself wrote Daniel Webster, "If Gen. Cass had been elected, Hawthorne would probably have been removed for his lukewarmness and apathy in their behalf."[55]

The real answer was surely between these extremes. Hawthorne was no stump speaker, but he used O'Sullivan and other party connections to secure his job, and professed a lifelong attachment to Jacksonian principles. Even when denying his political convictions to Hillard, he displayed an impressive knowledge of the Byzantine factions involved, and he was always aware of the political maneuvers taking place around him. The locofoco surveyor summed up his history of the affair by affirming he "was not altogether ill-pleased to be recognized by the Whigs as an enemy."[56]

In short, to go the full distance toward an understanding of Hawthorne, it is important to comprehend the Democratic milieu within which he chose to work, whether he was extroverted in his convictions or not. That is why the closeness of his friendship with O'Sullivan was significant. The two men were not merely fond of each other, but saw themselves as ideologically aligned, and useful to each other. When Hawthorne wanted to please the Salem Democracy and improve his chances for a job, he edited the manuscript of one of its leaders, which O'Sullivan thereupon inserted for publication within the *Review*. Following this shrewd slight-of-hand, where once again literature served as a tactical weapon, Hawthorne wrote Horatio Bridge, "I have grown considerable of a politician."[57]

Hawthorne even echoed O'Sullivan's religious construction of the Democracy in "The Hall of Fantasy," one of the few stories of the period he did not publish in the *Review*: "'Perhaps your faith in the ideal is deeper than you are aware,' said my friend. 'You are at least a Democrat; and methinks no scanty share of such faith is essential to the adoption of that creed.'" True, Hawthorne parodied O'Sullivan's zeal to change the world in that story, and perhaps in Holgrave, but he also felt real empathy for O'Sullivan's causes, an empathy that shows through in each of these characterizations. If Holgrave has a buffoonish quality, he is far less offensive than Judge Pyncheon, the very model of the unctuous Old Fogy loathed by Young America. As Hawthorne confessed, tongue in cheek, in "Old Esther Dudley" (published in the January 1839 *Review*), the story was transmitted to the reader through the agency of "a thorough-going democrat."[58]

Many critics from different backgrounds have posited Hawthorne's political ambivalence, and his careful cultivation of power-brokers to achieve literary success. In my opinion, these readings underestimate the boldness of his political stance, far less half-hearted than his begrudging comments would indicate. Hawthorne was no rabble-rouser, and political intrigue made him uneasy, but the official magazine of the Democratic party was indisputably his preferred forum. The facts do not lie; by the early 1840s, he was in a position to publish his stories in a variety of places, from the *Knickerbocker* to *Graham's* and *Godey's*, but he willfully consigned the bulk of them to the *Democratic Review* because he favored its general tone and direction, despite the ill repute such an association had brought George Sumner in Boston. Indeed, Hawthorne did get into hot water in 1849, when his writing for the *Review* and other Democratic papers was held a reason for his dismissal from the Custom House.

O'Sullivan knew that Hawthorne was no lapdog when it came to party doctrine, but he was delighted to receive his submissions and listed Hawthorne among "a number of the most able pens of Democratic party" in a list that was mainly composed of politicians and journalists. The 1842 essay, "Democracy and Literature," elaborated O'Sullivan's theory about how political liberty and original writing might serve each other's interests, and listed Hawthorne, along with Milton, Dante, Wordsworth, and Bryant as men who "expressed themselves plainly in terms of the democratic creed." Those who wrote for the *Review* were fully cognizant they were part of a cultural-political matrix in which party propaganda, political sympathies, job prospects, and publishing opportunities all went hand in hand. At the center of this matrix stood O'Sullivan and the *Democratic Review*.[59]

Whitman

In June 1839 the *Review* incanted the usual litany of America's literary resources, then issued a prophetic appeal: "Shall there not be one great poet—that man whose eye can roam over the borders of our land, and see these things of which we have spoken?" Four years later, the magazine was still expectant: "The great Poet of the People, the world-renowned bard, the Homer of the mass, has not yet appeared." There is a fair amount of evidence that Whitman, still Walter, was listening.[60]

Many critics have noted Whitman's Democratic idealism; some abstractly, others looking closely at his ties to New York's artisans and laborers. I would like to look into the issue further, again citing the *Review* as the intersection of these vague political sentiments and the production of literature. While Whitman's acquaintance with O'Sullivan was nowhere as deep as Hawthorne's, the *Review* had a profound impact on his career, providing both intellectual fodder and an early forum for his own writings. In 1845 Whitman opined that "all kinds of light reading, novels, newspapers, gossip, etc., serve as manure for the few *great productions* and are indispensable or perhaps are premises to something better." I do not wish to explore this metaphor too closely, but the *Review* provided potent fertilizer for the man who would publish *Leaves of Grass* a decade later. His admiration for the magazine was evident; in 1858 he reflected on the early 1840s, recollecting, "It was about that time that the *Democratic Review*, a monthly magazine of a profounder quality of talent than any since, was largely impressing the public, especially the young men. . . . Its corps of writers were all enthusiasts—believers in a 'good time coming.'" In 1842, writing in the New York *Aurora*, he wrote a whole editorial on the wisdom of the *Review*'s political philosophy and proclaimed it "the leading magazine published this side of the Atlantic."[61]

This praise was hardly accidental. Before August 1841, Whitman had been an obscure contributor to small Long Island newspapers. That month, O'Sullivan published his surprisingly gruesome story "Death in the School-Room," and suddenly the twenty-two-year-old writer had a national audience. Over the next few years, he wrote ten pieces under the *Review*'s auspices, a fairly impressive number for a writer with no academic pedigree. Most of these sentimental stories were uncharacteristic of the later writer we feel we know so well. But the importance of these pieces and their acceptance in the *Review* can hardly be overstated, for they brought the immature Whitman crucial encouragement and sudden standing in the community of New York journalists.[62]

He himself was later quite embarrassed by these early works. Interestingly, in view of his subsequent career, they betrayed an antiurban bias: "Man of cities! What is there in all your boasted pleasure—your fashions, parties, balls, and theatres, compared to the simplest delights we country folk enjoy?" Decades later, Horace Traubel recounted that when asked if these early stories were his, the elderly poet responded,

> Yes—I guess there's no doubt of that—they're mine, if I want to claim them—as I do not! I don't think much of 'em—they're better forgotten—lain dusty in the old files. . . . The Democratic Review was quite famous in those days—started in Washington by a young man—Sullivan, I think, was his name: I knew him well—a handsome, generous fellow. He treated me well. Hawthorne published some of his famous tales through the Review.[63]

As this last sentence implied, Whitman was well aware of the literary company he was keeping in the magazine. Beside sending in writings, he also read the *Review* voraciously, judging from the number of articles he clipped for personal use. Its worldview struck a chord with him, and like many young New York writers, he was excited to share its contagious nationalism. Whitman's background fit perfectly into the general pattern displayed by the *Review* crowd. Born on Long Island in 1819 to a Dutch-English family with Jeffersonian convictions (his father an ardent disciple of Thomas Paine and Fanny Wright), Whitman was well suited by geography and history to become a young Democrat. He fell under the spell of "the glorious Leggett" at an early age, and showed loyalty to the Jacksonian cause and the Young American program throughout the period. From domestic issues to foreign intervention in support of the 1848 revolutionists, it is difficult to find a single point of discord between the editor of the *Brooklyn Eagle* and his fellow travelers at the *Review*.[64]

Whitman's credentials as a Democrat stood up as well as any writer's in the 1840s; he published his first poem in the *Long Island Democrat* as early as 1838 and campaigned vociferously for Van Buren in the election of 1840. Appointed a Democrat "electioneer" in Queens County, he gave at least two speeches for the cause. In 1847, he claimed he spoke at a mass meeting of 15,000 Democrats in 1841. Whitman continued to work for Democratic papers throughout the 1840s, including contributions to O'Sullivan's *New York Morning News*, and loosely allied himself with the Barnburner branch of the party against its conservative Hunker wing. He was devoted to Silas Wright, and considered himself "one of the instruments" who helped bring about his gubernatorial nomination in 1844.[65]

As with Hawthorne, these partisan loyalties often entered into his fiction. The *Review* stories, even if unaccomplished by his later standards, reveal a complex psychology. A near-pathological distrust of fathers is evident in "Bervance" and "Wild Frank's Return." This "unnatural paternal antipathy," as he himself phrased it, may have been a comment on Whitman's own difficult relations with his father, but it also meshed with O'Sullivan's distrust of the elder generation. Likewise, "Death in the School-Room" contained a long aside denouncing "old-fashion'd schoolmasters" who indulge in "child torture."[66]

And like Hawthorne, Whitman repeated O'Sullivan's strong stand against capital punishment, in both his fiction and journalism. His story "Revenge and Requital," the tale of an unfortunate criminal who performed charity to assuage his guilt, ended, "Some of my readers may, perhaps, think that he ought to have been hung at the time of his crime. I must be pardoned if I think differently." "A Dialogue," published in the *Review* of November 1845, seemed to refer specifically to O'Sullivan's debate against Reverend George Cheever, warning, "'O, Bible!', says I, 'what follies and monstrous barbarities are defended in *thy* name!'" Whitman fondly recalled attending meetings in a room on Broadway where capital punishment was hotly debated: "A visitor there would have found a remarkable collection of 'heads.' The *Democratic Review* writers were frequently quoted—some were present to speak for themselves, or as listeners. We allude to Bryant, Judge Edmonds, O'Sullivan, Whittier, Hawthorne, old Major D'Aveza [sic], and others."[67]

Beyond publishing his juvenile pieces, the *Review* influenced Whitman's newspaper editorials, which often echoed O'Sullivan's. It would be boring to list all the areas in which the two men were in agreement, but a partial list would include the superiority of America's political institutions, the inevitability of their spread to foreign lands, America's destiny to overrun the continent, and the greatness of the American yeoman, whose spirit was first displayed in the American Revolution and kept alive through the agency of Andrew Jackson.

These thoughts, of course, were shared by a great number of Americans, but there were peculiar signs of Whitman's indebtedness. An article on "American Futurity" revealed a debt to O'Sullivan's 1839 essay on "The Great Nation of Futurity." Predicting a "holy millennium of liberty," he was confident the "masses of the down-trodden of Europe" would "achieve something of that destiny which we may suppose God intends eligible for mankind." Whitman was rhapsodic over the revolutionary change augured in 1848, writing poems about the excitement as it was happening and afterward (he predicted the revolutions as early as February 1847). Like O'Sullivan, Whitman developed an interest in Latin America after the failures of 1848 and wrote in 1850, "'Manifest destiny' certainly points to the speedy annexation of Cuba by the United States."[68]

The similarities can be pursued indefinitely. Whitman also promoted the cause of Ireland, the "source of the sunniest genius that has been diffused in the civilized world!" and offered fulminous editorials in the Young Ireland line. Like O'Sullivan, Whitman aligned himself with New York's Free Soil Democrats after the Wilmot Proviso, although he denounced extreme abolitionism. He also anticipated westward expansion with purple prose, and urged the annexation of the Yucatan: "We pant to see our country and its rule far-reaching, only inasmuch as it will take off the shackles that prevent men the even chance of being happy and good." In a similar vein, he dismissed England's claim to Oregon with the familiar youth metaphor: "America is full of young blood, young impulses and young ambition." Even his temperance novel, *Franklin Evans*, reverberated with the echoes of Manifest Destiny, foreseeing a sobered America stretching from "the frozen north" to "the hottest sands of the torrid south."[69]

And, of course, Whitman agreed body and soul with O'Sullivan's sense that a nation's political essence must be infused into its literature. He doubtless enjoyed *Review* articles like "Poetry for the People," which urged attention to labor and poverty, and checked the social backgrounds of great European writers for their relevance to ordinary Americans. Countless *Eagle* editorials averred the same philosophy, fearing that the sentimental "cataracts of trash" emanating from England were unworthy of Americans, "for they laugh to scorn the idea of republican freedom and virtue." An entire editorial, for example, was devoted to "Anti-Democratic Bearing in Scott's Novels." Like many Americans, Whitman was disappointed at Dickens' critique of America because of all foreign writers, he seemed the most likely to understand "Literary Democracy."[70]

I mentioned earlier that Whittier's first "Song of Labor," a poem entitled "The Shoemaker," appeared in an issue of the *Review* Whitman contributed to. Although Whittier's influence on Whitman has not come under much scrutiny, the "Songs of Labor" spoke an interesting new poetic language, filled with respect for the working class (not unlike "A Song for Occupations"). Whitman clipped an earlier *Review* article on the need for poetic treatment of the "dignity of labor" and "equality of men." In a moment of proletarian empathy, the *Review* had thrilled Whitman by calling for a poet with "mental energy answering to the strong right arm of the laborer." His words "should ring in every line like the short, quick blows on the anvil," and "breathe a right manly indignation toward the false control of social habits." It would be difficult to find an American writer who did more to sustain O'Sullivan's "democratic principle" in his work.[71]

More than most of the other *Review* writers, Whitman stayed true to Young American idealism long after the disappointments of the late 1840s and early 1850s. He certainly registered cynicism toward the regular system, but still emphasized the familiar touchstones of youth, liberty, and classlessness throughout his long career. In 1850, as the Compromise was being debated, his "Song for Certain Congressmen" contrasted the spirit of "young Freedom" to the depressing debate. Two years later, he wrote John Hale, a New Hampshire senator, urging him to save the Democratic party in terms resonating the Locofoco excitement of the mid-1830s. Introducing himself as "a young man, and a true Democrat," he urged Hale to accept the Free Soiler's nomination in the same revolutionary language Leggett and O'Sullivan loved:

> Look to the young men—appeal specially to them. . . . I know well, (for I am practically in New York), the real heart of this mighty city—the tens of thousands of young men, the mechanics, the writers, &c &c. In all these, under and behind the bosh of the regular politicians, there burns, almost with fierceness, the divine fire which more or less, during all ages, has only waited a chance to leap forth and confound the calculations of tyrants, hunkers, and all their tribe. At this moment, New York is the most radical city in America.[72]

During the next election, four years later, an identical generational radicalism overflowed Whitman's 1856 piece, "The Eighteenth Presidency!" Far more than O'Sullivan himself, Whitman retained the fervor of the *Review*'s early appeals to the Young Democracy. Calling upon "mechanics and young men," Whitman insisted, "the young fellows must prepare to do credit to this destiny, for the stuff is in them." As if it were still 1837, he repeated, "The young genius of America is not going to be emasculated and strangled just as it arrives toward manly age."[73]

Whitman's final paragraph repeated the early platform of Young America almost to the letter. With millennial tones, he seemed to expect war between the generations:

> The horizon rises, it divides I perceive, for a more august drama than any of the past. Old men have played their parts, the act suitable to them is closed, and if they do not withdraw voluntarily, must be bid to do so with unmistakeable voice. . . . What historic denouements are these we are approaching? On all sides tyrants tremble, crowns are unsteady, the human race restive, on the watch for some better era, some divine war. No man knows what will happen next, but all know that some such things are to happen as mark the greatest moral convulsions of the earth.

Citing "the common newspaper, the cheap book," and many other improvements, Whitman exulted that "frontiers and boundaries are less and less able to divide men." The new young American, like the old, discovers new places, expands communication, and even "re-states history." It is sad to contemplate that O'Sullivan, who articulated so many of these thoughts in his youth, would have found them laughably old-fashioned in 1856. By that point, exhausted by his long career inside cultural politics, he embodied the moral aimlessness his disciple denounced from the outside with such ferocious young energy.[74]

Melville

Ample evidence of O'Sullivan's sway with the literary crowd was given by the prompt decline in the magazine's writing after his departure in 1846. Hawthorne terminated the procession of works he had sent the *Review* since its inception. Whittier's last offering was another song of labor, "The Shipbuilders" (April 1846). No more was heard from Whitman (excepting his hilarious review of his own poetry in 1855), nor most of the writers in Duyckinck's stable. William Gilmore Simms continued to dash off inferior sonnets for a year or so, but the magazine's literary quality waned as it became embroiled in the petty schisms of the late 1840s and early 1850s.[75]

The nadir of this decline was reached in 1852, a year the magazine still inveighed against "Fogy Literature," but blindly attacked *Moby-Dick* in terms that might have been self-reflexively applied: "The field from which his first crops of literature were produced, has become greatly impoverished, and no amount of forcing seems likely to restore it to its pristine vigor." This devastating review, notorious to Melville scholars, is fascinating when one ponders the extent to which Melville was influenced by the quest for a Democratic literature. Although he never wrote a word for the *Review*, being slightly too young for the O'Sullivan-Duyckinck era, he considered himself a Democrat, like his brother Gansevoort, and fragmentary evidence indicates his acquaintance with the magazine's tenets.[76]

The relationship did not begin well. Evaluating *Typee*, his first book, the *Review* referred to the author as "Sherman Melville." But despite the slight, Melville participated meaningfully in the Democratic politico-literary matrix from the watershed year of 1845 until his rupture with the Young Americans in 1851-52. He was discovered and nurtured by O'Sullivan's ally, Evert Duyckinck, and borrowed a volume of the *Review* from Duyckinck in 1850, as he was writing *Moby-Dick*. He met the editor on at least one occasion, for Nathaniel Hawthorne and his wife invited O'Sullivan to Lenox on April 11, 1851, where they threw a dinner party to which "Mr. Melville came and brought bedstead and clock." Like *The House of the Seven Gables*, being written simultaneously, his romance contained both affirmative and antagonistic responses to Young American nationalism.[77]

Besides Duyckinck (to be discussed in the next chapter), many of Melville's literary acquaintances were writers who had contributed to the *Review* during O'Sullivan's tenure, including Cornelius Mathews, David Dudley Field, William Allen Butler, the Sedgwicks, and other extended members of the *Review* family. Until the *Moby-Dick* fiasco, his books were generally well received by the *News* and *Review*, and *Mardi* was the subject of an important essay upon its appearance.[78]

Like Hawthorne, Melville felt comfortable within the Democratic milieu even if he occasionally expressed distaste for it. Beyond the archeological evidence furnished by these sundry citations, he enjoyed a long foreground of youthful Locofocoism before meeting the Young Americans. Despite some anti-Jacksonism in their family (Old Hickory removed the Melville grandfather from the Boston Custom House in 1829), the fatherless Melville boys took to the Democracy early on, and may have known many of the *Review* principals as children. Gansevoort and Herman Melville attended a year of the Columbia Grammar School (1829-30) while living in Manhattan. No scholar has noticed that this would have placed the two children under the guidance of O'Sullivan, then a student-teacher at Columbia. His younger brother Thomas was a classmate of the two Melvilles. Furthermore, this would suggest a distant prior acquaintance with Duyckinck, then attending the Columbia High School, and explaining more easily the suddenness of their friendship in 1846.[79]

The Albany region, where the Melvilles moved in 1830, was warmly supportive of the Democracy (thanks in part to its native son from Kinderhook). Among Melville's earliest published work were the "Fragments from a Writing Desk" he had contributed to the *Democratic Press and Lansingburgh Advertiser* in 1839, and he could hardly avoid following his brother's extraordinary political career. Gansevoort Melville was extremely active in party circles before his untimely death in 1846, and many of the particulars of his life resembled O'Sullivan's. He early championed the cause of the immigrant Irish, attacked class privilege, and violently demanded the American prerogative to expand westward, causing great diplomatic unrest during his final appointment as secretary of the legation in London.[80]

The shadowy figure of Gansevoort Melville still eludes literary historians, but he clearly shaped his younger brother in ways that we will never completely fathom. My sense is that he was central to Melville's relationship with the Young Americans, and that their political machinations reminded him of the Democratic heritage his brother had bequeathed. Although he died as the term was gaining currency, Gansevoort Melville was in many ways a Young American himself, from his own relative youth (b. 1815) to his vituperative opinions. Indeed, it was he who in 1844 "rebaptized" James Polk as "Young Hickory," the same name that Franklin Pierce would adopt in 1852. The Young Americans were certainly aware of him; John Bigelow expressed jealousy of his new distinction in an 1844 diary entry.[81]

It would be hard to find two New Yorkers who worked more feverishly to elect Polk than O'Sullivan and the elder Melville. Gansevoort canvassed the country, gave countless speeches in support of Polk's candidacy, and single-handedly represented the disgruntled northern Democracy at many campaign events. Unlike his fellow New Yorkers, he ardently promoted the cause of Texas, as O'Sullivan would soon do as well. Gansevoort wrote long letters to Polk describing the situation in New York, and had almost become a household name when Herman returned from his travels in October 1844, just before the election. One can only speculate the effect Gansevoort's dramatic elevation had on his younger brother, coming at the exact moment his long and difficult voyage ended.[82]

Infinitely less political than Gansevoort, Herman Melville was caught nevertheless in the same vortex of escalating political tensions affecting other Young Americans. William Leggett influenced him early, as he did all of them, and when the Mexican War broke out, Herman wrote Gansevoort, already dead in London, that "something great is impending," insinuating the final struggle against England was in the air (he fantasized about a colossal naval engagement in the middle of the Atlantic). Throughout his life, especially when it was politically convenient for employment purposes, Melville would declare himself a Democrat. Indeed, when he was first mentioned in the *Review*, it was with the parenthetical note that he was "a brother, we believe, to the Secretary of Legation at London." Appropriately, the

New York Morning News, under O'Sullivan and Duyckinck, carried the first American announcement of *Typee,* and also its first review. Whether Melville agreed or not, the Young Americans left no doubt they considered him one of their own. It did not hurt that *Typee* was released at roughly the same moment as "Manifest Destiny" and conveyed similar Pacific longings.[83]

But beside these fleeting glimpses of Melville's interaction with O'Sullivan, there are teasing signs that the *Democratic Review* supplied material for his fiction. Melville's friend John Alexander Lockwood wrote a series of *Review* articles attacking flogging in the U.S. Navy in 1849, just as the finishing touches were being put on *White-Jacket.* A lengthy article on "The Whale-Fisheries" was published in 1846, including nationalistic statements concerning the superiority of American whalers. More impressive still is the similarity between the celebrated passage at the end of chapter 26 of *Moby-Dick* ("Thou who didst pick up Andrew Jackson from the pebbles; who didst hurl him upon a warhorse; who didst thunder him higher than a throne!") and an obscure sonnet to Andrew Jackson in the *Review* of May 1839: "Thou fearless man, of uncorrupted heart! / Raised, by the voice of freemen to a height / Sublimer far than Kings by birth may claim." And countless *Review* articles used the "Ship of State" metaphor for the rudderless federal government, particularly in the wake of the deliberations attending the Compromise of 1850.[84]

There were other hints of *Moby-Dick* in the *Review.* Melville was hypersensitive to its criticism and tortured by an 1849 review of *Mardi,* his ambitious political allegory. Though the book was praised in typical politico-literary terms (it affirmed "the life blood that belongs to the poor" and opposed "the rich"), its atheism was criticized. The magazine wondered if Melville would not profit from a "fiery baptism" that would leave him "washed white" (it even mentioned "calabashes"). Was *Moby-Dick* the author's perverse response to this critique? Other cryptic similarities appeared elsewhere in the *Review.* Just before the *Mardi* review an article described an ocean voyage on a ship called "Herman" that the anonymous author likened to "an American leviathan."[85]

As the *Review* moved toward a prosouthern position in 1850 and 1851 (with *Moby-Dick* underway), it compared Van Buren to Milton's Satan and urged that his son John Van Buren (already parodied in *Mardi*) be "cast forth, Jonah-like" to save the Democracy. It also quoted Calhoun's prediction that Mexico would become like a fast-fish attached to the United States. Finally, it ran a poem entitled "The Last of the Piquods" about the extinction of the doomed Indian tribe. No one of these references is terribly important, but they collectively suggest Melville's romance was informed by the strange new course the *Review* was charting.[86]

My point is not to show that scholars will always be able find obscure sources for *Moby-Dick.* Rather, I wish to show how Melville's cosmogony grew out of the Young American worldview and then proceeded to reject it. That Melville was attentive to contemporaneous politics is indisputable, as a glance at *Mardi* will allow. In that work, Alanno (Senator William Allen of Ohio) delivers a call for territorial expansion into the Northwest, with sarcastic commentary from Melville. Through Alanno, Melville echoed all of O'Sullivan and Gansevoort Melville's tropes, finding strength in America's youth ("You are free because you are young. Your nation is like a fine, florid youth, full of fiery impulses, and hard to restrain."). But he also took pains to hint at the dangers of empty rhetoric, and he strongly warned against "the grand error of your nation": the belief that history has somehow culminated in the American system of democracy. Like Hawthorne, Melville was not hesitant to decry the excesses of Young American political philosophy and repeatedly questioned the tenets of Manifest Destiny in the "Fast-fish and Loose-Fish" chapter of *Moby-Dick* as well as in *Mardi*. The tortured relationship between *Moby-Dick* and Young America will be taken up again in future chapters.[87]

The New Criticism

Beyond fostering relations with these writers, O'Sullivan took several steps toward the larger task of rejuvenating America's ossified literary infrastructure. He did this in several ways, from book advertising to the encouragement of new types of literary middlemen. First, he tried, with partial success, to promote the relatively obscure publishers he considered sympathetic to the cause of Democracy. Following the 1841 move to New York, it was logical to choose the firm of J. and H. G. Langley. The Langleys were Democrats and had published O'Sullivan's argument against capital punishment, Tocqueville's *Democracy in America*, and numerous other political works. In 1844, when Van Buren asked O'Sullivan to suggest a New York publisher to George Bancroft, he wrote, "I would not hesitate to recommend Langley, as at the same time a man of enterprise, capital, extended business facilities & connexions, and as the only *Democrat* I know in the trade, to whom it would be a labor of love to circulate it as widely as possible, with less care for private profit than political benefit."[88]

The Langleys received ample publicity not only on the magazine's title page, but also in its critical notices. Doubtless O'Sullivan considered this fitting, since Henry Langley shared his hot-tempered sensitivity to foreign criticism. When an American editor was given short shrift by an English review, Langley (with O'Sullivan's consent) wrote the victim asking for the names of English "small fry" poetasters, in order "to wield the omnipotent pen against them through the 'columns' and under the flag of the far-famed Democratic Review." Beside their liberal political works, the Langleys issued the novels of allied writers like William Gilmore Simms (*The Life of Francis Marion*) and Cornelius Mathews (*The Motley Book*), and boasted of their "truly democratic" books. In a publisher's note to the 1845 bound edition of the *Review*, Henry Langley freely used the first person plural to discuss the cause of democracy, boasting that "our opponents" had created the *American Review* "to counteract the pernicious influence of the Democratic Review." We have already seen how O'Sullivan tried to transfer the printing of Hawthorne's *Twice-Told Tales* to the Langleys after it failed to sell out its Boston edition.[89]

More importantly, O'Sullivan did all he could to advance the various publishing ventures of Evert Duyckinck, particularly his Library of American Books, which came to fruition just as Duyckinck officially joined the *Review*'s editorial staff. Generally, the *Review* supported any plan for the spread of literacy and critical discernment beyond the well educated. The *Review* also echoed Duyckinck's cry for a new type of professional literary critic to make sense of all the writing being done in the 1840s. William Charvat and other scholars have shown the majority of criticism in the early nineteenth century was deeply conservative, rejecting any works that questioned the mores of society on moral grounds before addressing their aesthetic qualities. Furthermore, the majority of active critics were older men, usually affiliated with higher learning, and hence their criticism had a didactic tone to it that grated on the ears of younger men like O'Sullivan and Duyckinck (or, further south, Edgar Allan Poe). The flood of written material published in the fourth and fifth decades of the century demanded more sophisticated and open-minded treatment, particularly by younger journalistic intellects.[90]

This the *Democratic Review* undertook from the start. Elizabeth Peabody, in her 1838 review of Emerson's "Nature," solemnly claimed the "critics are the priests of literature," an "intermediate class of minds" necessary for "the greatest minds" to communicate with "the great majority of minds." The magazine had borne out this prediction with many subsequent articles. Duyckinck and his allies aggressively fought the "dictatorship" of the old dogmatic criticism, arguing a critique should resemble a "prose-poem" or an "art-novel" in its wide and liberal treatment.[91]

In August 1844 Duyckinck's friend William A. Jones argued emphatically for the new type of critic, calling for "independency" rather than "erudition," hoping "to strip off the disguises of imposture, to reduce the bloated swaggerer to his original proportions," and insisting "the true position of the genuine critic is not yet acquired." As Jones envisioned it, the critic in a democracy would act as the all-important "middleman" between the people and the poet. Of course, in a pure democracy, the people would decide for themselves, but this was one of the many paradoxes of Young America. A subsequent article was more emphatic still, decrying the old-fashioned "literary eunuch" who reflexively deferred to wealth and standing, along with "the curse of blue-stockingism" and the "literary toryism" of the *North American Review*. Jones called instead for critics with a solid grasp of American culture, with "knowledge of life and character, dabbling in science and the arts, thorough knowledge of history and (at least) American politics and economy, with good sense and good feeling, honesty, tact, taste, judgment, and a style, clear, readable and attractive."[92]

Like much of Young America's thought, there was a secret motto behind this call for nationalism. Jones reasoned that improved, accessible criticism would result in a country whose increasingly incommunicative regions and classes would understand each other more readily:

> Hence we look for a better, a purer, a more enlightened and liberal school of criticism than has yet existed here. The materials for it are profusely scattered over the broad territory of these States; the spirit is not wanting in individual scholars, only an union and harmony of effort are requisite to establish a tone of thought and a standard of appeal, most especially necessary in the freest of modern states, where personal independence should be based on the wisest conscientiousness, to preserve liberty from degenerating into licentiousness, and democracy from falling into popular disorder.

By asserting what was true and good about American culture, then, the judicious critic could act politically to save the country from disuniting tendencies. Led by

O'Sullivan's relentless optimism, the *Democratic Review* was sensitive to this uplifting purpose, and Jones claimed a "unanimity of spirit existing between all the writers for it."[93]

"Union and harmony" were important concerns in the fall of 1844, when Jones wrote this piece. Americans were voting for a new president and northern Democrats, including O'Sullivan, were reeling from the rancor of the Baltimore convention. Even as Jones wrote these lines, the thin line separating democracy from disorder was becoming blurred. When the political weather of the late 1840s grew more threatening, young Democrats again asserted their faith in the unifying principle of their creed, even as they recoiled from the frightening effects of a popular sovereignty that was failing to work.

It remains difficult to evaluate the fusion of politics and literature, for the goals of statesmen and writers overlap inconsistently. Despite all their protestations of the need for literary democracy, the radicalism espoused by O'Sullivan, Duyckinck, Jones, and their friends did not translate into real political radicalism of any moment. These Columbia graduates were precocious in their advocacy of a fresh new literature that would place American letters on an equal footing with England, but they were reticent to applaud the subversive writing they were theoretically calling for when it actually appeared, especially when it impinged too directly on sensitive domestic concerns. O'Sullivan would not jeopardize the Democracy's fragile North-South coalition with a frank critique of slavery, and Duyckinck and Jones were indisposed to praise works that truly challenged their critical faculties and the standing order, as we shall see in the next chapter. Only Whitman would remain openly faithful to the democratic principle past the disruptions of the early 1850s, although he was hardly a card-carrying Democrat at that point.[94]

Yet despite this shortcoming, and the inevitability of its failure, it is necessary to recognize the great importance of the *Review* to the literary scene of the 1840s. O'Sullivan's reputation for political intrigue and the *Review*'s close adhesion to the Democratic party has clouded our vision somewhat, obscuring the magazine's deep commitment to a clearly articulated literary program. But it is obvious from a survey of the extensive literary liaisons cited above that the magazine was actively pursuing a program of writing excellence consonant with its political ideals, and that it achieved more lasting success than any other periodical of the 1840s. Even when they were confused and depressed by politics, the young writers of the *Review* asserted their belief in the restorative power of democracy to keep fast the ligatures of the Union, and particularly to shout down New England's domination of cultural politics. Jones wrote indignantly, "How can a puritanical New Englander manage to convey his impression of a theatrical performance, distinguish the meshes of a plot, or analyze the incidents of a ballet?" In so doing, he announced that New York held divergent critical views that could no longer be dismissed by rival arbiters of American taste.[95]

Although forgotten today, the magazine provided a format for some of the most important expressions of American thought in the period, along with the frenzied inanities that constituted so much of literary discourse in the antebellum era. Many of the greatest writers of the period expressed themselves under the Democratic party's umbrella. For these thinkers, and the "great mass of minds" affected by them, the *Democratic Review* was the bellwether of the period, and it is impossible to understand their work without a grasp of its political frame. "Poetry always conveys the truest and most striking features in the countenance of the time," the *Review* proclaimed, and "the predominant fact in the history of the nineteenth century thusfar" was "unquestionably the importance and elevation of the mass." Like much modern criticism, the magazine's adherents announced the "patriarchal" period was over, claiming "the present epoch of literature and popular sentiment must have its mouth-piece." This the *Review* conveniently found in itself.[96]

And through his connection with Duyckinck and other claimants to the Young America mantle, O'Sullivan was able to further his intentions, stated in the introduction to the first *Review* in October 1837, of creating an alternative cultural network to the Anglophilic one dominated by Whig New England. Like O'Sullivan, Duyckinck was frustrated by the inherent impossibility of supernationalism in a time of internecine discord. But he was able to take several remarkable steps toward the creation of a literary infrastructure, even if he was not entirely able to appreciate the import of his achievement, or what he inspired in others. For amidst the rubble of his ambition, an unruly protégé built a lasting monument to the hubris of Young America, celebrating and attacking it simultaneously. Melville, the last of Jackson's orphans, knew there was nothing manifest about destiny in a world where no one can truly divine what is "predestinated" until it has already happened.

3

Young America in Literature

Duyckinck, Melville, and the Mutual
Admiration Society

> It is a common thing to say that great genius will find its way out. This can never be proved. We know only such genius as does find its way out. And we so often see it scathed by the storms through which it has won its way, that we may reasonably doubt whether it is not often entirely silenced.
>
> —*Democratic Review* (November 1838)

> Not that American genius needs patronage in order to expand. For that explosive sort of stuff will expand though screwed up in a vice, and burst it, though it were triple steel. It is for the nation's sake, and not for her authors' sake, that I would have America be heedful of the increasing greatness among her writers.
>
> —Melville, "Hawthorne and His Mosses" (1850)

Predestinated

In personality the shy, retiring Evert Duyckinck was about as far from O'Sullivan's grandstanding as it was possible to be. Yet the bookworm and the firebrand forged a meaningful partnership in the mid-1840s, bringing their version of American culture to the New York masses and beyond. Duyckinck was no "Sub-Sub Librarian" either, but O'Sullivan's most trusted lieutenant in the heady days of the Polk campaign and its aftermath. His literary acumen combined with O'Sullivan's rabid political energy to briefly dominate the American book and magazine trade, before both turned to other projects. In his quiet way, he advanced O'Sullivan's "democratic principle" just as piously, and perhaps secured more lasting results than his easily distracted employer. In so doing, he laid the groundwork for the arrival of Hawthorne's "Master Genius" and Melville's "American Shiloh," the transformative literature so long expected by impatient nationalists.

In 1849 Melville prophesied to Duyckinck he was destined to write "such things as the Great Publisher of Mankind ordained ages before he published 'The World' — this planet, I mean — not the Literary Globe." Duyckinck was also biologically determined, in this case to edit the *Literary World* Melville was punning upon, for publishing was in his blood. His father, another Evert Duyckinck, was a bookseller and printer of the old artisanal school whose progeny grew up surrounded by antique volumes, along with books of his own making. Descended from an ancient New York family of artists and bookmen, Duyckinck's destiny was as manifest as Melville's, who told him, "We that write & print have all our books predestinated."[1]

Under these circumstances, the mystery behind bookmaking vanished, and the younger Duyckinck grew up with a love of literature and a solid grounding in the technology that produced it. Although he never wrote a piece of fiction, claiming his ambition in that area was precisely matched by his talent, Duyckinck's insightful understanding of the craft of authorship and his encyclopedic reading allowed him to become one of the most important taste-shapers of the nineteenth century. His friendship with important authors has resulted in occasional references to him in literary biographies, but few scholars have looked at his career in any detail.

Yet a close study sheds considerable light on the changes wrought in the profession during the seminal two decades before the Civil War. And his efforts to build a nationwide Democratic canon, in place of the New England-Whig orthodoxy, help us to see the complicated issue of canon-formation in something other than categories of race and gender. As much as O'Sullivan, Duyckinck played a crucial role in fostering a New York school emphasizing the touchstones of youth, Americanism, and democracy.

Specifically, I am interested in a groundbreaking series Duyckinck edited in the mid-1840s called the Library of American Books, surprising both for its broad compass and the lack of attention it has received. Announced in the *New York Morning News* the day after Jackson's death, the Library tried valiantly to elevate the people, bringing out new and different American writers in affordable paperback editions. These writers included many of our most celebrated literary artists, but the Library was largely met with indifference, and Duyckinck's subsequent efforts to create a protocanon encountered downright hostility from rival canoneers. The very bitterness of these quarrels suggests the complexity of canon formation, and the fallacy of assuming, as have some recent critics, that a "conservative" American canon emerged in the nineteenth century without challenge.[2]

Canonical struggles, while clearly connected to the expression of power, rarely pit one interest group against another in a clean, easily understood battle. More often, they consist of shifting personal allegiances based on self-promotion as much as loyalty to a great principle. All of these factors, present to a certain extent in any discussion of the canon, were exacerbated in an age when new technology of print media and a rapidly growing marketplace were utterly transforming the profession of authorship from a gentlemanly pursuit to the modern, chaotic vocation it has been ever since. Duyckinck's career spanned the disruptive transition introduced by the Industrial Revolution and brought him into contact with almost everyone claiming to be a literary artist in the mid nineteenth century. His location at the geographical and historical crossroads of American literature demands critical attention.

Duyckinck, if known at all by cognoscenti of American letters, is generally remembered, at best, as the man to whom Melville wrote some interesting letters, or
perhaps for introducing Melville to Hawthorne. Others, like Lewis Mumford,
looked upon him condescendingly as an "energetic hack," an obscure bibliophile
whose influence on Melville was hard to fathom. Born in Manhattan in 1816, he
came from an old Dutch-Knickerbocker family; hence the name, which Melville
spelled differently almost every time he wrote him (he apologized for translating
"your patronimick into the Sanscrit"). A seventeenth-century ancestor identified as
"Ever Duckings" once participated in a skirmish against the New Englanders, aptly
foreshadowing Duyckinck's work toward New York's cultural supremacy.[3]

Duyckinck's father died the day before his seventeenth birthday, in 1833. His
mother died four years later, adding to his sense of crisis in 1837. But his books
helped to weather all the problems confronting him as he faced adulthood. He
graduated from Columbia College just after O'Sullivan (1835), and a year later
founded the literary clique that metamorphosed into Young America in 1845. Appropriately, the Tetractys Club was formed with Duyckinck and three friends
(William A. Jones, Jedediah Auld, and Russell Trevett), and their circle was soon
enlarged to include Duyckinck's brother George, William Allen Butler (whose father helped launch the *Democratic Review*), and a high school chum named Cornelius Mathews. Like most young writers, they frittered away their time drinking
and playing small pranks on each other. An account of an early meeting revealed
that "slings are drunk" and "Babel-itish and super-human sounds" made by the ambitious intellectuals, already eager to disturb the older generation of writers.[4]

But the Tetractys had a serious side, despite these antics and their inability to
find a suitable name for themselves (they also called themselves "the Knights of the
Round Table"; hostile critics would later dub them "the Mutual Admiration Society"). On the eve of Van Buren's election in 1836, they put out a satirical magazine,
The Literary: A Miscellany for the Town, with a mixture of frivolous articles ("The
Life of Dr. Braindeath") and aggressive editorials about the need to rejuvenate literature. The *Literary* expired after one issue, but it contained in incubus all of
Duyckinck's later ideas. Remembering "when the author was wont to sit in stiff dignity in his high-backed chair" and act like an "icicle," the magazine was delighted
to proclaim a new era of "juvenile independence," adding "the age has altered from
the past, and the condition of literature has altered with it—for the better." The
new energies of the day required a more democratic system, and Duyckinck's anti-
European manifesto overflowed with Jacksonian symbolism: "There are no false
media of an 'Imprimatur' from closed inquisitions, or a royal seal 'by authority,' or
of fawning sycophancy upon wealth and station. The author attains his rank from
the force of his own character."[5]

The youthful clique was never as political as O'Sullivan, but clearly leaned toward the Democracy. One (Auld) identified himself as "a locofoco," and another
(Mathews) displayed an early obsession with satirizing the electoral process. Duyckinck's voluminous manuscripts, lovingly preserved in the New York Public Library,
reveal his voracious intellectual appetite concerning America and its revolutionary
legacy (an Anglophobic grandfather was active in the War for Independence). He
read everything he could get his hands on, especially esteeming writers like Leggett

and Thomas Paine ("the firmest of Democrats"). He collected unusual slang, jokes, "American Anecdotes," old ballads, and other bits of local folkore, and reiterated over and over again his love of Manhattan.[6]

But even at this early date, Duyckinck believed America to be the sum of many regional parts, each fascinating in its own right. In the summer of 1838, Duyckinck broadened his circle of literary acquaintances by traveling to Salem to visit a Democratic recluse whose stories he admired. Fifteen years later, at the height of his influence, Hawthorne reflected fondly on Duyckinck as the first individual "who ever thought it worthwhile to visit me as a literary Man." It was rather remarkable a New Yorker, not a Bostonian, achieved this distinction.[7]

Duyckinck may have known Hawthorne through the *American Monthly Magazine*, where they were both sending articles in 1838. From their earliest writings, the Tetractys revealed an urban sensibility that was notably different from the other writers in these cultivated magazines. Mathews wrote "City Sketches" about Manhattan, while Duyckinck (under the pseudonym "Felix Merry") confessed his love for rambles about town, visiting poor neighborhoods along with elegant ones. An early piece Duyckinck wrote for the *Knickerbocker*, "The Day-Book of Life," offered a metropolitan philosophy that was quite different from anything coming out of New England. Unlike, say, Emerson, Duyckinck actually liked crowds: "Nature is not enough: we need men and cities; we must join, in a certain way, in the throng and tumult; we must retire from solitude: the wave must return with the tide, or it is lost upon the shore."[8]

At the end of 1838 Duyckinck traveled through ancestral Holland with his friend James Beekman and Harmanus Bleecker, a prominent Albany Democrat (eventually Van Buren's minister to the Hague). Duyckinck praised him as "a sturdy Dutchman and a locofoco." The Knickerbocker junket intensified Duyckinck's patriotism, despite an embarrassing moment at Waterloo when he observed "some stupid American had scribbled the name of General Jackson on the inscription stone." He returned to the United States with a renewed sense of mission, and took steps to launch a second front in O'Sullivan's war against the conservative literary culture. Early letters to Bleecker reveal him brimming over with a sense "the past is gone" and "a popular literature is arising, one suited especially to the laborer."[9]

The first important undertaking of the Duyckinck clique was the monthly magazine *Arcturus*, which Poe called, with exaggeration, "decidedly the very best magazine in many respects ever published in the United States." Melville alluded to it in *Mardi*, and with more justice, when he wrote, "Ay, ay, *Arcturion*! I say it in no malice but thou wast exceedingly dull." James Russell Lowell paid it a left-handed compliment by calling it "as transcendental as Gotham can be." It ran from 1840 to 1842 and established the young critics, particularly Duyckinck, Mathews, and Jones (who did the bulk of the work) as bona fide New York literati. Articles ranged from politics to urban life (various "city articles") to reform issues of the day (pauperism, capital punishment) to the new types of culture enjoyed by New Yorkers (theater, art). Predictably, the magazine started with the usual insistence the world was beginning all over again for the American: "The Sky above him is a new sky, the earth beneath him is a new earth. . . ."[10]

The decision to commence adult life as a literary critic was no ordinary one, but the clubbish profession was grudgingly opening up in the 1840s. Duyckinck's friends felt the same generational energy O'Sullivan did, and wished to tear down all obstacles in their path. This mentality was easily applied to the New York literary scene, dominated as it was by an elitist cadre of conservative critics, publishers, and magazine editors, who indulged in a complicated pattern of mutual back-scratching that often made it difficult for new writers to penetrate the market. It applied even more easily to Boston, hardly known for its receptivity to outsiders.[11]

Duyckinck and his friends were champing at the bit for a new kind of American literature. They tried valiantly to describe what this writing would be like. Like America itself, the new books they expected would be big, reckless, and thoroughly "original," to use their most overworked adjective. A notebook fragment contains Duyckinck's hope that American culture would lead the country to "the healthy tone of a true republic," away from "European vanities," and toward "the wisdom and democracy and sober self-government of our American ancestors." Though mild-mannered, he loathed "the money element" springing up around him, as well as the ignorance of the American masses concerning culture. But he remained optimistic that a few smart critics could communicate with authentic Americans: "What have we not to hope from the true democratic element, if it be adhered to, little government, little agitation, free trade and low prices—'plain living and high thinking.'" This last phrase might serve as his personal motto.[12]

Amazingly, given Duyckinck's later fastidiousness, the clique considered itself "Rabelaisian." They boasted their love for "cakes and ale" and directed their thoughts toward America's "people" rather than the intelligentsia. They prized laughter highly for this reason, and an important critical essay Duyckinck wrote in 1840 claimed "the two most important desiderata for our country, are a great poet and a great humorous writer." Cornelius Mathews was anointed to the latter role, and Duyckinck especially urged him to strive for political satire: "The subject of political life is well-chosen for illustration; its capacity for mirth, its openness to ridicule, are perceived by the most implicit follower at the heels of the best crowd-compelling politician."[13]

Again, Duyckinck and his friends were never actively political to the extent O'Sullivan was. But the two friends were happy to use each other in their overlapping quests, and the *Democratic Review* impressed Duyckinck with its sense of America's destiny as a nation releasing a new, proletarian energy on the world, in literature as in everything else. In an 1845 article for the *Review* on "American Humor," W. A. Jones characterized Duyckinck as "almost rabidly American," and admired "the most enthusiastic style" with which he "talks of building up our literature, copyright, and the claims of American writers." Duyckinck's review of William Ellery Channing was transparently Democratic in its approval of "extending to all those blessings which have heretofore been thought the distinguished privilege of the few." Another clique member, J. B. Auld, wrote, "One reason I like E.A.D. is that he is such a good democrat at heart."[14]

Arcturus thus showed an intense interest in finding new writers, and generally disdained the established, older crowd of American writers such as Irving, Cooper, and James Kirke Paulding. Duyckinck continued to advocate Hawthorne with a glowing review of his "Grandfather's Chair" and a full profile in May 1841. When

Duyckinck and Mathews wrote Hawthorne at the end of the year to solicit material for the magazine, the writer wrote back of his "very deep gratitude" for the review and offered them some of his tales gratis for reprinting ("It would give me great pleasure to see them in a Magazine which I like so much as Arcturus"). The search for young authors continued with articles like Mathews's "Unrest of the Age," betraying the stir-crazy anomie felt by the rising post-Jacksonian generation. Like O'Sullivan, Duyckinck cultivated friendships with writers around the country, including James Russell Lowell (whom he called "one of the Young Americans" as early as 1843) and William Gilmore Simms.[15]

Mathews was probably the most ardent member of the clique, expressing his nationalistic ideas with an unmatched shrillness that brought contempt from many rival literati. He later became something of an albatross to Duyckinck, but he defined the clique's youthful stance early in its existence. In 1839, when Duyckinck was conducting his grand tour of Europe, Mathews wrote him, hoping "all of us, in our own way, contribute something to the state of good literature in our own country." With a defiant flourish, Mathews announced his intention of writing books "however rude," so long as they were "full of the elements of thought truly born and nurtured by the country in which I live." A speech he gave that year urged young intellectuals to pay close attention to the fascinating energies of the city and its Jacksonian crowds: "In the mighty metropolis a man's nature is fed and excited by a thousand sources. It is stimulated to action by the loud roar of the multitude." Mathews literally positioned himself in the street: "We will take our position in the thouroughfare and catch, with a pleased eye, the strange humors, the cunning dealings and actions of common men."[16]

Following his own advice, the great hope of the clique authored a plethora of instantly forgotten works from 1838 onward. It is a strange experience to enter the fictive world of Cornelius Mathews today. *Behemoth; A Legend of the Moundbuilders* (1839) was set in the remote North American past, featuring an Indian named Bokulla and a giant mastodon, locked in mortal combat. It utterly failed to arouse interest in America's pre-Columbian civilization. *Wakondah: The Master of Life* (1841) also stressed the Native American theme (Poe called it "trash" from beginning to end). His play *The Politicians* (1840), a novel called *The Career of Puffer Hopkins* (1842), and *Poems on Man in His Various Aspects Under the American Republic* (1843) offered burlesques of Jacksonian society, with some promising descriptions of New York politics, but little in the way of coherent plot and well-drawn characters. Despite successful episodes here and there (*Puffer Hopkins* wickedly parodied transcendentalist gobbledygook), his work was difficult to read. The *North American Review* would laugh, "He who has read it through can do or dare anything."[17]

Some were generous; the *Southern Literary Messenger* predicted in 1843, "We do not doubt he will hereafter become, one of the most prominent of the literateurs of the young America." In a way, this was right, for Mathews more than anyone else gave life to the term "Young America" when the clique adopted it in 1845. But today he is little more than a footnote to the bitter factionalism of the Manhattan literary scene in the 1840s. As difficult as it is to read Mathews's novellas, with their hackneyed plots and Dickensian dialogue, they offer a unique window into the Young

American psyche. Mathews had many inventive ideas, from the pseudo–science fiction of *The Behemoth* to his light satires of New York's annual electoral paroxysm. His books overflowed with love for old and new Manhattan and the city's increasingly frenetic pace. One could even say they reflected this pace, and also some of the disorganization of the growing city. With a little more discipline, he could have been an important mannerist of the mid-nineteenth-century urban scene. Each of his books went further than the last to fuse nationalism and literature; yet all lacked the imagination Whitman and Melville would bring to the task.[18]

History has not been kind to Mathews, and with good reason. His books remain more or less unreadable. But beneath the cardboard characters and stilted dialogue, one senses a vivid imagination, more daring than most writers of the period, and often sillier. It took courage to write about mastodons, and Perry Miller was right to insinuate that Melville remembered *The Behemoth* when he floated the equally outrageous idea of a white whale. If Cornelius Mathews failed in his quest to become the great American novelist, it was not for lack of trying.

Despite Mathews's limitations as a writer, he had few peers as a publicist. Unlike Duyckinck, he loved the limelight, and he was constantly finding authors' issues to complain about in the early 1840s. One cause the clique trumpeted loudly was international copyright, an issue that gave them a perfect forum to vent their patriotic spleen against the English and announce their own arrival on the literary scene. The lack of a copyright allowed inferior English novels to be imported and sold cheaply, to the detriment of struggling American authors. The issue was well-suited to their messianic sense of America's coming literary importance (although O'Sullivan, ever the laissez-faire Democrat, thought a copyright sounded like a tariff). And by forming a group of concerned authors, they created an infrastructural element for the profession, a protoguild whose organization Duyckinck urged with all the zeal of an unemployed cordwainer: "Union among authors, bringing together the force of their aggregate works, would create a sentiment, a feeling in their behalf, a voice to which booksellers would be compelled to listen."[19]

The copyright agitation began in the late 1830s, and its flames were dutifully flamed by *Arcturus*. In 1843 the American Copyright Club was formed with William Cullen Bryant as titular president, but driven by the energy of Mathews and Duyckinck. The former was particularly active, writing virulent articles and pamphlets, and haranguing audiences (a year earlier, he had almost spoiled a public dinner for Charles Dickens). Like O'Sullivan, he argued, "We are in a new country, with a new history," and predicted an impending struggle between "old" England and "America, roused to new duties in its youth" ("a great contest draws nigh!"). Many of Duyckinck's friends were invited into the club, including Hawthorne, Simms, James Russell Lowell, and Poe (there was impressive overlap with the *Review*'s stable of writers). Besides a lot of hot air, nothing of significance came from the Copyright Club (the law was not passed until 1891), but it showed the increasing degree authors were perceiving themselves as part of a distinct profession with economic considerations.[20]

The club was also significant because it gave Duyckinck the idea to publish a series of books promoting his vision of American literature and offering fair payment to authors. In early 1844, with Bryant's help, he undertook a series of inexpensive editions known as the Home Library, but it fizzled after a book of poems by Bryant and a travel essay by Joel Headley, another Duyckinck protégé. Despite the failure of the series, Duyckinck was learning how to seize control of the means of production, and he was making important friendships within the profession. Duyckinck's closeness to Hawthorne was also bringing him into nearer contact with O'Sullivan, and we can be sure that he was reading the reinvigorated *Democratic Review*. Indeed, he was part of its reinvigoration, for he and his friends had been submitting articles there ever since the demise of *Arcturus*.[21]

Literature for the Masses

Duyckinck and O'Sullivan were natural allies, not only because of their early schooling together, but because they both saw literature as a social instrument. In 1840, even before *Arcturus*, Duyckinck wrote W. A. Jones that American literature "must now be practical for the masses, original and ingenius [sic] for the educated." In a piece entitled "The Culture of the Imagination," Jones imagined a future America where "culture" (from plays to concerts and lectures) would be dispensed free to the populace, partly through "people's editions, cheap libraries without end." Duyckinck confided to his diary around this time, "The literary movement appears to come from the masses themselves who are purging themselves of small vulgarities & puerilities of thinking and are asking for something better." In the January 1842 issue of *Arcturus*, Duyckinck set forth his editorial policy: "There is no line in its pages that is not meant for the humblest reader, as well as the highest." He and his associates refused to see literature as the province of "monks"; rather, "they would have its pages spread in the market place; would scatter its leaves, if they could, far and wide, mingling them with the lighter issues of the day, and gliding through the throng with a benignant recognition of all that is good, noble and pure."[22]

Duyckinck's position was not merely the extension of his politics, but also the result of his perceptive reading of the publishing business itself, where improved technology was introducing literature to thousands of unlettered Americans. Enormous improvements in publishing and distributing technology had created a vast new audience for books over the same period the Democrats had taken over the White House. These improvements were on such a grand scale, collectively, as to constitute a communications revolution. As recent scholarship has shown, every feature of information-processing was modernized, from typesetting to bookbinding to paper-folding to stitching and myriad other functions. Instinctively knowing this earlier than most people made Duyckinck a good editor and a good Democrat. Unlike the curmudgeonly Thoreau (who complained, "The modern cheap and fertile press, with all its translations, has done little to bring us closer to the heroic writers of antiquity"), he foresaw with unusual clarity the uses of this new technology.[23]

These advances were felt nowhere more keenly than New York, the emerging commercial metropolis of the nation. Logically, New York's printers and publishers were the pioneers of the mechanical metamorphosis within their profession. Helmut Lehmann-Haupt found 345 publishers in New York in the period 1820–1852, compared to 198 in Philadelphia and 147 in Boston. Henry Wadsworth Longfellow was sensitive to this growing preeminence. He wrote George W. Greene, the consul at Rome, in 1839: "New York is becoming more and more literary. It will soon be the center of everything in this country;—the Great Metropolis. All young men of talent are looking that way; and new literary projects in the shape of Magazines and Weekly papers are constantly started, showing great activity, and zeal, and enterprise."[24]

From a personal and a geographical perspective, then, Duyckinck was perfectly situated to bring American literature to its climacteric. But despite the young literary energy flowing toward the emporium, there were obstacles in Duyckinck's path. New York literary culture was dominated by a network of older critics and publishers, most of whom had reigned unchallenged since their golden day in the 1820s. The Harper Brothers ran the top publishing firm, which was galling to Duyckinck for several reasons. Not only did they flout the copyright laws, denying American authors a fair chance to compete with pirated imports, but James Harper had apprenticed to Duyckinck's father before surpassing him. The Harpers disliked Duyckinck as much as he disliked them, and subverted his projects.[25]

Despite his growing influence in the early 1840s, Duyckinck's campaign to redirect American literature toward the people began as an outsider's assault on the citadel of established culture. Many recent critics have overlooked this, however, preferring to identify Duyckinck with the hegemony he was competing against. Jane Tompkins, for example, citing his early alliance with Hawthorne, called Duyckinck "arguably the most important literary man in New York." Not only is this inaccurate from a historical perspective (Duyckinck was twenty-four years old and almost entirely unknown at the time); it fails to consider the extent to which Hawthorne and Duyckinck saw themselves struggling against the arthritic Whiggish literary network.[26]

No better testimony can be given to the importance of the political subcurrent beneath the literary criticism of *Arcturus* than the dismal reaction of George Templeton Strong, a local Whig to whom Duyckinck gave a bound copy in 1848. A horrified Strong found the magazine "pervaded by the progress instinct with the lies of 'liberality' and enlightenment and the like twaddle." His opinion is worth printing in full:

> *Arcturus* would unsex woman and destroy the Idea of Womanhood on Earth by removing their "disabilities" and "elevating" them into a race of disagreeable, effeminate men in petticoats. It holds capital punishment cruel, barbarous and unnecessary, the diffusion of useful information a panacea for all social evils, and so forth—anybody can gulp its doctrines on all subjects from those specimens.[27]

Arcturus probably did not deserve the full measure of Strong's scorn, for in truth it was not as revolutionary as its proponents hoped it would be, and failed after two years. Poe was delicate in his criticism, saying that "the magazine was, upon the whole, a little *too good* to enjoy extensive popularity." But Strong was not entirely off the mark in detecting a social conscience beneath the polite veneer, for Duyckinck's cabal felt strongly that their literature should somehow limn the ordinary people on whom Strong rained his contempt.[28]

It was at this moment that O'Sullivan stepped in to revive Duyckinck's flagging fortunes. Following the demise of *Arcturus* and the copyright agitation, Duyckinck's literary reputation gained him several offices which forced him into an even closer rapport with the *Review*'s network of writers. He increasingly assisted with O'Sullivan's newspaper, the *New York Morning News*, providing a mouthpiece for his friends to explore their rowdy nationalism in everything from theater to art, music, and politics. Announcements of America's impending "Manifest Destiny" appeared alongside reviews of Mathews and Longfellow, deciding to no one's surprise that the former "has the more vivid genius, and approaches nearer to the energetic spirit of the age." Articles repeatedly described the transfer of literary energy from Boston to New York. William Gilmore Simms, becoming an ally of the clique, echoed the anti-New England message by calling on New York to become the nation's literary capital.[29]

An important article written by Duyckinck at this time outlined his ambitious plans for the new year. Ironically, it also revealed some of the cracks beginning to form in the Democracy's intellectual coalition. Entitled "Literary Prospects of 1845," it echoed some of his earlier statements of literary radicalism, looking forward to "a fresh and youthful year," declaring "the old is worn out, the reign of humbug is extinct," and recalling the Battle of Culloden O'Sullivan's forebear had planned: "Like its predecessor, one hundred years ago, let it be a year of Rebellion, of protest against all shabbiness and unworthiness in literature—fighting not *for* Pretenders, but against them." Yet Duyckinck also hinted at his deep discomfiture over O'Sullivan's expansionism: "The opening of a new department of literature may be as well worth talking about as the acquisition of Texas—with this little difference in the subject matter of the two, that while one is an enlargment [sic] of the freedom of the mind, the other is a question of the slavery of the body." It was a crucial distinction.

Duyckinck increasingly relished the prospect of a literature free of the distractions of "party politics" and the "unwholesome insects" they bring with them. Significantly, this essay was published not in the *Democratic*, but in the new *American Review*, which had been launched by the Whigs to reclaim some of their lost edge since the *Democratic*'s arrival. Duyckinck concluded the piece with a call for "union," not only among guild-conscious authors, but among all Americans in a "stronger than political" sense, dependent on "a common sentiment breathed by the fresh original books of the land." While O'Sullivan defined expansion as the glue that would hold the country together, Duyckinck looked to the genius of American literature. The extent of this "little difference" would become clear in a few years.[30]

But if Duyckinck had misgivings about militarism and slavery, he concealed them for the good of the cause. In April 1845 Duyckinck moved even closer to O'Sullivan as he became literary editor of the *Democratic Review*. In Duyckinck's first issue as editor, he enlisted a number of friends to write articles and wrote a politically charged review of Hawthorne, suggesting his allegiance to the Democratic party had earned him a government appointment. Duyckinck urged the Polk administration to adopt a "Literary Pension Fund" to support indigent writers, since it was unfair for politicians to grow "fattened in their lifetime" while a poet "lives and starves."

Hawthorne got the job, and riding the wave of enthusiasm following Polk's election, Young America was finally in a position to begin flexing its muscles.[31]

At this moment, on June 30, 1845, Cornelius Mathews gave the address that articulated all the nationalistic feelings he had been storing up for years. "Americanism," as he declaimed before New York University, was sweeping the world, redefining the realms of literature, humor, art, music, and theater. All the emotions of 1837 came rushing back as he announced the arrival of his generation, "the first generation reared, from infancy to manhood—along the whole line of our lives, minute by minute, year by year—in the doctrine and under the discipline of Republican Truth." This generation refused the path of "plodding, careful, hankering, money-getters," but chose something better for itself. Young America was born.[32]

Clearly, Mathews had that rare, exciting feeling that different forces and ideas were converging and culminating in a particular place. His Young America was simultaneously regional, national, and international, beginning in New York and emanating to the rest of the world, "revolutionizing slowly under our example" (O'Sullivan would have struck the word "slowly"). Mathews explained: "Here, in New York, is the seat and stronghold of this young power: but, all over the land, day by day, new men are emerging into activity."[33]

In short, Mathews was proclaiming Manifest Destiny in literature alongside O'Sullivan's proclamation of geopolitical Manifest Destiny. The resemblance was uncanny; he even used the same words, issuing a "manifest demand to the country" to accomplish its "intellectual as well as physical destiny." Like O'Sullivan (and unlike Duyckinck), Mathews was comfortable defining literature in martial terms, linking creativity to geographical expansion. He warned belligerently: "The spirit which disdains defeat in war . . . cannot much longer rest content with an ignominious vassalage in literature." If there were a way to express "54-40 or Fight!" in literary terms, he would have thought of it. For the time being, all seemed right in the Young American universe, although history would prove that these two types of Manifest Destiny, physical and metaphysical, were hardly one and the same.[34]

The Library of American Books

In the same speech, Mathews hinted at Young America's next step. He demanded that publishers go further to publish books that were both affordable and first-rate, "to be placed within the reach of every American citizen for his library" in order to satisfy his "American desires" (whatever that meant). Around the same time, Duyckinck became an editor with Wiley and Putnam, an aggressive New York publishing house eager to win some of the expanding literary market dominated by the Harper Brothers. He had met George Putnam in London in the course of his European journey seven years earlier, recording in his journal the pleasure of Putnam's company, with whom he enjoyed "a relishing talk on John Bull, New York and Literature." Putnam was also the London distributor of the *Democratic Review*, and had joined Duyckinck and Mathews in the copyright agitation. Unsurprisingly, O'Sullivan's newspaper was effusive in its praise for "the junior member of the firm, whose enterprising liberality . . . has been of eminent use to American authors in the introduction of their works in England."[35]

Like everyone else in the Duyckinck circle, Putnam was young (b. 1814) and eager to leave his mark on the world, especially if he could promote American cultural independence along the way. He even took matters into his own hands by writing a book for his own house entitled *American Facts* (1845) that attempted to redress various English slights of American culture. Duyckinck did not especially like the book, finding it pedantic and Bostonian. As he phrased it in the *Review*, "He is the most amiable and well-meaning of men, but he was born in New England." Putnam was also a Whig, which probably disturbed Duyckinck less than it would have O'Sullivan. This disadvantage was outweighed by the fact he was Sophia Hawthorne's first cousin.[36]

Duyckinck was charged with the general editorship of two important series to be put out by Wiley and Putnam. The first, the Library of Choice Reading, would focus on bringing out foreign classics in affordable volumes (its reductionist slogan: "Books that are books"). The second series, the Library of American Books, was more daring. Although it has received relatively little attention from modern commentators, it was a watershed in American literary history for several reasons. Not only did it introduce many of the country's most exciting young authors, it was the first series to even consider the radical notion Americans might be interested in reading a set of books by their own writers. An advertisement for the series boldly issued "an appeal for the literature of America—such a one as it has the right to make in its own behalf, with the expectation of a hearty response."[37]

Duyckinck was clearly assembling what he considered to be a top-notch cross-section of American writers, from as many regions and backgrounds as possible. He wrote William Gilmore Simms, it was "better to have the dryest chronicle of facts than those digests of feeble invention and imitative description in the old American magazines." Thoreau was not alone as he bewailed reading "the nine thousandth tale about Zebulon and Sephronia, and how they loved as none had ever loved before," specifically querying, "Why should we leave it to Harper & Brothers and Redding & Co. to select our reading?"[38]

As he had done with *Arcturus*, Duyckinck avoided the older totemic figures, such as Cooper and Irving, and instead sought younger types, both male and female. To an extent, Duyckinck's series foreshadowed present debates about canons, for he was clearly trying to posit a new group of writers to displace the older group, who, if not exactly "canonical," were more established and less representative of the rising generation of the 1840s. The elder Richard Henry Dana might have sensed the political underpinnings of the planned series, considering it yet another example of "the curse of that great Curse, Democracy!" In certain ways Duyckinck's efforts adumbrated the rejection of genteel culture undertaken by young critics like Mumford and Brooks after World War I. But unlike his Americanist successors, Duyckinck was more than just an influential critic; he was charged with the direction of an important publishing series through which he could enact his ideas.[39]

By 1845 Duyckinck had become a shrewd literary savant and was in a good position for such a coup. He wrote Putnam, "I had long, whether from infant and boyish years having been passed in my father's bookstore, had an eye on the trade and written many schemes for them on the empty air when Mr Wiley applied to me for counsel—so the apple had not ripened in a day though it was ready for shaking." The books in the series were affordable, a key point in the competitive market and in his populist ideology. As Duyckinck wrote in an advertising circular, "Books in the United States must hereafter be cheap," because common sense, new technology, and democracy dictated it. The *American Review* showered praise: "We regard the starting of this series, in the cheap yet beautiful form in which they are issued, as a new era in our publishing history."[40]

Another vital way in which the Library of American Books signaled a breakthrough was its sympathetic treatment of writers. Poe praised Duyckinck highly for providing "unwonted encouragement to native authors by publishing their books, in good style and good company, without trouble or risks to the authors themselves, and in the very teeth of the disadvantages arising from the want of an international copyright law." The amount paid varied according to the writer's stature (the firm was willing to waive all profit to woo Emerson), but writers were allowed to keep a 10 percent profit and their copyright after the editions were paid for. The cheapness of the editions placed them within the budget of ordinary readers, essential in a day when pirated editions of popular English novels could be sold cheaply to the American public, but they also managed to pay back something to the creator of the product. Duyckinck even placed quotations from the American Copyright Club on the wrappers and front pages of books in the series. For all these reasons, the series would have been important to the history of American literature even if the authors included had been utterly destitute of talent.[41]

This, however, was hardly the case. Duyckinck lined up a formidable cast of allied thinkers for his cause, a list that still impresses a century and a half later. One of the first enlistees, unsurprisingly, was Nathaniel Hawthorne, who served the Library of American Books in a quadruple capacity. He edited the first book in the series, the manuscript of his close friend Horatio Bridge's travel adventures, entitled *Journal of an African Cruiser*, which Hawthorne had originally suggested as a set of *Democratic Review* articles. Hawthorne also contributed a new collection of his short stories, most of which had appeared in the *Review*, along with an introduction, and called it *Mosses From an Old Manse* (other titles bandied about, and mercifully rejected, were *Wallflowers from an Old Abbey*, and *Moss and Lichens from an Old Parsonage*). Third, he did his best to advance the cause of the series by casting plaudits upon the books as a newspaper reviewer.[42]

Finally, Hawthorne helped Duyckinck as an adviser and a link to the New England writers. Living in Concord in 1845, he was in an ideal position to witness the first springtime signs of the American Renaissance, and he translated this information to Duyckinck in several fascinating letters. One in particular, on July 1, 1845, reveals that Hawthorne was sounding other members of the Concord community for possible contributions to the Library. Concerning Thoreau, for example, Hawthorne was prescient in his assessment:

> As for Thoreau, there is one chance in a thousand that he might write a most excellent and readable book; but I should be sorry to take the responsibility, either towards you or him, of stirring him up to write anything for the series. He is the most

unmalleable fellow alive—the most tedious, tiresome, and intolerable—the narrowest and most notional—and yet, true as all this is, he has great qualities of intellect and character. The only way, however, in which he could ever approach the popular mind, would be by writing a book of simple observation of nature.[43]

Indeed, two years later, Thoreau offered Duyckinck precisely such a book for the series. In 1847 he wrote Duyckinck announcing the readiness of his *A Week on the Concord and Merrimack Rivers* for publication. Emerson wrote a fulsome letter of praise for the work, citing its "originality" and noting "the great advantage of being known which your circulation ensures." But despite his efforts, and Thoreau's testy letters, Duyckinck seems to have remembered Hawthorne's advice, and only offered to publish it at Thoreau's risk, which the latter refused.[44]

The attempt to snare Emerson himself for the series was more complicated, with Hawthorne again mediating. Duyckinck almost won him over him with his enthusiasm. Having heard of the "Representative Men" lectures in preparation, he nearly salivated in supplication, confessing "my desire for a genuine book for the series of American books he has placed under my charge is like the thirst of the parched traveller in the wilderness." He also impressed him with promises to "pay liberally for a new work," preferably something "entirely new, written in a popular manner for the class of readers *virginibus puerisque*." Stressing the democratic theme, Duyckinck continued, "I would urge the proposition as important to the literature of the country which needs the example of the few original authors." He reminded him, perhaps gauchely, that "New York is the true publishing center." After agreeing to publish a volume of poetry, the deal fell through when Emerson calculated his muse was more profitable under his current publishing arrangement.[45]

Nevertheless, their correspondence is interesting for confirming Emerson was no flighty transcendentalist when it came to money matters. It also revealed Duyckinck's increasingly confident understanding of the business end of publishing. He boasted of New York's market, and promised the firm would "give you any advantages in their power in mode of printing, advertizing, etc." Not entirely unmindful of profit, Duyckinck reminded Emerson of the need to have his book out by December, "ready for the Christmas purchases throughout the country."[46]

Along with the vision of literature as commerce that emerges from Duyckinck's correspondence, it strikingly linked creativity to the new technology of printing and distribution. Duyckinck's contention that New York was the true center of publishing was not so much an intellectual boast as an insider's assessment of the changing literary marketplace. Even more interesting was a letter to Hawthorne urging him to finish "The Old Manse": "Think of the whistle of the expectant steam press and the 'virgins and boys' who are waiting for that story introductory."[47]

Despite his fondness for old English authors and genteel conversation, Duyckinck was a modernist when it came to an understanding of the new profession of authorship. Indeed, his dream of an original literature, cheaply disseminated with fair dividends paid to the author, was utterly dependent on the new mechanical improvements at his disposal, all of which had reached New York before Boston. Unlike the displaced author of legend, threatened by technology's disruption of the republic, Duyckinck yoked his intellectual program to an entrepreneurial understanding of the new system.

Hawthorne may have worried about the railroad in his fiction, but he was no shrinking violet about machines in their correspondence. Lamenting Emerson's decision not to join the Library, he wrote Duyckinck, "I wish he might be induced to publish this volume in New York. His reputation is still, I think, provincial, and almost local, partly owing to the defects of the New England system of publication." By cultivating the New York editors, Hawthorne took steps to avoid this provinciality, for as one of them later reflected, "He understood such advertisement of New England products was essential for their sale beyond the limits of the Eastern States." Although Duyckinck was unable to entirely win over the Concord community, it is significant that a New York firm came within a hair's breadth of publishing *Representative Men* and *A Week on the Concord and Merrimack Rivers* alongside the many famous works it *was* able to secure.[48]

A letter Duyckinck wrote Hawthorne on March 21, 1845, showed clearly the interconnectedness of Duyckinck's many different projects. He revealed he had been reading "Rappacini's Daughter" in "the next Democratic," no doubt in connection with the puff of Hawthorne O'Sullivan had asked him to prepare to help the job search. He added that this had fueled his desire to publish Hawthorne's stories with Wiley and Putnam as a volume of "Once Told Tales." Duyckinck stressed the modernity of the Wiley and Putnam firm, with its "neat and elegant" stereotype, its supportive publicity campaign, and its transfer of copyright to the author. The letter ended with a reminder that George Putnam sent regards to his "fair cousin," Hawthorne's wife. In microcosm, Duyckinck revealed the touchstones of his Young American universe: the *Democratic Review*, presided over by a sympathetic editor, supporting the call for original American writing; the ambitious publisher eager to nurture American culture; and the young writer interested in native themes and closely acquainted with the editor and publisher.[49]

Other books in the series included critical works, such as Margaret Fuller's *Papers on Literature and Art* and William Gilmore Simms's *Views and Reviews in American Literature*. These fit in well with Duyckinck's view of a vigorous new American literature. Fuller included an obligatory paean to the cause with her essay on "American Literature," reviewed Hawthorne's *Mosses* favorably, and even went beyond the call of duty by praising Cornelius Mathews. Simms, despite his southern perspective, offered perhaps the most urgent expression of Young America's nationalistic aims with his essay "Americanism in Literature." Simms also contributed a collection of original fiction, *The Wigwam and the Cabin*. Western writers were represented by Caroline Kirkland's *Western Clearings* and James Hall's *The Wilderness and the Warpath*. New Englanders included not only Hawthorne, but John Greenleaf Whittier, who published *Supernaturalism in New England* for Duyckinck. Like *Mosses*, this book had originated within the *Democratic Review* and had first been urged on Hawthorne as a fitting topic. As it was, Hawthorne reviewed Whittier's work in the *Literary World*. According to a squib in the *Review*, Duyckinck even planned a volume of "Indian literature."[50]

Not all of Duyckinck's writers shared his conception of America's literary destiny. An unusual ally was found in Edgar Allan Poe, who despised "the gross paradox of liking a stupid book the better, because, sure enough, its stupidity is American," but who despised even more the effete critics Duyckinck's forces were arrayed against. Poe denounced Longfellow, with "a whole legion of active quacks at his control," and following a round of abuse at the hands of the older critics, he thanked his Young American supporters as "the choice and magnanimous few who spoke promptly in my praise." Poe was supported by other writers in the Library, including Simms and Margaret Fuller, who shared his desire to dislodge the established writers. Far from a random publishing event, it was a politicized struggle for literary representation.[51]

The Library counted among its offerings two of Poe's most important publications, *The Raven and Other Poems* and his *Tales*, both issued in 1846. He did not entirely agree with Duyckinck's selection of tales, but this version of the tales became the standard text. Like Hawthorne, Poe also performed yeoman duty as a reviewer of kindred works in the series. He must have really wanted to please Duyckinck, because he swallowed his critical scruples to call Simms's *Wigwam and the Cabin* "decidedly the most American of American books." He probably even meant it as a compliment. A few years after their collaboration, Poe was again critical of the cant of Young America's nationalism ("toadying Americans & abusing foreigners right or wrong"), and snickered at their "Mutual Admiration Society," but his temporary alliance with the group was more meaningful than most of his literary friendships.[52]

Perhaps most important of all, the first book published by Herman Melville in America was released by Duyckinck to great acclaim in 1846. Duyckinck announced the impending arrival of *Typee* to Hawthorne on March 13, 1846. Hindsight lends poignancy to his condescending assurance this new acolyte was not "over philosophical":

> Next week a Frenchy coloured picture of the Marquesan islanders will appear in the library from the pen of a Mr. Melville, who according to his story, was graceless enough to desert from a New England whale ship, preferring the society of cannibals to the interminable casks of corned beef and impracticable bread which so afflicted his imagination in the hold of that vessel. It is a lively and pleasant book, not over philosophical perhaps.[53]

And of course, no series of American books, in the eyes of Young America, could be complete without a contribution from Cornelius Mathews, who penned *Big Abel and the Little Manhattan* expressly for the cause. Given the book's timing and theme (two vagabonds, the descendants of New York's original white and Indian settlers, walk around the city, exclaiming at its modernity), it should have been Mathews's masterpiece. Sadly, it was not. Poe kindly applied the cherished adjective "original" to the windblown narrative, and even called it "a book especially well adapted to a series which is distinctly American." We will never know if he was damning with faint praise.[54]

Duyckinck's catholic taste and levelheadedness served him well during an increasingly fragmented period in American history. His fairness can be seen by the fact many of Duyckinck's less rational friends castigated him for supporting rival regions. Simms, for example, objected to the inclusion of Whittier, and considered Duyckinck almost southern in his sensibilities: "The truth is (if the truth were known) all your affinities in New York are with the South rather than New England. You have not their frigidity, lack their peculiar & hard featured training, own none of their selfishness, are less homogeneous, and have ten times their imagination." Simms frequented Duyckinck's literary salon whenever in New York, where a perplexed John Bigelow once encountered him, noting "he looks upon his particular section of the South as the geographer of the fourteenth century looked upon Jerusalem—the centre of the world." At the same time, Simms recognized, as he confided to Duyckinck, that New York was "the true publishing city." He blamed the sorry state of American literature on "the influence of English and Yankee authorities," and like Melville, thought a good war with England might clear things up.[55]

New Englanders like Hawthorne and James Russell Lowell, on the other hand, considered him to be more New-English than most boorish New Yorkers. In his *Fable for Critics* (1848), Lowell rhymed, "Good-day, Mr. Duyckinck, I am happy to meet / With a scholar so ripe and a critic so neat." E. P. Whipple called him "the most Bostonian of New-Yorkers." This reputation for balance was a crucial attribute at a time when each section's literati were beginning to disdain the other's creative efforts on what were basically political grounds alone.[56]

To his credit, Duyckinck's vision of American literature embraced all of its regions, expanding beyond the exclusive domain of Boston, Philadelphia, and New York. The works he picked for the series showed a wider perspective, insisting there was more to American culture than the pale abstractions of northern heterodoxy and the English-New English continuum. William Gilmore Simms essentially made this point when he argued the "Anglo-Norman" tradition to be as meaningful as the Anglo-Saxon, and Margaret Fuller likewise posited that the American genius would not rise "till the fusion of the races among us is more complete."[57]

It is odd to fathom Margaret Fuller and William Gilmore Simms as allies, but so they were, for the moment, joined by their respect for Duyckinck's achievement. And if Duyckinck was not quite a crusading feminist, he still championed female authors on a few important occasions. True, Young America desired "virile" literature, but the Library's inclusion of important works by Fuller and Caroline Kirkland was a declaration of faith in the woman writer, and conferred higher status than they had previously enjoyed.[58]

An interesting measure of the success of the Library of American Books is the excitement it generated in the like-minded young literatus watching them from Brooklyn. Walter Whitman, then of the *Brooklyn Eagle*, vented his enthusiasm for a "Home Literature" in several editorials written in the summer of 1846, as the project was underway. Several weeks after *Mosses from an Old Manse* was issued, he denounced the aristocratic tendency of English writing, then wondered, "Shall Hawthorne get a paltry seventy-five dollars for a two-volume work?—Shall real American genius shiver with neglect while the public runs after this foreign trash?"[59]

Whitman frequently clipped articles from the *Democratic Review* on Young American themes, including an article on "Nationality in Literature" from March 1847. This article must have quickened the young editor's pulse, with its invocation:

> If there is anything peculiar in our institutions and condition, we would have some native bard to sing, some native historian to record it. We would have those who are born upon our soil; who have faith in republican governments; who cherish

noble hopes and aspirations for our country; whose hearts beat in unison with our countrymen, to manifest their faith, their hopes, their sympathies, in some suitable manner.[60]

Despite the harmony of interests, Whitman never joined the Duyckinck clique, probably because Duyckinck's taste in friends was more genteel than his literary philosophy. Whitman concealed a sense of hurt in later life when he joked to Traubel about Duyckinck's "clerical looking" and "proper" appearance, but he clearly supported the Library's goals. He wrote editorials in favor of copyright and observed Duyckinck's fair treatment of authors made it "the imperative duty of every honorable man" to purchase these editions.[61]

But if Duyckinck failed to act as Whitman's mentor, he still had much to be proud of in 1846. By using his network of friends and publishing connections, including Putnam, the *Democratic Review*, Hawthorne and other young Democrats, he had reconceived American literature. Thanks to his efforts, new writers across the land were invited to help define the national experience for a new generation. It was truly a landmark in American publishing history.

It would be nice to follow this point with an accounting of the Library's vast success. Sadly, it did not produce the popular acclamation Duyckinck expected. Putnam's son wrote a memoir of his father in which he asserted the combined Libraries resulted in a "deficiency rather than a profit," owing largely to Duyckinck's "tendency to over-estimate the number of readers whose taste in literature was as high as his own." This criticism was echoed decades later by Duyckinck's fellow Young American William Allen Butler: "While Duyckinck was the most genial of companions, and the most impartial of critics, he was too much of a recluse, buried in his books, almost solitary in his life, and entirely removed from the circle of worldly and fashionable life, to judge of my work as a palpable hit." As many others have learned since then, high critical standards do not always coincide with the wishes of the Democracy.[62]

Despite his modesty, Duyckinck was also beginning to arouse the enmity of rival critics. The din of Americanism accompanying the series nettled many in the publishing world, particularly those who were not young and Democratic. Like Poe, Lewis Gaylord Clark, the editor of the *Knickerbocker*, ridiculed the Young Americans as a "Mutual Admiration Society," and sarcastically wondered if anyone was aware "a new dynasty has been established in the American Republic of Letters." Mathews especially annoyed people; Clark said *Big Abel and the Little Manhattan* was as deep as a thimble. O'Sullivan warned Duyckinck to beware "your too devoted friendship as a critic." Even Duyckinck's friend James Russell Lowell wrote him that he laughed when he saw an advertisement for Mathews's work "with the effervescence about 'Young America.' Do you not yourself see something droll in it?" Chances are, he did not. The *New York Tribune* jokingly called Duyckinck and Mathews "the Castor and Pollux of Literature—the Gemini of the literary Zodiac—the Damon and Pythias of the drama of real life."[63]

From Lowell's Boston, the *North American Review* also passed harsh judgment. Mathews wrote "dismal trash," and the entire call for nationalistic literature was "at war with good taste." Pinching its nose, the *North American Review* said exactly what it thought of the Young American projects, from Manifest Destiny to legal codification to the Library of American Books:

> But certain coteries of would-be men of letters, noisy authorlings, and noisy in pro-portion to their diminutive size, waste their time and vex the patient spirits of long-suffering readers, by prating about our want of an independent American litera-ture. Of course, all this prating is without the faintest shadow of sense, and resembles the patriotic froth which the country was favored with from high senato-rial quarters while the Oregon business was under discussion in the national legis-lature. From the vehement style in which these literary patriots discourse, it would seem that they lamented the heritage of the English language and its glorious trea-sures, which are our birthright, as a national calamity. Like the codifying commis-sioners of a neighboring State, they almost appear to recommend the adoption of the American language as the language of literature, without specifying what par-ticular one of the thousand dialects spoken on this continent they intend to honor with their choice.[64]

Over the next decade, Duyckinck would have his work cut out fending off at-tacks from the established critics he had alienated with his advances. Yet despite the relative financial failure of the series, the Library of American Books set a precedent of the highest importance. American literature was now a marketable commodity, controlled by the conditions of the bustling economy, and sufficiently important that publishers were looking out for new works to capture the growing audience of readers.

The *Literary World* and the *Moby-Dick* Fiasco

Following the Library of American Books, Duyckinck turned with characteristic alacrity to a new venture, one that grew out of the ashes of the last project (Lewis Mumford wrote, "They were busy little moles, these Duyckincks"). Perhaps be-cause of his Library's disappointing sales, Duyckinck saw the need for a weekly trade magazine devoted to advertising, literary gossip, and publishing information. Interested in bibliophilic matters his entire life, he had already written extensively on the profession of authorship in *Arcturus* and the *Democratic Review*. In 1844 he had expressed interest in starting a panoramic literary magazine called the *Home-Critic*, which never got off the ground. The *Democratic Review* was an important pioneer in giving "Literary Intelligence" its own section, but Duyckinck was more ambitious. His experience with Wiley and Putnam had strengthened his circum-spect grasp of the literary industry, and it was at the urging of John Wiley that he commenced his new undertaking, to be published jointly by Wiley and Putnam and Appleton & Company.[65]

The *Literary World* came out in February 1847, and soon became, according to its editor, "a centre of information for the booksellers of the whole country." Once again, the trumpet peal of Americanism blasted as Duyckinck rushed into the fray against old enemies like the *North American Review*, "that calm old adder slumber-ing upon the lawn of Harvard." But chastened somewhat by his failures, he con-jured a frontier metaphor for his struggle: "There is a generous appreciation in store, we believe, for the humblest laborer in the cause of American Literature. The forest has a good soil under it, though here are brambles and thorns, foxes and wolves on the surface."[66]

Within a few months, Duyckinck encountered more of these brambles and thorns. He and Wiley quarreled over the inclusion of Cornelius Mathews in the project, and Duyckinck left the magazine for a year, until he and his brother could buy it outright in October 1848. From that point until the end of 1853, when it folded, the *Literary World* was entirely a Duyckinck production. These five years, covering almost exactly the lustrum analyzed by F. O. Matthiessen in *American Renaissance*, allowed the weekly magazine to comment on almost all the important works of the period.[67]

Accordingly, the *Literary World* is extremely valuable as a tool for literary archeology. Even today, its criticism seems fresh. Duyckinck knew "people do not wish to be lectured, but talked to," and he consistently maintained a friendly, intelligent tone. The only time an edge crept into his writing was when he tried to fend off the mediocrity invading his profession. He angrily insisted that literature was "something more than the vicissitudes of Amanda Jenkins's affections" or "the wonderful narrative connected with Penelope Smith's new bonnet and all that flatulent kind of thing, which is so interesting in the Milliner's Magazines."[68]

The most famous article published in the *Literary World* was Melville's pseudonymous review of "Hawthorne and His Mosses" in August 1850. Many scholars have looked into the long relationship between Melville and Duyckinck, but I would like to bring out a few nuances that have been overlooked in the stampede to discover every fact relating to Melville during this period. Among other things, I would like to probe their changing natures over the course of the five-year period leading up to *Moby-Dick*. The poignant story of that book's inspiration and rejection has a great deal to do with Duyckinck's earlier career as a Young American, and his sudden discomfort with nationalism and rash experimentation around 1850. As he retreated from his youth, finding comfort in parenthood and old books, his disciple raced toward a final confrontation with Young America that left both men bloodied.

Since publishing *Typee* in the Library of American Books, Duyckinck had acted as a mentor to the young novelist, protecting him under the aegis of Young America from the fierce backbiting of the New York literati. In many respects, Duyckinck filled the role Gansevoort Melville had played before his death, becoming a gentler Young American role model. Together they enjoyed the bonhomie of Duyckinck's well-appointed home, drinking and playing whist together, and laughing at less convivial authors like Emerson, who saw himself "above munching a plain cake in company of jolly fellows, & swiging [sic] off his ale like you & me."[69]

The sounds of mirth and bonhomie resonate from many descriptions of Duyckinck's salon, along with words like "genial," confirming their youthful good nature. When Cornelius Mathews took over a humor magazine, *Yankee Doodle*, in 1847, Melville was pressed into service, offering sarcastic accounts of Zachary Taylor in Mexico, with stories of the general sitting on tacks and the like. As he was finishing *Moby-Dick* in Pittsfield a few years later, Melville movingly remembered the "cigars & punch" and "the old tinkle of glasses" accompanying his intellectual maturation. He not only learned how to behave like an author in Duyckinck's home (i.e., get drunk), but also how to become one, for these Young American tutorials changed Melville, feeding his thirst for knowledge and new forms of creativity. And yet the transition was not an easy one, for as these references to bibulous geniality indicate, Young America was not entirely prepared for its disciple's ambition, grandiose even by its own standards.[70]

Melville responded to this crash course in authorial behavior by producing exactly the kind of unrefined writing Duyckinck and Mathews had always called for, and *Typee* and *Omoo* were among the best-selling books of any of Duyckinck's intellectual progeny. Furthermore, when Melville began to explore the murky depths of his sailor metaphysics in *Mardi*, Duyckinck encouraged his ambition, privately praising its "poetry and wildness" and writing a positive review in the *Literary World*. Grandly announcing that "the question of his intellectual stamina is to be decided," Duyckinck adjudicated Melville's standing with the highest measure of his praise: *Mardi* was "a purely original invention."[71]

Appropriately, Melville had named the ship on which he started his allegorical journey "Arcturion," in probable tribute to Duyckinck's first magazine. And when he offered Duyckinck a copy of the book in 1850, he did so in the Young American phraseology a fellow clique member would have found witty in the extreme: "Political republics should be the asylum for the persecuted of all nations; so, if Mardi be admitted to your shelves, your bibliographical Republic of Letters may find some contentment in the thought, that it has afforded refuge to a work, which almost everywhere else has been driven forth like a wild, mystic Mormon into shelterless exile."[72]

More important, Duyckinck allowed Melville free access to his large library, where Melville was able to pillage Sir Thomas Browne, Rabelais, travel narratives, and other esoteric source materials. As Melville continued his prolific writing, he adopted many of the mannerisms of the Young Americans and the *Review* writers. His work often addressed young men, criticized elders, dwelt upon the "democratic" themes of poverty and labor, and attacked arbitrary systems of punishment. Like Hawthorne, he knew enough of Young America to distrust its excesses, but he still participated in much of its enthusiasm. As he wrote Duyckinck, in a letter that revealed both his devotion and his independence, "The two things yet to be discovered are these—The Art of rejuvenating old age in men, & oldageifying youth in books." Another letter recalled the old Locofoco belief that "the Declaration of Independence makes a difference."[73]

Over the course of his development as an author, Melville inserted many passages into his work that reflected his tutelage with Young America. At times, he almost seemed to be apprenticing to become the next Cornelius Mathews, if not O'Sullivan himself. In *White-Jacket* (1850), he gave his friends what he thought they wanted. At the end of an attack against whipping, he flogged the *Democratic Review*'s favorite themes, singling out America as the owner of futurity:

> The Past is dead, and has no resurrection; but the Future is endowed with such a life, that it lives to us even in anticipation. The Past is, in many things, the foe of mankind; the Future is, in all things, our friend. In the Past is no hope; the Future is both hope and fruition. The Past is the text-book of tyrants; the Future the Bible of the Free. . . .
> And we Americans are the peculiar, chosen people—the Israel of our time;

we bear the ark of the liberties of the world. Seventy years ago we escaped from thrall, and besides our first birth-right—embracing one continent of earth—God has given to us, for a future inheritance, the broad domains of the political pagans, that shall yet come and lie down under the shade of our ark, without bloody hands being lifted. God has predestinated, mankind expects, great things from our race; and great things we feel are in our souls. The rest of the nations must soon be in our rear. We are the pioneers of the world; the advance-guard, sent on through the wilderness of untried things, to break a new path in the New World that is ours. In our youth is our strength; in our inexperience, our wisdom.[74]

At this exciting moment in Melville's career, his mentor introduced him to the man who would help him to reexamine all these beliefs, having been in Young America's camp before. Literary historians are cognizant of the enormous intellectual debt Melville owed Nathaniel Hawthorne, but because Duyckinck is less famous, few have paused to reflect that it was he who introduced the two writers. Given the historical context, it makes perfect sense; both had written for the Library of American Books, both were interested in the problem of "original" American source material, and both were nominally on the Democratic side of the political equation that Young America sided with. This explains Melville's love for "A Select Party," the story Hawthorne worked up especially for Young America when he needed a job in 1845.

In retrospect, the introduction of the two men seems like anything but a random social event. Rather, it fit into Duyckinck's elaborate calculus for a vigorous American literature, and he introduced them to each other order so they might provide assistance to each other, to him, and to the cause uniting them. Duyckinck paved the way for their friendship by providing their works for each other. In 1846 he sent *Typee* to Hawthorne, which the latter reviewed in the *Salem Advertiser* and told Duyckinck he liked "uncommonly well." Then in July 1849 Melville borrowed *Twice-Told Tales* from Duyckinck while writing *White-Jacket*.[75]

The crucial stage came in August 1850 when Duyckinck's visit to western Massachusetts resulted in the famous climb up Monument Mountain with O'Sullivan's friend David Dudley Field (see chapter 5). This social occasion, unofficially sponsored by Young America, cemented their acquaintance, and Duyckinck asked Melville to review the *Mosses* for the *Literary World*. Indeed, Melville's famous review of Hawthorne seems to have been tailor-made for Duyckinck. Written by one Library of American Books author, it was a review of another book in the Library, anonymously published by the Library's editor in his own magazine. Its strident nationalism was mimetically Young American, and its specific observations about Hawthorne echoed many of those in Duyckinck's earlier Hawthorne reviews. Not so incidentally, Melville had borrowed volumes of both *Arcturus* and the *Democratic Review* from Duyckinck that very summer. He was also receiving the *Literary World* each week, thanks to a subscription from Duyckinck (Melville thanked Duyckinck, writing, "In the country here, I begin to appreciate the *Literary World*. I read it as a sort of private letter from you to me."). In short, Duyckinck's fingerprints were visible all over "Hawthorne and His Mosses."[76]

From this extraordinary review, we are afforded a glimpse into the workings of Melville's mind as he undertook the writing of his masterpiece. During the hike up

Monument Mountain, he delivered a homily against Oliver Wendell Holmes's taunts of American inferiority. Now he continued the battle in print as if it were 1845 all over again: "Let us away with this Bostonian leaven of literary flunkeyism towards England." He even performed the politico-literary link: "While we are rapidly preparing for that political supremacy among the nations, which prophetically awaits us at the close of the present century; in a literary point of view, we are deplorably unprepared for it." Melville seemed to specifically refer to Duyckinck's clique by alluding to a "hot-headed Carolina cousin" (Simms), and he voiced their common political background by declaring his Jacksonian fondness for "that unshackled, democratic spirit of Christianity in all things, which now takes the practical lead in this world, though at the same time led by ourselves—us Americans." Evidently, he had replaced Cornelius Mathews (also present at Monument Mountain) as the Young American mouthpiece.[77]

But if the story ended here, *Moby-Dick* would only be a finny *Behemoth*. The more one reads the review, the more one feels its tortured quality, as if Melville was trying to fulfill what was expected of him, but half-doubted himself. The geniality of Young America faded as he admitted Hawthorne's blackness "fixes and fascinates me." Admiring tragedy for the first time, and King Lear specifically, Melville now rejected the more clearly Young American qualities of Shakespeare's "popularizing noise and show of broad farce." Toeing the Young American line in much of the essay, he strangely qualified it elsewhere, advising writers not to "studiously cleave to nationality" just before his most nationalistic passage. The story that most excited him, Hawthorne's "A Select Party," combined the same mixture of ambivalence and zeal for the "coming of the literary Shiloh of America." Simultaneously attracted and repulsed by Young America, the bifurcated writer seemed already to know, in his ruminations on failure, the inevitable disaster awaiting his own experimentation in "deep far-away things."[78]

Following the excitement of August 1850, Melville returned to his study to finish the new book he was working on, incorporating the principles outlined in "Hawthorne and His Mosses." When *Moby-Dick* was published in late 1851, Duyckinck was of course among the first to review it, which he did in the *Literary World*. All the pieces should have been in place for the triumphant vindication of Young America. The book, written by a protégé and dedicated to a close ally, seemed to offer everything the Duyckinck faction had ever hoped for. It was original in the extreme, it was erratic and decidedly un-English, it dealt with native subject matter, and even seemed here and there to be an elaboration of some of Mathews's earlier works. It borrowed from a work in the Library of American Books, J. Ross Browne's *Etchings of a Whaling Cruise*, which Duyckinck had asked Melville to review, and it even echoed an editorial Duyckinck had written about the "insular ishmaelitish people" who had settled America.[79]

Like Melville's previous work, the book featured a young man with "little or no money," who felt disdain when ordered about by "some old hunks of a sea-captain." The book brimmed over with democratic tension alongside this generational unease, criticizing the "high hushed world" of elite culture, attacking monarchy and aristocracy in many instances, and famously defending Andrew Jackson and his "democratic God." It criticized overweening individualism and its correlative, venture capitalism, emphasizing instead something akin to the old Locofoco ideal of a fraternal society, based on artisanal labor, before succumbing to the black pessimism Melville had discovered in his Hawthorne review.[80]

Like that review, it is the combination of idealism and cynicism that gives *Moby-Dick* its frightening energy, and defines it as the culmination and end of Young American innocence, and the hopeful worldview it sprang from. For all the Locofocoism there may be in the book, Melville is also saying "no, in thunder" to the tiresome rhetoric of nationalism. He is deeply suspicious of politics, distrusting Ahab's oratorical skills, and throwing out cryptic references to "loose-fish" like Mexico that imply his disapproval of expansion. It would be hard to write about Mathews's furry behemoths in *Moby-Dick*'s wake.[81]

But at this moment of supremacy for Young America in literature, an extraordinary anticlimax occurred. Duyckinck wrote a tepid review that belittled all the parts of the book Melville cared for most, faulting him for "this piratical running down of creeds and opinions," and for drawing out Ahab too long. Hawthorne wrote Duyckinck to chastise him, saying, "What a book Melville has written! It gives me an idea of much greater power than his preceding ones. It hardly seemed to me that the review of it, in the Literary World, did justice to its best points." And the *Democratic Review*, aimlessly drifting toward anti-intellectualism under new owners, attacked the book with brutal hostility, enraged by its "bad rhetoric, involved syntax, stilted sentiment and incoherent English." In fairness to Duyckinck, he later reassessed the novel in his *Cyclopædia*, admitting it to be "the most dramatic and imaginative of Melville's books," but he failed to see the power of *Moby-Dick* at the crucial moment of its appearance.[82]

Melville was crushed by the relative failure of his masterpiece; even while writing it, he warned Duyckinck of his hypersensitivity to criticism. Then in January 1852 he wrote his former mentor that he could not fulfill an appointment with him, and on February 14 dispatched a cool notice to the "Editors of the Literary World" to cancel his subscription. Melville's next work, *Pierre* (1852), devoted a full chapter toward the venting of his spleen. "Young America in Literature" did not skewer Duyckinck exclusively, instead castigating the entire profession for its blind devotion to passing literary fads. Yet there were cryptic references to Duyckinck that indicate Melville's deep disappointment. For example, Pierre's refusal to be daguerreotyped for "Captain Kidd's Magazine" duplicates a similar refusal Melville made to Duyckinck in early 1851, and the term "Captain Kidd" may refer to Duyckinck's use of the word "piratical" in his *Moby-Dick* review. Melville seemed to speak to his former mentor when he wrote, "And believe me you will pronounce Pierre a thorough-going Democrat in time; perhaps a little too Radical for your fancy." Needless to say, this work fared even worse than its predecessor. Duyckinck was predictably horrified, though he did his best to see *Pierre* as a mere "eccentricity of the imagination."[83]

The obvious question is why did Evert Duyckinck and his allies let down their most ambitious and talented friend when he was attempting all they had ever urged? There is no equally obvious answer, except to posit that there was always some latent conservatism beneath the veneer of Young American radicalism, and further, that

Duyckinck was mellowing as he grew older. The successful editor of the 1850s was a far cry from the rabble-rousing young journalist of the 1840s, and more comfortable with his place in the literary establishment (he also had three growing children to support). Melville may have been addressing Duyckinck on the first page of *Moby-Dick*, berating him for the failure of his promised revolutions:

> So fare thee well, poor devil of a Sub-Sub, whose commentator I am. Thou be-longest to that hopeless, sallow tribe which no wine of this world will ever warm; and for whom even Pale Sherry would be too rosy-strong; but with whom one sometimes loves to sit, and feel poor-devilish, too; and grow convivial upon tears; and say to them bluntly, with full eyes and empty glasses, and in not altogether un-pleasant sadness—Give it up, Sub-Subs! For by how much the more pains ye take to please the world, by so much the more shall ye ever go thankless! Would that I could clear out Hampton Court and the Tuileries for ye![84]

A significant event around the same time of the *Moby-Dick* debacle was Duyckinck's acquisition of *Holden's Dollar Magazine* in early 1851. This maga-zine was the opposite of what the early Young America movement had stood for, embracing no issue of substance and devoted merely to commercial success and reading of a browsing nature. Duyckinck had denounced precisely this sort of magazine after the demise of *Arcturus*, blaming the "spawn of fashionable monthly magazines" and "Milliner's Magazines" for his failure. The brothers Duyckinck wrote to Melville to ask him to be contribute, but he tartly refused, an-swering, "I am not in the humor to write the kind of thing you need—and I am not in the humor to write for *Holden's Magazine*." Melville added a dose of bile: "To see one's 'mug' in a magazine, is presumptive evidence he's a nobody." Other scholars, moved by Melville's denunciation of the "eminently safe man," have seen glimmers of Duyckinck in "Bartleby the Scrivener" and "The Fiddler" as well.[85]

With his good Episcopalian upbringing and antiquarian bent, Duyckinck was intellectually unready for Melville's dramatic experimentation, particularly his ob-session with evil. Despite his critical acumen in stylistic matters and his canny un-derstanding of literary production, there is little evidence Duyckinck was a deep thinker in the metaphysical strain, and he retained a New Yorkish disdain for tran-scendentalism throughout his life. As early as 1845, he had written, "nothing kills men sooner than an active intellect," and he was well known even in his youth for well-meaning fastidiousness (a friend wrote, "All loved him, and he loved all nice men of letters who were not uproarious Bohemians"). Ironically, the "genial" man who boasted of swigging ale with his literary friends and who lent Melville Rabelais was terrified of real experimentation, beyond the two-dimensionality of Mathews's work. There was some truth to Whitman's remark the Duyckincks were "men of a truly proper style—God help 'em!"[86]

Melville, exhilarated by his intellectual tutelage in Duyckinck's salon, had sim-ply moved beyond Young America's ability to understand him. In a *Literary World* article from March 1850, Duyckinck had used a familiar vocabulary to praise *White-Jacket* ("thoroughly American and democratic"), but capped his remarks with a telling apostrophe: "In regarding, too, the spirit of things, may he not fall into the error of undervaluing their forms, lest he get into a bewildering, barren, and void scepticism [sic]!" Reviewing *Pierre* two years later, Duyckinck intended to poke fun at Melville, but instead revealed the truth of the situation: "Mr. Melville may have constructed his story upon some new theory of art to a knowledge of which we have not yet transcended."[87]

It is also important to note Duyckinck's Young Americans were softening their nationalism at the very moment a new breed of Young Americans was hardening its own in the early 1850s (see chapter 6). This would have rendered Melville's politico-literary experimentation even less digestible. In fact, while many scholars have linked "Hawthorne and His Mosses" to Young America, few have observed that Duyckinck's nationalism had peaked years earlier, and Melville was awkwardly unsynchronized with them. Despite Young America's enthusiasm for the 1848 revolutions, witnessed in person by George Duyckinck, there was a progressive attenuation of rhetoric across the six-year span of the *Literary World*, and when Longfellow attacked Young America in *Kavanagh* (1849), it barely paid notice. Unlike Melville, probing "the almost frantic democracy" to its death agonies, Duyckinck and Mathews simply stopped writing about American politics around 1850.[88]

To be fair, democracy had changed too. Abroad, the failure of the European revolutions had dampened Young American ardor, as had the terrifying Astor Place riot in New York in 1849. Both Melville and Duyckinck signed a protest against the mob's behavior, almost the only Democrats to do so. Other Young Americans were also backtracking. Duyckinck's friend Joel Headley later denounced the riot in his history of the subject. Even Mathews was criticizing mob behavior in the early 1850s. His play *Witchcraft* contained some of the old inanities (i.e., a character named Pudeater), but it was far gloomier than his early work, denouncing journalists, politicians, and unruly crowds. Near the end, as the hero dies, he cries out in a language that condemns the futility of Manifest Destiny, aimless and no longer democratic:

> Look on that fair young Hope, it pines and dies
> An outcast on the threshold of the world.
> Thou Land, Colossus-Like, that spread'st thyself,
> Until, a foot on either shore, thou may'st
> Thy neck unconquerable stoop, and bathe
> Thy sinewy arms wide as thou wilt and as deep,
> In the salt greenness of the two great seas,
> And have no watcher of thy lonesome sport!
> Ye masses of mankind, thou Populous heart![89]

Another shock was registered with the depressing debate over the Wilmot Proviso and the Compromise of 1850, suggesting New England's old warnings about the Slave Power were more accurate than New Yorkers had wished to believe. The Young Americans had never really cottoned to the Mexican War, and now they saw just how harmful extremism could be. From South Carolina, Simms complained of the regional hatreds and also revealed Duyckinck's lack of interest in the ugly politics of the new decade: "We are all absorbed in politics, the cauldron bubbling up furiously, and about to boil over. That it will do so, someday, to the great terror of the country, you may be certain. But, I will not distress you with a topic with which, I take it, you have no sympathy."[90]

Duyckinck tried to retain his old generosity, writing, "We desire to know no section, no party. . . . While jealousies and heartburnings are indulged elsewhere, New York stands central; knows all men of all sections as brethren, welcomes all with an equal hand." But even the best-intentioned Democrats now had trouble feeling the millennial expectancy that came so naturally in 1845. Terms like Young America, Democracy, and Manifest Destiny suddenly acquired a bad odor at midcentury, and the need for a great American novel deteriorated along with them. The *Literary World* cautiously staked out middle ground, preferring "taste and judgment" to "nationality," and adding, "There is something in the consideration of this question of American literature, which has a singular power in affecting the understanding, and to some degree unsettling the reason of all who engage in it."[91]

For all these reasons, *Moby-Dick*, with its fierce curiosity about America's moral purpose, struck Melville's Young American friends as a disturbing work. In other words, the masterpiece that resulted from the crisis in the national mood was undermined by the degree to which it mirrored the crisis. As everyone else ran from nationalism, sensing that it led to disaster, Melville weirdly embraced it, fatally out of step with his peers. He also offended their sense of style. If Duyckinck's dream was genial literature for the masses, then it is not difficult to see why Melville's perverse dabblings in tragedy would have discomfited him. The Young American campaign for national literature expected nothing greater than the comic, mock-Dickensian novels that flowed from the pen of Mathews, a realism rooted in tiny jokes of no significance, and without an ounce of the cosmic pessimism Melville brought to the fore.

Finally, a prosaic explanation for Duyckinck's unreadiness to embrace *Moby-Dick* may lie in the dull arena of publishing politics. Duyckinck tried repeatedly to procure the book for a house he was friendly with, but Melville chose to give it to the Harpers, which may have slightly rankled his old acquaintance, especially given his ancient animosity toward that house. Duyckinck wrote his wife during a subsequent visit to Pittsfield in August 1851, "By the way tell Henry [Panton, his brother-in-law] that Harpers are to publish Melville's whale book. I have said a great deal for Redfield but it appears to have been concluded." As the erstwhile publisher of Mathews, Simms, and Poe, J. S. Redfield was obviously allied with the Duyckinck camp to some extent. And we know Duyckinck had high hopes for the book from a letter he wrote his brother a year earlier: "Melville has a new book mostly done—a romantic, fanciful and literal and most enjoyable presentment of the Whale Fishery—something quite new." While there is little of intellectual drama in the scenario of a reviewer tendering a lukewarm review out of jealousy toward the publisher, it is as good an explanation as any in this turbulent era.[92]

In this critique, I do not mean to indict Duyckinck, despite the tone I am taking. Rather, I wish to point out the constantly shifting human politics that are always at play in literature. David Reynolds, looking at the same scenario, simply decided that Melville was courageously patriotic and Young America effete and weak. Reynolds even quoted Duyckinck allegedly declaring his desire for a literature "immune from democratic enthusiasms," although a check indicates Duyckinck never said this (Reynolds was quoting Michael Rogin about Duyckinck, and Rogin had cited Perry Miller out of context). Duyckinck may have retreated from his early radicalism, but in the heyday of Young America a literature of "democratic enthusiasms" was precisely what he wanted. No friend of Cornelius Mathews could possibly think otherwise, as this was the one redeeming feature of his work. Why else would their position papers find such easy acceptance in the *Democratic Review*? Duyckinck's critics should remember that Melville's nationalism was inflamed by the Young American teachings of the 1840s, and that *Moby-Dick* never could have been written without them, whether Duyckinck recognized its genius or not.[93]

Closing out the early chapter of Young America, *Moby-Dick* confirmed O'Sullivan's old idea that American novels would have democracy at their core. But it did so in a way no one would have imagined, taking all the energy of young Locofocoism and turning it back on the meandering American ship of state, which the book accused of losing its bearings through excessive reliance on its perceived "destiny." In other words, O'Sullivan's original message was turned against what O'Sullivan had come to stand for in 1851.

The *Cyclopædia of American Literature*

Despite his backsliding from the jingoism of the 1840s, Duyckinck made one last important contribution to the construction of a Democratic canon, suggesting he had not abdicated all of his nationalism with the *Moby-Dick* review. In 1855–56, as *Leaves of Grass* was published across the East River, he and his brother George brought out their massive two-volume *Cyclopædia of American Literature*, the largest and most comprehensive book of its type then written, and still a useful reference work. The *Cyclopædia* was a tremendous undertaking in scope, profiling writers throughout American history, from all different backgrounds. Many women were included, and the book was an important step toward the balanced and well-informed perspective needed to adjudicate a modern American canon. Duyckinck had also gone to great lengths to assure geographical balance, including dozens of Southern writers (thanks to the research of William Gilmore Simms), an indication that "Americanism in Literature" still meant something as the regions were being rent asunder.

Surprisingly, this helpful opus still managed to excite controversy, indicating again the political currents pulsing beneath the surface of American literature. Rufus Griswold, the executor of Poe's estate and executioner of his reputation, raised a tremendous ruckus over the *Cyclopædia*, publishing a bitter critique that denounced small errors and the omission of New England writers. It was one of the most destructive reviews in the history of American criticism, charged with an animus that is difficult to comprehend unless one recalls the earlier Young American program and the ire it provoked.

Griswold's angry campaign betrayed the last gasps of Jacksonian factionalism. Predictably, Griswold was a Whig in the 1840s, attacked by the Young America clique at that time for neglecting them in his own attempt at canon formation,

Prose Writers of America (1847). He had been friendly to the literary nationalists in the early forties, proposing their participation in a book he was preparing on "The American Spirit of the Age." But Duyckinck's response may have alienated Griswold by volunteering chapters on predictably Democratic topics—Bryant, Forrest and the Drama, Hawthorne, Willis, Leggett and the Newspaper Press, Periodical Literature, Mathews, International Copyright, and The Future.[94]

The Young Americans also had a history of dismissing Griswold's efforts to define American culture. O'Sullivan likened the compiler to a "curious entomologist gathering up a few of each kind as specimens, from time to time; spreading out the filmy gauze of their bright little wings, and preserving them pressed and dried for immortality between the leaves of a book." Another Young American review was crueler, stating that A. J. Downing's *The Fruits and Fruit Trees of America* "is a larger volume than Mr. Griswold's *Poets and Poetry of America*, and may be thought by some people to contain a great deal more poetry."[95]

As the decade progressed, it became evident that Griswold and Duyckinck had very different definitions of literary nationalism, differences that, if not explicitly "political," were nonetheless connected to their divergent literary-political orientations. Duyckinck, a Democratic New Yorker, believed in a pan-American nationalism, one that embraced the South and West alongside the North, women alongside men, and the young with the venerable. Griswold, a Whig New Englander, preferred New England divines and hegemonic figures like Daniel Webster and Andrews Norton, few of whom represented to Duyckinck a meaningfully "national" tradition. A review, probably by Duyckinck, in the *New York Morning News* asserted, "The so-called American poets of Mr. Griswold do not as a body represent the nation."[96]

On a smaller scale, they were also on different sides of the ideological fence within the microcosmic world of the New York literary scene. As noted earlier, Duyckinck was antagonistic toward the elitist magazines personified by Lewis Gaylord Clark, the editor of the *Knickerbocker,* an early friend and supporter of Griswold. These Whiggish rivals viciously attacked Duyckinck's "Mutual Admiration Society," and New Englanders like Longfellow and Lowell joined the feeding frenzy, carping away with glee at the foibles of Young America. Richard Henry Dana also expressed his disapproval of Duyckinck's "Very-Americanism," writing, "You are a modest man personally—why cannot you be so nationally?" A satire written by Charles F. Briggs, close to Griswold, parodied a buffoonish character like Mathews seeking "a pure, bold, original, strong, vigorous, indigenous and native literature," and slaving over a work entitled *The Life, Adventures, Fortunes, and Fooleries, of Christopher Cockroach, Citizen.*[97]

The result of this ideological cleavage was a long-standing feud between Duyckinck and Griswold, and the two thinkers, with equally sincere hopes of promoting American literature, undermined each other's efforts with savage efficiency. Latent insecurities became overt hostilities in 1847 with the issue of Griswold's *Prose Writers* anthology. Griswold seems to have taken the lead, writing the Boston publisher James T. Fields before the book came out, "Young America will be rabid." His prophecy was accurate; four days after publication, he wrote Fields again, "E.A. Duyckinck, J.B. Auld, and the whole mob of 'Young Americans' (pish!)

'swear terribly' that they're omitted, and that the amiable Cornelius, centurion of the sect, is so 'abused.'"[98]

Duyckinck was surprised to see that a chapter on Mathews he had prepared for the volume had been replaced by Griswold's pejorative commentary. Angered by the slight as well as the injury to his friend's reputation, his review in the *Literary World* was uncharacteristically vituperative. Ridiculing *Prose Writers* as a "big and little book," Duyckinck asserted Griswold's compilation was "dry and chaffy, meagre, and unprofitable." On the question of literary nationalism, Duyckinck rejected Griswold's Whiggish formula with Democratic bluntness: "The principle seems to be to find nationality where it does not exist as such, and to deny it where it does." Whitman was sufficiently moved by Duyckinck's harangue that he clipped the article for safekeeping when it appeared in the May 1847 *Democratic Review*.[99]

What is remarkable about their mutual contempt is that, to the untutored eye, Duyckinck and Griswold were cut from the exact same cloth. Both had been magazine editors in the 1840s, and they were fellow members of the New-York Historical Society and the Copyright Club. Griswold's preface in *Prose Writers* went to great lengths to support the copyright agitation and establish his concern for an "original" American literature. When he came to defining it, however, he subtly rejected the Young American platform, arguing that "some writers, by no means destitute of abilities, in their anxiety to be national have merely ceased to be natural." Although Griswold admired works dealing with American subject matter, he did not feel it a prerequisite to native literature, arguing "a 'national work' may as well be written about the Pyramids as about the mound builders." This was not a haphazard observation, but a specific slight to Duyckinck's ally, Cornelius Mathews, who had written a lengthy and unreadable work on precisely that topic. Discussing Mathews by name later in the anthology, Griswold went even further to dismantle Young America:

> The most servile of our copyists have thus far been those who have talked most of originality, as if to divert attention from their felt deficiencies in this respect. Our 'Young America' had not wit enough to coin for itself a name, but must parody one used in England; and in its *pronunciamento* in favour of a fresh and vigorous literature, it adopts a quaint phraseology, that so far from having been born here, was never known among us, except to the readers of very old books and the Address of the Copyright Club.[100]

Mathews's interest in New York's proletarian scenery was introduced as evidence that he possessed "a mind accustomed to the contemplation of vulgar depravity." It would be difficult to find a more Whiggish observation about America in 1847. Duyckinck responded by criticizing Griswold's neglect of antielitist writers, such as Thomas Paine and William Leggett (and interestingly, Herman Melville), further suggesting that Griswold's personal canon was dangerously selective and posited a very different vision of America than the democratic culture Duyckinck would recognize. In other words, this was a more political dispute than immediately met the eye.[101]

Following the veiled exchange of insults attending the *Prose Writers*, Griswold bore a deep and lingering animus toward Duyckinck and his program. Duyckinck added fuel to the fire by comparing Griswold to a literary zoologist chasing "minnows" and "insect buzzings" in a review of his *The Poets and Poetry of America* (1849). Griswold retaliated in his infamous Poe memoir, cruelly doctoring a letter written by the late poet to read that he considered Duyckinck "one of our great cliquists and claquers," when in fact he had never written anything of the kind. Duyckinck suspected this, and wrote as much in the *Literary World*. The stage was thus set for a renewal of hostilities when the Duyckincks offered their larger, more ambitious anthology in 1855–56. Unsurprisingly, Griswold excoriated the editors for their attention to Thomas Paine, "whose abilities and services are absurdly exaggerated." After a dizzyingly pedantic list of obscure facts neglected in the two volumes, Griswold concluded, "Every thing appears to have been done carelessly and feebly . . . it may be doubted whether the annals of bookmaking furnish more melancholy examples than are to be found in this work, of an utter incapacity to write intelligibly, perspicuously, or even grammatically."[102]

A modern reading of the Duyckincks' work finds little or no justification for Griswold's vindictive condemnation, but such were the extraordinary pressures brought to bear on the definers of the emerging canon in the antebellum period. The episode provides another illustration of the inevitable intrusion of petty personal grievances and political squabbles into what ought to be, but never can be, a purely literary matter.[103]

Duyckinck's career as a literary ombudsman continued successfully into the 1860s and 1870s, although his productions were increasingly devoid of editorial substance until he became rather a parody of the distinguished, complacent old man of letters he had tried so hard to displace in the 1840s. Contrary to legend, he and Melville remained friendly after their misunderstanding, although it is interesting to note that when Melville borrowed some books in 1860, the latter made a point of denouncing "the mealy mouthed habit of writing of human nature of the present day."[104]

Heedless, or more probably oblivious, Duyckinck put out several handsome but uninteresting gift books on the order of *National Portrait Gallery of Eminent Americans* (1861) and the ambitiously titled *History of the World from the Earliest Period to the Present Time* (1869–71). In 1869 he wrote his old friend Simms, whose acquaintance he had joyfully renewed following the rebellion, that he was no longer interested in new books, "the old ones supplying generally much better food for the imagination." Old Fogydom had irrevocably set in, and when Duyckinck died in 1878, the former literary radical was buried at the very citadel of polite literary gentility, alongside Irving's grave in the Sleepy Hollow Cemetery at Tarrytown, overlooking the Hudson.[105]

Despite occupying an obscure position in the wings of the American Renaissance, Duyckinck's life teaches much about the complexity of canon formation, and the randomness of a life in literature. In his early days an ardent nationalist, in his prime a seasoned arbiter of all species of literature, and in his dotage a genteel type with the best of them, Duyckinck wore many hats and should not be pigeonholed. Furthermore, he often adopted positions and forged alliances (with Poe, for example) that were at odds with his stated ideals but which served him well in the constantly shifting battleground of the New York literary scene. In 1875 he wrote a moving eulogy of Poe in his journal that casts light on his own troubled career, successful by some standards, but not nearly as influential as he once dared to hope: "Poe came into the world, for America a little too soon, at a period when there was the least possible encouragement for a man of genius; when the public was indifferent and in an inverse way of mending the matter the writers themselves were often absurdly antagonistic to each other. Now when there is better pay there is more mutual cheer."[106]

Looking at the *Moby-Dick* fiasco and the *Cyclopædia* dispute, it seems fairer to call Duyckinck a pioneering but flawed broker of American culture, incapable of going the distance with Melville but important for inspiring him. Despite their prematurity, both the Library of American Books and the *Cyclopædia* deserve attention as halting steps toward an inclusive national literature worthy of the adjective "American." At every stage of his career, Duyckinck toiled valiantly to create the necessary infrastructure for a modern American culture. He oversaw and even commissioned the writing of some of the greatest literary works in the country's history, calmly nudging the profession of authorship into the modern age. With his panoptic critical vision, he perceived important new developments across the American cultural map, including art and drama, and strengthened the national "ligaments" the *Democratic Review* had set out to define. In so doing, he anticipated later arguments over American culture, particularly the rejection of the genteel tradition in the 1920s. Lewis Mumford would have been surprised at how much he had in common with the "busy little mole" he abruptly dismissed.

The Fighting O'Sullivans, featured in *The Royalist*, October 1894.
From left to right: General John William O'Sullivan (great-grandfather,
architect of the disastrous Battle of Culloden), Major Thomas Herbert O'Sullivan (grandfather, forced to leave the French army after a fight with John Paul Jones), and John Louis
O'Sullivan (Harvard University Library).

Henry Inman's painting of the O'Sullivan family (from a reproduction in the O'Sullivan
family genealogy at the Historical Society of Pennsylvania). John Louis O'Sullivan is third
from left, holding a book.

Silhouette of O'Sullivan, October 5, 1840 (The Metropolitan Museum of Art, Bequest of Glenn Tilley Morse, 1950).

Mr. and Mrs. John L. O'Sullivan, the Count and Countess of Bearhaven (The Historical Society of Pennsylvania).

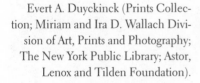

Evert A. Duyckinck (Prints Collection; Miriam and Ira D. Wallach Division of Art, Prints and Photography; The New York Public Library; Astor, Lenox and Tilden Foundation).

Urban Realism: F. O. C. Darley's street urchins in the *Democratic Review*, 1843 (Harvard College Library).

Distribution of the American Art-Union Prizes, 1847 (Museum of the City of New York, The J. Clarence Davies Collection).

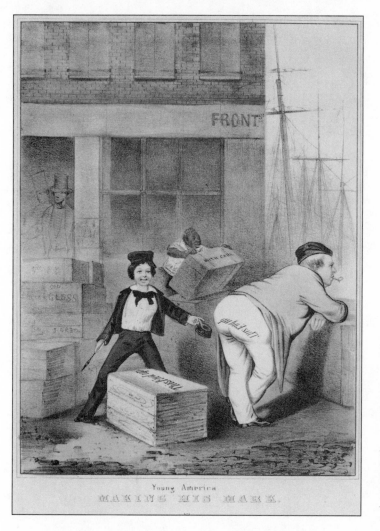

Young America
MAKING HIS MARK.

A satirical print capturing the spirit of Young America (The Metropolitan Museum of Art, The Edward W. C. Arnold Collection of New York Prints, Maps and Pictures, Bequest of Edward W. C. Arnold, 1954).

VID DUDLEY FIELD, New Yo
ONAL LAW—ME

L. O'SULLIVAN, United States

David Dudley Field (left) and John O'Sullivan (right), reunited on the front page of *Harper's Weekly*, November 14, 1874. (Harvard University Library).

4

Representation without Taxation

Art for the People

It is a remarkable fact in the history of art, that, in most countries, the epoch which witnessed the growing influence of the popular element was also marked by a great achievement in art.

—*Bulletin of the American Art-Union* (September 1849)

Genre

In 1834 the sculptor Hiram Powers was commissioned to create a bust of Andrew Jackson, but paused before rendering the president's toothless mouth. Never much for self-pity, Jackson admonished the nervous artist and ordered the portrait executed with military precision and unblinking realism. "Make me as I am, Mr. Powers," he commanded, "and be true to nature always." These words might serve as the slogan for an era that witnessed the rise of a legitimate artistic infrastructure in the United States, and a corresponding preference for American reality, as expressed in landscape and genre art, over the faux-European gentility of elegant portraiture.[1]

Genre painting has risen in stature recently, with a spate of scholarly works supplying much needed information about the conditions of painting in the nineteenth century. The more ambitious of these have also attempted to render the strands connecting art to national ideology and politics. I hope to do something similar, although I will look a little more closely at the historical context than at the art itself, arguing once again that New York provided an unusually electric atmosphere for the young creative thinker of the 1840s. By now, the reader can probably guess I will reassert the surprising interest taken by Democrats in this creativity. For despite our new knowledge about genre, I feel scholars are still reluctant to probe the full extent of its relationship to the complex politics of the era.[2]

The aggressive expansion of American intellectual activity in the mid nineteenth century was hardly confined to literary matters. Indeed, many of the political currents discernible behind Young America's literary coup were also at play in the American art scene, particularly in the mid-1840s. Again, New York was the locus of much of this intellectual agitation, both as the dominant marketplace and the center for a group of painters bringing a youthful populism to the profession. Like the *Democratic Review* writers, a generation of rising painters searched valiantly for an American idiom, employing a similar intellectual strategy and a common language. And like their literary cohorts, they occasionally betrayed contradictory aspirations in their staccato march toward cultural nationalism. Most of New York's genre painters believed in O'Sullivan's Democratic future in the 1830s and 1840s, but renounced this belief around 1850, when history turned out differently than expected.

The resemblance was not purely coincidental, for Duyckinck and his literary cronies took a deep interest in painterly matters. As the most successful genre painter of the day, William Sidney Mount, wrote to a friend, echoing Durand's tribute to Cole and Bryant, "You are right, we are brothers. Poets, and Painters, are one family—we see nature with kindred eyes." Unsurprisingly, the Democratic politico-literary continuum visible in Young American journalism was also evident in the background of the movement for a modern American art. Besides Mount, many of the principal players in the New York art scene of the 1840s were Jacksonians, and these new types of creators and collectors redefined the way Americans perceived themselves. As with literature, these victories were paradoxically both fleeting and important.[3]

When the *Democratic Review* was founded, it specifically included art in the litany of categories wanting an infusion of the "democratic principle." Samuel Langtree had dwelt on the subject since his early days in the country. O'Sullivan, too, collected recent American art and particularly supported the New York painter Henry Inman, who was commissioned to do a portrait of O'Sullivan's family when the editor was just a boy (appropriately, O'Sullivan had a book in his hands). When Inman ran into financial trouble in the 1840s, O'Sullivan served on a committee to help his family. Throughout the entire decade, the intellectuals clustered around the *Review* urged the spread of art, along with literature, to the people.[4]

If anything, Duyckinck and his friends were even more eager to launch an ancillary artistic movement. Duyckinck, after all, came from a long family tradition of humble portraiture, including several Evert Duyckincks who had painted portraits around New York in the seventeenth century. In his landmark speech on "Americanism" in 1845, Cornelius Mathews called for "the true spirit of Young America" in sculpture, painting, and engraving:

> And in art, shall we not have schools of our own? Partaking of the climate, the rocks, the woodlands, the rivers and the human faces of our own country? Chosen from whatever region of the world the subjects may be, will there not be something in the form and spirit, in the skill and kind of execution, to inform us that their origin is in the American heart and the American genius?[5]

Despite Emerson's claim that the age was ocular, the fine arts had never really received their full measure of respect in the United States, for a variety of complicated reasons. Republican antipathy to monarchical courts and state-supported churches annulled the chief sources of traditional patronage, presenting a conundrum for democratic artists. Who would pay for an art that failed to glorify the rich, and even in extreme cases, questioned their right to wealth? Whitman wrote coyly, "Here is a case for the imperial scepter, even in America."[6]

Beyond that, something in the aggressive American character seemed antithetical to the beaux arts. Tocqueville trenchantly observed a preference for the useful to the beautiful. In his mind, there was no doubt this was linked to the American social system, where increased participation was inevitably attended by decreased quality ("the production of artists are more numerous, but the merit of each production is diminished"). As American intellectuals never tired of complaining, there was no reserve of tradition to refer to in the New World, and American artists traditionally visited Europe to complete their formal education before returning to the United States. What small support there was in the early republic was largely found among the privileged classes of Philadelphia. New England, with its Puritan hangover, did not promise much in the way of an aesthetic sensibility.[7]

A number of European commentators on the American scene acidulously noted the awkwardness of the early attempts to foster a native art. Frances Trollope could hardly believe "the utter ignorance respecting pictures to be found among persons of first standing in society." She found American artists terrified to draw from life models and everywhere decried "a profundity of ignorance almost inconceivable." After visiting several New York exhibits, she sneered, "The Medici of the Republic must exert themselves a little more before these can become even respectable." At the same time, a deep interest in the pictorial arts was spreading among rank and file Americans, as confirmed by Mrs. Anna Jameson, yet another of the flock of snooping Englishwomen, who observed "the country seemed to me to swarm with painters," many of whom were "outrageously bad."[8]

The situation slowly improved in the third and fourth decades of the century, particularly around New York. Samuel F. B. Morse assessed it as the capital of American art as early as 1818, and within a decade no one would disagree. The American Academy of the Fine Arts was founded there in 1801, although dominated by wealthy merchants rather than bona fide artists, and in 1826 the more accessible National Academy of Design was inaugurated. It helped that New York's triad of eminent writers of the 1820s, Irving, Bryant, and Cooper, all took a deep interest in the visual arts, as did many of the lesser intellects who orbited around them.[9]

One of the more important was Gulian Verplanck, a New York writer and politician who did much to spread art enthusiasm, especially in his capacity as distributor of federal patronage while in Congress. Verplanck realized that a democratic polity required a populistic approach to the arts. A fiery speech of 1824 pleaded, "Let us not look back to the past." Rather, the cultivation of genuinely American art required that "taste must become popular. It must not be regarded as the peculiar possession of painters, connoisseurs, or diletanti [sic]. The arts must be considered as liberal, in the ancient and truest sense . . . as being worthy of the countenance and knowledge of every freeman."[10]

With much fanfare, the emergence of the Hudson River School in the late 1820s and 1830s, dominated by Thomas Cole, Thomas Doughty, and Asher B. Durand, constituted the first indigenous artistic achievement of major significance. There was some irony in the Hudson's emergence as a theme for narcotic landscape paintings, as it was the chief source of New York's wealth following the completion of the Erie Canal, and hence the unconscious agent of the rapid change transforming the metropolis (the year the canal opened, 1825, was the year of Thomas Cole's celebrated debut). In other words, the commerce supplied by the river made an artistic community possible, although one would never know it from these sleepy Arcadian tableaux.

Coeval with the rise of Jacksonian democracy in the 1820s and 1830s, there arose another artistic movement, loosely organized, but no less committed to its own version of representation. Disdaining the sublime vistas of Cole and Durand, a growing number of genre painters committed to the canvas an important vision of American life, simultaneously modern in its realism and simplistic, even nostalgic, in its humble focus. This vision was unoccluded with grand concepts of nature; rather, the genre artists merely painted the ordinary citizens they saw at work and play about them. Like the Hudson River School, they were for the most part settled about New York, but even those who were not, like Missouri's George Caleb Bingham, made the pilgrimage to Manhattan to better distribute their work.

Separate from Young America, yet sharing many formative influences (and briefly annexed by them), these artists were devoted to a philosophy of commonplace art that quietly carried a potent political message. Rejecting traditional themes of history and religion, and refusing to treat European subjects altogether, their focus on comic domestic scenes and rural life was not exactly revolutionary, but it did carry a judgment that unexceptional Americans should participate in the emerging cultural process. Emerson corroborated the legitimacy of this tendency with his essay on art, insisting "the artist must employ the symbols in use in his day and nation to convey his enlarged sense to his fellow-men," and that painters must paint the "new and necessary facts" of America, "in the field and road-side, in the shop and mill." The enactment of this vision turned out to be less radical than its promise. But a few superior artists stood out for their ability to capture the peculiar tension of a time and place caught between the preindustrial past and the ultramodern future.[11]

No one can deny the Hudson River painters were championing the cause of nationalism, but genre artists offered a very different philosophy of composition. Not only were the Hudson River painters fond of brighter colors than the drab earth tones associated with genre, they preferred to couch their message in the natural setting, with as few living, breathing Americans as possible. In other words, they were antiurban, despite their need for Manhattan patronage. Cole wrote that New York filled him "with a presentiment of evil" and urged Durand to leave Manhattan so he would not feel "surrounded by our fellow-men." The dislike of humanity implied by their unpeopled vistas was an important statement in its own right.[12]

The genre painters were a breed apart. If they were not exactly obsessed with the city, they were fascinated by the way in which Americans lived together, and the way they looked at ordinary, interactive moments in their lives. Although often considered humorous and nostalgic, their work nevertheless reflected the tension of the changing social landscape and hence much of the political landscape as well. While the landscape painters retreated from modernity, the genre artists labored awkwardly to capture the tension of the transitional moment, and often limned the same subjects Young America found interesting.

Genre work was not unprecedented in the United States. Earlier in the century, isolated artists like John Louis Krimmel, John Neagle, and John Quidor had painted the quirky American types about them. But the spread of young genre artists around New York in the 1830s constituted a more serious movement. The trend toward increased social realism was undoubtedly accelerated by rapid improvements in representational technology, including the lithograph (Nathaniel Currier opened his shop in New York in 1835), and the photograph not long thereafter. From a geographical, economical, and social perspective, New York was well-suited to foster a new consciousness of American art. And what better vehicle than genre painting, which traced its ancestry to seventeenth-century Holland, just as New York itself did?[13]

Mount and Whitman

Among the new genre painters of the 1830s, several especially struck the fancy of the American public, and the Young Americans particularly. William Sidney Mount, born at Setauket, Long Island in 1807, had grown up fatherless like O'Sullivan. His first critical mention, in William Dunlap's pioneering 1834 history of American art, recorded him remembering, with pleasing humility, "to the age of seventeen I was a hard working farmer's boy." Despite the rural focus of his work, Mount wrote in his journal, "New York is the place for an Artist if he can put up with the noise." Unlike Thomas Cole, Mount prodded himself "to see a variety of character, and colours, the City is the place." Even more important, he placed the American people in the foreground, considering them an integral part of his work, rather than tiny background figures bowing down before a sunset.[14]

Mount's career has been studied in detail by art historians, but rarely with much attention to his participation in the social and political struggles of his generation. Yet in many ways, Mount's achievement embodied the concept of Artist-as-Democrat, and the parallels to Whitman's career are striking. F. O. Matthiessen first recognized the convergence in *American Renaissance*, but it has been little noted since then, except for a short section on Mount in David Reynolds's Whitman biography.[15]

Born near each other on Long Island, they grew up in Arcadian settings and in each case the child was instilled with a deep faith in rural democracy. Like the Whitmans, Mount's family was zealous in its plebeian nationalism. In 1824 his uncle Micah Hawkins composed the first American comic opera, *The Saw Mill or a Yankey Trick*.[16] The same year, the seventeen-year-old Mount went to New York to learn the craft of sign painting from his older brother Henry. He profited from New York's increasing artistic consciousness, attending classes at the new National Academy of Design, and began to create his own work, mostly landscapes and mediocre biblical allegories. Then in 1830, he completed a painting that would set the course for his entire career. *Rustic Dance After a Sleigh Ride* depicted a crowd of partygoers laughing and dancing to the spirited fiddling of a young black musician. Hardly a sophisticated work, its pervasive humor and realistic depiction of American mores nonetheless struck a responsive chord. Another painting from

1830, *School Boys Quarreling,* indicated that Mount had unquestionably found his niche.[17]

Besides Hogarth and David Wilkie, Mount was doubtless inspired by the seventeenth-century Dutch genre painters, an easily available influence in Washington Irving's Manhattan. Seventeenth-century Holland fascinated Americans of the early nineteenth century as a miniature simulacrum of themselves. As John Lothrop Motley discovered in his monumental history of the Dutch republic, the Dutch had simultaneously established their political independence and developed an imposing commercial empire overseas, all while nurturing a vibrant national culture. The connection between mercantile and artistic success was intoxicating to American onlookers, particularly the nervous humor with which the best of Dutch genre poked fun at the new, domineering business types populating the social horizon. The Dutch vogue was even more appealing for allowing Americans to indulge the anti-British feelings necessary for cultural independence while affirming their Protestantism.[18]

The Dutch heritage was keenly felt in Manhattan, for obvious reasons, and had been shrewdly exploited by Irving and Paulding. Even in the 1840s, it excited the nostalgia of thoroughbred Knickerbockers like Duyckinck, half-castes like Whitman and Melville, and a whole range of artists and writers tired of grand historical scenes. The list of popular Dutch topics was virtually the same that American genre painters found tempting. James Jackson Jarves provided an excellent catalogue in *The Art-Idea* (1864):

> It loves beer, and tobacco; boar-hunts and rough games; bar-rooms, pipes, brooks and kettles; jewelry and satins, civic rank and commercial pride; scenes of avarice, lust and fierce brawling; a flat, monotonous, unspiritual landscape, redolent with the fat of kine and herbage; foul kitchens and dirty maids; . . . —in short, whatever a thrifty, vulgar-minded race of fighters and traders, proud of their ingots, their tables, and their freedom, delighted in.[19]

How could Duyckinck and company fail to delight in such a list? Mathews's mock-Dickensian novels were overpopulated with exactly these types. As Jarves noted, its organizing principle was clearly political. The earthy vulgarity of Dutch genre, even when dwelling on "foul kitchens and dirty maids," proceeded from "democratic liberty of choice as opposed to aristocratic exclusiveness and ecclesiastical rigor of selection." The very crudeness of the art allowed it to touch on "common sentiments and feelings, and failings, too, for it was essentially human, and loved the earthly natural, and spoke out, in earnest sincerity, what the people believed and liked, good or bad, just as their hearts dictated." This was a powerful rationale in Jacksonian America.[20]

Like the Dutch, Mount set about bringing a realistic approach to the scenery surrounding him. Rejecting historical painting as unprofitable and unsuitable to his genial temperament, he wrote candidly, "I retired into the country to paint the mugs of Long Island yoemanry [sic]." As William A. Jones, one of Duyckinck's original clique, wrote in the first article written about Mount, the painter rejected the prevalent idea of visiting Europe for inspiration, and instead "made Long Island his Italy."[21]

Throughout the 1830s and 1840s, Mount prolifically painted genre scenes representing the American character. As he became more successful, Mount was finally offered a chance to see Europe by a wealthy patron, Luman Reed, but he declined on patriotic grounds, "For fear I might be induced by the splendor of European art to tarry too long, and thus lose my nationality." Yet Mount was no nineteenth-century Norman Rockwell, searching out rustic virtue only for the self-affirming light it would cast back on the viewer and the society at large. Even more compelling was the peculiar mix of affection and anxiety pervading many of the images. Like Hawthorne and many other young artists, Mount perceived and recreated an American reality characterized by a compelling combination of bucolic innocence with a less naive craftiness, a sharp alertness, even a deceitfulness that seemed no less a part of the national personality. Mount pursued a complex realism, undermining the surface comedy of his works with more disturbing elements.[22]

An 1853 list of unattempted paintings is fascinating for its unnerving topics, including "A Dog pissing against the skul [sic] of a Horse"; "Workmen looking out of a window to see the military"; "An old Man standing at the grave of his mother"; "A colored woman (a white girl) drawing water out of a pole well." The real paintings were also disconcerting. *Truant Gamblers* (1835) depicted four schoolchildren about to be caught by a frightening man while playing hooky. Similarly, *The Disagreeable Surprise* (1843) and *Boys Caught Napping in a Field* (1848) offered images of mischievous children, but with presentiments of inevitable punishment for inattentiveness to responsibilities. If the Marxist term "alienation" is too strong to convey what could more accurately be characterized as apprehension, it is nonetheless important to recognize that Mount's work was not always as good-naturedly "American" as many critics have acclaimed it.[23]

Taken as a whole, the genre painting of the period reflected the same curious mixture of democratic aspiration and nervousness the Young Americans betrayed. Even while projecting messages of rural happiness and youthful energy, it often betrayed a painterly awareness that appearances could be deceiving. Several sweeping categories dominated genre, each the source of considerable unease at this transitional moment for the republic, and particularly for the Jacksonian persuasion. Broadly stated, they were (1) the restlessness of the young; (2) the rise of commerce and its intrusion into the countryside (a volatile issue after the Panic of 1837), and (3) the national obsession with newspapers, political sloganeering, and information dissemination. A long article might be written simply on paintings of newsboys in the 1840s, at the exact moment Young America was advancing its many territorial claims through the new journalism. An even longer one might be written on race and genre.

Mount's work revealed all these concerns. As the paintings listed already suggest, children and young men, often unruly ones, were central to his work. His early *School Boys Quarreling* (1830) inaugurated his long practice of rendering groups of young Americans in problematic situations (often with African-Americans situated awkwardly in the margins). A number of paintings also reflected the artist's fascination with the awkward moment of the commercial transaction, another problem of timely significance. The trader was a popular type in American mythology, yet beneath his humorous depiction lay anxiety over the country's economic transformation. Mount correctly located the nation's psychological epicenter in the shrewd machinations and finagling that constituted antebellum commerce, even in its relatively innocent rural manifestations. *Bargaining for a Horse* (1835) was perhaps the supreme example of this carefully orchestrated tension. Depicting two men whittling on sticks as they negotiate the sale of a horse, the scene is relatively placid except for the distant and strangely unnerving presence of a woman, the wife of the one of the men, yelling something shrilly over a fence. *Raffling for a Goose*, the year of the Panic (1837), showed seven men, in various conditions of alertness, waiting for a man to pull raffle tickets from his hat. *Coming to the Point* (1854) was essentially a copy of *Bargaining for a Horse*, with one of the traders much younger than the other. In all these, we can see the divided consciousness of an artist who is nostalgic for the arcadian past, but intrigued by the unsettling societal forces of encroaching modernity.[24]

Several of Mount's paintings lend themselves especially well to political interpretation. *Cider Making*, completed in 1841 on commission, seems at first nothing more than an innocuous rural scene, but several critics have argued persuasively for it as an allegory of the recent "Hard Cider and Log Cabin" presidential campaign that had placed Harrison and Tyler in the White House. Besides internal references to the campaign, an article in a New York newspaper deciphered the references the year the painting was finished, indicating clearly the Democratic painter's interest in the political process.[25]

Over a decade later, Mount painted another overtly political canvas, *The Herald in the Country* (1853), also known as *The Politics of 1852, or Who Let Down the Bars?* The painting depicted an encounter in the woods between a farmer and a more gentrified newspaper reader who appears to have been surprised in the act of poaching. Behind the innocent facade of this playful scene were a number of pressing anxieties. One explanation of the painting's second title is that Mount was concerned about the growing fuzziness of the lines demarcating the Whigs and Democrats in the election of 1852. Again, he appeared to single out the urban-rural differential as a source for both humor and tension, and repeated the frequent antagonism between youth and age.[26]

In her recent work, the art historian Elizabeth Johns has devoted much attention to the question of politics in the work of Mount and other genre artists, subjecting paintings like these to minute analysis. But Johns, quick to interpret his art, and vociferous on the subject of the party struggles of the 1840s, is strangely quiet when assessing Mount's ardent political views, dismissing him merely as "a Democrat but neither a Cassandra nor a crusader." I would argue he was a bit of both. There is no doubt about the strength of his private convictions, or that he was a lifelong Jacksonian, though he occasionally painted for Whig patrons. His own correspondence and journals easily corroborate the fact. He continually urged his friends to vote the Democratic ticket, considered the Democrats "the true sons of God," and strongly distrusted the Whigs. Despite the undeniable tension that existed in his artwork, as delineated above, in no way did it undercut his fundamental faith in democratic art or the right of the people to govern themselves. For this reason, his art was unstintingly praised by the *Democratic Review* community.[27]

Surely an appreciation of Mount is enhanced by a sense of the common political inheritance he shared with other Democratic artists and thinkers. Matthiessen's link between Mount and Whitman is worth exploring further. Their work manifested a number of thematic parallels, particularly that of the young Whitman whose sentimental stories about rural America appeared in the *Review* in the early 1840s. A passage from *Specimen Days* on "Two Old Family Interiors" is remarkable for evoking Mount's images, from the ancient Long Island farm interior to cider drinking and clamming parties. Dozens of Mount's scenes suggest kinship with the poet, from loafing farmhands to the mischievous young boys snickering in the background of so much of his work. Some scholars attribute a painting to Mount titled *Walt Whitman's School at Southold, 1841*, which if true would suggest they knew each other years before Whitman mentioned him in his writing.[28]

The Long Islanders also enjoyed a common enthusiasm for folk music. Mount's fascination was not limited to the canvas; he played several instruments and even patented a violin with a concave back that he labeled "the Cradle of Harmony." When the Civil War began, Mount expressed the naïve hope the nation's love of music would heal the breach, and he proposed that bands be placed in the Congress to play patriotic music whenever debate grew acrimonious. Whitman would have understood, given his opinion that "the subtlest spirit of a nation is expressed through its music." Perhaps there was some reason Long Island inspired these feelings; in *Moby-Dick*, Melville almost re-created a Mount painting with a "Long-Island sailor" who sings out for music in expectation of a corn harvest.[29]

Beyond these thematic links, the two artists knew and liked each other. Whitman immensely enjoyed genre painting, as was appropriate for a proud descendant of "far-off Netherlands stock," and he professed admiration for Mount on many occasions, particularly these musical paintings. Reviewing a show in the *Evening Post*, he praised the usual "Americanism," but curiously disapproved of "exemplifying our national attributes with Ethiopian minstrelsy" (though Whitman was more of an abolitionist than Mount ever was). Duyckinck's *Literary World*, in an 1850 review of Mount, anticipated the conceit Whitman would use in *Leaves of Grass*: "Long Island has always appeared to us a sort of little volume by itself, in watered binding, and with leaves of perennial green and freshness."[30]

Whitman frequently borrowed painterly metaphors in his early poetry, hanging "pictures" in the "gallery" of his mind, and wrote enthusiastic art criticism for the *Brooklyn Eagle* in the 1840s. Many of these "pictures" were similar to Mount tableaux, such as "a husking-frolic in the West," or "an old black man . . . humming hymn tunes." He counted several artists among his close friends, gave a speech before the Brooklyn Art-Union, and composed militant reveries about a rising "phalanx, ardent, radical, progressive" led by "the young artist race!"[31]

As hinted by the last quotation, Whitman's enthusiasm for democratic art was inherently political, shaped by the general Young American enthusiasm for the European revolutions. He believed that men like Kossuth and Mazzini were artistic for their perception of "moral beauty" and that "there can be no true Artist, without a glowing thought for freedom." Like most readers of the *Democratic Review*, including Melville, Whitman and Mount abhorred physical and capital punishment, as we can assume from a note that Mount intended to paint on the subject of

"Floging [sic] in the Navy." Had he painted it, he would have been ensured a favorable notice in the *Review*.[32]

Even in his method Mount resembled the poet. He enjoyed painting outdoors, and wrote, "Of painting in the open air—I am the first American I know of that painted directly, that is, made studies in the open air with oil colors." In this he was lucky, for the screw-top paint tube was only invented in 1841. In 1848 he wrote in his journal, "Painting out of doors will make at once an old painter out of a young beginner. . . . It requires courage to go right to nature." Another journal fragment read, "Five years from nature is better than twenty five spent in fancy." "Fancy" painting was the term for art conceived in an artist's head, rather than from something he actually beheld before his canvas, and the word quietly conveyed Mount's disdain for the inherited European approach to art. As the humorist Seba Smith noted, reviewing Mount's *Long Island Farmer Husking Corn*, a painting "drawed from real life" is the summit of realistic representation, "and there ain't no more nateral picters in the world, than them that's drawn from nater."[33]

Representing social reality honestly, paying little heed to high culture, Mount's "nateral" art propelled the cause of popular representation within American painting. Through his persevering efforts to depict the simple world around him, Mount also advanced a political ethos, one linked to both a particular party and the larger culture. Simple but dignified, comic but unmocking, apprehensive but open-minded, Mount's work vividly recapitulated the complex optimism about human character that marked so many Democratic thinkers in the antebellum period.

Edmonds, Darley, and the Urban Scene

Several other genre artists of the 1840s profited from their situation within the milieu of the New York Democracy. Another important painter of the period was Francis Edmonds. Like Mount, he was a New Yorker and a Democrat, but in this case he came from the upstate town of Hudson. Born a year before Mount (1806), Edmonds became more of an urban cosmopolite, working as a Manhattan banker while dabbling as an artist, but their artistic backgrounds were similar. He attended the new school of the National Academy of Design in New York in the late 1820s, where he met fellow students Mount, William Page, and several other artists and engravers.[34]

No study of Edmonds has delved deeply into his political background, or for that matter the important career of his older brother, John Edmonds, a distinguished New York jurist. Both were Democrats solidly in the Van Buren camp. Hudson was near Van Buren's Kinderhook, and a citizen recalled the Democratic Club of the town in terms reminiscent of a painted Dutch interior: "Round a red hot stove in an atmosphere blue with smoke, seated on old pine benches and wooden bottomed chairs, met the great anti-Federal fathers of the city." John Edmonds grew up in this atmosphere, undergoing an informal education in the local power system by studying law and living with Van Buren in Hudson and Albany. After practicing law, editing a newspaper, and serving in the state senate, he moved to New York in 1837, where he joined the reform efforts endorsed by the *Review*. Edmonds and O'Sullivan served on several political committees together, including an important one studying New York prisons, and later in life they shared an intense interest in spiritualism. Mount also participated keenly in this fad and owned one of Judge Edmonds's works on the subject. In 1845 Edmonds was appointed circuit judge on O'Sullivan's recommendation, and thereafter became a New York Supreme Court justice.[35]

Like his brother, Francis Edmonds drank deeply from the well of Jacksonism, and was even appointed the city chamberlain of New York in 1854, although his career was less public than his brother's. Edmonds's uncle was a close supporter of Van Buren, and the banks in which the nephew made his career were Democratically inclined. He laughed at himself "for uniting in my person that strange compound—a Bank officer and a Democrat," and apparently he was several times dismissed from bank positions for being "such an infernal Loco Foco." Significantly, many of his art patrons were influential Democrats, including John Van Buren and Edwin Forrest, the famed tragedian. In 1851 Edmonds, John Van Buren, and Melville's brother Allan signed a public invitation urging Stephen Douglas, the emerging hope of Young America II, to visit New York (see chapter 6). It appeared in the *Review*.[36]

Despite Edmonds's close proximity to the world of finance, his art reflected the same empathy for the American folk Mount felt. His early paintings, exhibited pseudonymously in the late 1830s, represented earthy domestic scenes. One of the first, *The Epicure* (1838), painted in the immediate aftermath of the Bank war and the Panic, showed a distinctly Whiggish looking gentleman pinching snuff and inspecting a suckling pig while servants scurried to prepare his meal. In 1839 *The Penny Paper* (also called *Newspaper Boy*) reflected some of Mount's concern with newspaper reading and was described by a contemporary as "a large room thronged with men, women and children, into the midst of whom a ragged boy has entered to sell his Sunday morning papers." The same year, he scored his first major triumph, *Sparking*, which revealed with comic tenderness a young couple wooing each other before a fire while an elderly woman nervously washes dishes in the kitchen. It was exhibited at the National Academy with *The City and the Country Beaux*, again showing a young woman trying to decide between these two different types of suitors, and strongly borrowing from Mount's 1835 work *The Sportsman's Last Visit*.[37]

Like his more famous predecessor, Edmonds was often cited for the warm affection pervading his domestic scenes, but the modern observer cannot help noticing an undercurrent of nervousness in the work of both painters. The rendering of rural and urban types together is always amusing, of course, but also reflected anxiety over the incursion of new American types into the traditional family setting. In both *The Sportsman's Last Visit* and *The City and the Country Beaux*, the attention of the young woman is directed toward the more sophisticated Whiggish type. The entire situation offered a painted metaphor for the choice being made between two parties and two types of Americans, particularly in the bitter election year of 1840 when the latter was exhibited. In each case the oafish but endearing country representative looks on suspiciously while the more elegantly tailored city gentleman seems to win the day through contrived poses and elegant cajolery. Edmonds's hidden anxiety was especially interesting because it was directed against the money-lending types that Edmonds presumably worked with all day long. In 1838, the year after the Panic, he drew a simple but fascinating wash drawing entitled *The Paper City* revealing a speculator promising wealth to a gullible pair of rubes by simply showing them a legal document.[38]

In the 1840s, following an extended trip to Europe, Edmonds painted some of his most memorable works. While traveling, he reinvigorated his nationalism by reacquainting himself with the Dutch Masters and spent time with George Putnam, Duyckinck's publisher. *The Image Pedlar* (ca. 1844), borrowing from antecedents by Durand and Wilkie, depicted a traveling salesman who holds a group of plaster statuettes of famous leaders (including Jackson), showing once again the obsession with trade marking the paintings of the 1840s. George Putnam included a reproduction in his *American Facts* of 1845.[39]

Less prolific than Mount, doubtless because of the demands of his bank duties, Edmonds nevertheless offered several important works in the early 1850s that continued early themes. *The Speculator* (1852) exposed a suspicious blackguard holding a list of "valuable lots" before a gullible rural couple. *Taking the Census* (1854), somewhat similar in composition to *The Speculator*, limned with a mixture of warmth and ambivalence the intrusive visit of a government representative to register the existence of an inarticulate rural family. Like Mount, Edmonds continued to place a high emphasis on Americans left out of the metaphorical picture, including blacks, the elderly, and laborers in *The Scythe Grinder* (1856), *The Thirsty Drover* (1856), and an unemployed man in *Hard Times* (*Out of Work and Nothing to Do*) (1861). More economic tension surfaced in the wake of the Panic of 1857 with *Bargaining* (*The Christmas Turkey*) and *The New Bonnet* (both 1858), which pictured an elderly couple grimacing at the bill for their daughter's frivolous new purchase.[40]

Several other genre artists betrayed Young American themes, or at least the same youthful ennui toward the moneylenders of the older generation. Richard Caton Woodville's *Old '76 and Young '48* (1849), depicting a young soldier listening to an old revolutionary veteran tell war stories, captured perfectly the complicated reverence and disgust for the past many youthful Americans felt in the 1840s. The intermediate generation (a father with a watch fob) is shunted into the background, while the revolutionary ancestor and the youthful warrior heroically dominate the foreground. No stranger to revolutionary iconography, Whitman was particularly enamored of this painting when it was exhibited at the American Art-Union, and wrote, "The whole picture is good, and free from that straining after effect whose attempt is too evident (that's the fault), which mars most of the pictures here." Another celebrated Woodville opus, *War News from Mexico* (1848), showed an enthusiastic crowd gathered outside a tavern devouring a newspaper for recent military news. This image, widely reproduced, effectively captured the transformative effect of the modern print media, galvanized by its first war coverage. Like Mount, there lurked a political subtext beneath much of his work, from the obvious *Politics in an Oyster House* (1848), in which a young man yells at an older figure, to other genre works like *Waiting for the Stage* (1851).[41]

One of the most popular genre themes from the mid-1830s to the early 1850s was the newsboy, a new type of American embodying the generational energy and urban élan cultivated by the Young Americans. It would be difficult to list all the painters who rendered newsboys. Francis Edmonds might have begun the trend in 1839 with *The Penny Paper (Newspaper Boy)*; he was soon followed by Henry Inman's *News Boy* of 1841. Others included David Gilmour Blythe and James Henry Cafferty. Even more obscure, Thomas Le Clear's most famous work, *Buffalo Newsboy* (1853), showed a sturdy adolescent of that city eating an apple before a wall covered with handbills. Le Clear had trained in New York with Henry Inman in 1839, and exhibited at the Art-Union in 1846. Although it has been lost, a scene he painted entitled simply *Young America* apparently captured much of the bluster and bravado wrapped up in the term. A contemporary witness, Henry T. Tuckerman, described it for posterity:

> "Young America," which contains over a dozen figures, is remarkable for its skilled grouping and the harmony of tone which pervades it. The chief interest of the work centers in "Young America," a lad who, from the top of a dry goods box, is making a speech to the boys gathered about him. The figures are drawn from a true perspective, and each is evidently a study from life. The basket , and the old woman with apples, are especially noticeable. The locality is a street in Buffalo, and the man on the sidewalk evidently engaged in counting up his gains is a portrait of a well-known operator in stocks, who goes by the name of "three cents a month."[42]

If not all of these obscure painters were "Young American" in the strict sense of working for the *Review*, they certainly shared the national hopes of O'Sullivan and Duyckinck, often linking youth and revolution. Martin Johnson Heade scored an early success with a painting drawing on the excitement of 1848. Titled *The Roman Newsboys* (ca. 1849), it presented two exuberant Young Italians spreading revolutionary propaganda through newsbills and graffiti, the chief weapons of their cause. The same year, an obscure New York painter named Frederick R. Spencer completed *The Newsboy*, an enthralling work showing a young urbanite before a wall of paper announcements ranging from advertisements to announcements of the Astor Place Riot, with a large sign proclaiming "SOMETHING COMEING." The vicarious thrill American audiences felt before these newsboy images reasserted their enthusiasm for youthful rebellion and probably reflected a little nervousness about the power of the press. Some of these feelings were present as late as 1916, when George Bellows painted *The Newsboy*, faintly connecting the Ashcan School to its Young American antecedents.[43]

The same revolution in printing technology that propelled O'Sullivan and Duyckinck to prominence also brought about a pressing need for competent magazine draftsmen. The preeminent illustrator of the 1840s was an early contributor to the *Review*. F. O. C. Darley, born in Philadelphia in 1822, began doodling on the side while a clerk, and his sketches of disheveled urban types soon drew the attention of that city's prominent literati, including Poe, who took a formative early interest in Darley's career. Like Mount, he was more or less an autodidact, but despite a lack of formal training, he quickly became one of the most successful illustrators in the crowded American magazine scene.[44]

The Young Americans pounced on him, sensing a kindred spirit. All of New York was under the spell of Charles Dickens in the 1840s (Cornelius Mathews especially), and Darley's work was well-suited to this vogue. He was skilled at recreating the variety of shady characters springing up with the metropolis, and in 1843 he illustrated a volume of urban sketches by Joseph Neal entitled *In Town and About; or, Pencillings and Pennings*. The volume was well received, and the *Democratic Review* was sufficiently impressed that it included three Darley scenes in 1843. "The News-Boy," "Corner Loungers," and "The Card Players," depicted the new sociological types flooding New York and marked the first art work published in the *Review*. Darley's savvy street urchins perfectly captured the saucy "b'hoy" qualities O'-Sullivan wanted to translate into literature. Duyckinck, too, was impressed, gladly lending Darley books from his enormous library. Darley returned the favor in several ways, working on Young American projects later in the decade.[45]

Not every genre artist of the 1840s participated in the Democratic cultural network, of course, but even those who did not acknowledged the dominance of the Manhattan market. George Caleb Bingham, for example, was an ardent Whig for most of his career; although that meant a very different thing in rural Missouri than it did in New York. Despite the western focus of his work, he tried repeatedly to sell his art through New York brokers, with mixed results. Bingham's Whiggery may explain the antipathy Duyckinck's *Literary World* displayed toward him on occasion (it found *Jolly Flat-Boat Men* "a vulgar subject, vulgarly treated"). Even more than Mount, he peppered his work with political references, and devoted a major series of paintings to the electoral process in the early 1850s, more cynical than Mount's interpretation would have been. As with the writers, artistic party lines became blurry after 1850, when Whigs and Democrats both lost faith in their respective ideologies.[46]

Long before that, in the days when party animosities were sharper, Young America perceived clear affinities between its own aspirations and genre's delineation of everyday America. The *Democratic Review* praised Mount's work to the skies, finding there the "stamp of freshness that the foreign works are sadly deficient in" and admiring him for "drawing upon our own resources." Besides publishing Darley's sketches, the *Review* featured an important 1843 article by Horatio Greenough disdaining the elitism of European patronage, encouraging young artists, and predicting the "new impulse" the profession was about to feel from the United States.[47]

O'Sullivan enjoyed art, and he had inserted art articles in the magazine almost since its founding. One of the most interesting appeared in November 1838, a long diatribe against artistic elitism that argued a new, Jacksonian approach to art education. Despite favoring limited government in most respects, O'Sullivan proposed public funding for art schools and individual artists, almost a century before anything like that happened. In his reasoning, the arts were "never playthings," but vital means of elevation for the people, like libraries and universities. By removing art from its elite guardians, he suggested, the Democrats might spread happiness among the people and "the fever of the times may in some degree abate." There was even a touch of Manifest Destiny in his appeal, urging that American art works be "scattered everywhere" across the continent.[48]

O'Sullivan was not the only one thinking this way. In 1843, at his urging, Charles Sumner wrote an article on their mutual friend, the sculptor Thomas Crawford, and even he borrowed the trope of expansionism: "The star of Art, perhaps, shall follow that of Empire in its westward way." O'Sullivan's friendship with the young Julia Ward introduced him to the Ward family's art collection, one of the largest in New York. The Sedgwicks were interested in art as well, and Bryant recorded meeting Cole and Morse through their hospitality.[49]

Duyckinck and Mathews always championed the fine arts with ardor. The first issue of *Arcturus* proclaimed, "Next to poetry, of all the fine arts we would prefer to see Painting truly loved in this country," and regular gossipy features were offered on "the fine arts." The would-be cosmopolites were especially eager to seize on art because it allowed them to exercise the liberal thought they felt lacking in the book world. While Bostonians might recoil from undraped figures, open-minded New Yorkers would accept art as yet another sphere where the American mind could expand. In the *Democratic Review*, William A. Jones questioned whether the "puritanical New Englander" could even enjoy art.[50]

Basking in their Rabelaisian conviviality, the Young Americans especially admired the rough comic quality of the rising genre painters. In Mathews's address on Americanism, he specifically demanded a "school for comic design, here at New York, which shall be truly national." He and his friends felt that the "genial" Mount (Duyckinck's favorite adjective) was conducting a parallel struggle to their own. When he moved to Manhattan in 1847, they were strongly supportive. The *Literary World* praised him incessantly, arguing art does not "belong exclusively to subjects and characters of an elevated kind," and asserted *The Power of Music* alone would "insure Mount a permanent reputation, if he fishes for clams the rest of his life."[51]

For Duyckinck, who privately owned works by Mount and other local artists, the interest in genre painting had a deeply personal meaning. As early as 1838, in the course of his ancestral pilgrimage through Europe, the young twenty-two-year-old had relished the simple humor of the Dutch Old Masters and the skill with which "they copy everyday life in everyday colors." Regarding some tavern scenes, the young nationalist predicted they would someday be equaled by "our own Mount."[52]

Many of Duyckinck's friends were equally enthusiastic. One of the old Tetractys, William A. Jones, led a one-man public relations campaign for Mount. His important article on "American Humor" in the *Review*, which praised Duyckinck and Mathews as a matter of course, also took pains to exalt Mount and Edmonds in the same breath. If Duyckinck was "almost rabidly American," so "Mount, Deas, Edmonds, are honestly national." Divining "the sources of American humor," Jones offered a list that applied as much to genre painting as to writing:

> the Camp meeting, the negro music, the auctioneers and orators, and fashionable clergy, life on the Mississippi and the Lakes, the history of every man's life, his shifts and expedients, and change of pursuits, newspaper controversies, fashions in dress, military trainings, public lectures, newspaper advertisements, placards, signs, names of children, man worship, razor-strop men. The trait creeps out in numberless ways. So far from being a dull people we are eminently cheerful.[53]

In August 1851 Jones wrote the first major critical biography of his fellow Long Islander, an eight-page biography in the *American Review* that stressed the comic qualities the Young Americans flattered themselves expert in, and also praised Mount for work of "a strictly national character." Repeating the Duyckinck refrain, Jones continued, "In painting, as in literature, familiar history is in general far more valuable and directly interesting than the so-called heroic phases of art." The word *familiar*, with its root in the family scene Mount enjoyed depicting, was well-chosen. Mount favored his literary benefactor with a small portrait in 1853, one of the few that allows us to see what a Young American looked like.[54]

Mathews also caught the art bug, and in 1853 he wrote an entire book that sustained the poet-as-painter metaphor. A *Pen-and-Ink Panorama of New York City* limned the local scenery with the same affectionate humor the genre painters savored. It began with Mathews's usual bluster: "In the little canvas I propose to open before you, ladies and gentlemen, I have attempted to paint a home picture . . . I shall endeavor to body forth something for your entertainment, by unrolling before you the streets of and characters of a great city." He disparaged traditional "historical paintings" along with "historical romances" and instead presented the new urban images of firemen and other specimens of modernity, both beautiful and ugly. When Melville tried to insult Young America in *Pierre*, he ridiculed its antiaesthetic of the "povertiresque" (and then proceeded to outdo anything Mathews wrote in the way of urban squalor).[55]

Like the Young Americans, Mount and the genre artists were concerned with the essential premise of a democratic art, which was simply how to bring as much of it to as many people as possible. Duyckinck must have recognized something of himself in Mount's hope for democratic acceptance outside the academies and wealthy salons. The literati would have appreciated the succinct way he stated the case: "Painting of familiar objects has the advantage over writing by addressing itself to those who cannot read or write of any nation what-so-ever. It is not necessary for one to be gifted in language to understand a painting if the story is well-told—It speaks all the languages—is understood by the illiterate and enjoyed still more by the learned."[56]

This was the same imperative that drove O'Sullivan's cultural politics and launched Duyckinck's quest for an accessible, affordable literature. If Mount was not exactly a member of the *Review*'s inner circle, he was admired as a fellow toiler in the vineyard of cultural nationalism. With a lively genre tradition established in New York, all that was needed was a proper network of distribution to spread the new art across the land.

The American Art-Union

As Duyckinck learned through his heroic efforts to shore up the American literary infrastructure, mere talent was not enough to penetrate the thick defenses of cultural elitism. Institutional support was also needed, along with financing and a proper system of national distribution. For the genre painters of the 1840s, this was largely provided by the American Art-Union, one of the landmark institutions in the history of American representation, whose existence from 1838 to 1851 ran parallel to O'Sullivan's tenure at the *Democratic Review*. Like transcendentalism, the idea of the Art-Union was borrowed from Germany, but held peculiar affinities for Americans. Before the Art-Union, the few American art academies that existed were elitist in tone, and restricted generally to wealthy gentlemen who funded them and established artists who lent them prestige. As John Trumbull, president of the American Academy of Fine Arts, put it in an 1833 address, "Artists are necessarily dependent upon the protection of the rich and great." To the extent they held exhibitions, they were limited in duration and accessibility. James Herring, an artist who helped found the Art-Union, wrote in 1838 of "a vast amount of artistic talent not known or appreciated, because it had no means of expansion."[57]

The problem was aggravated, in the minds of young painters, by the stupid acquisitiveness that generally marked the collecting efforts of the arriviste American, a genus swarming New York since the Era of Good Feelings. These recently enriched connoisseurs scoured Europe for the Old Master paintings they felt would convey social acceptability. Cornelius Mathews parodied a parvenu's letter to a son traveling in Europe: "Dear Son: Well, the house is done, and very fine it is too; . . . Now I want to fill it with pictures from the old masterz and enclose you a draft for $150 to buy them. I like to patronize the arts, and I'd build a church, but that's got vulgar." Duyckinck wrote in his journal, "The builders of fine houses begin to look for something to cover their walls. The first taste was for European copies of the old masters—now, within a very few years, a desire to possess the original works of modern, and latterly—greatly through the Art-Union—of American works has sprung up."[58]

Around the country, young artists were frustrated by these obstacles, but the situation began to improve by degrees in the late 1820s, just as genre enthusiasm rose. The National Academy of Design was founded by artists piqued at the American Academy's exclusiveness, and the Sketch Club brought together an eclectic group of "artists, authors, men of science and lovers of art" with a common interest in American culture. Even if this group preserved some aloofness, it placed a lower premium on wealth than any art organization previously in existence. A partial list of its more famous members indicates a respectable Jacksonian presence, including Bryant, Mount, and Edmonds, along with luminaries such as Irving, Morse, Cooper, Cole, Durand, Darley, and many others. The Duyckinck brothers were occasional guests as well. Significantly, several merchants, including Luman Reed, were allowed into the club for their support of the artistic community.[59]

Reed, a self-made merchant, was one of the patrons of the nascent Hudson River School, commissioning major works from Cole and Durand. Appropriately, he was also one of the chief beneficiaries of the river's connection to inland markets and the region's sudden rise to economic predominance. Raised in Coxackie, a Hudson River town not far from Van Buren's Kinderhook, he had spent his entire life working the river in some capacity. His personal empire expanded rapidly, and as he entered middle age, he sought to surround himself with tokens of success. Accordingly, around 1830 he began to collect and commission works of art, and before his death six years later, he had over fifty paintings, the majority of which were

American. He built an elegant townhouse with an entire floor for gallery space, and generously allowed public access one day a week.[60]

In many senses Reed, though not a creator in any sense except the economic one, stood as an important transitional figure in artistic circles of nineteenth-century New York. Earlier American patrons had displayed a clear preference for stylized portraits and European scenery, assuming European art was vastly superior, and purchasing it as a status symbol. Reed was probably as pretentious in some senses, but he represented a new type of collector, and suddenly the vogue for Old Masters seemed old indeed. Unlike the average connoisseur, he inclined toward the Democracy. He explained that he "exhibited very little interest in politics—he however liked the decission [sic] of and actions of President Jackson" and "did not favor the policy and doctrines of Webster and Clay, especially in respect to a 'U.S. Fiscal agent' or U.S. Bank." He even commissioned a portrait of Jackson at the hands of Asher B. Durand. This was hardly typical patronage.[61]

Reed was also genuinely interested in the painting of American scenery, befriending and subsidizing local, living artists without prior reputations. Durand was merely an engraver when they met, and Reed urged him to strive for higher ambitions: "Let us make something of ourselves out of our own materials & we shall then be independent of others. It is all nonsense to say we have not got the materials." In all of these respects, he was personally more invested in his collection than his elite predecessors. The accessibility of his collection also helped generate a heightened public interest in art.[62]

Reed's taste was equally important for giving an impetus to the rise of genre painting. In addition to his landscapes, Reed enjoyed scenes from commonplace events and local history and purchased works such as Durand's *Peter Stuyvesant and the Trumpeter* (1835) and *The Pedlar* (1835–36). Despite the brevity of his career as a collector, he was typical of the new type of American who considered his country's artistic achievement a matter of personal honor. When he died, his collection was preserved intact, and appropriately, the merchant-artist Francis Edmonds supervised its removal to the New York Gallery of the Fine Arts.[63]

For all the welcome informality of the Luman Reed collection, the public need for art access was largely unfulfilled at the time of his death in 1836. Accordingly, the Apollo Gallery was created in 1838 by James Herring, instantly aiming for a more democratic audience than previous galleries and academies, and cultivating artists from all over the nation, rather than the Northeast alone. An engraver and literary gadfly like Duyckinck, Herring realized that the depression of the late 1830s made it difficult for wealthy individuals to advance American art on their own. In 1839 he and some like-minded citizens formed an artistic joint stock company of sorts, the Apollo Association.[64]

Despite a slow start, the association evolved into a popular success by any index of measurement. It was incorporated by the New York legislature as a semipublic institution in 1840, and members began enlisting slowly, encouraged by voluntary "honorary secretaries" spreading the gospel in principal cities. In 1842 a revamping of the Committee on Management resulted in a determination to increase the accessibility of art to the public. Not only was a prize offered for the best painting "of a national character," but the art was placed in a permanent setting where people could see it free of charge. These actions not only resulted in a dramatic membership surge, they served as the bedrock of the modern notion of the free public art museum.[65]

The enlarged horizon of expectations was reflected in the grander name of the American Art-Union, adopted by the Apollo Association in 1844, by which time there were 2,080 members. Bryant was president from 1844 to 1846, adding to its draw for young Democrats. In 1849, its peak year, there were 18,960 amateur connoisseurs flung across the republic from Athens, Maine, to Zebulon, Georgia. The *Bulletin* boasted, "From one end of this great nation to the other—on the Atlantic and the Pacific—from the Gulf to the Lakes—there is hardly a city or a village that through this institution has practically an Art-Union of its own."[66]

It is difficult to overestimate the importance of the Art-Union in the history of American art patronage. Within the brief compass of thirteen years, it accomplished two very important objectives, both harmonious with Young American goals. It encouraged a rudimentary appreciation of art in circles and places where such a thing was unprecedented, giving the lie to the dictum our utilitarian people were too crass for aesthetic reflection. Second, it offered much-needed institutional encouragement to living artists from all regions, many of whom were desperately obscure until its founding. Charles Dudley Warner considered the Art-Union "one of the most significant phases of the general tendency towards what may be called the democraticization of art in modern times" and rated its influence as "something really prodigious." From the more genteel perspective of the late nineteenth century, Warner added superciliously, "Though very naturally it was affected in no slight degree by the homely tastes of the public that supplied the greater part of its clientage." Many of the more radical Young American theorists would have posited that this was precisely the point, and that "homely" was the perfect double-entendre to describe their aims.[67]

The Art-Union was less rigid than preexisting art societies in almost every conceivable way, from financing to membership promotions to the display of the art itself. Subscribers paid five dollars per annum, and for this they were sent a print of an American artwork and became eligible for an annual lottery of original art held every December. They also received the Art-Union *Bulletin*, the first magazine devoted exclusively to American art. Not only did painters and sculptors benefit, but also the engravers and die-casters enlisted to prepare the prints. Beyond the obvious dividends the Art-Union produced for the rising artists of the period, it served as a boondoggle for hundreds of craftsmen and tinkerers in related fields, many of whom were able to make the leap to painting after first succeeding at a humbler artistic career. John Kouwenhoven has argued "an extraordinarily large percentage of American artists were originally apt in, or dependent upon mechanical skill."[68]

It is impressive how many American artists of the mid nineteenth century had engraving experience. Ironically, much of the credit belonged to Andrew Jackson, for the proliferation of state banks that followed his Bank war created a huge market for new bank notes. Besides Edmonds and Mount, who both dabbled in currency design, Asher B. Durand was one of the most prominent engravers in New York. James Herring, the art fancier who started the Apollo Gallery in 1838, was also

an accomplished engraver before shifting careers. In each case, the Art-Union facilitated the interpenetration of the engraver's craft and the artist's more dilettantish
world, in addition to the volume of business it brought to engravers for the annual
printing jobs. A *Bulletin* article of 1849 resembled trade protectionism in its claim
the Art-Union promoted all crafts ancillary to the profession: "None but American
artists are employed; American workmen in all departments receive the money
which is expended in connection with it."[69]

An Art-Union speech in 1845 spelled out this philosophy more specifically, urging the Art-Union to cultivate the boy who yesterday was "a poor apprentice, to a
cutter of tombstones, a carver of dials, or a painter of signs" and who now "feels the
divinity of genius stirring within him." A year later, Hawthorne published his story
of the inspired carver, "Drowne's Wooden Image," for Duyckinck's Library of
American Books (in *Mosses from an Old Manse*). Echoing this idea, Drowne illustrated the premise that "in every human spirit there is imagination, sensibility, creative power, genius, which, according to circumstances, may either be developed in
this world, or shrouded in dulness until another state of being." By opening wide
the dialogue between craftsmen, artists, editors, and the public, the Art-Union
briefly enacted this premise, and in so doing modernized the vocation of art in a
way the vast majority of its constituents were only dimly aware of. This was an
achievement of real moment, and one that outlasted the Art-Union's brief tenure in
the vanguard of American taste.[70]

On the strength of these ideas, and the general ebullience of the 1840s, the Art-
Union soon was transformed from a loosely organized society into an enormous,
far-reaching national concern, dealing in thousands of artworks a year and expanding geographically as rapidly as the people it served. George Putnam enlisted as an
"Honorary Secretary" from as far away as London, a fact he trumpeted from the title
page of his *American Facts*, which included a section on art. The annual lottery
drawing in December became a popular social event in New York, with mobs of patrons jostling each other in a frenzy of would-be connoisseurship. Blustery speeches
were given on these occasions, boldly calling for "American Æsthestics" and announcing, in O'Sullivanesque cadences, that "a new race enters on the arena, with
the ardour of youth, and strong both in talents and in numbers." American art, it
seemed, was driven by a manifest destiny of its own.[71]

The official documents of the Art-Union offer a fascinating glimpse at the intellectually acquisitive mentality of the period, demanding a new type of cultural
representation in surprisingly angry language for a group of bourgeois New Yorkers.
Charles F. Briggs, an author who drifted in and out of the Duyckinck set in the
early 1840s, delivered the annual address of 1842, the pivotal year of reorientation.
Like a Young American, he complained about the elitism of earlier academies: "We
have no public galleries; our high-ways are ornamented with neither monuments
nor statues; the men of wealth and taste among us, who possess works of art, shut
them up within the walls of their houses, where they are as much lost to the world
as though they had never existed." Under the proposed system, "the humblest individual in society, and the most remote parts of the Union, may become possessed of
the choicest works of art," and "the great mass of the people can learn to appreciate
the true value of works of Art."[72]

Briggs spoke volumes about New York's claims to represent the entire nation; he insisted the Art-Union was growing in a nonsectional way "by a constant adaptation of its every change and feature to the peculiar characteristics and wants, not of a *single city*, but of the *whole republic*." The point was hammered home tautologically: "We seek to establish a National School of Art. Ours is an American Association, founded upon American principles, fashioned by experience after American views, sustained by American patronage; and our aim shall ever after be to promote the permanent and progressive advance of American Art."[73]

Much of the Art-Union rhetoric overlapped with Young America, including its anticlerical stance. The 1843 *Transactions* again featured Briggs, arguing that the people themselves had to assemble together to fill the patronage void in America: "Our churches are now the last places where an artist would look for encouragement." Briggs insisted it was of "much greater consequence" when patronage came from the people rather than "popes and princes," for then the painter "may feel himself under vassalage to no one master." O'Sullivan, with his chronic distrust of priestcraft and kingcraft, could hardly have said it better.[74]

Briggs particularly identified the novice painter as the object of the association's ministrations: "It is the young artist who is struggling to plant his feet on the lowest rung of the ladder of fame who most needs the helping hand of a friend to sustain him in his first step; and the most important aid that can be rendered to Art is given to the young beginner." He even shuddered at the emasculate phrase "Fine Arts," because "the very term fine would exclude from the number of objects deemed worthy of serious consideration, any subject to which it might be applied." For the manly cultural nationalist, the arts were too important to remain as mere "luxuries to be indulged in only by the rich and effeminate."[75]

Like Duyckinck, Briggs's radicalism served several purposes, occasionally contradictory. He insisted it was time for "the vulgar poor" to view the artworks "rarely found but in the houses of the rich, or else shut up carefully in galleries." But he also betrayed nervousness about their growing numbers, especially in New York: "To the inhabitants of cities, as nearly all the subscribers to the Art-Union are, a painted landscape is almost essential to preserve a healthy tone to the spirits, lest they forget in the wilderness of bricks which surrounds them the pure delights of nature and a country life." It could be argued there was something inherently conservative in Briggs' appeal, but he was diagnosing a sickness in the entire urban social fabric, and not just its lower tier. He thought "such a sight might improve the digestion of the dyspeptic merchant as he sits at his pampered table, after a day of harassing labor, the labor that wearies without strengthening the body, because it makes the inside instead of the outside of the head sweat."

In other words, a creeping sense of alienation and a distrust of industrial capitalism were as much the engines of art nationalism as the more innocent patriotism so vociferously articulated. A minister repeated these themes in an Art-Union speech that reversed the political excitement Young America felt:

> President-making, and money-getting, together, stir up all that is bitter, sectional, or personal in us. We want some interests that are larger than purse or party, on which men cannot take sides, or breed strifes, or become selfish. Such an interest

is Art. And no nation needs its exalting, purifying, calming influences, more than ours. We need it to supplant the mean, utilitarian tastes, which threaten to make us a mere nation of shop-keepers. We need it to soften the harsh features of political zeal, and party strife, the other engrossing business of the people. And therefore, let us rejoice in The *American Art-Union.*[76]

But this antipolitical argument should not blind us to the Art-Union's populistic significance. The Art-Union not only revised thinking about patronage and the right of the people to behold art, it also, by virtue of its approach, dictated its own aesthetic strategy. Understandably, the tidal wave of nationalistic rhetoric brought with it a call for domestic representation, from revolutionary scenes to genre to landscapes. The committee made no bones about soliciting "subjects illustrating national character, or history, or scenery," and in 1849 the president announced his hope to found "an American School which may yet take its place with the Italian, the Dutch, and the Spanish." European imitation was frowned on, as was the larger field of portraiture, or any interest in the events of the distant past ("Modern Artists have no hope but in Modern Art"). Echoing Mount's disdain for "fancy painting" the Art-Union urged artists to work "more immediately from nature, and less through other pictures" so "their canvas smacks of fresh air, rather than of dingy galleries."[77]

The genre painters especially profited from the Art-Union, for they understood the need for national self-expression that the Art-Union was addressing in the first place. Fittingly, the crowds of unschooled art fanciers who flocked to the Art-Union were especially moved by the humorous realism they saw in the new art. Duyckinck's *Literary World* made the important observation that genre scenes like Edmonds's *Strolling Musician* were more popular with plebeian visitors than Durand's "misty noontide of landscape."[78]

Edmonds was particularly fortunate in his association. He had joined the upstart organization from its inception, serving as treasurer in its first year, and on the Committee of Management throughout the 1840s. From this vantage point, and through his Democratic newspaper connections, he was able to exert considerable influence, securing favorable reviews for fellow painters in sympathetic places like Bryant's *Evening Post.* He exhibited seven paintings there, including a humorous lampoon of an old man with a young bride that was purchased by John Van Buren. More important, the Apollo Association conveyed its highest honor on Edmonds by engraving his celebrated *Sparking,* sent to all members in 1844. Taking note of the genre style, the *Transactions* of 1844 specifically praised its "homely" but "universal" interest, and labeled the painting "the best of the kind yet produced in the country."[79]

The year before, all the members had received an engraving of Mount's *Farmer's Nooning.* Yet ironically, this painter, of whom it was universally observed that he was the most American of Americans, conducted only a minimal business through the Art-Union. The aloofness was largely personal (the Art-Union balked at paying what he felt were fair prices, and also spurned the work of his brother Shepard Mount). One of the hundreds of curious notes he wrote to himself summed up his view: "Never be trameled [sic] by societies. They serve as clogs to genius." Another fragment contained a list of works he hoped to paint someday, including one provocatively titled, "A young artist leaving the Art-Union with a rejected picture."[80]

For the most part, the career of every other genre artist was significantly advanced by the Art-Union and its advanced notions of publicity and distribution. George Caleb Bingham profited greatly from the assistance of the Art-Union. Richard Caton Woodville, whose *Old '76 and Young '48* was admired by Whitman at the Art-Union, was another favorite, and at least three of his works were engraved for members. Even F. O. C. Darley entered the picture, though not as a painter. In 1848, as the Art-Union was expanding dramatically, he illustrated a special volume of Washington Irving's "Rip Van Winkle" to be given free to all subscribers. The next year, he repeated himself with "The Legend of Sleepy Hollow." Darley also drew scenes from Cooper novels for the *Bulletin* and donated his original drawings to the annual auction. Besides facilitating the sale of work by established artists, the Art-Union did much to nurture talent. The young Frederic Church took a studio in the Art-Union building at 497 Broadway, where he was able to immediately immerse himself in the emerging art scene.[81]

The Art-Union's attention to ordinary Americans soon produced dividends in attendance, and reports continuously boasted of the volume of "citizens of the laboring classes" tramping through its halls. As hinted before, some of this self-congratulatory reporting was sanctimonious, hoping art would instill the people with "the impressive lessons of history and the sacred truths of religion." Echoing Briggs, a speaker in 1847 hoped the Art-Union would provide a "living landscape" for "men pent up in the dark streets of cities."[82]

Yet beneath the admonitory quality of these reports, there was a strong current of good faith in the experiment, and for every cautious statement there were ten celebratory ones. In 1851, even after the withering effect of the Compromise of 1850, one Art-Unionist still could sound optimistic about the democratic potential of American art:

> as giving expression to the aspirations and sympathies of a nation, to social and po-
> litical wrongs and errors, . . . of those traits in which we differ from any or all
> other nations, . . . in the delineation of the modifications of class (not of artificial
> rank); in the fiery democratic impulses of the masses; the calmer elevation of the
> statesman; the purified feelings of domestic life; all the outbursts and aspirations,
> the energy and fiery enthusiasm which belongs to the nation. These mark what our
> school must be.[83]

These, of course, were political as well as artistic claims. As with Young America's literary campaign, the call for national art indicated not only enthusiasm for democracy, but also fear of the splintering effects of regional culture, particularly the dominion of New England. It is striking how many members of the American Art-Union came from the South (hundreds from each state), indeed, from every region, including the expanding frontier and soldiers stationed in Mexico. Furthermore, the paintings chosen for distribution carefully represented a regional balance, especially in the late 1840s, repeating Duyckinck and O'Sullivan's concern

that American culture be defined with broad latitude. There were discernible political subcurrents in almost all the major addresses at the Art-Union drawings, from
those pleasantly recapitulating the American creed of democratic opportunity, to
others that were truly contemptuous of the artistic elite. One eager writer even promoted an aesthetic system based on the federal government, with compositions
"where each part is in perfect keeping with all the rest, and the result is a single irresistible impression formed out of many, *e pluribus unum*." Fortunately, few artists
felt compelled to go to this extreme of Americanism in their work.[84]

Young America and the Art-Union

Given this ongoing politico-artistic dialectic, it is unsurprising that all of the major personnel of Young America and the *Democratic Review* enlisted in the association: Benjamin Butler became a member in 1839, along with Bryant, George
Putnam, and the Edmonds brothers. Van Buren himself joined in 1840, along with
the Duyckincks, and William Gilmore Simms became an "Honorary Secretary" in
1841. O'Sullivan enlisted in 1843, with David Dudley Field and Cornelius Mathews, and Samuel Tilden signed up two years later. This is not to argue the American Art-Union was exclusively Democratic in sympathy, but almost all the young
literary Democrats were sympathetic to its ancillary efforts in the art world. It is also
noteworthy that Duyckinck's Whiggish rivals in the area of cultural nationalism,
Rufus Griswold and Lewis Gaylord Clark, were more active in the National Academy of Design, and glaringly absent from the Art-Union's membership rolls.[85]

The convergence of the artistic and literary programs became especially pronounced in the middle of the decade. In 1845, the same year Duyckinck launched
his Library of American Books, his old friend, Joel Headley (the author of a work in
the series), delivered an impassioned address on the "Americanism" of the Art-
Union. The address was typically orotund, swollen with the bombast craved at public gatherings, but Headley made several compelling points, and in the process revealed how closely allied the Young American plan was to the Art-Union's.

Headley began with a simple patriotic statement, "It is an American institution—with a *home* feeling and a *home* purpose, and therefore I love it." He then
continued in something like eloquence:

> If there ever was a people on the face of the earth with peculiar and striking char-
> acteristics, it is the American people; and if we could only release ourselves from
> that strange infatuation about foreign arts and artists, and foreign literature, and
> foreign everything, and dare and love to be ourselves, we should soon have an
> *American* literature, an *American* school of art, as well as a peculiar form of self-
> government.[86]

Warming up to the subject, Headley continued, forcibly interjecting politics
into the issue, with a sneer at the favorite topics of Whiggery:

> Give me the control of the *art* of a country, and you may have the management of
> its administrations. There can be no greater folly than that committed by our
> statesmen, when they treat art and literature as something quite aside from great

national interests. The tariff, internal improvements, banks, political speeches and party measures, are put paramount to them, and yet they all together do not so educate the soul of the nation.

For Headley, who conjured up the interesting example of a young Italian imprisoned for painting the struggle for republicanism, all art was inherently political, and more specifically, "ever on the side of liberty" and "popular feeling." Youth was essential to the new art, for "he that muses and dreams over the past, calling feebly on the classic age to come again, commits a folly that after years can never repair." Acknowledging his Young American cronies, Headley concluded his dramatic plea with the peroration: "So must genius always do, and doing this successfully is what makes a *school* both in poetry and art."[87]

Headley had written art criticism in the *Democratic Review*, including a spoof on ignorant American cultivation of Italian art, published around the time of his speech. Of course, the *Review* supported the Art-Union throughout the decade, approving its nonsectional focus and repeating its usual expansive rhetoric: "Every state in the Union, from the extreme north to the distant south, and from the Atlantic to the remote west, contains choice specimens of American Art, forming a nucleus for budding genius in every quarter."[88]

The magazine shared other personnel with the Art-Union as well. Quite a few writers worked for both organizations. One of the more prominent, John Bigelow, recorded an amusing incident where he was prevailed on to give a speech about art and democracy at an Art-Union drawing, but the noisy crowd was too restless to listen to him, probably saying more about the issue than his speech ever could. Even the overworked O'Sullivan grew interested. Beside enrolling as a member, in 1846 he signed a petition of writers and artists who supported a gallery named after Henry Inman, his favorite artist. He also used the Art-Union for political favors, as Duyckinck recorded in his diary:

> A little incident came off today when Woodville's carefully varnished "Game of Chess" was knocked down to John Van Buren. "That's not my bid" says he. "A friend has bought it for you." It passed to be John O'Sullivan, who wishing to make the lawyer a present—for the relief his talents had given him from the United States marshals, for his filibustering difficulties and having overheard his wish to possess this painting, had taken this method of putting him in possession of it.[89]

Duyckinck became more involved still. Having already perceived that genre painting complemented his literary ambitions, he strongly supported the Art-Union in person and in print. His brother George even won a painting in the 1844 drawing. *Arcturus* had praised the original Apollo Gallery in its first issue and approved the idea of sending prints to the people around the country who could not make it to a Manhattan gallery. Like the Library of American Books, this seemed an effective way of bringing culture cheaply and efficiently to the American masses, and promoting American artists in the meantime. In his important article "The Culture of the Imagination," W. A. Jones recommended cheap culture as a necessary corollary of democratic polity, because "the numberless improvements in the art of engraving have brought the choicest works within the reach of even the laborer. People's editions, cheap libraries without end, furnish the means of mental culture to all." Jones even called on the state to further this trend by financing "free lectures, free concerts, free admission to galleries of paintings and sculptures, to libraries and reading-rooms."[90]

Duyckinck's later magazine, *The Literary World*, was also effusive. It wrote of the Art-Union, "We may date the dawn of popular feeling in favor of art from the morning of the existence of this institution." With customary hyperbole, it added, "We believe we are now upon the verge of an era, which will eclipse even the brilliant glory of the sixteenth century." Americans were ready to move beyond effete European art like "gilded and beflowered China ware and highly ornamented snuff-boxes." The *Literary World* was especially proud the Art-Union had "removed that ancient landmark of '25 cents admission' which had existed so long, a perpetual barrier between spectacles and spectators."[91]

Beside the nationalistic art it supported, the Art-Union, acting like a magnet for all the disparate social types of the big city, transfixed the Young Americans with its Dickensian literary possibilities. A moonstruck writer in the *Literary World* opined there was no better place than the Art-Union "to give a stranger a notion of the physiognomy of the various phases of New York society," from "gentlemen of careful toilets and anxious eyebrows" to the "B'hoy" and the "belle of the Bowery." The magazine took pains to praise the Art-Union's evening hours, for that was when the museum was open to working-class visitors. Looking at the crowd and the new gas lights there, the writer, very likely Duyckinck, gazed in awe at the spectacle of modernity:

> It is in the evening, when the red glass over the door beams like a lurid, extra-sized, semi-circular planet over the drifting current of Broadway, and the tide of visitors draws incessantly through the well lighted tunnel that leads from the pavement to the pictures, that the Art-Union is in all its glory. Then it is that it counts its friends and finds amongst them the representatives of every section of the social system.[92]

One of the old Tetractys, William Allen Butler, even wrote a poem about class mixing, titled "The Free Gallery of the American Art-Union:"

> Here at last the arts of beauty
> in their fittest home abide,
> Not beneath the gilded ceilings
> Of the palaces of pride;
> Not in lordly shrines sequestered.
> For the favored few alone,
> But in simple halls whose portals
> Open to the world are thrown!
>
> Close beside the whirl incessant
> Of the city's ceaseless din,
> Free to all who choose to enter,
> Is the wealth of art within;
> And the rich man and the poor man,
> Turning from the crowded street,
> In the fellowship of feeling,
> Here as equals still may meet![93]

On a few occasions, the *Literary World* recalled O'Sullivan's attempts to fuse Manifest Destiny and culture, particularly in 1848 when the revolutions had everyone briefly optimistic. Reviewing F. O. C. Darley's Rip Van Winkle drawings, distributed free to members that year, Duyckinck's sheet borrowed the rhetoric of expansion to contemplate the "delighted faces" across the continent as the Art-Union "scattered these leaves, in tens of thousands, from the St. John to the Rio Grande." Fusing art and politics even more closely, a friend of Duyckinck's ran for ward representative on the platform of supporting democracy and the Art-Union. He was strongly supported in the *Literary World*.[94]

Earlier in this chapter, I argued that Elizabeth Johns had understated the strength of Mount's Democratic convictions in her recent work on genre. In a similar way, she misrepresented the politics of magazine coverage, confusing Duyckinck with his archrival Lewis Gaylord Clark, the Whig editor of the *Knickerbocker* magazine. Clark's *Knickerbocker* was not "Democratic" in any sense. That magazine's celebration of the Art-Union as a form of social control, instilling "motley crowds" with "minds elevated by what they have seen, with manners and feelings refined, with new checks fastened upon coarse and unruly passions," was unmistakably in the nervous Whig tradition. Duyckinck's *Literary World*, which she cites as "less democratic," was just the opposite. Its reviews consistently praised the fluidity with which all classes and types mixed at the Art-Union.[95]

Beyond praising the Art-Union with his pen, Duyckinck also lent his administrative talents to the understaffed enterprise, corresponding with artists, and influencing the Art-Union's decisions about purchases. He served on its Committee of Management during its peak years, from 1848 to 1851. On one convivial occasion, he brought Herman Melville to the grand opening of new rooms for the Art-Union, where they were delighted to meet Mount. Duyckinck recorded the event for posterity in his diary: "Lanman introduced me to Mount the humorous painter, of a fine and even beautiful countenance." They enjoyed an alcoholic punch ("nowhere spoken against in scripture"), they compared a nude to *Typee*'s Fayaway, and Duyckinck observed that his artistic acquaintances were pleased by the human pictures before them: "Mount and Melville were delighted with the living tableaux." It was probably the most Rabelaisian evening Duyckinck ever spent.[96]

This passage seems the basis for F. O. Matthiessen's claim that Mount was "an occasional drinking companion of the Duyckincks and Melville." He exaggerated, but both Melville and Mount, in their different democratic ways, regarded Duyckinck as an important ally. Recent evidence indicates that Melville was more interested in art, and particularly Dutch genre, than he has been given credit for. In 1850, when Melville wrote "Hawthorne and His Mosses" for *The Literary World*, he commented: "For poets (whether in prose or verse), being painters of Nature, are like their brethren of the pencil, the true portrait-painters, who, in the multitude of likenesses to be sketched, do not invariably omit their own." Although never a member, Whitman applauded the Art-Union from Brooklyn and wrote an article in 1850 about a visit to the gallery.[97]

The dénouement of the Art-Union proved surprisingly abrupt, occurring at the moment of its peak success. Growth continued at an extraordinary rate throughout the decade, culminating in 1849, when 1,010 works of art were distributed among almost nineteen thousand members. Imitative Art-Unions sprang up in other regions, earning the original the dubious title of "the mother of Art-Unions." In 1848 it was estimated that half a million people availed themselves of the free gallery, an extraordinary number roughly equal to the entire population of New York.[98]

But at the height of success, several problems combined to sound the death-knell of the organization. First, the Art-Union was run on unsound financial principles. Every year, a large number of subscribers would join at year's end in order to be eligible for the lottery, but the art had to be purchased ahead of time, so that a great deal of guesswork was involved. In 1851 much more money was spent than was received back in subscriptions. At the same time, powerful enemies of the Art-Union had accumulated, from the rival art associations who watched its success with jealous eyes, to the disgruntled artists whose creations were spurned. One of the latter, an Englishman named Thomas Whitley, was joined by James Gordon Bennett of the *New York Herald*, who was able to bring legal proceedings on the simple grounds that lotteries were illegal in the state of New York. In May 1852, a court upheld the suit, and the Art-Union closed its doors after a brief, tumultuous, and important existence.[99]

Despite its abridged history, the Art-Union irrevocably enlarged the nation's art consciousness and facilitated the emergence of a professional class of artists and art-mongers. Besides the encouragement it provided genre painters like Edmonds, it gave younger artists a place to learn their craft. If it did nothing else, it brought art appreciation out of the few private salons it had inhabited and forced it out into the open. No matter how the resulting art itself was evaluated, this was a pathbreaking achievement.

As a postscript, it is interesting to note a decline in genre art's popularity from its peak in the mid-1840s to the early 1850s, when it was preempted by the more genteel preference for landscapes. While this may have been transitory fashion, it resembled the attenuation of Young American rhetoric over the same period. Reviewing Woodville's *War News from Mexico* (1848), the *Bulletin of the Art-Union* cringed from its realism, writing, "There is also something painful in the truth with which the squalor and rags of the poor negro girl are rendered." Two years later, the *Literary World* reviewed Mount's work somewhat mincingly, admiring its truthfulness but complaining "the subjects are low, low, very low," distressed particularly by all the shabby clothes (the breeches are "exceedingly questionable") and rickety barns. With all too much realism, this review revealed Young America's retreat from reality, and foreshadowed, to use an artist's term, the disastrous reception *Moby-Dick* was about to receive.[100]

The return to landscape was simply part of the general defalcation from a Democratic idealism that had become untenable in the early 1850s. In the wake of the failed European revolutions and the tarnished Compromise, Young American nationalism became yesterday's news. As the Art-Union scrambled to distribute pleasant and regionally balanced prints to its members, it sacrificed some of the antielite energy that had fueled its early phase and began to look again to the familiar realm of nature for inspiration. Confirmation of the new attitude toward art was revealed in George Putnam's *Home Book of the Picturesque*, issued by Duyckinck's former publisher in 1852. Despite Putnam's excitement over genre in 1845, the

Home Book emphasized instead the serenity of the American landscape and the calm it brought to the leisured contemplator. Described as a "presentation-book" in the publisher's notice, the book had little agenda except to serve as an commodity of exchange among "our liberal, gift-giving people." Snobbery oozed from its turgid prose, utterly dismissive of the human dimension in art: "Oceans, mountains, rivers, cataracts, wild woods, fragrant prairies, and melodious winds, are elements and exemplification of that general harmony which subsists throughout the universe, and which is the most potent over the most valuable minds."

All the gains achieved by democratic art seemed to slip away as the nation's cultural movers, frightened by the disturbing political weather of the early 1850s, refocused their attention on the "harmony" of the unthreatening natural realm. In this new hierarchy, the people held little value, and cities were positively "evils to be shunned, since they vitiate if not destroy that purity and calm which are essential to the best growth of mind." There was simply no room for genre painting in a book like this. In the same decade, the American Art-Union was replaced in popularity by the more international Cosmopolitan Art Association, a change in nomenclature that spoke volumes about the shifting intellectual climate.[101]

But despite the backsliding of the 1850s, it is important to recognize that a crucial new plateau of artistic awareness had been achieved in the United States during the 1840s. Outlasting vicissitudes in taste, an infrastructure of galleries, journals, and public interest was firmly in place, ready for subsequent artists and art-brokers to build on. Before the American Art-Union, Asher B. Durand observed, the number of artists "could be counted on one's fingers," and after its demise they constituted "a large body." He continued, "The institution, if not the creator of a taste for art in the community, disseminated a knowledge of it and largely stimulated its growth. Through it the people awoke to the fact that art was one of the forces of society."[102]

As political troubles forced attention toward more serious matters, cultural nationalists like Mount were left without much wind in their sails. During the 1850s, he continued to paint, but less prolifically, and with less originality, often repeating themes he had employed earlier. Like many other ex-Jacksonians, O'Sullivan and Judge Edmonds among them, he became intensely interested in the fad of spiritualism, believing it possible to communicate with expired spirits through mediums. As Whitman was in the ascendant, putting the final touches to *Leaves of Grass* in the spring of 1855, his painterly *camerado* was excitedly transcribing messages he believed sent to him by the spirit of Rembrandt van Rijn.[103]

The letters were pathetic, of course, but fascinating in their insistence on the value of earthy nationalism in painting, with "Rembrandt" comparing his Holland to Mount's America. Specifically, the spirit wrote, "I endeavoured notwithstanding all sorts of fierce and malignant criticisms to make my pictures purely Dutch both in deliniation [sic] of costume and figure out of love for Nationality—so my dear friend I am drawn towards you by a kindred sympathy, seeing that you are the best National painter of your country."[104]

But beyond some interesting advice on coloring technique, and a timely warning not to repeat his imagery overmuch (a warning Mount neglected), the communication revealed little more than the disordering tendencies that befall an Artist-

Patriot without a country. The Civil War, of course, relegated all talk of national art somewhat moot. It is striking how many of the aggressive cultural expansionists of the 1840s faded from sight during the war, as if crushed into submission by the national failure at reconciliation. Unlike Whitman, Mount took no active role in the war, and his creativity diminished every year the struggle continued. His lingering Jacksonian sympathies made it difficult to accept Republican dominion, and in 1867 he painted his final political paintings. Entitled *Politically Dead* and *Dawn of Day*, they lamely denounced the Republican use of the freedman issue by depicting a sleeping black man whom a rooster was trying to awaken. The unheeded rooster might more truthfully be said to have represented the decline of Mount's own constituency. The young post-Jacksonians of the 1840s, having crowed their hearts out, were no longer relevant to the complicated American scene.[105]

Despite the melancholy note of this dénouement, the great struggle to introduce art into the lives of the hustling and bustling American people in the 1840s was by no means an unmitigated failure. True, if we look at the Art-Union with a cursory glance, it does not appear to have been especially successful, having endured the grand total of thirteen years. But from a wider angle, we can see the influence it had sparking interest around the nation, and helping to build a network for distribution. For several years, in an age dominated by intense political, social, and economic anxieties, the Art-Union achieved unprecedented success in bringing its mail-order philosophy of fine art to the people. To quote J. J. Jarves again, "There was but little high art in this; but it was a right beginning, leaving the popular mind to choose its own loves, and, through its own experience, to advance gradually from lower thoughts and feelings to higher."[106]

Resembling and befriending the Young Americans, the chief exponents of nationalist art in the 1840s were a difficult, irascible lot, important not so much for the lasting quality of their work as for their rejection of any previous generation's monopoly on taste. Like Melville, Whitman, and other thinkers in the *Democratic Review*'s orbit, the genre painters intuitively recognized the value of what Melville called the "unvarnished" truth (an artist's word). The novelist articulated this notion of a flexible, populist expression, dependent upon the will of the people, in his public lecture on art:

> May it not possibly be, that as Burns perhaps understood flowers as well as Linnaeus, and the Scotch peasant's poetical description of the daisy, 'wee, modest, crimson-tipped flower,' *is rightly set above* the technical description of the Swedish professor, so in Art, just as in nature, it may not be the accredited wise man alone who, in all respects, is qualified to comprehend or describe.[107]

If the widespread representation of ordinary, unposed Americans did not in itself constitute an extraordinary artistic achievement, then the increased participation of those same people in the larger art-distribution process did. Together, the human realism of the genre artists and the widely felt influence of the American Art-Union enhanced the lives of countless numbers of "unaccredited" citizens whose lives had never been touched by art previously. Despite the brevity of this participatory moment, it introduced the democratic principle into what had been an ill-defined and aristocratic enclave of American culture.

5

The Young American Lexicon

Field and Codification

It has been said a thousand times, and will bear to be said a great many times again, that the history of a people may be gathered, and best-gathered, from its statute-books.

—David Dudley Field

And thus there seems a reason in all things, even in law.

—Herman Melville, *Moby-Dick*

Monument Mountain

On August 5, 1850, a group of mildly inebriated American intellectuals, in a rare display of physical hardihood, clambered up Monument Mountain, just south of Stockbridge in western Massachusetts. True, the "mountain" in question was only 1,640 feet high, but its ascent marked an important opportunity for several Young Americans to gather together and descant on their favorite topics. Indeed, this humble mountaineering expedition may well have signaled the apogee of Young America. The climbers included city slickers on vacation (Duyckinck, Mathews, Boston publisher James T. Fields), writers residing in the Berkshires (Hawthorne, Melville, Oliver Wendell Holmes), and two Stockbridge natives, Henry Dwight Sedgwick and David Dudley Field.

Everything about the outing was highly symbolic, as we might infer from the exhilaration with which the Young Americans dilated on it in the press afterward. The mountain had been chosen as the subject of Bryant's earlier poem of the same name, which Cornelius Mathews declaimed magniloquently during a cloudburst. A "considerable quantity" of champagne was consumed, and the Young Americans bantered incessantly about the superiority of American letters to England, a subliminal way of asserting New York's preeminence over Boston. Appropriately, the New Yorkers fared better on the hike than the New Englanders. Holmes "peeped about the cliffs and protested it affected him like ipecac," and Fields later claimed the mountain was six thousand feet high. Melville impressed Duyckinck as "the boldest of all" as he "bestrode a peaked rock, which ran out like a bowsprit, and pulled and hauled imaginary ropes." Perhaps sensing his irrelevance to the younger set, Holmes went home and composed a rather mean-spirited poem about the insignificance of Manhattan in the Bostonian scheme of things, which he read publicly a mere nine days after Monument Mountain. He particularly ridiculed the "titanic pygmies" of New York's "pseudo-critic-editorial race," fed on "Æolian beans" and therefore given to loud, windy opinions about national greatness.[1]

Melville scholars will recognize this event instantly, for it has been enshrined as one of the defining moments of his career, a vital gam before the completion of *Moby-Dick*. Annoyed by Holmes's taunts of English cultural superiority, he took up the gauntlet for the Young Americans and asserted the coming excellence of American letters, an excellence he was in the act of enacting. Two days later, Duyckinck correctly gauged his "presentment of the Whale Fishery," as "something quite new." A week later, chock full of patriotic invective, Melville began his famous encomium "Hawthorne and His Mosses." Hawthorne, whom he had met the day of the climb, was also enjoying his major phase, so the timing of the climb was highly propitious, representing in a sense the culmination of literary Young America. Or more accurately, its last gasp.[2]

For all the attention the outing has received, our understanding of it is still incomplete. The presence of Mathews, Duyckinck, and Hawthorne, all contributors to the *Democratic Review* and the Library of American Books, and all friendly with Melville, is accountable and has been duly noted by literary historians. The stuffy Bostonian element, represented by Holmes and Fields, makes less sense in this New Yorkish context, but can be explained by the former's property adjacent to Melville's in Pittsfield, and the latter's business relationship with Hawthorne. But the role of Field (and to a lesser extent Sedgwick) has never been properly interpreted, nor even much noticed. Yet Field was the presiding genius over the entire affair, and it was under his roof that the long-overdue rendezvous between Hawthorne and Melville was finally transacted.

A forty-five-year-old lawyer in 1850, Field was no novelist, yet his contribution to American intellectual independence was original and profound. Field's contribution lay in the area of jurisprudence, a region few literary theorists have explored, except to look specifically where it intersects with writing (i.e., copyright law), or to note the general phenomenon that a great number of American authors in the early republic were also trained as lawyers. Likewise, most legal historians, while cognizant of Field's eminence within their own discipline, have injudiciously overlooked his early dabbling in literature and politics, and his specific alliance with the Young America clique. Yet these literary friendships were entirely consonant with his desire to reduce American legal dependence on England and, in Melville's phrase, to make the people "all justiciaries in the same case themselves."[3]

A close look at the Berkshire outing reveals that Field conceived, organized, and subsidized the entire event. A resident of both Manhattan and Stockbridge who had written frequently for the *Democratic Review*, Field was well-acquainted with O'Sullivan and the Young Americans. When he bumped into Duyckinck and Mathews on the train from Manhattan (on their way to visit Melville), it was his idea "at once to arrange an admirable excursion in the neighborhood of the Mountain of the Monument." The group convened at his suggestion, departed from his house, and after the climb retired there again for the dinner at which Holmes and Melville debated.[4]

For *Moby-Dick* scholars, the Stockbridge outing is fascinating when one considers Melville's writing stage and the fact that a "Sea-Serpent" was discussed at dinner. There were even references to the event in *Moby-Dick*, as when Melville mentioned an "Icy Glen" in passing, the name of a local attraction the intellectuals visited after their meal. Surely there was a good deal of Young American bantering in the air, and Mathews, the author of *Behemoth*, would have had much to say on the subject of oversized fictitious animals. Holmes taunted the New Yorkers, aping Young America; "in less than twenty years it would be a common thing to grow in these United States men sixteen and seventeen feet high; and intellectual in proportion." These were the sarcastic remarks Melville attacked "vigorously," according to an admiring Duyckinck.[5]

During the three-hour dinner, the bibulous party was joined by other Berkshire personalities, including the erstwhile Young American Joel Headley. Headley, who had been a minister at Stockbridge before turning to literature, had written for Duyckinck's Library of American Books and delivered Young America's stinging attack on imitative art at the American Art-Union in 1845. Later in the day, Catharine Maria Sedgwick dropped in, giving Duyckinck, the former lawyer, a "cross examination" on *Hope Leslie*, which he wrote his wife, "I did not stand very well on."[6]

Another guest at Field's dinner, never before noticed, completed the sense of convergence felt in Stockbridge that day. The guest, whom Cornelius Mathews described only as "a most lady-like and agreeable conversationalist, mother of a distinguished democratic reviewer," was almost certainly O'Sullivan's mother, the celebrated Madame O'Sullivan. Not only was she a long-term Stockbridge visitor, and close to the Sedgwicks, but her presence makes sense when the overall composition of the group is considered. For Field, Duyckinck, Mathews, and Hawthorne had a common bond in their *Review* experience, and Melville was no stranger to their machinations.[7]

Several nights later, Melville held a drunken masquerade for his wordy friends, one of whom, "a sturdy man, some six feet in height, and a practicing attorney withal," committed an execrable pun and was forcibly defenestrated from the premises. With childlike relish, Mathews related it was "an awful pun, portentous, ill-timed, rude, unseemly, mean, inhospitable, villainous, and so complicated in its scoundrelism as to cause the sudden and violent ejection of its maker out of a back door into the door-yard grass at midnight." It boggles the mind to realize this tipsy punster was likely the six-foot-tall David Dudley Field, shorn of his usual dignity.[8]

In this chapter I hope to provide a sense of the ligaments connecting Field's nationalistic legal reform with the Young American quest for a self-generated literary culture. This *Review* contributor, as "Young American" in his way as O'Sullivan and Duyckinck, devoted his life to the codification of American law, the rejection of English precedent, and the substitution of fresh language for stilted legal prose. As the frivolities atop Monument Mountain indicated, the two movements overlapped meaningfully. Ranging afield of their expertise, legal and literary thinkers trespassed into each other's bailiwicks, and as usual, O'Sullivan was mixed up in it all. Whether a lawyer or not, everyone who ascended Monument Mountain in August 1850 was concerned with the "construction" of American culture. From Catharine Sedgwick giving Duyckinck a "cross examination," to the incessant wordplay indulged in by Field, Mathews, and Melville, all the players in this mid-century drama felt the interconnectedness of law and language.

In other words, Field's presence that day on Monument Mountain was entirely consistent. In the 1840s, the rhetoric of legal reform dovetailed with the Young American campaign for a new American literature, and the *Democratic Review* served as the linchpin connecting these intersecting nodes of intellection. In the process, it gave voice to the aspirations not only of a specific generation, but also of an interesting regional combination of thinkers in western Massachusetts and upstate New York. Furthermore, there is evidence that many writers, including Melville and Whitman, were listening to the debates over legal language. In both law and letters, aggressive thinkers in the Young American camp advanced the case that American reality was new, and that therefore a different linguistic and legal apparatus was needed to define it. These efforts fit comfortably alongside Manifest Destiny, which was nothing if not a legal argument against obsolete claims to the land.

Precedents

Like most things juridical, the codification movement, so distrustful of the past, enjoyed a long prehistory before Field arrived on the scene. He mirrored O'Sullivan's paradox, for his futuristic yearnings were linked to latent beliefs handed down from previous generations. In fact, judging from his early influences, it was almost inevitable he would take an interest in legal reform.

The codification movement was one of the great themes of nineteenth-century American legal history. It achieved only partial success, at best, yet it still excites attention as an unusually daring exertion of the cumbrous legal mind. Groaning under the weight of ancient English law, the codifiers tried to modernize the profession by reducing a millennium's worth of legalese into compact, comprehensible written codes of procedural and substantive law. The movement was most lively in New York, where the shortcomings of an outdated legal system were rendered acutely visible by the pressures brought to bear amidst turbulent social change and explosive growth. Field argued in 1852: "The number of souls in this city in 1846, was about 400,000; it is now about 600,000. . . . This city is the center of commerce, the point of exchange, of the State and the Union, nay, of the continent itself."[9]

More than a specific question pertaining to a narrow discipline, the debate over America's legal inheritance invited judgment on literary and intellectual matters with profound ramifications for ordinary citizens. The argument over the degree to which "new" American law should be rooted in "old" English custom evoked bitter struggles over cultural values and the role of language in determining reality. From simple word choices to the applicability of remote Latin phrases, the topics debated by American legal theorists resembled nothing so much as an exegetical quarrel among literary critics.

Indeed, the law was often likened to literature. For many Americans, the mere sound of ancient English precedent was enough to render it void of meaning. Hatred of feudalism was an old American complaint, particularly common among the revolutionary generation. Thomas Jefferson complained of the "verbiage, the barbarous tautologies and redundancies which render the British statutes unintelligible," and longed for the simpler code the founding fathers had not dared implement for fear of disruption while the new government was tested.[10]

For all its vaunted independence after the Treaty of Paris, the United States still followed the unwieldy body of English precedent known as the common law. As Field defined it, the common law was "the customary law of England, as it existed before the coronation of Richard the First, which was in 1189." Despite their bluster, postrevolutionary Americans were still governed in their daily actions by obscure medieval cases and the opinions of feudal judges handed down centuries earlier.[11]

Making matters worse, many Americans were particularly disturbed by equity, an adjunct branch of the law created in the thirteenth century to provide special attention to cases where the common law was unclear. Though designed to increase the fairness with which justice was meted out, equity (or chancery, as it was also referred to) suffered from its historic link to the monarchy. In the English Revolution, the Chancellor and the chancery judges had largely supported the crown while the common law judges had gone with Parliament. Many Americans, revering Cromwell as the inspiration for their own revolution, were attuned to these associations, and found the outdated terminology required in chancery actions even more galling than the common law.

Following the Revolution, the states moved in varying degrees to modernize their legal systems, but the feudal taint of the common law still lurked near the surface. There were many reasons this disquieted Americans, and not only because of the predilection for un-English thinking favored by Anglophobes like the Young Americans. The difficulty of learning the common law tended to confer unnecessary distinction upon lawyers, to separate them into what Tocqueville observed as a false aristocracy. As he noted, "the bulk of the nation is scarcely acquainted" with its legislation. In contrast to England and the United States, France since Napoleon had encouraged popular apprehension of legal principles. As with literature, this was a function of reading:

> The French codes are often difficult to comprehend, but they can be read by everyone; nothing on the other hand, can be more obscure and strange to the uninitiated than a legislation founded upon precedents. . . . The French lawyer is simply a man extensively acquainted with the statutes of his own country; but the English or American lawyer resembles the hierophants of Egypt, for like them he is the sole interpreter of an occult science.[12]

Yet another, more baldly political reason for sentiment against the common law was its concentration of power in the conservative hands of the judges appointed to interpret it. These magistrates were by nature more reactionary than the legislative bodies enacting statute law. Worse, from the Democratic perspective, they were particularly aggressive in the Jacksonian period, dominating juries and attempting to mold the common law into a set of precedents that allowed unchecked economic expansion at the expense of personal liberty. Conservative judges, for example, were particularly hostile toward the insurgent labor consciousness of the period. Equity law was even more dependent on judicial caprice, as confirmed by Chancellor Kent's remark, "I most always found principles suited to my views of the case." For all of these reasons, the idea of an American Code, loosely modeled on the Code Napoléon, grew into a powerful desideratum among populistic thinkers.[13]

Codification received important impetus early in the century from the unlikely hand of Edward Livingston, descended from one of New York's old patroon families. Livingston was elected to several political offices as a Jeffersonian, but in 1803 he removed to the newly American city of New Orleans after an underling misused public funds (he was mayor of New York at the time). Here he learned a good deal about the problems of inefficient jurisprudence. New Orleans was a babel of cultures and jurisdictions, or as the *Review* later put it, "a vast miscellany of Spanish customs, French decrees, English precedents, and conflicting legislative enactments." It was a perfect laboratory for the effects of uniform American law on a multiform people.[14]

Livingston enjoyed a long and fruitful career in Louisiana, allying himself with Jackson, for whom he became secretary of state and minister to France. In his second identity as a Louisianan elder statesman, Livingston did much to retool the state's legal apparatus, introducing a state penal code in 1825 and writing widely read treatises on the need for simplified law. His words resonated for the new generation of Jacksonians: "Your criminal code is no longer to be the study of a select few: it is not the design of the framers that it should be exclusively the study even of our own sex; and it is particularly desirable, that it should become a branch of early education for our youth."[15]

Livingston's message was continued by his brother-in-law Auguste Davezac (or D'Avezac), a Haitian-Louisianan lawyer living and breathing among New Yorkers in the 1840s. In his advanced age, the indefatigable Davezac became a *Review* contributor on literary and political matters, served in the New York legislature, and helped O'Sullivan in his campaign to abolish capital punishment. He brought a peculiar Gallic humor to the deadly serious business of reform, and of course had no special respect for the English common law. Whitman admired his "bald head" and "significant individuality." Duyckinck knew him also, and during his European travels, they held a long, reverential conversation about Andrew Jackson.[16]

But even before Davezac's arrival in New York, Livingston's reforms had inspired many young Americans. Democrats, frustrated by the conservative stranglehold on the judiciary, were always interested in new strategies of fighting Whiggery, and two of the politicians who helped launched the *Review* were special admirers of Livingston. Henry Gilpin, Van Buren's attorney general, was a devoted acolyte and authored Livingston's necrology, as well as his profile in the *National Portrait Gallery*. Benjamin Butler, attorney general under Jackson, devoted the early part of his life to emulating the Louisiana codes.[17]

In the early 1820s, there was a mounting sense around the United States that legal reform was both necessary and imminent. The agitation was acute in New York, just entering the meridian of its influence. The state constitution had been revised in 1821, and as its organic law went into effect on the first day of 1823, it became apparent to many observers that a revision of statute law was also necessary. With the massive influx of commerce following the Erie Canal, New Yorkers expected sea change in every category of existence, and a legal infrastructure flexible enough to accommodate it. Swept along by the nineteenth century, anxious Gothamites recognized the need for a streamlined, comprehensible system of jurisprudence to impose order on what was becoming a bewildering social reality.[18]

As this provincial seaport became the American emporium, it found the old guidelines regulating commerce and expansion restrictive. Indeed, there was often a direct correlation between the pace of growth and the antipathy young entrepreneurs felt toward the trammels of the common law. They felt special hostility toward the chancery courts, where the backlog of cases was enormous and, as we have seen, judicial power and linguistic antiquity were both concentrated.[19]

The New Yorkish impatience for reform was hastened by the influx of a number of radical foreign lawyers in the early decades of the nineteenth century. Forced to emigrate from Europe in the reactionary years following the French and Irish revolutions, these incendiaries had no place to go except the United States. Thomas Addis Emmet, for example, came to New York in 1804 following his participation in the United Ireland movement of 1798 and brief exile in France and Holland. Another refugee was William Sampson, who was imprisoned after joining the United Ireland movement and emigrated to New York in 1806 after six years in Napoleonic France. Sampson gained prominence soon after his arrival for his 1810 defense of journeymen cordwainers, which articulated the union concept of the closed shop.[20]

In 1823 Sampson leapt into the fray of legal reform with an "Anniversary Discourse" he delivered before the New-York Historical Society. This address, purporting to show "the Origin, Progress, Antiquities, Curiosities, and Nature of the Common Law," was one of the earliest to state clearly the case for American codification and was partly inspired by Livingston's progress in Louisiana. The failed Irish revolutionary insisted the American Revolution, too, was somehow incomplete, that "one thing should still be wanting to crown the noble arch—A NATIONAL CODE."[21]

Sampson's speech before the Historical Society instantly adopted the juvenescent tack that would become so familiar in the 1840s:

> It is perhaps to be regretted, that the youth who dedicate themselves to the study of our legal constitutions, should be greeted on the threshold with phrases strange to the ears of freedom: that they cannot enter the vestibule without paying constrained devotion to the idols which their fathers have levelled in the dust. . . . Impressions thus stamped on young minds, are not quickly eradicated, and if once taught to believe, that excellence is only to be found abroad, they will not care to seek for it at home.[22]

Sampson attacked the common law with all the tropes of feudalism: It was a "mazy labyrinth" with "grotesque forms," the "wild result of chance and rude convulsions." He ridiculed those who esteemed the "pristine vigour" of the common law by likening this ancestor worship to druidical human sacrifices and "magic astrology." Sampson's conjuring of these mysteries was brilliantly satirical:

> These people, (it may be said), long after they had set the great example of self-government upon principles of perfect equality, . . . had still one pagan idol to which they daily offered up much smoky incense. They called it by the mystical and cabalistic name of Common Law. A mysterious essence. Like the Dalai Lama, not to be seen or visited in open day; of most indefinite antiquity; . . . to be worshipped by ignorant and superstitious votaries.[23]

After ridiculing the notion that ancient British law supported popular liberty, Sampson reverted to the simple but essential statement all codifiers would revert to: "Our condition is different from theirs." Adumbrating O'Sullivan, he called for Americans to enact a system "worthy of our destinies." Indeed, the peroration of Sampson's address cast the argument in the same metageographical language that would thrill Manifest Destinarians two decades later. Combining legal progress with the whiff of westward expansion, Sampson invoked the nation of futurity:

> When this is done, and our untrammelled jurisprudence shall expand to the measure of our growing fortunes, its history will . . . be imaged, if we must speak in metaphor, by a mighty river, which in some lonely barren desert, first issues from its native rock. When yet a slender stream it only serves to slake the tyger's thirst, and that of his fellow savage man. Next a foaming torrent, wild as the scenes through which it drives its headlong desultory course. By a predestined ordinance descending still, it gains the fertile plain. Uniting there with kindred waters and tributary streams it takes a milder aspect, and on its polished surface stand reflected, commerce, and arts, and all that can embellish sublunary schemes, till last of all it feels the ocean's swell, and bears upon its heaving bosom the wealth of nations and treasures of the earth.[24]

In the immediate aftermath of the speech, several events took place that would involve future players in the Young America scene. Benjamin F. Butler, twenty-seven years old at the time, launched the first serious attempt to introduce the principles of codification into the state's jurisprudence. Butler had already been writing on the extension of the suffrage, and this appeared to him a new area in which to enlarge the sphere of democracy. With the support of his law partner, Martin Van Buren, Butler proposed that "the mass of disconnected statutes" be replaced by "a new and complete system of original laws." Disdaining the "prolixities, uncertainties and confusions" of the English common law, Butler promised to write in clear, modern American.[25]

The strategy worked, and Butler was appointed by the legislature to a small committee to revise the state statute law from 1824 to 1828. The resulting "Revision," as it was called, was a great achievement of verbal simplification, although it deliberately shunned the term "codification" to avoid stirring up specters of the French Revolution. The Revision appeased judicial conservatives with its respectful maintenance of certain elements of the common law, but it did revolutionize the language of the law. Reviewing it, the Albany *Argus* reflected, "Among the multitude of new things, perhaps there is no good reason we should not have new words."[26]

Butler would use this great achievement as the springboard for his subsequent political career. He maintained an interest in legal theory throughout his life and organized the law school of the University of New York in the mid-1830s. In a sense, he too was represented in Stockbridge in August 1850, for his son William Allen Butler, a close friend of the Duyckinck brothers, and a lawyer and writer like the rest of them, arrived four days after the climb up Monument Mountain. Immediately "captured" by Melville and Duyckinck at the Pittsfield station and whisked off to Melville's masquerade, he shared in the Young American frenzy of chestbeating in western Massachusetts as *Moby-Dick* was nearing completion.[27]

Another after-effect of Sampson's speech, related to Butler's Revision, was the galvanization of energies among a small but influential clique of lawyers hailing from Stockbridge. Almost as soon as Sampson's speech was delivered, the prestigious *North American Review* decided to review it from Boston. The assignment was logically doled out to Henry Dwight Sedgwick, a Stockbridge lawyer with a successful practice in Manhattan, familiar with the vagaries of both Boston and New York. Sedgwick had impeccable credentials for the task, having written a treatise on the common law. He was the son of the old Federalist judge Theodore Sedgwick, the leading lawyer in western Massachusetts.[28]

But despite the patrician lineage, the Sedgwicks were beginning to turn out contrarian opinions, as the editors of the *North American Review* learned to their chagrin in 1824. Sedgwick did not take Sampson to task for his fiery speech; indeed he rather admired it. Less incendiary than the Irish revolutionary, he still agreed that American expansion and rapid social change would produce a "revolution in its jurisprudence," and that it was ridiculous to apply "old rules" to "new relations and new things." Before relocating, Sedgwick had practiced in Massachusetts, which had reformed its jurisprudence somewhat, and he found New York's befogged system "absurdly technical and embarrassing." Like Benjamin Butler, he was also represented by a son in August 1850; Henry Dwight Sedgwick II accompanied Field, Duyckinck, Melville, and Hawthorne up Monument Mountain.[29]

Henry was not the only Sedgwick to show an interest in "new things." Indeed, a progressive interest in world liberalism united the entire brood. Henry and his brother Robert went to great lengths to assist embattled Greek revolutionaries to secure a frigate in New York in the 1820s. His sister Catherine Maria Sedgwick helped settle a small band of recently freed Young Italians in Stockbridge in the late 1830s. Bryant remembered the Sedgwick salon vividly even decades later: "The houses of the two brothers . . . were the resort of the best company in New York, cultivated men and women, literati, artists, and occasionally, foreigners of distinction." As the poet recalled, Henry Sedgwick's legal thinking was very much caught up in this intellectual ferment, and he took a "vivid interest" in young Benjamin Butler's revisions. Indeed, the whole group did; Bryant wrote, "How much we all admired him."[30]

Several other Sedgwicks offer an interesting glimpse at the sustenance of codification in the Housatonic Valley before Field came along. Yet another sibling of Henry's, Theodore Sedgwick II, continued the family iconoclasm by declaring himself a Jacksonian partisan. He also authored several works which he expressly dedicated to his unsophisticated readers. In his *Hints for the People* he stated, "I desire to write so as to be understood by the *people*." Likewise, in *Hints to My Countrymen* he stated, "I write primarily for the American labourer." Henry Sedgwick had voiced the same concern in his 1822 pamphlet on the common law, arguing that it was a question of reading comprehension: "I wish to be clearly and distinctively understood, by men of plain common sense." Similarly, Catharine Maria Sedgwick would devote her 1839 novel *Home* "to farmers and mechanics."[31]

This point should not be dismissed immediately, for a desire to elevate the common reader's understanding of the law was at the root of codification. In this campaign, the Sedgwicks were not far removed from the early Young Americans, either ideologically or personally. Sedgwick's long-term law partner in Albany was the amiable Dutchman, Harmanus Bleecker, who served as a mentor to the young Evert Duyckinck. The elder lawyer accompanied Duyckinck during his rite-of-passage through Holland, France, and England in 1839, and he exerted a lasting influence on his young charge. Reveling in their common ethnicity, Duyckinck wrote filial letters to Bleecker filled with reform instincts. He quoted Channing's address on labor, approved of literature for the working class, and added a Young American flourish, "We have to cope with a new state of things and must make the best of them."[32]

This was certainly the philosophy of Theodore Sedgwick III, the son of Theodore II, and a legal reformer in his own right, acting as a linchpin between the activism of the 1820s and the 1840s. A missing puzzle piece of sorts, Theodore III knew O'Sullivan well, and graduated two years ahead of him at Columbia (1829). His Young American credentials were impressive. In 1840 he edited the works of William Leggett for publication, a true labor of love. Sedgwick also served as an attaché of the American Legation while Edward Livingston was minister to France in 1833-34. In the latter capacity, he provided important assistance to Tocqueville, whom he had met previously in Stockbridge, as he was assembling *Democracy in America*. Their acquaintance may explain the freedom with which the Frenchman criticized American dependence on the common law. Like the other young Democrats, Sedgwick ardently endorsed the French along with the American Revolution, believing they were "parts of the same vast drama, commenced here at Lexington, and closed at Waterloo."[33]

Sedgwick devoted himself to egalitarian politics and pamphleteering on his return from France. In 1845 he answered the Locofoco query, *What is a Monopoly?* From there it was a short step to legal reform. In 1838 another tract of his attacked the slowness of legal proceedings in the New York court of chancery, and he retained an interest in legal reform throughout his life. Sedgwick also wrote a memoir of his forebear William Livingston, New York's original legal compiler.[34]

From Henry to Theodore III, the Sedgwicks kept the question of codification alive until Field, their young protégé, took it up again in the 1840s. Beyond this specific lineage of legal dissent, Field's early political orientation was strongly affected by the geographical and cultural configuration of the Berkshire region. It is more than coincidental that the codifiers—Livingston, Butler, Sedgwick, and Field—all hailed from within fifty miles of each other. Despite its ancient status as a stronghold of congregational polity, the Berkshire region was far removed from the New England seaboard and the dominance exerted by Boston. Only three dozen miles or so inland from the Hudson River, and closer still to Van Buren's Kinderhook, many of these western Massachusetts intellectuals looked to New York and Albany for ideological sustenance. Henry and Robert Sedgwick emigrated to

Manhattan to accelerate their legal careers, and other Berkshiremen traveled just across the border to Columbia County and the Albany region, where they in turn exerted a strong influence on upstate New York and its peculiar politics.

Many ambitious young intellects in the Stockbridge-Albany-Manhattan triangle gravitated toward the Democracy, in rather the opposite pattern of the young gentry of Boston. Butler wrote of Kinderhook, "I was born and cradled under the principles of democracy." The younger Henry Sedgwick, who ascended Monument Mountain, cherished an early memory shouting a lusty "Hurrah for Jackson!" as Van Buren was visiting Stockbridge in 1835. The vice president patted his head, adding, "How interesting it is to see the instincts of Democracy sprung up at this tender age!" Sedgwick added humorously he especially loved a regional confection known as "Jackson Balls." Many Democratic visitors, from Van Buren to Silas Wright, Thomas Dorr, and O'Sullivan, spent time in Stockbridge as it became a fashionable summer retreat. Appropriately, the *Review* praised it as a simulacrum of the perfect democratic society, where "the poorer and richer classes mutually respect each other, according to individual character and desert."[35]

Needless to say, the nearby presence of a great party chieftain like Van Buren could turn an ambitious young man's head, and a regional axis of sympathetic Democrats wielded power until well after the Civil War. The way in which this group perpetuated itself is fascinating in its own right, for it developed a sophisticated network of placement and apprenticeship for new thinkers, almost all of whom appear to have been trained to dislike the common law. Talented young men like Samuel Tilden, John Bigelow, and John Edmonds were identified early as promising prospects, then given training in a law office before becoming Democratic politicians.[36]

Kinderhook had already supplied a remarkable number of talented lawyers before the Jacksonian period. Even before Butler, two other villagers had revised New York's statutes (Peter Van Schaack in 1773, and W. P. Van Ness in 1813). But Stockbridge left an even better tally. At the end of the nineteenth century, it had supplied two Supreme Court justices, both from the Field family (Field's brother Stephen and his nephew David Joseph Brewer). Another hailed from neighboring South Lee (Henry B. Brown). If one adds Oliver Wendell Holmes, Jr., who spent summers at his father's house in Pittsfield, the list of Berkshire jurists is truly daunting.[37]

Considering the antecedents and internecine entanglements of the codification movement just before its champion appeared, it becomes clear that Field was working in a long-standing continuum, one in which geography and family played a large role. It is not important to know the whereabouts of each of these isolated thinkers at every moment, but an awareness of the Berkshire-Upper Hud-son alliance enhances an understanding of codification and deepens our grasp of the Monument Mountain excursion. In an attempt to link these many fragments, I hope to argue once again the centrality of the *Democratic Review* to the situation.

Field and Young America

Looking at the Anglophobic tradition of attacking the common law, beginning with Francophiles and Irishmen like Livingston, Davezac, Sampson, and Butler, and sustained by the Sedgwicks and David Dudley Field, it is difficult to imagine how O'Sullivan and his friends could have been anything but sympathetic. The *Democratic Review* paid lavish attention to Livingston's reforms, even well after the fact. Besides printing fragments of his "Unpublished Reminiscences," the magazine frequently cited Livingston's latitudinarian spirit, particularly when O'Sullivan undertook his quest to eliminate capital punishment in the early 1840s. In July 1841, a two-part article on "Edward Livingston and His Codes" inaugurated the newly refurbished *Review* in its New York incarnation. The two articles called out for adoption of a similar code in New York, arguing that American dependence on unwritten law from the murky past was "the primal, vital, radical error." The *Review* even took the rare step of criticizing the revolutionary generation for not having gone far enough in abolishing English customs. In a nutshell, it renounced "judge-made law," which leaned toward conservatism, particularly in matters relating to labor, and promoted a more populistic "legislature-made law." One *Review* writer proposed eliminating "the whole mass of English law" and all judicial opinions, relying instead on trial by jury as the closest approximation of democratic government in meting out justice.[38]

O'Sullivan was trained in the law, as were Duyckinck and many of the lesser luminaries working for the *Review*. One of O'Sullivan's earliest articles attacked the conservative Anglophilia of the Supreme Court. As usual, he did not mince words. He called the Dartmouth College case a "monstrum horrendum," and extending his Latinate parody of legal discourse, lamented the Supreme Court had "gravely resolved that laws may be retrospective, unjust and despotic, ad libitum — ad deliquium — ad nauseam."[39]

Admiration for English jurisprudence especially infuriated him as "an Ostrogrothic halt in our march" toward the glorious American future. He continued the critique in 1839, attacking "our British-law-trained legislators" for pro-English policies and lamenting the "imitativeness" of those who study "the laws, institutions and antiquities of other nations." Law and literature were wrapped up together in the problem, and "the irrational stuff of law libraries" was as detrimental to American progress as "the metaphysics of colleges" and "the theocracy of priests." Put simply, old English law was Whiggish: "Taught to look abroad for the highest standards of law, judicial wisdom, and literary excellence, the native sense is subjugated to a most obsequious idolatry of the tastes, sentiments, and prejudices of Europe. Hence our legislation, jurisprudence, literature, are more reflective of foreign aristocracy than of American democracy."[40]

Like the Sedgwicks, O'Sullivan believed that a body of law, to be meaningful, must be "perfectly intelligible to the commonest of the common people." American law was found wanting: "Our laws are hidden from us in such a multitude of books, and couched in such uncouth phraseology and technicality, that when we happen to read any of them, they are utterly beyond the comprehension of the people." O'Sullivan's conclusion was surely strengthened by his long familiarity with Stockbridge and the Sedgwicks. When he exhausted himself in 1839, he recuperated there, and his correspondence suggests he had visited many times previously. An 1836 letter to Thomas Dorr, for example, mentioned Stockbridge, where the genteel rabble-rousers probably met.[41]

At any rate, O'Sullivan was sufficiently part of the Stockbridge milieu to throw "Berkshire" parties in his Manhattan dwelling, according to Catharine Maria Sedgwick:

> Last evening was a Berkshire at the O'Sullivans'. Alexander Everett is staying with them. They are living at one end of the University, the prettiest rooms in New York, with pointed Gothic windows and paneled doors, and the loveliest silver lamps lighted with gas. The pictures of five generations of the O'S's over the mantel-piece in little, encircling a Madonna portrait of M. and A. — in short, everything in keeping with these most picturesque of all the moderns.

The moderns were less picturesque to the *New York Herald*, which poked fun at the Berkshire set: "Mr. O'Sullivan has been working very hard for five or six years to get into the *Evening Post* and Sedgwick clique of the city — and alas! he has succeeded. Poor young man! He really deserved a better fate."[42]

Shortly after his Berkshire idyll, when he relocated the *Democratic Review* to New York, O'Sullivan began to work closely with Field. They had undoubtedly met previously, for both were writing their mutual friend Thomas Wilson Dorr in the mid-1830s and musing on common topics and acquaintances. Field was eight years older than the editor, born in 1805, but he fit the Young American profile despite the slight seniority.[43]

Like the Sedgwicks, he sprang from Federalist stock. His father, from whom all three of his names came, was an eminent New England divine with an antiquarian bent. He had been the Congregational pastor at Haddam, Connecticut, and Stockbridge and authored histories of the Berkshire region. Despite, or more probably because of this respectable background, the junior Field failed to graduate from Williams College after leading a student insurrection against harsh disciplinary practices. Judging from early diaries, he was always obstreperous. Of his college days, he wrote, "No man's authority was acknowledged. Opinions which had become long current in the world, dogmas that had been handed down from our forefathers, even the writings of the greatest men, were no authority with me." It is small wonder he was expelled.[44]

Also like the Sedgwicks, the Fields were strangely attracted to insurgency. Field's sister Emilia had witnessed the Greek Revolution while traveling with her missionary husband in the 1820s; another, Mary, saw the Hungarian and Italian revolutions of 1848 and described them for the *New York Observer*. Likewise, his brother Henry Field was in Paris in 1848 and sent his own reports of that revolution to the *Observer*. Henry Field later wrote a book on the Irish uprising of 1798. When Field himself traveled to England in 1836, he noted with relish a rabid speech by O'Connell in Parliament. Could O'Sullivan have failed to admire a family after his own heart?[45]

Following the ignominy of his hasty departure from Williams, Field apprenticed to become a lawyer, looking westward to New York rather than eastward to Boston. Encouraged by Theodore Sedgwick II, he clerked for six months with Harmanus Bleecker in Albany, then continued to train in the offices of his fellow townsmen Henry and Robert Sedgwick in Manhattan. In September 1825, he recorded arriving in "the great capital of wealth and power," sounding like Rastignac at the end of *Père Goriot*: "The world was all before me. I was now beyond, not only the roof, but the care of my father. Everything depended upon myself, whether I should sink into obscurity and want, or make myself and mine comfortable and respected. There were but two or three whom I could call my friends, in a city of two hundred thousand people."[46]

Of course, those "two or three" happened to be the influential Sedgwicks, which lessened the hardship considerably. He boarded in the same house as another Berkshire emigrant, William Cullen Bryant. Field also lived in French and Spanish boardinghouses to improve his linguistic skills, and he recorded in his journal the contempt he felt for "poor souls" with only "English ideas and English prejudices," formed from "English books." Since college, he had believed "the French are in advance of the rest of the world," and he nurtured the same democratic obsessions that characterized the other Young Americans ("In my politics I am throroughly, even democratically republican"). He loved American history, adding, "That of our revolution is, it seems to me, the most eloquent story in the annals of the world." But the revolution had not extended yet to American culture: "The people of this country do not yet fully comprehend their situation. The philosophy of their own government has not yet been sufficiently developed to their eyes. When that philosophy shall be well unfolded, how interesting, how welcome, how glorious will it be!"[47]

It was inevitable the ambitious young apprentice would interest himself in an issue embroiling his legal mentor in controversy. Henry Sedgwick's sanguine review of Sampson in the *North American Review* had been published shortly before Field's arrival. Field began reading on the subject and was impressed by Livingston's 1822 report on the feasibility of codes in Louisiana and Sampson's speech the year after. In 1836 Field underwent a personal crisis when his wife died. He left his children with his parents and took a long trip to Europe, where he studied foreign law closely. Disgust crept into his voice when he saw the "grotesque" wigs and gowns of the English judges, "whose favor had extended over my own continent." Upon return, he was further tested by the Panic of 1837 (he was "embarrassed for several years"), but he now knew his destiny. As O'Sullivan began the *Review* and Duyckinck started his publishing projects, Field committed himself passionately to legal reform.[48]

Interest in the question was heating up again in many quarters. The Massachusetts statutes were revised in 1836, and there was increased agitation for codification among moderates like Joseph Story and more radical (usually Democrat) reformers who felt workingmen were at a disadvantage under common law jurisprudence. Robert Rantoul, Jr., for example, was valiantly pursuing the same triumvirate of issues Livingston had explored, and which O'Sullivan and Field would shortly discover. He proposed penal reform, abolition of capital punishment, and codification in the 1830s and continued to do so until his premature death in 1852. In a speech he gave on July 4, 1836, Rantoul excoriated the common law as a vestige of "the dark ages," replete with "folly, barbarism, and feudality." Disdaining the retrospective tendency of judges who consider "precedents are everything: the spirit of the age is nothing," he intoned, "We must have democratic governors, who will appoint democratic judges, and the whole of the law must be codified." In his journal, Emerson had noted "the Volume of Revised Statutes" as one of the "genuine works of the times." More publicly, he proclaimed in the first paragraph of *Nature*, "There are new lands, new men, new thoughts. Let us demand our own works and laws and worship."[49]

The issue was lively in New York as well. In 1839 Field plunged headlong into the cause. That year, Gulian Verplanck, the erstwhile Democrat who supported copyright and American art, gave a speech in the New York Senate urging that Americans learn from the "experimental jurisprudence" of their own reality rather than build a simulacrum of foreign life. Verplanck was a moderate, rejecting drastic overhaul of the system, but even more strongly disdaining the "fancied wisdom" that refuses to profit "by the experience of our own times." Inspired, Field wrote a supportive letter demanding reform of an overburdened legal system that denied justice to "great numbers of people." He had found the cause to which he would devote his career.[50]

By this point he was actively running with O'Sullivan. Following his trip to Europe, he published five "Sketches over the Sea" in the *Democratic Review*. These were for the most part simple travel articles about Scandinavia, but Field could not pass an opportunity to criticize Swedish jurisprudence, which had too many different courts and needed to be "opened up to the people." He became a frequent *Review* contributor thereafter. The two men were well suited for each other, and each adopted the other's pet reforms. O'Sullivan, elected to the state legislature in 1840, was amenable to Field's legal crusade and the two linked forces to draft statements on New York's need for a more expeditious system. Field publicly addressed a letter to O'Sullivan on January 1, 1842, urging him to introduce proposals for the "speedy administration of justice," which O'Sullivan did in the way of an appendix to a committee report. Field himself drafted three bills for legal reform, which O'Sullivan then submitted. Field ran for the assembly in 1841, but his cantankerous personality, so effective in the courtroom, did not endear him to voters.[51]

At the same time, O'Sullivan's chief passion was the abolition of capital punishment. The two issues were twinned together throughout the nineteenth century, and support for one usually translated into support for the other. Livingston had done much to popularize both causes in Louisiana, as had Rantoul in Massachusetts. Indeed their origin went back to the beginning of American codification, when Pennsylvania and Virginia revised their colonial statutes after the Revolution to reduce executions.

The similarity was evident in O'Sullivan's 1841 legislative report on capital punishment, with its citation of Rantoul and Livingston. The central tenet of his argument was that the old morality embodied in the Mosaic Law of the Bible had run its course and become atavistic in modern society. His dismissal of the old covenant paralleled Field's animus toward the common law: "It was the height of absurdity to claim any authority as applicable to other nations and tribes."[52]

Following his early travel pieces and their legislative collaboration, Field wrote more frequently for the *Democratic Review*, often venturing well beyond the law. Among other topics, he addressed the Dorr Rebellion and the Oregon question, two vital issues to the Democracy in the early 1840s. Field gained favor in the eyes of young Democrats in April 1841 with his ringing defense of Theodore Sedgwick's edition of the William Leggett papers in the conservative *New York Review*. Praising

Leggett particularly for his "AMERICAN PRINCIPLES" (in upper case, no less), he forecast his codification argument: "That there breathes in the institutions of this country a peculiar spirit, a spirit nowhere else to be found, no one can gainsay. A great fundamental principle lies underneath our polity." Lamenting that "we are a new nation with old opinions," Field urged "a new code of rights and duties" that would bring "new motives, new hopes."[53]

Field also seized the opportunity to treat the need for fresh literature: "Not being provided with a literature of his own, the American is subjected to two opposite systems of training; one from books, the other from the life which he sees around him." He derided the classics of romance and poetry, "which the old man holds above all price," and the young man is deceived to covet, as "useless" for the forward-thinking American. Like O'Sullivan and Duyckinck, he yearned for a national literature that avoided the "aristocratical" elements of European culture. Speaking of Leggett, and obviously also of himself, Field voiced the aspiration that united the Young Americans: "One who wishes to speak to the American people a language that they will all understand, and sentiments to which their hearts shall answer, must have studied much that the schools of Europe do not teach."[54]

This sort of writing pleased the young Democrats venerating Leggett's memory. Having accredited himself, Field stepped up his own literary activities. Perry Miller wrote that Field's "extracurricular" writings were "rare enough to make each word resounding," yet he wrote prolifically on a number of Young American themes, both political and literary. One of these themes was the study of Native American language, a subject directly related to the quest for indigenous literary material. America's pre-Columbian heritage was enjoying a vogue in the 1840s, stirred primarily by the researches of Henry R. Schoolcraft. Field jumped on the bandwagon, perhaps impelled by his interest in Stockbridge history. The *Democratic Review* pushed the cause cheerfully. An 1843 poem (possibly by Field) sang the praises of "The Indian Names of Stockbridge" with extensive footnotes explaining the localities, including Monument Mountain. A year later, Field wrote "The Journey of a Day," the story of a sightseeing tour of the Berkshires.[55]

This ethnological hobby culminated in one of Field's least persuasive arguments, but one that shows how intoxicating the climate of New York nationalism was in the mid-1840s. Field suggested the country adopt the unlikely name "Alleghania" to avoid confusion with other claimants to "America," a name he disliked for its European origin. The issue was buffeted around by the New-York Historical Society, where O'Sullivan, Field, Butler, Sedgwick, Bleecker, Duyckinck, and other *Review* principals were members. In 1845, at Field's suggestion, the society appointed a committee to study the national name, including him of course (along with Schoolcraft and the writer Charles Fenno Hoffman). This episode briefly aroused great interest in the press. O'Sullivan lavished attention through the *Review* and the *Morning News*, but the new name was doomed from the start.[56]

Nevertheless, the literary allies sprang into action. Caroline Kirkland prefaced her 1846 edition of *Western Clearings* (for Duyckinck's Library) by referring to "the United States of Alleghania." And William Gilmore Simms grew so absorbed in the topic that he wrote a lengthy letter to the society that digressed into a full-blown call for Manifest Destiny, showing once again how Young America's causes overlapped.

The "Anglo-Norman" people, he proclaimed, were "destined, in process of time, to swallow up, absorb or subject, all of the miserable, peevish and paltry people south of us. . . . Help us to secure Texas to our farthest southern boundaries!! Help us to gain a literary independence by a proper law of copyright, and be sure that we shall glory in the exclusive appropriation of the American name." Evidently, the ramifications of the Alleghanian debate extended at least as far as the Rio Grande.[57]

Trivial as this issue may seem from the legal perspective, it raised interesting questions. Like O'Sullivan, apprehensive about sectionalism after 1844, the lawyer asserted that American cultural conditions were unique, and that nationalistic expression would promote harmony between the regions:

> We believe that the people of all the states of this Union are one people; that they have national characteristics, and national ideas; that they are one in heart as one in character; with sympathies and bonds older than governments, and stronger than laws; and that if they were today broken into a score of republics, they would remain, like the Germans, one people, though many nations. What we want is a sign of our identity. We want utterance for our nationality.[58]

Furthermore, Field's lexical obsession with Indian language displayed a clear literary bent that joined him more closely with the writerly Young Americans. Cornelius Mathews had dwelt upon Native American themes in several works in the same period, from *Behemoth: A Legend of the Mound-builders* (1839) to the ambitious work he wrote for Duyckinck's Library, *Big Abel and the Little Manhattan* (1845). Simms's response shows even more emphatically the connections between literary patriotism and foreign policy. At the same time Field was engaged in these cultural projects, he was a member of the American Art-Union, where he saw all the other *Review* staffers.[59]

Although he opposed the annexation of Texas in 1844, Field also wrote two bellicose articles on the Oregon question in 1845, cheek by jowl with O'Sullivan's fulminations on Manifest Destiny (themselves an argument against the "cobweb tissues" of old precedents). The articles detailed the American legal claim to the territory and attacked the English quarterly reviews as "insane in their hatred of America and everything American." Foreseeing a day when American trading would open up the Pacific region and "the Asiatic mind," Field borrowed O'Sullivan's tropes to present his vision of a cultural empire stretching "from the ancient seat of the Aztecs to the Arctic Sea," and representing "the complete and final emancipation of the American mind from English influence." From his futuristic foreign policy to his literary dalliances, Field showed all the symptoms of full-blown Young Americanism.[60]

Amidst all this journalistic activity, Field also reconcentrated his effort to reform American jurisprudence. In April 1844 he prepared for the *Review* an article entitled "Study and Practice of the Law," which contained many of the ideas he would wrestle with over the next forty years. Despite its legalistic niceties, the article was consonant with the generational anxiety already displayed by O'Sullivan and Duyckinck. Field remembered the old bewigged, knee-buckled attorneys of his father's day, then stated: "The bar is now crowded with bustling and restless men. . . . A new race has sprung up and supplanted the old."[61]

Field's aperçu was not quite as dramatic as O'Sullivan's grandstanding, but it revealed the Young American ideology applied to law. By eliminating "all the jargon," indeed by wiping away "nine tenths" of the procedural forms through which justice was meted out, Field argued that a more conversant populace would gain immeasurably. As reported by his brother, his twin goals were "that the law as enacted by human governments should be founded in natural justice," and "that it should be set forth in the simplest and clearest language, so that it should be 'understanded [*sic*] of the people.'"[62]

Interest in legal reform was spreading in the 1840s, and not just in New York. The Rhode Island radical Thomas Dorr favored codification (despite his apprenticeship to Chancellor Kent in the 1820s), and he and Field exchanged mutually supportive letters from 1834 until Dorr's death in 1854. These letters, never before cited, force a reappraisal of each man and the degree to which they perceived their causes as related. Dorr has traditionally been dismissed as a power-hungry demagogue, yet he cherished many of the tenets held by the cerebral Young Americans. And Field's distinguished reputation did not prevent him from offering legal counsel to Dorr in 1844, adding, "I was never convinced of anything more firmly, than I am that the principles of your movement were the principles of our revolution."[63]

But despite Rhode Island's temporary relevance to Young America, Manhattan was always the epicenter of the struggle. New York was growing at breakneck speed, and the infusion of different cultures and ethnicities accentuated the need for modern, un-English jurisprudence, as it had in Livingston's Louisiana. In an intriguing history of New York constitutions written in 1848, Butler boasted of "the effects of the intermixture of the different races—the Dutch—the English, Scottish, and Irish—the French, Swedes and Germans—the Anglo-Americans, from the eastern colonies." This alembic atmosphere naturally promoted open-mindedness, and if it made New Yorkers "less homogeneous" than other states, it "also made them more liberal in their opinions, and more ready to adopt and to carry out, the spirit of progress and reform."[64]

The other Young Americans attached themselves to the cause with great zeal. Duyckinck and Mathews, lawyers of a sort, supported the allied issues of capital punishment reform and codification simultaneously. Early numbers of *Arcturus* raved over O'Sullivan's capital punishment report and Livingston's antecedent efforts. Duyckinck also ridiculed old common-law punishments: "Barbarous customs of the old English common law, the severities of trial by battle, the tests of witchcraft, are stories now for the amusement of children."[65]

The *Democratic Review* never ceased its enthusiasm. From John Bigelow's diary, with its record of dinner parties with O'Sullivan, Field, and the Sedgwicks, it appears a coterie of *Review* personalities were clustered around this one issue. Well after O'Sullivan's departure in 1846, the magazine supported Field's call for codification, declaring "the freshness of youth is around everything except the gnarled and misshapen trunk of law." It angrily denounced "the legerdemain of lawcraft," claiming it derived "its spurious wisdom from the age in which witches were burnt." The magazine even took the step of advocating popular election of the judiciary, which Field himself hesitated at. In the language of '48, it called judges "despots" and branded life appointments to the judiciary "a shoot from the doctrine of the divine right of kings."[66]

This leads to an important point about codification; its potency as a political weapon. Given the perception of most common law judges as older men with a conservative bent, young Democrats eagerly embraced a system that would reduce their influence. Dorr warned Field, "You are more merciful to the recreant judges, who seek to kill the new practice by misconstruction, than they deserve . . . do not resist too sparingly." Like his militant friend, Field felt no pity for the old men blocking his path: "The judges are usually advanced beyond the middle period of life; trained from their majority in habits of subservience to precedent; reposing on other men's studies, thinking the thoughts of their predecessors; looking only at the past."[67]

Field's star rose quickly in the late 1840s, and he gained attention as the nation's leading legal reformer. As the New York constitution of 1846 was debated, Field wrote furiously to urge specific reforms, and his influence was felt everywhere behind the proceedings. In 1846 he published a widely read series of articles on "The Reorganization of the Judiciary" in the *Evening Post* and *Morning News*. The fame he hungered for as an adolescent was suddenly on the horizon.

The new constitution was approved in November 1846, and it went into effect the first day of 1847, suddenly enacting many of Field's ideas. It eliminated barriers to the unification of law and equity, making that merger finally possible, and it created a three-man commission to further simplify state law. It was exactly the mandate he was looking for. The legislature appointed him to this commission, and he worked furiously at stripping away the legal flotsam and jetsam of centuries. The commission's first report was issued February 29, 1848, the same week that John Quincy Adams died, Walt Whitman arrived in New Orleans, and a revolution ignited in Paris.[68]

Field would have liked the timing, for he surely considered his work revolutionary. The report, which quickly became known as the Field Code, proposed a more streamlined law than had ever existed. The historic step was finally taken of unifying the common law and equity procedures, so the rights of all parties in an action might be adjudicated at once. Complex formalities and prolixities were alike subject to ejectment (the old feudal practice of evicting an unwelcome tenant, and one of the first words to go in the new American scheme). Foreign terms were eliminated, including ancient English words that were no longer comprehensible. The writ of habeas corpus, for example, was changed to "the writ of deliverance from prison." As Field wrote, in characteristically terse prose:

> Custom only has made them tolerable to the profession, while they have always been a jargon to the mass of the people. Our own language is rich enough to express all our ideas, and, especially in the construction of a new system of law, it should seem in better taste and wiser to make it wholly in the mother tongue of those who are to read it and be governed by it.[69]

The alternative Field proposed resonated with the optimism Young America temporarily felt in 1848 and also revealed Field's debt to the Sedgwicks. A litigant would now state his case "in ordinary and concise language, without repetition, and in such a manner as to enable a man of common understanding to know what is intended." After some consideration, the legislature enacted the first report into law on April 12, 1848 (to be operative July 1, 1848). As revolutions were sweeping away the aristocracies of Europe, the edifice of the common law finally appeared to be teetering on its foundations, ready for the death blow.[70]

It never came. Despite the excitement of the moment, the code's full implementation was delayed and complicated by foot-dragging legislators and lawyers reluctant to abandon their old frame of reference, as well as by several defects in its application to real life. Field continued to work feverishly, supported by his brethren in the Van Buren wing of the party, including Sedgwick, Butler, and Edmonds, all of whom evaluated the long-awaited reforms favorably. But he was never a very good politician (an early notebook said it all: "Can political problems be solved with mathematical precision?"). And after 1850, as American hopes for European liberalism waned, interest declined in codification. No one could know it then, but 1848 marked the high-water mark for Field's movement, just as it did for democratic idealism everywhere.[71]

For all the acclaim Field was achieving as a legal reformer, his attachment to the Democratic party was shrinking, largely as a result of the disgust most Van Buren Democrats felt after the 1844 nomination and their increasing anxiety over Texas. More than O'Sullivan, he had always spoken out against slavery, and he was one of the first Young Americans to find the Democracy unbearable. As late as September 1847 Field was giving Jacksonian speeches on the importance of strict construction to the *Review*, but he was simultaneously leading the migration of antislavery Democrats away from the party. At the Democratic state convention in Syracuse that month, he was ruled out of order when he urged a resolution endorsing the Wilmot Proviso. Following this insult, the antislavery "Barnburners" held their own convention at Herkimer, which overwhelmingly passed his motion, and set the foundation for the rise of the Free Soil party in 1848. In January 1848, Field, Sedgwick, and Butler further stressed the connection between codification and popular liberty by speaking at a rally in favor of the Roman states, then beginning their agitation. The tremendous excitement caused by the 1848 revolutions was easily translated into the codification struggle.[72]

But like most Young Americans, Field's later career did not bear out its early radical promise. As he gained stature, he issued fewer Jacksonian diatribes, particularly as the Democratic party disintegrated in the 1850s. He joined the Republicans in 1856 and was instrumental in shifting support away from Seward and toward Lincoln at the 1860 convention. He also participated in efforts toward a peace conference between North and South in 1861. Enriched by a second marriage, as well as his lucrative practice, he became a fixture of New York society, and George Templeton Strong described one his soirées as "a chaos of ill-assorted people and a babel of clack—enough to unsettle one's intellects permanently." Indeed, in old age he became very different from the young lawyer crusading against precedent. With his disputatious personality and his superior knowledge of legal arcana and obscure technicalities, he was known as the "king of the pettifoggers," a title the young Field would hardly have relished.[73]

After the war, Field acquired even more wealth as the highly paid counsel for clients of dubious moral standing, including Boss Tweed, Jay Gould, and James Fisk. He boasted, "My practice was the largest and my income from it the most that any lawyer had at the New York Bar, and probably at any Bar in the country." In 1872, responding to an anonymous critique by Henry Adams, he lashed out at those who asserted lawyers were required to only serve moralistic causes. His argument was neatly the opposite of the more idealistic one he himself had advanced in the *Democratic Review* in 1844, when he called law without morality a "revolting doctrine." It was said that he "would take retainers from Satan himself" and was often portrayed by the cartoonist Thomas Nast in exactly that position. His 1894 obituary read, "Mr. Field was not a popular man in any sense."[74]

Despite these changes, he never lost his attachment to codification and pushed for it until the end of his long life. He led several conferences on international law and negotiation, one of which he invited O'Sullivan to. His codes were more successful the further away from New York they were deployed, particularly in the West. He continued to revise his masterpiece, the 1848 Code, poring over it year by year as Whitman did with *Leaves of Grass*. It expanded likewise until by 1880 it had 3,356 sections. New York did enact his penal code in 1881, but rejected his civil code repeatedly. Like most of the Young Americans, Field's great legacy was his lasting rhetoric rather than a tangible achievement recognized at home.[75]

Yet the less savory aspects of Field's later career should not obscure appreciation of his achievement. In his 1848 Code and its later revisions, Field tried to reshape the course of American law, and he almost pulled it off. For all his later venality, Field was driven by a passion to revive the democratic intent of the Revolution. It was no coincidence the Field Code was released as revolution was breaking out all over Europe, for he and his fellow Young Americans saw the progress of world democracy as a united phenomenon, with American culture in the vanguard.

In 1852, shortly before he died, Thomas Dorr wrote to Field on the subject of his reforms. Field had kept Dorr informed of his work throughout the 1840s, and now Dorr gave his final imprimatur to the cause (he died two years later, just after Field visited him):

> It gives me great pleasure to see that you are making an American name by your well directed and persevering efforts to complete and secure the long needed reform in legal practice. Do not relax in your exertions till all the paths of the People shall be made strait and plain to the Temple of Justice, and the enormous system of chicanery under which they have groaned so long shall be fairly prostrated. Then the good time will have come for reaching the great reforms in the law itself which the People require. . . . I congratulate you upon the honor of leading what was once the forlorn hope, in the attack upon the hoary abuses of the law, but is now the People's Young Guard, carrying the standard of reform toward the center of the enemy's camp.[76]

This is not to say Dorr did not appreciate the businesslike reasons for codification. Himself the victim of a state government weighted down with arcane legal technicalities, and dominated by sluggish agricultural interests, he must have admired the code's emphasis on swift economic transactions. Following his abortive 1842 revolution, this paragon of working-class sympathy had joined the capitalist stampede, and he understood the legal needs of free enterprise. In 1849 he made a rare visit to Manhattan to ask Field and O'Sullivan to suggest investors (preferably Democrats) for a business venture.[77]

It was not exactly the "revolution" they sought earlier in their careers, but as these old friends would argue, there was no paradox here. In different ways, and with very different results, Dorr and Field gave their lives to modernize American thinking. Eighteenth-century solutions were no longer sufficient for the increasingly unwieldy scope of nineteenth-century problems. Each devoted himself to seeking answers that would minister to the country's complicated economic demands while at the same time satisfying its ideological destiny. To enlarge public participation in political and social life while simultaneously facilitating the earning of wealth, surely that was and is about as close to a national purpose as the United States has ever had.

Unsealing the Books

Field often likened the common law to a sealed document, and used metaphors of reading and literacy to explain the need to open what had been a closed text to the public. In a speech near the end of his life he opined, "The law with us is a sealed book to the masses; it is a sealed book to all but the lawyers, and it is but partly opened even as to them." This was not only a convenient comparative device; it had a factual basis, for he had almost lost a case once when he had failed to notice that a document had a seal, and therefore dictated a different procedure under the old rules of common law pleading.[78]

The whole question of codification has an intriguing relevance to the literary scene, and not merely because so many writers were incidentally lawyers. As all lexicographers know, law, like prose, is a "construction" of reality, in both senses of the word. Interpreting the past, of course, was and is a vital function of jurisprudence. But the construction metaphor could also apply to the American intellectual infrastructure Field, O'Sullivan, and their cohorts expended so much energy trying to build. In all their pronouncements, Young Americans did their best to advance the linked causes of law and literature, to nurture, as it were, an American "lexicon." Field himself had posed the question, "What indeed is literature, but the voice of society?" Discussing the distinction between common law and equity, he reasserted the entire question was "little more than a play upon words." And wordplay could have serious ramifications, as he learned when his execrable pun resulted in his ejection that drunken night in 1850, with *Moby-Dick* half-completed in the same building. Across the spectrum of lawyers and editors who composed the Young America clique, there was universal interest in what we might call the letter of the law.[79]

Among other things, the call for codification was a cry for a curb on the romantic imagination, and for a heightened realism related to an improved understanding of modern America. The very language of the Field Code left little room for whimsy. It stated boldly: "The Pleadings Must be True"; "Facts Only Must be

Stated"; "All Statements Must be Concisely Made, and When Once Made Must Not be Repeated." In other words, it was an attempt to demystify a body of expression that had lost its relevance to an evolving populace.[80]

When reading the arguments of the legal reformers in the Jacksonian period, one notices how many found the "fictions" of the common law objectionable. The *Democratic Review* was often a plaintiff. An article on Bentham lamented, "One fantastic fiction became the excuse of a fiction still more fantastic . . . until the whole mass seemed like a vast pile of rubbish, or rather like some of those ancient structures which are seen in Italy, with here a broken column, there a shattered portico." A year later, the magazine renewed the complaint: "It abounds in the absurdest fictions" and "in wild and extravagant doctrines," always "expressed in language carelessly defined" and "difficult to be understood." Assessing the Field Code in 1848, John Edmonds praised its displacement of "the tide of fiction and redundancy" and the "useless verbiage" of the previous generation.[81]

As Field himself wrote in the magazine, the "antique phraseology" inherited from "our forefathers" had grown so obsolete "as no longer to command the respect or answer the wants of society." Ironically, he used the language of Natty Bumppo, himself somewhat outdated, to condemn the old ways:

> And thus it happened that a most artificial system of procedure, conceived in the midnight of the dark ages, established in those scholastic times when chancellors were ecclesiastics, and logic was taught by monks, and perfected in a later and more venal period, with a view to the multiplication of offices and the increase of fees, was imposed upon the banks of the Hudson and the quiet valley of the Mohawk.[82]

This was parallel to the antifeudal argument for the "democratic principle" advanced simultaneously by O'Sullivan. Field's obsession with Indian words likewise revealed his hope for a vital new American language. Rather than a mere acquaintance of the Young American group, as he has been portrayed, his message was part and parcel of the larger concept they were advancing.

Just as codification did not originate with Field, so literary interest in the question antedated the 1840s. Many prominent writers of the twenties and thirties had addressed issues of legal pettifoggery in their fiction. James Kirke Paulding wrote an interesting tract in 1826 entitled *The Merry Tales of the Three Wise Men of Gotham*, a satire of three different types of idealists. The second of them, nicknamed "Quominus," came from a country with a massive body of obscure precedent, which intimidated people away from the courts and preserved the status quo. Paulding summed up the feeling of many writers toward Latinate legal terminology: "It is all settled by the *hocus in quo*—which I suppose is what we call *hocus-pocus* in English." There was also an important ethnic component behind Paulding's Dutch antipathy toward the English common law. He disliked those who venerated English judges as "high-priests" of reason while suggesting "that a French, Italian, German or Dutch judge knew no more about managing the common law than they did about boxing."[83]

Joseph G. Baldwin may have best captured the tenor of codification with his *Flush Times of Alabama and Mississippi* (1853). Anti-English feeling was especially strong in the Southwest, where "the iron rules of British law were too tyrannical for free Americans," and Baldwin perfectly conveyed the link between the cult of Jackson and the distrust of periwigs:

> If Sam had a contempt for anyone more than another, it was for Sir William Blackstone, whom he regarded as "something between a sneak and a puke," and for whose superstitious veneration of the common law he felt about the same sympathy that General Jackson felt for Mr. Madison's squeamishness on the subject of blood and carnage. . . . He had no respect for old things, and not much for old persons. Established institutions he looked into as familiarly as into a horse's mouth. He would, if he could, have wiped out the Chancery system, or the whole body of the common law.[84]

More to the point, Baldwin wrote, "In the new country, there are no seniors: the bar is all Young America." Literary Young America returned the compliment, dwelling frequently on the bar in its fiction. Cornelius Mathews borrowed liberally from his legal training in his fiction. His first work, *The Motley Book* (1838), described an odious lawyer named Peter Doublet who personified everything Young America objected to. The "best part of his life had lain in the eighteenth century . . . all his thoughts and feelings dated back forty years." Citing the dated procedure Field detested, Doublet planned to possess a disputed farm "by livery of seisin under the old law," but desisted when an angry local threatened him. Mathews's *Chanticleer* was reviewed in the *Literary World* in 1850, and the reviewer considered it refreshing to find a comprehensible book when so many diffuse novels were like "old Chancery Papers, to be read by glancing at a catch worked here and there and in a dozen folios." The law also impinged on the canonical debates Duyckinck engaged in with his rival Griswold in the 1840s. When the latter issued his *Prose Writers of America* anthology in 1847, the *Democratic Review* strongly criticized him for neglecting Livingston and Leggett, whom they perceived as crucial apostles of the anti-English tradition in American letters.[85]

But none of this would be particularly interesting if the campaign for legal reform had not also had some bearing on the great writers of the period. In my opinion, it did, particularly on Whitman, who followed Field's crusade closely, and on Mathews's successor as the literary champion of Young America, Herman Melville. Both wrote early works addressing the illegitimate exercise of authority, the central problem of the Revolution. But more specifically, each was well-informed about legal dynamics of the 1840s. While commentators have investigated Melville's interest in the law, especially through his father-in-law (Lemuel Shaw, the chief justice of Massachusetts), few have examined his interest in the intellectual history of the Berkshire region, and hence legal history.[86]

Field and Melville were certainly familiar; when Melville applied to become consul to Florence under Lincoln, Field signed a letter praising his patriotism. *Typee* contained comical passages on the long history of taboos and the wordiness needed to justify them. The "Fast-Fish and Loose-Fish" chapter of *Moby-Dick* revealed Melville's reading of legal precedent, and in *Mardi*, written the year of the Field Code, he jocosely referred to an analogous legal edifice: "Regarded section by section, this code of laws seemed exceedingly trivial, but taken together, made a somewhat imposing aggregation of particles." Later, in *The Confidence-Man*, he wrote, "In short, a due conception of what is to be held for this sort of personage in fiction would make him almost as much of a prodigy there, as in real history is a new law-giver."[87]

Other scholars have noted that "Bartleby the Scrivener" also raises interesting legal questions. The narrator is a former master at chancery, an office reformed when the distinction between law and equity was abolished by the 1846 constitution and the Field Code. Melville seemed to approve the change, since the narrator's anger at the "sudden and violent abrogation of the office" merely proceeds from his disappointment at not receiving "a life-lease"of its profits. Intriguingly, Gansevoort Melville had applied for the office of examiner in chancery in New York in 1842, working the Democratic network through John Edmonds. "Bartleby" also echoed Field's fierce complaints in the *Review* that old systems of legal procedure were wasteful of the mind: "The labor is thrown away, and so many fine heads and strong hands are condemned to the servile, the belittleing [sic] employment of writing out old jingles of words, invented somewhere about the times of the Edwards."[88]

There is some fleeting evidence that Melville read some of the documents in the quest for codification. William Sampson would seem an unlikely influence, but his writings echoed faintly in *Moby-Dick*. One of Sampson's early publications was a record of a case he was involved in, entitled simply, *Is a Whale a Fish?* (1819). The case, a lengthy legal inquiry into that pressing question, discussed Jonah, sperm whales fighting squids ("krakens"), and other finny topics to surface in *Moby-Dick*. The book has never been cited in any of the standard histories of Melville's reading and influences, yet there are strong pieces of evidence that he read it. Chapters 24, 89, and 90 of *Moby-Dick* show clear borrowing, even citing the same quotations word for word that Sampson had already excavated, and it must have detained Melville at some point around 1850.[89]

Yet another obscure work Melville may have glanced at along his tortuous path was the "Lay Sermon at Sea" Auguste Davezac gave to the *Democratic Review* in 1840. Alongside an excerpt of Dana's *Two Years Before the Mast*, the article meditated on the relationship between a ship's compass and religion, in language reminiscent of "The Quadrant" and "The Needle" chapters. Davezac also hinted at the famous passage from "Knights and Squires," wondering, "perhaps this good ship now bears on its deck another Jackson—a further avenger of American wrongs, a redoubtable champion of freedom in the coming days." There are also resemblances between their vision of the ocean as a metaphor for the American West. Davezac compared the seas to "blooming meadows, yielding to each breeze the treasures of their various and perfumed blossoms" and "the spreading prairies of the far west, rolling, like this ocean, their flexible undulating grass, as waves tossed about by the winds." Melville, in "The Gilder" chapter, likened the ocean to "so much flowery earth; and the distant ship revealing only the tops of her masts, seems struggling forward, not through high rolling waves, but through the tall grass of a rolling prairie."[90]

I do not propose to dwell overlong on these minute echoes, but I would like to briefly expound on the significance of Melville's presence in the Berkshires in 1850. While specific causes and effects are impossible to determine, it seems fitting that Melville and Hawthorne wrote their masterpieces in a place that understood the

Young American struggle for intellectual independence, and also gave them some peace of mind. The region's self-sufficiency and quiet antipathy toward English culture must have seemed the perfect tonic to the two overwrought writers after the struggles of the late 1840s. For Melville, the 1850 return to Pittsfield, where he had happily passed summers with his uncle, was a welcome homecoming.[91]

If, as I suspect, Melville was aware of the rich legal and intellectual tradition linking disparate Democrat reformers from Butler to the Sedgwicks and Field, then it is unsurprising he developed the nationalistic sentiments that issued forth in "Hawthorne and His Mosses" following the hike up Monument Mountain. Notably, he began that pivotal critical work, "Some charm is in this northern air," as if the climate had as much to do with his thinking as he did. For what it's worth, he purchased the 1829 history Field's father had written about Berkshire County immediately after his return to the region in 1850. The volume was not only read and annotated by the novelist, but supplied the plot for "The Apple-Tree Table." The Berkshire writer J. E. A. Smith, commenting on Melville's many perambulations in the area, wrote "picnic revelers may be sure that whatever romantic camping-ground they choose in Berkshire, Herman Melville has been there before them."[92]

The influence of legal reform on Whitman was also notable, judging from the wealth of materials he collected on the subject and his own writings. Among the many articles he clipped for personal use were several on the legal profession in the 1840s. As a transplanted New Yorker in Louisiana in 1848, he took a natural interest in Livingston's legacy, and his admiration for Auguste Davezac was already mentioned. Years later, he recalled him with a storyteller's flair to Traubel in Camden: "Did I ever tell you of D'Avezac, my old French friend there in New York? It was long ago that I knew him—I was a very young fellow—but I can see him now, just as he was, with all the aroma of life upon him—and such a life! D'Avezac was a French Radical—too Radical to stay over there."[93]

Whitman did all the little things expected of a Young American foot soldier. He went to hear Field and Sedgwick speak at a Tammany Hall rally on April 6, 1842. In 1847 he reviewed Sedgwick's *American Citizen* with enthusiasm: "It is a noble discourse!" Presumably, he sympathized with Field's zeal for Algonquin nomenclature, as he remained fascinated by Indian words throughout his life. He called himself "I, habitan of the Alleghanies" in "To a Historian," and in 1846, a year after the Alleghania hubbub, he wrote an article on "Indian Life and Customs," concluding, "Are *these* not the proper subjects for the bard or the novelist?" Doubtless, he would have responded to Field's earlier invocation in his Leggett article:

> Would to heaven that there might arise some master-spirit, who should teach this doctrine of quality to our countrymen as it might be taught, and as they will one day understand it; to show them how it leads to the abasement of none, but to the elevation of many; how it infuses into countless multitudes, who might otherwise have lived despairingly, new hopes, self-respect, and energy to labor and to bear; how the haughtiest spirit and loftiest mind may be purified and exalted by universal sympathy.[94]

I do not mean to suggest that Whitman and Field, so utterly different, had identical aspirations, but there were important convergences in their thought that help us to see both in a wider context. The culmination of their parallel development occurred in 1855. As Whitman was putting the finishing touches to *Leaves of Grass*, Field urged codification in the perfervid prose required of commencement orators:

> May it be so resolved as that we shall win the well-deserved prize; that we shall have a book of our own laws, a CODE AMERICAN, not insular but continental, as simple as so vast a work can be made, free in its spirit, catholic in its principles! And that work will go with our ships, our travelers, and our armies; it will march with the language, it will move with every emigration, and make itself a home in the farthest portion of our own continent, in the vast Australian lands, and in the islands of the southern and western seas.[95]

This address, before the Albany Law School where he started his career, not only repeated O'Sullivan's cultural definition of Manifest Destiny, it foreshadowed Whitman's evolving concept of "rondure," a term signifying worldwide empathy and communication. Field had a special interest in this concept, for his brother Cyrus was then working on the submarine telegraph that linked Europe and North America, and which Whitman would himself celebrate in "Passage to India" ("the seas inlaid with eloquent gentle wires"). Field himself alluded to it in the Albany speech, mentioning "the world's girdle" as an instrument for the expansion of American dominion, and finally asking aloud, "Whence shall come the lawgiver of the new time? From our own soil, I would fain hope and believe. The materials are at hand, and the time is propitious." Though a different kind of lawgiver, Whitman could not have agreed more. When he anonymously reviewed *Leaves of Grass* in the *Democratic Review*, he was characteristically ebullient, claiming "every phrase announces new laws."[96]

Codification Decoded

Like Young America, the codification movement is not always easy to decipher. Both movements were frustrated in the short term, although they inspired some lasting monuments. Field was thwarted in his attempts to promulgate a single code of procedure, but his persistent promotional efforts increased American sensitivity to the question of common law dependence, and resulted in the streamlined legal proceedings adopted by many western states (as well as the British Empire in India). Further, the idea of an elective judiciary, though not exactly his, outlived codification to bring real change to the courts. As the *Review* wrote in 1852, "Young America held that its ultimate jurors and arbitrators should not be powers outside of its control, but at least on an equality with its law-makers—of its own election."[97]

In all of these endeavors, the codifiers complemented the Young American literati, who likewise saw language as a determinant as well as a reflection of social reality. Praising texts for their understandability was another way of distributing them to as many Americans as possible, just as Duyckinck and O'Sullivan hoped to do with their print projects. By debunking the past, and specifically the English past, these politico-literary reformers were also indulging a chance to reenact the culminating moment of American culture: the Revolution. John Edmonds wrote with exhilaration: "The Revolution of 1776 established only our independence of the government of England. Our independence of her laws, her language and her literature was yet to be wrought out . . . the great work, had, however, at length fairly been commenced."[98]

Like all aspects of cultural nationalism in the 1840s, the codification movement derived much of its impetus from a sense that if American culture were not organized and promoted, it would become fragmented, pulled apart by its powerful centrifugal tendencies. Field betrayed this fear in many of his utterances, not only in his paeans to American uniqueness, but in his conception of the law itself. The American lawyer, according to Field, needed to know not only the intricacies of the law, but how they were combined into a meaningful, united entity: "He must have comprehended the greatness of the whole, the harmony of its parts, and the infinite diversity of its particulars." More important, he had to bring "order out of this chaos," to collect its parts into "one consistent and harmonious whole." Hence Field's admiration for the Allegheny mountain range, which "binds the country together, as with a band of iron."[99]

This theory of union would have been easily grasped by Abraham Lincoln, who never surrendered a Whiggish distrust of Young American jingoism, but who knew the value of simplified language and the binding effects of patriotic rhetoric. When he delivered his compendious interpretation of American history, the 1860 Cooper Union address, he was escorted to the platform by David Dudley Field, by then a full-blooded Republican who dismissed the Democratic party as the "tool of the slave-holding oligarchy."[100]

Was codification as radical as it seemed to lawyers of the older generation? In some ways, it was not. Surely it appealed to Field for personal reasons. Like all the Young Americans, he wanted nothing so much as a chance to prove his mettle, to achieve power without waiting until middle age. The sweeping rhetoric of the codification campaign was not a bad way to accomplish this. As his friendship with Lincoln would indicate, as well as his kingmaker role in 1860, Field was intensely ambitious. And despite his hot-headed words, codification had the same fundamental goal its opponents had, the better administration of justice in a modernizing society. Much of Field's anger was directed against the backlog of cases accumulating as New York applied outdated English legal concepts to the bustling nineteenth century.

Some might even argue that codification had more to do with commerce than with democracy. There is some truth to the charge. Unlike gentler and more radical Young Americans (Duyckinck and O'Sullivan), Field was never shy about advancing mercantilist causes as a New York lawyer, and part of his rationale was simply to clear out the obstructions to business in the booming 1840s. Similarly, Butler started his law school because the sheer volume of transactions demanded it, with commercial cases in New York "more constantly arising . . . than in any other part of the Republic." Like Duyckinck's publishing ventures, codification represented an attempt to impose a new organizing structure on a society no longer playing by eighteenth-century rules.[101]

The Young American context is also useful to explain Field's contradictory psychological imperatives. For all the Democratic rhetoric he generated, it sometimes seemed, as it did with Melville, Duyckinck, and even O'Sullivan, that Field was driven as much by an animus against elderly Whiggish money brokers as truly proletarian sympathy. Many of the Stockbridge-New York liberals were descended from Federalist stock, despite their Jacksonian apostasy. Some of them may have discovered, accidentally or not, that ultra-Americanist rage was an effective device for muting the nouveau-riche elements in American society, rapidly gaining supremacy through undisciplined financial speculation.

In their attack on a court system that was, as Morton Horwitz has shown, increasingly disposed to protect the new industrial-entrepreneurial elites, the Young Americans shared the disgust that their ancestors felt at a money-grubbing wealth made not from the land or the sea, but from stock manipulation and dehumanizing industry. And worshipping the Revolution, as the codifiers did, allowed them to express generational disaffection and worship their elitist grandparents at the same time, to be both radical and conservative. This shifting dialectic helps explain why some moderate conservatives like Joseph Story supported codification along with their ideological opponents.

In short, codification was a revolution that did not always live up to its rhetoric. But for all its limitations, it was still a revolution, with a radical message only slightly blunted by these extenuating circumstances. Looking backward to 1776 *and* anticipating a glorious future for the expanding republic, Field was a true Young American, simultaneously embracing tradition and change. In law, as in art and literature, New York was large enough to contain these contradictions. The city relentlessly promulgated visions of a new, modernistic American culture, if only because its rate of growth demanded it. Theodore Sedgwick III stated the assumption that underlay all Young American thought in an 1858 address:

> New York, in both its virtues and its vices—its excellences and its defects—its immense material progress, its gayety and good humor, its active and eager intelligence, its intense energy, its vast treasures of wealth and knowledge, its presumptuous audacity, its reckless lawlessness, its organized disorder, is the very symbol and type of the country. New York is the quintessence of America.[102]

An even deeper excursion into the historical background provides more food for thought. Few bother to read the deadly dull genealogical histories of the nineteenth century, but a striking fact of the Young American configuration is how many of them were descended from forebears who had fought against the English crown. The ancestors of the Sedgwicks and Benjamin Butler had been prominent Cromwell supporters; and the Livingstons and Rantouls were originally from Scotland (like the Melvilles), where there was a long tradition of anti-English codification. Disaffected Irish like O'Sullivan and Sampson were sympathetic, and perhaps the New York Dutch felt the same stirrings, albeit more quietly. Despite the disparate elements of Young America, its members were united by an antimonarchical reverence for the English, American, and French revolutions.[103]

If Field was not exactly Cromwell or Robespierre, there was still a strong sense of historic drama attached to codification. To dwell exclusively on Field's limitations is to cheapen the truly reconstructive thrust of his reforms, and the feeling that a battle going back centuries was about to be won. An insincere Democrat could never have written Thomas Dorr of "our revolution," nor would Dorr have celebrated his leadership of "the People's Young Guard." Like the other Young Americans, his youthful radicalism disintegrated somewhat under the pressures of aging and the disillusion following the failures of 1848. Yet this did not indicate a wholesale abandonment of the cause.

And we do Field a disservice if we overlook the sincerity of his efforts to enlarge the discourse of legal procedure, to bring its language within the ken of the ordinary citizen. Even to the end of his long life, he retained a lively interest in words, writing articles on the beauty of Native American place-names. Like Whitman, he could be moved to rapture by the mere mention of "Mannahatta" or "Mononga-hela." In 1888, while strenuously urging a house committee to name New Mexico "Montezuma" and Washington state "Tacoma," he reached back into his memory and cited his 1840s correspondence with William Gilmore Simms to persuade the reluctant lawmakers. It was one of his few unsuccessful arguments, but it showed that even at the end of the century, as Whitman and Melville were finishing their life's work, and O'Sullivan was languishing in obscurity, the embers of Young American nationalism still flickered quietly.[104]

To Field and his fellow codifiers, words were not empty sounds to be memorized and misinterpreted by a tiny body of legal hierophants. Rather, they were vital living instruments of communication that ought to be comprehended by as many as possible in order to describe and improve social reality. His fury at obscure Latin phrases and medieval English legal terms masked a deeper contempt for an outmoded polity in which the few had prescribed rules for the many. In the end, Field's eulogy of William Leggett, the radical who motivated so many Young Americans, might well be applied to himself: He "rejected the trammels which a false taste and a wrong education impose upon too many minds among us; because he embraced with all his heart the fundamental principle of American institutions."[105]

Young America Redux

Young America is *not* the offspring of old fogydom. Being wise in our generation, and being determined not to be burthened with more fathers than there is any need for, we declare that the young democracy, either in its principles or its action, has no connection either in blood, policy, consanguinity or look, with those antiquated, stiff-cravated personages.

—*Democratic Review* (1852)

It was the devious-cruising Rachel, that in her retracing search after her missing children, only found another orphan.

—Melville, *Moby-Dick*

Tragedy and Farce

In 1852, reflecting on the failure of the revolution in France, Karl Marx paraphrased Hegel to remark that history enacts itself twice, the first time as tragedy, the second time as farce. His ruminations were originally published in New York, where at that very moment a bastardized Young America was rising up to reassert America's Manifest Destiny in even more strident language than 1845. Its reincarnation darkly confirmed Marx's pithy observation.[1]

This latter-day Young America, which I call Young America II, is the version studied by most historians, who rarely address its literary antecedents. The second Young America shared rhetorical elements with the first, but there were important divergences, and only a broad construction would define them as part of the same unilateral movement. Reflecting and propelled by the increasingly angry tone of American politics, Young America became a watchword around the country for a dangerously aggressive, unstable nationalism with complete disregard for polite sensibilities. What had been "tragedy," the well-intentioned but doomed attempt of New York intellectuals to create a meaningful democratic culture in the 1840s, was supplanted in the 1850s by the stupid farce of third-rate politicians using "democracy" as a catch-all slogan for their unprincipled schemes to wrest foreign territory and divert attention from the slavery issue. The first Young America expected American culture, by force of its excellence, to peacefully spread American influence as an intellectual Manifest Destiny; its successor expected American force alone to exercise this influence, along with whatever mediocre culture was attached to it. Beside their origin in the *Democratic Review*, they had little in common beneath the surface.

As we might expect, the key player linking the two Young Americas was John O'Sullivan. After he sold the *Democratic Review* in 1846, he bounced around New York and Washington, still welcome in prominent Democratic circles, but lacking the central purpose the *Review* had given him. Without this compass, he began displaying strange ideological vicissitudes, wandering Ishmael-like from one position to another. His early indecision about the war was short-lived. As American troops won dazzling victories, O'Sullivan grew cocksure. Unsatisfied with the massive acquisition of Mexican territory, he harangued the Polk administration about Cuba, urging the island's purchase as the further unraveling of Manifest Destiny. He had always been fascinated by warmer climates, and in 1846 he wrote his old comrade in arms, Thomas Dorr, of the geographical restlessness each felt as they entered middle age: "It must be confessed too that the shores of the Pacific do present an attraction for the steps of men of our school and stamp. I feel strongly tempted toward California."[2]

O'Sullivan's pet interest in Cuba soon blossomed into a full-fledged monomania, nurtured by the marriage of his sister Mary (Langtree's widow) to a prominent Cuban planter, Cristobal Madan y Madan. Having helped as much as anyone to elect Polk, O'Sullivan was granted considerable access to the president. He first brought messages for his old New York patrons, Van Buren and Butler, but soon was visiting the White House for his own reasons. Despite his impressive lobbying credentials and a fair measure of success at gaining the president's sympathy, no progress was fast enough, and he wrote Dorr, "I am disgusted with Polk, and hold the War accursed." This was of course the same war he had helped to launch with his editorials on Manifest Destiny, all the while insisting on his "peace" principles to his antislavery friends in the northern Democracy.[3]

True to his ancestry, the inconsistent O'Sullivan had always harbored delusions of grandeur and ambitions for political intrigue. Now he had a scope for them, and he congregated with all manner of renegade "filibuster" elements plotting to wrest slave-owning Cuba from Spain in the name of some peculiar definition of liberty. He spent his honeymoon in Cuba in 1846, and returned frequently thereafter to consult with Madan and other plotters for annexation. Following the easy conquests of the Mexican war, Cuba beckoned temptingly to the growing American land lust.

Lust is not an inappropriate term, for the annexationists boasted of the island's, "rosy, sugared lips," and even more luridly, advised: "She is of age—take her, Uncle Sam!" These allurements were economic as well as aesthetic and were probably intensified in O'Sullivan's mind by his father's failed adventures in South America thirty years earlier. Appropriately, the Spanish ambassador to France labeled him with the same epithet the senior O'Sullivan had earned, calling him an "entrepreneur pirate." Now was his chance to invoke the family destiny. After years of apostrophizing revolution as an intellectual phenomenon, O'Sullivan was finally experiencing real diplomatic intrigue of his own.[4]

On July 6, 1847, he drafted a long memorandum to James Buchanan, the secretary of state, on the desirability of purchasing Cuba from Spain. With his old flair for hyperbole, and a heightened sensitivity to financial considerations, he wrote that the purchase "would stamp the term of the Administration which should effect it, as one of the great epochs, not only of our country, but of the commercial history of the world." The perpetually underfinanced O'Sullivan stood to gain considerably by annexation, or so he thought. O'Sullivan proposed a purchase price of $100–$150 million, to be defrayed by wealthy Cuban planters chafing under the yoke of colonial authority. There was an anti-English element in his thinking as well, for England had been making noises about acquiring Cuba and Puerto Rico. Strangely, he thought that Cuba's entry into the Union would bring about Canada's annexation, preserving the balance of power between North and South. He ended the memorandum by volunteering to serve as a secret agent to sound out the Spanish. Like his ancestors, he was growing restless.[5]

By the spring of 1848, O'Sullivan's tone was belligerent, inflamed by the European revolutions. ("The French Republic [God bless it!] would be on our side, and England will have enough to do to mind her own business at home.") He was wrong about this, as he was increasingly wrong about many things; no one wanted to see the United States acquire Cuba, not even the republicans of Young Europe. Oblivious, O'Sullivan threatened Buchanan, "Further delay would be criminal—imbecile—almost treasonable to the destiny and policy of the United States." He repeated the absurd argument that Cuba's acquisition would please North and South, thinking the growing tension over slavery would be placated by additional territory:

> In a party point of view, it will be an excellent move. We Barnburners will be as much pleased at it as the Southerners themselves. To the Abolitionists, we can point out that it is the only mode of stopping the slave trade; which is the fact. If the object can be consummated before the Election, it would have an electric effect. . . . It will give great moral force to the party whose measure it will be, as contributing to prove that to be the true American party, the party entrusted by God and Nature with the mission of the American policy and destiny.[6]

Despite the faulty logic, O'Sullivan met repeatedly with Polk that revolutionary spring, and almost convinced him. On May 10, he and Stephen Douglas, the young Illinois senator who shared his hunger for expansion, visited the president in tandem, and Polk, apparently persuaded, confided to his diary: "I am decidedly in favour of purchasing Cuba and making it one of the States of the Union." Despite the ultimate failure of the purchase plan for a variety of diplomatic reasons, O'Sullivan's admission into the highest government circles whetted his growing appetite for action. As his plan was obstructed, the frustrated agitator turned his sights to more immediate means of liberation. On June 2, he returned to inform an unimpressed Polk that plans were afoot for violent seizure of the island.[7]

Just as his father had fallen in with the Venezuelan Francisco Miranda, O'Sullivan now dedicated himself to the leading Cuban revolutionary, Narciso Lopez, whom he knew through Madan. He was playing a dangerous game. Though he supported Van Buren and Free Soil, he grew fonder of the South as Cuba loomed larger. He wrote Calhoun in 1849, urging him to "rouse all the youth and manhood

of the Southern States in particular to rush down to help the Cuban Revolution."
As he argued, "If I, a 'New York Free Soiler' am so deeply interested in behalf of
this movement, what ought not to be the enthusiasm of Southern gentlemen?"
Calhoun was probably suspicious of O'Sullivan, who had opposed him strenuously
in previous struggles with Van Buren, but O'Sullivan's new devotion to the South
was sincere, even if erratic. With other Americans, most of whom were from Kentucky and the Southwest, he concerted efforts to raise money and troops for Lopez's
invasion of the island.[8]

Like most of his exploits outside journalism, O'Sullivan's foray in military ad-
venturism was a disaster. Two steamships with the unthreatening names *Fanny* and
Sea Gull were purchased, along with the statelier *Cleopatra*, and the invasion utterly failed. Abortive efforts were attempted in 1849 and 1850, from which Lopez escaped, only to return and be executed following crushing defeat in 1851. O'Sullivan
was arrested by federal authorities on charges of violating American neutrality, and
tried in both New Orleans and New York. The "Cuban State Trials" were sensational affairs, and O'Sullivan profited from the circus atmosphere to elude convic-
tion. David Dudley Field and Samuel Tilden were his character witnesses, and
John Van Buren defended him.[9]

But despite his release, O'Sullivan's monomania alienated many of the intellectuals he had enlisted for the *Review* in the 1840s. Over the course of the 1840s,
his principles changed subtly but significantly, to the point where he was quite different from his former colleagues. Specifically, his new project showed little concern for two former guiding truths; the pacifistic idea that Manifest Destiny should
be unforced, and the unreliability of the Calhounites, whom he had labeled "the
world of traitordom" after they subverted Van Buren's campaign in 1844. Despite arguments about extending democracy, many Northerners saw the lust for Caribbean
dominion as yet another encroachment of the Slave Power. There was good reason
for this, for prominent southern expansionists were corroborating the worst northern fears with their unapologetic need to expand in order to preserve the peculiar
institution. As the other Young Americans expressed new anxieties about democracy, brought on by causes ranging from Mexico to Astor Place to the 1850 Compromise, O'Sullivan seemed to be speaking in tongues.[10]

In 1854 John Greenleaf Whittier, one of O'Sullivan's old contributors, wrote
"The Haschish," a poem comparing the drug to the cotton plant and its power to al-
ter men's minds. Seeming to speak directly of O'Sullivan, who was clearly abandoning his pacifism, Whittier wrote:

> The man of peace, about whose dreams
> The sweet millennial angels cluster,
> Tastes the mad weed, and plots and schemes,
> A raving Cuban filibuster!
>
> The noisiest Democrat, with ease,
> It turns to Slavery's parish beadle;
> The shrewdest statesman eats and sees
> Due southward points the polar needle.[11]

Sanders and Young America II

O'Sullivan's Ahablike inversion of the compass owed much to the new company he was keeping, particularly George Nicholas Sanders, who acquired the *Democratic Review* in late 1851 and brought O'Sullivan back into the fold as an editor. Under Sanders, however, it was a very different magazine than the one that had published Whitman and Hawthorne. J. C. Breckinridge, from Sanders's home state of Kentucky, noticed the new stridency immediately in 1852 and denounced it in a speech on the Senate floor: "The Democratic Review has been heretofore not a partisan paper, but a periodical that was supposed to represent the whole Democratic party . . . I have observed recently a very great change." Under Sanders the *Review*'s jingoism achieved an even higher pitch than O'Sullivan's dog-whistle stridency. Sanders summed his editorial policy: "The more fire the better as we intend to make the times hot."[12]

Like O'Sullivan, Sanders was a fascinating character with both political and literary aspirations, seemingly everywhere and nowhere at once. Born in western Kentucky in 1812, the descendant of yet another declining but well-bred family with curious foreign interests, Sanders had grown up admiring Calhoun much as O'Sullivan had Van Buren. He took a keen interest in Manifest Destiny, and early became involved with local Democratic politics, strongly urging the 1844 presidential candidates to support the admission of Texas.[13]

If his intellectual wattage was less than O'Sullivan's, Sanders was even more of a revolutionary. In the late 1840s he had become friendly with the steamboat magnate George Law, and when the French Revolution burst out in 1848, Sanders and Law were deeply committed. Unlike most Americans, who supported the insurgents with good will alone, Sanders tried to sell them forty thousand old muskets, but arrived in France too late to consummate the deal (although rumor had it he constructed barricades in the streets of Paris). He returned more determined than ever to enlist American support for the young revolutionaries of Europe, cognizant also that this might bring business for Law's shipping lines.[14]

Men like Sanders were increasingly audible in the early 1850s. The 1848 revolutions had galvanized Americans to a new interest in the fate of republicanism abroad. As the European forces of reaction consolidated their victory, Americans were outspoken in their condemnation. At the same time, the events following the Mexican War confused Americans and drove a wedge between them. The Wilmot Proviso and 1850 Compromise shook the two-party system severely, and American faith in the democratic system was undermined at home at the same time it was being trumpeted abroad in reference to 1848. This strange combination of hopes and fears, when intensified in a mind like O'Sullivan's or Sanders's, screwed American righteousness to a new notch. The result was an unprecedented interventionism, one that urged American military involvement not only in the Caribbean, but in Europe as well, and before Woodrow Wilson was even born.

As is often the case with foreign intervention, an important reason for this sensitivity to foreign oppression was the volatile world financial situation. American merchants stood to make a great deal of money from foreign adventure, no matter how it turned out. The discovery of gold in California increased attention to the

promise of wealth in the acquired territories, and many of the new Young Americans were directly involved in business ventures in California and Latin America.
One can almost feel the money lust in O'Sullivan's Cuban plans, a far cry from the
disdain for wealth he had shown in his early *Review* pieces. He had forgotten the
magazine's early message, in the simpler days of Van Buren and subtreasuries: "You
cannot worship God and Mammon, nor kneel at the shrine of liberty while grovel-
ing at the hoof of the golden calf."[15]

Another reason for the resurgence of Young America was simply demographic.
The combination of massive immigration in the 1840s and natural population growth
created a widespread sense that a new generation was entitled to political power, one
that could better address the new American situation following 1848. This feeling of
generational entitlement was only heightened by the near-simultaneous demise of
Calhoun, Webster, and Clay in the early 1850s. The nervous rapidity with which
revolutions and wars were being taken up and dismissed was exacerbated by a fear
that the old regional and partisan balance was giving way to a new disequilibrium in
which anything might happen.

Into this leadership void Young America II plunged happily. After purchasing
the *Democratic Review* in December 1851, probably with George Law's funding,
Sanders set to work, with assistance from O'Sullivan and a board of editors including recent European revolutionaries. In January 1852, he launched the new *Review*
with éclat. A portrait of Mazzini graced the frontispiece, opposite an editorial on
"Eighteen Fifty-Two and the Presidency" warning the new year would see the ful-
fillment of the promise glimpsed in 1848. Sanders made two points repeatedly. First,
Americans were prepared to intervene in the struggle ("our armies are on the
ground, ready on the soil of Europe to fight for the triumph of Republicanism"),
and second, the "young generation" needed a new leader, "a statesman who can
bring young blood, young ideas, and young hearts to the councils of the Republic."
He denounced Louis Napoleon ("The Usurper!") and called for Americans to support the revolutionary struggles stretching from Ireland to Hungary and Italy. Using
a questionable metaphor, the *Review* declared its fraternity: "Something we owe to
'Young Europe.' Let us seek it diligently, and with honest hearts, to find out what it
is, and how to pay it. We owe her our example, let us see there is no spot on its
snow. We owe her our encouragement, our brotherly sympathy."[16]

With these feelings of familial camaraderie, Young America II was born. It
quickly became a specific term applying to Sanders's political interest group. He
used the phrase repeatedly in editorials, and it soon entered the popular argot. In
February, the *Review* declared, "We are not for all the young men before the country, but only for the bold, active honor and talent of Young America." The *Review*
then veered off on a course of adolescent hostility toward all its enemies, real and
imagined. Even older Democrats were suspect, and the magazine renounced its
former purpose of profiling the party's elder statesmen, the "venerable fogies" who,
in their portrait sessions, "sat for hours contorting and pursing their lips, so as to
look implacably stern, and awfully democratic, and powerfully Jacksonian."[17]

In April, the magazine composed one of the most important statements of
Young America II. In an article on "The Progress of Democracy," Sanders offered
his theory of American history, always admiring those who "advance" rather than

"stand still or retreat." With Whitmanesque sweep, he praised everything he could think of that was important about America, from John Paul Jones to Jefferson to westward expansion to young artists to anti-English lawyers to the yacht *America*, embracing each under his umbrella:

> That unseen influence, that development of the *anima mundi*, which we term American Democratic Progress, or Young America, actuated, impelled, and led all the triumphs of the republic, whether or not the immediate agents were conscious of the inspiration. The same soul, the same impulsive idea, expansive and withal beautiful in art, and intensely romantic and virtuous in action, alike realized the dream of ages in a pacific empire, whose "waters turn to gold upon the lips," and the statue of the Grecian slave.[18]

Like O'Sullivan, who presumably was abetting him, Sanders not only combined political and cultural projects in his mind, he did it in a way that sold magazines. The invigorated *Review* performed well in his tenure, and despite its irrational, almost desperate energy, it provided entertaining reading. In the same issue, Sanders penned a comic etymology of the term *old fogy*, even setting old gothic type to spell out "Ye Kategorie of Ye Olde Fogies." The definition, too, was typical: "If a solemnly fat old gentleman, or a sententious, dogmatic, and owl-like, or supercilious, vain, namby-pamby young one, asks you to define him the phrase, 'old fogy,' lend him sixpence to buy a pocket looking-glass."[19] With uncharacteristic self-effacement, Sanders even stood the trope upside down, suggesting that someday even the *Democratic Review* might be so defined: "This *Review* even, this the most go-ahead and grandest literary creation of our time, may in the twentieth or twenty-first century, falling perchance into incompetent hands, as we cannot hope to live so long, be called 'an old fogy,' and treated as such."[20]

As usual, exaggeration colored the assessment of the "grandest literary creation." In this rabid political climate, the *Review*'s intellectual side was neglected. Bluntly illustrating the new format, Sanders used a graphic metaphor to rain contempt on the magazine's old policy of encouraging authors. The new *Review* had "taken a vow of literary chastity, declared its determination not to accept the office of a literary prostitute, and to take to its fresh and virgin sheets none but those worthy of immortality's embrace." Any Democrats seeking literary gratification would have to turn to less virtuous magazines, inexplicably equated in Sanders's mind with an elderly mulatto prostitute, a "dingy African": "the old harridan; with her dingy, red, and wizened face, her weak and unsteady body dizened out with the huge "Washington-head" brooch, on her quadroon and wrinkled bosom!" A veiled joke concluded the unamusing allusion to flaccid fogydom: "No Review, conducted on such lax principles of literary morals, could be the 'organ' of any political principle or party, or the efficient advocate of any good cause."[21]

Despite these high moralistic claims, the real reason for the diminished focus on literature was the semiliteracy of the editorial board, none of whom, besides O'Sullivan, had much training in that department. In Sanders's first issue the magazine published the most hostile of *Moby-Dick*'s many severe reviews, dismissing it as "the very ultimatum of weakness to which its author could attain." The magazine that had inspired Manifest Destiny was not impressed by the romance responding to it:

Mr. Melville is evidently trying to ascertain how far the public will consent to be imposed upon. He is gauging, at once, our gullibility and our patience. Having written one or two passable extravagancies, he has considered himself privileged to produce as many more as he pleases, increasingly exaggerated and increasingly dull . . . if there are any of our readers who wish to find examples of bad rhetoric, involved syntax, stilted sentiment and incoherent English, we will take the liberty of recommending to them this precious volume of Mr. Melville's.[22]

Soon after this hatchet job, hardly any book reviews were included at all. The late Margaret Fuller earned a gracious eulogy, mainly because her revolutionary credentials were intact, but almost all other literature was suspect. An extraordinary article on "Fogydom in Literature" simply attacked everything. Dismissing polite, Anglo-imitative fiction, Sanders was blunt:

Young America does not require such pap. Better the silver spoon which free institutions entail on it as a birthright, should stick in its throat and choke it, than it should grow elfin on the hemlock which fogy nurses would tender to it. It must have fresh, wholesome mother's milk, strong as the blood which flowed in '76, not the green tea of parvenu society, nor British concoctions of chalk and water.[23]

The violence of the *Review's* extreme literary theory could only be expressed in painful bodily metaphors: English writers were "diarrhetic," the *North American Review* was "that superannuated dust-box into which old Fogydom expectorates freely," and American servility forced "a swimming sensation of the head and a somersetting of the stomach." Punning on "constitution," the *Review* concluded, "We do not want such a disgusting and sickening literature. The American constitution will not be strengthened by swallowing such emetics."[24]

Ironically, the emetic writer targeted by the article was William A. Jones, who had written extensively for the *Review* as part of Duyckinck's original Young America clique. Jones was skewered mercilessly as "the most obsequious toady," salaaming before English writers "after the most approved oriental custom." Nothing was remembered of Jones's former work except the "distinct recollection of having been put to sleep some years since" by it. Much of this work had actually been performed within the pages of the *Review,* including Jones's courageous endorsement of Melville's *Mardi* in July 1849, less than three years previous. But the new Young America had a short-term memory and a limited attention span. Its indifference to one of Duyckinck's most reliable foot-soldiers indicated how far apart the groups had wandered, and how little in the way of culture the infantile new Young America needed to gratify its immediate needs.[25]

1852

The new Young America came to a sudden boil in 1852, not just for the chance to unseat an elderly Whig president, but because of a number of external pressures acting on nationalists from all backgrounds. These pressures combined to destroy what little consensus there was among northern Democrats, and Young America II emerged as little more than a screen for southern expansionists, even though it maintained its base in New York. Sanders inadvertently revealed the anger creeping into Young Americanism when he announced, "The year '1852' has come to be universally regarded as a liberator and an avenger."[26]

An interesting comparison might be made between the Cuba excitement of 1850–52 and another issue Young America tried to rally behind around the same time. In 1851, the Hungarian radical in exile, Louis Kossuth, came to the United States seeking support for his failed revolution. His visit was one of the spectacular events of the period, evolving into a grand tour reminiscent of Lafayette's excessive visit in 1824. Kossuth was a failure as a soldier and statesman, but Americans overlooked these details in their haste to again participate in the unfolding of democratic history. Huge crowds heard him speak, and enormous amounts of money were subscribed to the Magyar cause. Sanders was closely involved, even promising an armed steamship to Kossuth, an offer the latter called "the greatest made to me since I came to the U.S." Almost everyone in the country was wildly enthusiastic, except Herman Melville, who noted that "if he left home to look after Hungary the cause in hunger would suffer." Even the Duyckincks were moved, remembering George's Paris adventure in 1848.[27]

But for all the pomp of Kossuth's visit, it also revealed the increasing inability of the North and South to agree on anything. While Cuban annexation was led by Southerners, eager to intervene abroad for democracy, the Kossuth excitement, defined in the same terms, was largely confined to the North and West. The key difference, of course, was slavery, the problem that was beginning to shape everything in American politics. Although Kossuth maintained scrupulous neutrality on the subject, Southerners perceived his emphasis on "liberty" to be Abolitionist. Cuban democracy was different altogether, since it only applied to the slaveowners chafing under monarchical Spanish rule. In fact, it was secretly a ruse to promote southern, rather than American notions of empire. Mike Walsh, the New York Irish leader, wrote John Quitman that revolution and annexation were the only ways "Cuba can be saved to the South."[28]

Thus the European revolutions, which all the Young Americans had celebrated in 1848 as the culmination of democracy, began to cause internal discord in the 1850s. Southerners remembered their old distrust of the French Revolution, which they believed had led to the Haitian Revolution. More outspoken than Kossuth was Mazzini, who did not hide his hatred for slavery, leading southern Young Americans to distrust him. Kossuth was furious in 1853 when a large gun order (probably made through Sanders) was canceled because of Mazzini's abolitionism. A letter Hawthorne wrote George Sanders in 1854 revealed the unresolved tension of the issue. Hawthorne shared Sanders's outrage that Mazzini was harming his cause in the United States, but then went on to excoriate Kossuth for his equivocation, wishing for "a sturdier condemnation of slavery," which of course Sanders would have deplored. Young America was losing its bearings.[29]

A survey of old and new *Review* writers reveal the growing inconsistency of the Young American position in the early 1850s. As O'Sullivan and Sanders grew more bellicose, many of the old New York clique began to reexamine their commitment to annexation and the Democratic party. Field, Sedgwick, and Bigelow were antislavery, and none of the Van Burenites had forgotten the slings they had suffered at the hands of the southern wing of the party. Even Parke Godwin, who wildly cheered Kossuth and laughed at O'Sullivan's Cuban shenanigans as the misbehavior of "a few wild fellows," became righteous over the aggressions of the slave power. Perhaps no sentence better conjures Young America's rhetorical dilemma than Sanders's idiotic rant that Old Fogies were "treating Liberty like a nigger."[30]

But if the difference between the Kossuth and Cuba excitements revealed a widening gulf, Young America II pressed on undeterred, calling for American intervention wherever needed. The British minister, trying to explain Young America for his superiors, defined it as "those who profess extreme democratic doctrines . . . and also those who urge it to be the duty as well as the true Policy of the United States to intervene in the Affairs of Foreign Nations in support of Democratic and Republican Principles." Identifying imperial Russia as the source of reaction in Europe, the new Young Americans resembled cold warriors a century before their time. In a disconcertingly modern tone, they urged American arms be deployed against Russia in third countries to prevent the spread of alien principles contrary to democracy. Spurred on by Kossuth, who saw the American and Russian systems as fundamentally "antagonistic," the American annexationists harshly criticized the czar for his own land hunger. As late as 1953 Russians were citing Young American invective to convince the world of the long history of American ambition in the Pacific.[31]

Despite these worldwide ambitions, the local drift of Young America was unmistakably southward, as evidenced by one menacing definition of American territorial ambition: "East by sunrise, West by sunset, North by the Arctic expedition, and South *as far as we darn please.*" Whereas the *Review* of 1837 had been a discreet instrument of the Van Buren administration, the 1852 *Review* became a renegade organ of extreme annexationist opinion with a distrust of Washington politicians. A writer wrote, "*Young America* is to speak out & is to be heard," proving "it is not necessary to be professional men in *Politics* or *science* to be felt in the country."[32]

The one exception was the man who personified the new concept of Young America: Senator Stephen Douglas of Illinois, the "Little Giant" and "the Lochinvar of the Young Democracy." Douglas enlisted Sanders to help his forthcoming presidential campaign and arranged financing for him to purchase the *Review*. Their admiration was mutual. He praised Sanders as "a man of remarkable vigor of intellect," and wrote privately, "I profit more by your letters than any I receive," but he also wondered if his friend had "the requisite prudence to conduct the Review safely." His forebodings were amply confirmed.[33]

Douglas had devoted a life of public service to the expansion of democracy, and he looked and acted the part of a Young American. Born the same year as O'Sullivan (1813), small and barrel-chested, he was gifted with powerful oratorical skills, especially when roused to the righteous indignation that defined the Young American persuasion. Like many of the other Young Americans, he grew up fatherless. He was likened to "a steam-engine in breeches" and appropriately enjoyed the support of George Law, the wealthy steamboat magnate who had tried to supply arms to the French insurgents of 1848.[34]

Beyond his youth and bluster, Douglas thrilled the Young Americans with his national scope of vision. His supporters reveled in his continental grandeur. A New Yorker supposed the candidate, "with his eastern birth, his western residence and his southern marriage will be regarded in those sections as a less sectional man than any other." O'Sullivan had admired him since they together urged Polk to purchase Cuba, and in 1845, Douglas had endorsed Manifest Destiny before it was even coined: "I would exert all legal and honorable means to drive Great Britain and the last vestiges of royal authority from the continent of North America, and extend the limits of the republic from ocean to ocean. I would make this an ocean-bound republic, and have no more disputes about boundaries or red lines upon the map."[35]

Even to neutral onlookers, Douglas was the personification of the blustery attitude denominated "Young America" around the nation, though increasingly centered in the South and West, with a stronghold in New York. He admitted this verbal identification in a Senate debate with Lewis Cass, revealing that many Americans were suspicious of it: "It is the vocation of some partisan presses and personal organs, to denounce and stigmatize a certain class of politicians, by attributing to them unworthy and disreputable purposes, under the cognomen of 'Young America.' It is their amiable custom, I believe, to point to me as the one most worthy to bear the appellation."[36]

Douglas was right about the critical tone many were taking toward his supporters. Andrew Johnson called him "the candidate of the cormorants of our party," and elsewhere the faction was defined, not inaccurately, as a congeries of "adventurers, politicians, jobbers, lobby members, loafers, letter writers, and patriots which call themselves 'Young America.'" J. C. Breckinridge denounced it in no uncertain terms: "I want no wild and visionary progress that would sweep away all the immortal principles of our forefathers—hunt up some imaginary genius, place him on a new policy, give him 'Young America' for a fulcrum, and let him turn the world upside down. That is not the progress I want."[37]

Despite these unsavory associations, Douglas did not disavow the "Young America" nickname and even enjoyed considerable popularity as the rising political star of the new generation. He was joined by many important politicians, who with Sanders marked Young America's shift southwestward. An Ohio supporter wrote, "Douglas is the man, *Young America*, the word." Prominent allied senators included the former Jacksonians William Allen of Ohio and Robert Walker of Mississippi, John Weller of Ohio and California, and Pierre Soulé of Louisiana. Soulé, like William Sampson, was a former European republican who had been forced to emigrate to the United States, and he was hot-blooded in his support of the '48ers. He explained his support of Douglas in revolutionary terminology: "In siding with Douglas, I was prompted to give my help in a struggle whose object was the overthrow of the old party-dynasties that had assumed power, and lost all elasticity of mind, all energy of will, all courage in action, so necessary to those who wish to govern a great people."[38]

Douglas shared many of O'Sullivan's old tenets. He was deeply Anglophobic, and in 1853 uttered a classic denunciation of European antiquity in almost precisely the terms Hawthorne would use, to opposite effect, in his preface to *The Marble Faun* seven years later: "Europe is antiquated, decrepit, teetering on the verge of dissolution. When you visit her, the objects which enlist your highest admiration are the relics of past greatness; the broken columns erected to departed power. It is one vast grave-yard."[39]

Fittingly, Douglas enjoyed appealing to American youth with his messianic sense of American destiny. His whole identity was rooted in it: "From early youth, I have indulged an enthusiasm, which seemed to others wild and romantic, in regard to the growth, expansion and destiny of this republic." Despite his own diminutive stature, he proclaimed, "You cannot fetter the limbs of the young giant. He will burst all your chains." It was inevitable that someone, in this case Thomas Hart Benton, would note the slapstick absurdity of Douglas's attempt at self-enlargement: "He thinks he can bestride this continent with one foot on the shore of the Atlantic, the other on the Pacific. But he can't do it—he can't do it. His legs are too short."[40]

Despite this literal shortcoming, Douglas also mirrored O'Sullivan in the high premium he placed on American culture as a means of extending the sway of United States. He supported copyright legislation, wrote amateur poetry, and personally defrayed the expenses of a young American artist's education in Europe. Democracy's "mission" was "the great mission of progress in the arts and sciences— in the science of politics and government—in the development of human rights throughout the world." He issued a number of Whitmanesque pronunciamentos on the American "right to think freely and boldly." Indeed, his motto, "resurgam," echoed Whitman's 1850 poem "Resurgemus" to the European radicals.[41]

Appropriately, the Little Giant was permanently enshrined in the literature he anticipated, although not, perhaps, as he might have expected. In my opinion, Melville, the great debunker of Young America, referred cryptically to Douglas and the decline of Young America in *Moby-Dick*. In the chapter on "The Whiteness of the Whale," he wrote paradigmatically of two horses crazed by a desire to run westward. The first, the White Steed of the Prairies, had a Jacksonian majesty:

> a magnificent milk-white charger, large-eyed, small-headed, bluff-chested, and with the dignity of a thousand monarchs in his lofty, overscorning carriage. He was the elected Xerxes of vast herds of wild horses, whose pastures in those days were only fenced by the Rocky Mountains and the Alleghanies. At their flaming head he westward trooped it like that flaming star which every evening leads on the hosts of light.[42]

With warm nostrils and a flashing cascade of white hair, added to a circle of aides and marshals, the White Steed possessed all the military grandeur of the Hero of New Orleans and struck Melville as "a most imperial and archangelical apparition of that unfallen, western world." In other words, he evoked all of the heroic qualities of the man originally celebrated by Young America I in its halcyon period.

Moving into the present tense of 1851, Melville was less sanguine about Jackson's successors. A new horse, younger, possessed the same westward instinct, but with far less dignity, less "spiritual whiteness," and indeed with a disturbing element of "demonism." Remembering that Douglas had been born in Vermont before moving westward to make his career as an orator of Manifest Destiny, consider the following passage as Melville's damning judgment on Young America II:

> Tell me, why this strong young colt, foaled in some peaceful valley of Vermont, far removed from all beasts of prey—why is it that upon the sunniest day, if you but

shake a fresh buffalo robe behind him, so that he cannot even see it, but only smells its wild animal muskiness—why will he start, snort, and with bursting eyes paw the ground in phrensies of affright? There is no remembrance in him of any gorings of wild creatures in his green northern home, so that the strange muskiness he smells cannot recall to him anything associated with the experience of former perils, for what knows he, this New England colt, of the black bisons of distant Oregon?[43]

Despite shaking the buffalo robe often in 1851 and 1852, Douglas narrowly lost the campaign for the nomination and presidency. He was chiefly defeated by the aggressive support voiced by Sanders and the Young Americans, which alienated almost everyone else in the ring. Sanders simply excoriated Douglas's rivals for the prize. Of Lewis Cass, the ultimate "Old Fogy," he wrote, "Age is to be honored, but senility is pitiable." Winfield Scott was "a vain military fop," Van Buren "a beaten horse," Buchanan "a mere lawyer, trained in the quiddities of the court," and others were "imbeciles," "nincompoop(s)," and "vile toads." This was Young America II in all its juvenile glory.[44]

Douglas implored Sanders to soften his tone, even begging him to "select someone else as your candidate, and bend all your energies to elect him." It was to no avail. After Sanders had alienated all the important power brokers in Washington, Douglas was, in Andrew Johnson's poetic expression, "a dead cock in the pit." Mirroring Melville's parable, Douglas wrote Sanders to denounce "this course which represents me as an Ishmaelite with my head against every-body." The day after the election, a supporter wrote Douglas, "Pierce is President-Elect, as you this day would have been but for some indiscreet (or pretended) friends."[45]

The defeat of Douglas, while disappointing to Sanders, was not a complete defeat for Young America. The Douglas effort may have even played into the hands of Franklin Pierce, the war hero who was less incendiary than Douglas but still had some credit among *Review* readers for his relative youth. As his campaign biographer noted, he was not an old soldier like Winfield Scott, "indelibly stamped into the history of the past," but "a new man" with "a life of energy." The biographer was O'Sullivan's old helpmate, whom the *Review* praised as "Nathaniel Hawthorne, politician." It praised the biography in literary and political terms, boasting that Hawthorne's modest and direct tone perfectly matched the candidate, who would never approve "the lucubrations of the high-falutin order of literary genii." Using Hawthorne as a model, Sanders seized upon Pierce's "young strength" and "faith in youth" to attach Young America to his bandwagon.[46]

Another friend had written Pierce in the summer of 1852, "The grand ideas which are the most potent in the election are sympathy for the liberals of Europe, the expansion of the American republic southward and westward, and the grasping of the magnificent purse of the commerce of the Pacific, in short, the ideas for which the term *Young America* is the symbol."[47]

Pierce took the lesson to heart and profited from friendly overtures to the Young Americans without fully embracing their zeal. The *Review* strongly endorsed him throughout the summer of 1852 as "O K," which was slang for a strong position on Cuba and Canada. Appropriately, he adopted the filial nickname Young

Hickory, the same Gansevoort Melville had bestowed upon Polk in 1844. With Pierce's election, many conservative Europeans actually feared American invasion, and the *Revue des Deux Mondes* predicted "la *Jeune Amerique*" would bring "a violent and perhaps bloody solution." European republicans like Mazzini and Kossuth were overjoyed at their candidate's victory, having actively helped to elect him through their influence on foreign voters in the United States. They expected reciprocity, and Pierce would not disappoint them. As Young America II grew blunter and stupider, it seemed to be gaining power. Despite Sanders's complete mismanagement of the Douglas campaign, he and his allies, including Hawthorne and O'Sullivan, were about to enjoy their last moment in the spotlight.[48]

Young America Abroad

Despite Young America's failure to elect its first choice, its influence was everywhere in the early 1850s. The word *Young* was freely affixed to all sorts of politically volatile groups, many of which had nothing to do with each other. A group of radical German '48ers formed a Socialist group called Jung Amerika, reading Marx's New York articles. The Cuban filibusters, the very definition of crass capitalism, gathered under the banner of "Young Cuba." A branch of Young Italy, headquartered in New York, made louder and louder noises as dispatches came back from Rome about the republican struggles.[49]

Despite their early opposition to him, Pierce rewarded Young America with an assortment of plush diplomatic jobs. Mazzini wrote this was done to reward the efforts he and Kossuth made in Pierce's behalf during the campaign. Most famously, Hawthorne was given the lucrative Liverpool consulship, but O'Sullivan was made chargé and then minister to Portugal, and a host of other Young Americans were given prominent appointments, almost all of which offended the host governments.[50]

Pierre Soulé, who had virulently attacked Spanish reactionism and favored the annexation of Cuba, was appointed minister to Spain. A journalist observed, "Mr. Soulé was probably the most obnoxious man that could have been chosen to represent us at Madrid." One of the Young Italian émigrés Catharine Sedgwick had invited to Stockbridge, E. F. Foresti, was sent to Genoa, where he was at first refused by the Sardinian government. The financier August Belmont inherited the position held by Harmanus Bleecker and Auguste Davezac at The Hague. Edwin De Leon, who had given one of the earliest "Young America" speeches in 1845, became chargé at Alexandria, Egypt.[51]

Most obnoxious of all was George Sanders, who served briefly as consul to London before being recalled. This was almost the same position Polk had given Gansevoort Melville in 1845, and like his predecessor, Sanders took a perverse delight in upsetting the applecarts of polite diplomacy. Among other misdeeds, he wrote a letter to the *London Times* expressing his hope Napoleon III would be assassinated and allowed American diplomatic pouches to be stuffed with revolutionary communications between European antimonarchists, whom he also gave passports to. Unsurprisingly, the Senate refused to confirm him. Nevertheless, he left a lasting memory among the Old Fogies of Europe, if only how not to be a diplomat.[52]

Sanders's most famous *faux pas* was a Washington's Birthday dinner he gave in London on February 21, 1854, to which all of the prominent radicals of Europe were invited. It was an unprecedented event, both for its boldness and its questionable political wisdom, which of course defied everything George Washington stood for. Mazzini, Garibaldi, Orsini, Kossuth, Ledru-Rollin, Arnold Ruge, and Alexander Herzen all supped at the invitation of the United States, and Minister James Buchanan even conferred his blessing with an appearance. To quote Gansevoort Melville's brother, this was verily an "Anacharsis Clootz deputation," bringing "the world's grievances" from "all the ends of the earth." Buchanan expressed a fear that the house would explode with all the "combustible materials" about. The message was sent to Europe that American diplomacy would do all it could to support the popular revolutions brewing. Predictably, the radicals themselves bickered whom to invite (Socialist Louis Blanc was refused), revealing the limitations of revolutionary *realpolitik*. Kossuth was always grateful for recognition, but as he wrote Mazzini, in a tone that indicates what he really thought of Young America, "It is a great bore this dining. But these Americans are like that—like children."[53]

This assemblage of antimonarchical radicals, sent to the European capitals recovering from 1848, was perhaps the least effective diplomatic corps ever marshaled by the United States and startled the shaky nerves of their hosts at every step. They cavorted with republicans working to subvert the established governments and held secret conferences to promote these ends. European newspapers were aghast at the American "conclave of cuteness," and denounced the nettlesome envoys. There is some evidence that O'Sullivan, Sanders, and Soulé were plotting on their own to foment revolution in Spain (by which Cuba would become American) and the rest of Europe. Sanders was still the conduit for thousands of guns, but his recall diminished this activity. The crowning achievement of Young American diplomacy was the Ostend Manifesto of 1854, which again stated the case for Cuban annexation and threatened the United States "would be justified in wresting it from Spain if we possess the power." European governments were convinced a plot was afoot for an American-sponsored "general insurrection" leading to a "Universal Republic." But after this high-water mark, the American interventionists retreated and Soulé, their leader, resigned his post. Americans were finally growing tired of bluster and expansion.[54]

When Sanders was recalled, some impressive Europeans lamented his departure, including the obvious beneficiaries of his attentions (Kossuth, Mazzini, and Ledru-Rollin cosigned a letter of regret). Victor Hugo inscribed several novels to him as his "concitoyen de la république universelle," and wrote, "You are worthy to speak to France, and to speak to her in the name of America. . . . My admiration rises to affection for you." Sanders also corresponded freely with Hawthorne, as fellow American diplomats in England, and the latter expressed his "regret and mortification" when Sanders was recalled, even inviting him to stay with him for a few days before returning. Hawthorne had attended a Washington dinner with "the fastest of the Young Americans" in 1853, and admitted that "some men possessed a kind of magnetic influence over him which he could not resist, however it might lead him," though he was "not of the same rabid politics."[55]

Throughout this period of intense political activity, O'Sullivan nominally kept up his interest in literature (he became friendly with Victor Hugo,who gave him a plaster model of his hand), and he never lost his attachment to Hawthorne. He was one of few to enjoy the privilege of dining with Hawthorne and Melville together, which he did in Lenox on April 11, 1851. His friendship with Hawthorne would prove one of the few constants of his life, as it turned out. In 1853 he wrote again to Dorr, then dying in Rhode Island, to inform him "you are one of the three nearest and dearest friends whose portraits framed are constantly before my eye." The other two were Nathaniel Hawthorne and Narciso Lopez. It is difficult to conjecture what impressions were formed in O'Sullivan's mind by this unlikely triptych, but he evidently still considered literature to be one of the instruments of bringing about the revolution he craved.[56]

Hawthorne for the most part reciprocated the affection, although there were several strains upon their friendship. Forgetting O'Sullivan's chronic inability to understand money, Hawthorne lost ten thousand dollars in one of his hare-brained investment schemes. On another occasion, Hawthorne was forced to invest in New York real estate, buying O'Sullivan's wife's property to avoid having to lend him money.[57]

As fellow diplomats in Europe under Pierce, the old acquaintances renewed their friendship in the 1850s, even vacationing together in their new official capacities. O'Sullivan stayed with Hawthorne for three weeks in Liverpool on the way to assuming his post in Lisbon, and O'Sullivan invited Sophia Hawthorne to Portugal for an extended visit to improve her health. Her stay proved good medicine, and Hawthorne, writing a friend, revealed that O'Sullivan's financial problems had not dimmed his social aspirations: "She is delightfully situated with the O'Sullivans, and sees kings, princes, dukes and ambassadors, as familiarly as I do Liverpool merchants." Hawthorne, much relieved, wrote, "I never felt half so grateful to anybody, as I do to them." At one point, Hawthorne even contemplated taking over the Lisbon post from O'Sullivan. It would have been a congenial appointment, for the king regent of Portugal was "a great admirer of The Scarlet Letter" and O'Sullivan presented him with a set of Hawthorne's works.[58]

O'Sullivan thrived in the role of diplomat, which catered perfectly to his need for public recognition and showy patriotism, as well as his gift for foreign tongues. For all the leveling democracy he had preached over the years, he gloried in the monarchical setting and was well received by the Portuguese royal family. He remained steadfast in his attachment to American culture, however, taking pride in the simplicity of his ceremonial attire.[59]

Around this time, Hawthorne composed several reflections on O'Sullivan's character that stand as the most penetrating assessment left to historians. Prompted partly by his deep gratitude, and perhaps also by jealousy over Sophia's closeness to him (Una wrote her father that O'Sullivan was second only to Hawthorne in her mother's affections), he left a bittersweet portrait, probably accurate, of a man with deep literary sensibilities who had been irrevocably tarnished by his political adventuring. In a note to a friend, he called O'Sullivan "one of the truest and best men in the world," adding "he has wasted much of his life in politics, but is a scholar, and might have been a poet."[60]

Writing Sophia in February 1856, he was more penetrating still. Hawthorne admired his "quick, womanly sensibility—a light and tender grace, which, in happy circumstances, would make all his deeds and demonstrations beautiful." He confessed, "I have a genuine affection for him, and a confidence in his honor; and as respects his defects in everything that concerns pecuniary matters, I believe him to have kept his integrity to a degree that is really wonderful, in spite of the embarrassments of a lifetime." As hinted by the last comment, Hawthorne disapproved of O'Sullivan's political machinations, although he had not hesitated to profit from them earlier in their friendship: "It has sometimes seemed to me that the lustre of his angel-plumage has been a little dimmed—his heavenly garments a little soiled and bedraggled—by the foul ways through which it has been his fate to tread, and the foul companions with whom necessity and politics have brought him acquainted."

Hawthorne tempered the critique, adding, "To do him justice, he is miraculously pure and true, considering what his outward life has been." But there was a fundamental flaw in O'Sullivan's character that Hawthorne had trouble articulating. He suggested that O'Sullivan, despite his charisma, was not sturdy enough, that his "quick, genial soil produces an abundant growth of flowers," but not the stern Alpine vegetation Hawthorne preferred. This may simply have been the opinion of a jealous husband, but Hawthorne's judgment rings true of the entire Young America movement:

> Thou talkest of his high principle; but that does not appear to me to be his kind of moral endowment. Perhaps he may have the material that principles are manufactured from. . . . I like him, and enjoy his society, and he calls up, I think, whatever small part of me is elegant and agreeable; but neither of my best nor of my worst has he ever, or could he ever, have a glimpse.[61]

Despite his critique of O'Sullivan, they remained close to each other, and the old Young American literary alliance was briefly revivified in 1856 when Hawthorne and Melville (who was visiting) wrote worried letters inquiring about George Duyckinck, who had broken his leg in a train crash in England. Hawthorne had not fulfilled the promise he made to Duyckinck of writing articles for the *Literary World* from England, as "a slight return for your favors toward me, of such ancient date, and so persistingly kept up," but he maintained warm feelings toward his old friend.[62]

Hawthorne and O'Sullivan remained in their official posts through the Pierce administration, then stayed on in Europe afterward, unsure when or how to return to the country they had done so much to represent. Having missed much of the tension of the 1850s, they were not conditioned to it as their friends were and were unprepared for the complex situation greeting them upon their return. Both waited until 1860 to repatriate themselves, and O'Sullivan, deeply conflicted about his loyalties, returned to Europe soon thereafter. In December 1861, Hawthorne wrote Franklin Pierce about him: "Poor fellow! I am not sure that the fate he half-anticipates would not be the best thing for him—to be shot or hung."[63]

Cracks in the Bell

> Upon its disinterment, the main fracture was found to have started from a small spot in the ear; which, being scraped, revealed a defect, deceptively minute, in the casting; which defect must subsequently have been pasted over with some unknown compound.
>
> —Melville, "The Bell Tower" (1855)

> When some magnificent architectural structure crumbles in an instant into ruin . . . we know that there were latent causes, in certain flaws or points of weakness, which it then becomes of the first necessity to discover before we can reconstruct.
>
> —John L. O'Sullivan, *Union, Disunion and Reunion* (1862)

A casual observer might have reflected on the variety and vigor of Young American pronouncements in the 1850s and concluded that cultural nationalism had never been stronger. But a closer examination reveals there were important structural defects in the architecture of Young America, deceptively minute signs of weakness that gave clear warning of the national crisis impending. Despite rhetorical similarities on the surface, the two Young Americas had strongly divergent definitions of Manifest Destiny. For Duyckinck in 1845, it was the extension of a benign American culture led by youthful writers and artists. For Sanders and O'Sullivan seven years later, it was the forceful acquisition of foreign territory in the name of "democracy," but little better than European imperialism.

This militaristic muscle flexing had little to do with the arts, and even struck many of the original Young Americans as downright anti-intellectual. Not only was the American republic stooping to the level of European monarchies in its power games, it was doing so in the name of extending slavery. For all their anti-English-ness, many old Young Americans found this step intolerable. Thus the Young America movement, vaguely defined even at its height, became the site of intense confusion and soul-searching about the mission of American culture. In the North and South, nationalists continued to expound on the need for extending American culture around the world, but they did so for very different reasons.

At the same time this crack was widening within Young America, the term was expanding to embrace several new meanings in the 1850s. A group of free-wheeling businessmen and foreign investors found it a convenient expression for their desire to extend American influence into new markets. Besides the gun-running steamship owner George Law, prominent members of this financial Young America included August Belmont and George Francis Train. Belmont, a German who had learned business under the Rothschilds, had a certain Young American credibility in that he was a loyal Democrat and had spent several years pursuing riches in Havana.[64]

Train was a Bostonian who had carved out wealth at home and abroad. Among other accomplishments, he had financed the clipper *The Flying Cloud*, built by Donald McKay, whom F. O. Matthiessen idealized as the type of Whitman's "Man in the Open Air." Besides that imaginary literary connection, Train was a self-proclaimed Young American who wanted to extend American culture around the world as part of a shrill theory he called "Spread-Eagleism." He wrote several books tracing his adventures, including *Young America Abroad* and *Young America in Wall Street*, using mercantile terms to define "that Young America which pours its energies through all the channels of commerce in all quarters of the globe." According to his definition, it was a distant forerunner of the businessman's power of positive thinking: "Young America . . . likes joy, gladness, bright colors; growling, ill-nature, scowls he detests. . . . Young America believes in a good hearty laugh."[65]

There had always been a strong economic component behind Young American jingoism dating back to O'Sullivan's opposition to the tariff. These businessmen, too, believed in Manifest Destiny, although they defined it in a more material sense than any intellectual would. It was American capital, not culture, they wished to extend, and they pioneered the concept of a financial empire reaching across the Pacific. Not only were the early 1850s the time of the great California migration, but Matthew Perry reached Japan in 1853, a year after an article in the *Review* predicted the "naturally enterprising" people of this feudal empire would prefer unfettered capitalism to the despotic state reducing them to "little more than automata in every affair of life." With condescension, Sanders also praised the Chinese immigrants already learning to be "good, provident money-making citizens of this great republic." Equally enticing was Australia, then striking a number of observers, including Melville, as "that great America on the other side of the sphere," and not only for its gold boom. Train spent years there, then traveled extensively through Asia and Europe, always commenting on ways American businessmen might cultivate profitable relationships with the natives.[66]

Many other strains of Young American ideology persisted among disparate groups, and there were even several humorous magazines in the 1850s titled *Young America* that were largely apolitical. But as the term spread, its meaning became diffuse. The advocates of free land, led by George Evans and many of the radical German "48ers," also called for western expansion, but their egalitarianism was the opposite of Train's investment strategy. The Evans clique was also strongly opposed to slavery. Mike Walsh, on the other hand, the leader of New York's Irish rowdies, repudiated his old ally Evans as he gravitated toward a pro-Southern position. William M. Corry, a Cincinnati journalist, also switched from an early position against slavery to a later one in favor of it. This widespread pattern of erratic behavior concerning expansionism helps to put O'Sullivan's foibles in a larger context.[67]

As Young America's volume expanded, its substance diminished. Like Manifest Destiny, the term embraced so much that it became difficult to define, although for some it retained a pejorative edge. Orestes Brownson, reflecting on American history, defended "Mr. Cotton, the stern but well-meaning old Puritan, who had infinitely more mind and heart than Young America, that has learned to laugh at him." In 1854 Theodore Parker wrote a sermon on old age that demonized Young America, even linking it inexplicably to Aaron Burr, "Perhaps the worst great man Young America ever gendered in her bosom." The phrase also entered everyday parlance as slang for energy, as evidenced by a baseball coach's 1858 injunction to his lazy team to put more "Young America" into their play. An interesting definition offered by George William Curtis revealed its contradictions, embracing laziness and vigor, conservatism and radicalism simultaneously:

> What is popularly called "Young America" is a spirit appearing chiefly in politics and society, differing widely in each. In society it is timid and conservative, in politics audacious and radical; on the one side are those who have, on the other those who hope. . . . In the Bowery it takes the form of the b'hoy; in Broadway it appears in trowsers with a slight stiffening of limb—dances by night, and lolls at hotel-windows by day—believes that to be idle is to be gentlemanly, and to be tipsy and frequent gaming-houses, manly.[68]

One need only canvas the far-flung Young Americans at the time of the Civil War to see how differently they turned out. Duyckinck and Mathews drifted into cultured gentility, removed from politics, although certainly supportive of the Union war effort, as Duyckinck demonstrated with his gift-books on the war's progress. One wonders if they ever remembered the "Song of the Tetractys" Mathews had composed at the beginning of the mutual admiration society, way back in 1836. The lyrics were accidentally accurate: "Shall we not weep when joyous Youth is dying— / And broken hopes around us wither'd lying?"[69]

Bigelow, Bryant, Parke Godwin, and Field became leading Republicans, ardently opposed to slavery. Samuel Tilden, Stephen Douglas, William Allen, and Robert Walker maintained their allegiance to the Democratic party, but supported the Union (the Mississippian Walker was more opposed to slavery than the Ohioan Allen).

Theodore Sedgwick III, long opposed to the spread of slavery, also lent his support to the Union. Despite Young America's southern drift in the 1850s, he still drew upon its rhetoric in an 1858 address before the Columbia alumni, although he added a word on the need for "restraints." Addressing the "young and ardent intellect" assembled before him, he proclaimed,

> If, submitting to the restraints of discipline, and trampling under foot excesses of opinion, they cling fast to the great central idea of Nationality; who will doubt or deny or regret our manifest destiny? who will fail to salute our progress with affectionate admiration? who will not hail with delight the spread of our influence westward, southward, in every direction in which the active intelligence of America shall guide her indomitable energies?[70]

Far away from New York, William Gilmore Simms could never abandon South Carolina, despite his dislike for Calhounites, and he stayed there throughout the war. As the war ended, and mail service reunited the regions, he wrote Duyckinck, "Has politics killed literature?" It was an excellent question. In his case, the answer was yes (his enormous library was destroyed by Federal soldiers, little caring he once stood as a lone voice for Americanism in South Carolina). He and Duyckinck happily resumed their old correspondence, entering their dotage with all the enthusiasm of young pen pals.[71]

All of the leading Cuban annexationists supported the Confederacy. Among the Pierce appointees to Europe, the majority became Confederates, performing diplomatic service for the South during the war (including Pierre Soulé, Edwin De

Leon, and George Sanders). Hawthorne stayed true to the Democracy, earning widespread contempt for his ambivalence to Lincoln, and publicly defended the unpopular Franklin Pierce, in whose company he died in 1864. In 1862, when he published a poorly received critique of the war in *The Atlantic*, the editors denounced him with a subtle dig at his former Young Americanism. After deleting Hawthorne's remarks about Lincoln because they lacked "reverence," the editors added a bitter postscript, chiding Hawthorne for his past political sins: "It pains us to see a gentleman of ripe age, and who has spent years under the corrective influence of foreign institutions, falling into the characteristic and most ominous fault of Young America."[72]

More than most writers, Whitman indulged freely in jingoistic sloganeering of a Young American sort throughout the 1850s, although the deep rage he expressed in "The Eighteenth Presidency" revealed a creeping pessimism beneath his beatific persona. Melville was diffident, perhaps because he had seen his brother's Young Americanism kill him at an early age. He was probably horrified to be identified as one of "Our Young Authors" in a *Putnam's* profile in 1853. Following the euphoria of the Monument Mountain climb and his review of Hawthorne, his youthful nationalism abated until he was celebrating antiquity in "I and My Chimney" (published 1856): "Old myself, I take to oldness in things; for that cause mainly loving old Montaigne, and old cheese, and old wine; and eschewing young people, hot rolls, new books, and early potatoes." The newly venerable author pitied the "infatuate juvenility" that led seekers after new things like "the Spirit Rapping philosophy" O'Sullivan was discovering. In *The Confidence Man*, he poured out more venom, dismissing the excitements of Young Europe along with the gun-running journalists (Sanders and O'Sullivan both) who had promoted them: "In fine, these sour sages regard the press in the light of a Colt's Revolver, pledged to no cause but his in whose chance hands it may be. . . . Hence, for truth and the right, they hold, to indulge hopes from the one is little more sensible than for Kossuth and Mazzini to indulge hopes from the other."[73]

His poetry, too, betrayed his cynicism. In his supplement to *Battle-Pieces*, there was a flicker of the old rhetoric, when he theorized that "Secession, like Slavery, is against Destiny." But there was no doubt his Young American days were over. *Clarel* was long and morose, blaming those who sought to create "an Anglo-Saxon China" for bringing on "the Dark Ages of Democracy." More to the point, a brief quatrain entitled "Greek Architecture" neatly inverted everything Young America ever stood for:

> Not magnitude, not lavishness,
> But Form, the Site;
> Not innovating willfulness,
> But reverence for the Archetype.[74]

Most confused of all among this welter of ex-nationalists was O'Sullivan, whose odd peregrinations in Europe through the war confirmed that he had become a man without a country. Officially pro-South, he seems never to have gained the full confidence of the Confederate hierarchy, and always harbored the dream of returning to New York. He dashed off letters to the leaders of both American governments, but no one took him seriously. It is small wonder he became a spiritualist, trying to commune with a happier past when his nationalism meant something.

There were loomings of his personal crisis as early as 1860, when he returned to New York from his long European stay. His former comrades were shocked at his intellectual transition, or more accurately, his failed transition. John Bigelow, now an important editor in his own right, was distressed to find his former mentor at a dinner "avowing himself a pro-slavery man and declaring that the Africans in America ought to erect the first monument they were able to erect by voluntary subscription to the first slave-trader." O'Sullivan's old friend Samuel Tilden, who had also grown in importance, was doubtless embarrassed by O'Sullivan's letters and requests for loans.[75]

Everywhere the former shaper of opinion turned, he was greeted by the sight of his old partners and underlings, grown more influential than he, all in disagreement with him, and symbolic of a new American order he was unable to understand. He tried to persuade prominent northerners to compromise with the truculent South, but no one was interested in his opinion. Frustrated by his inability to find a sympathetic audience, he returned to Europe in February 1861, before Lincoln even took office. When he heard the news of Fort Sumter, he broke down with "convulsions of tears," then wrote Tilden in agony: "Gracious God, that we should have lived to see such things! . . . What doom is sufficient for the mad authors of all this!"[76]

The following months were not easy for O'Sullivan. Despite investing in a Spanish copper mine that supplied European military needs, he had little money, having been "ruined for Cuba." He found it difficult to decide where he stood on the calamity, or whether even to come home (he now considered Switzerland "the only respectable republic left"). Despite growing southern sympathy, he could not get New York out of his mind and chafed "terribly" at his removal from the American theater. His loyalties seemed unfocused, despite their strong expression: "Just as I would have shouldered a Northern rifle to unite in the defense of Washington, against menaced invasion from the South, so would I now, were I at home, stand up in aid of the rightful defense of the Southern soil against this equally unjustifiable invasion from the North."[77]

In June, O'Sullivan declared, "I am frankly and decidedly with the South now in their stand of resistance against subjugation and for independence." He wrote Tilden, "I have pretty well made up my mind never to return to live at the North again," and confirmed Hawthorne's fears by telling Tilden "Republican mobs . . . would infallibly hang me were I in New York." But his thoughts always returned to Manhattan, despite suspecting "the North will be too hot to hold *me* hereafter." The lynch mob was a recurring theme in his letters, and he plaintively hoped "though I might myself be hung for a traitor on the streets of New York, for my sentiments on the subject, there would still remain somebody willing to cut me down and give me a decent burial." He appeared to almost wish it to happen.[78]

Once an incurable optimist, O'Sullivan now saw little hope for the future. He wrote Tilden, "Our Union is doomed." The formerly irrepressible democrat denounced the fictitious "mobs" and politicians who had precipitated the conflict ("majority is as bad a tyrant as imperial despotism"). Lincoln was both a dictator and "a third-rate village attorney" (he could not figure out which). He lumped all his enemies togethers, and his "blood boiled" at the "Republicans and old Federalists and Whigs" who had always stood for force over logic. For all his dabbling in warfare, he loathed the "Military Centralization" of the new administration, and thought it "more pregnant of future mischief" than even secession and separation. Returning to an old theme, he argued the "insanity" of the war was "manifest." Manifest Insanity never caught on.[79]

As the war continued, O'Sullivan grew ardently attached to the Lost Cause, thereby fulfilling a complex manifest destiny of his own. True to his lineage, he wrote Jefferson Davis, "The darker may be the gloom of the clouds resting on the Southern cause, the brighter and warmer burns the flame of my attachment to it." He volunteered to carry a "musket," but confessed he knew nothing of military matters (including the fact "muskets" had been upgraded to rifles). He still sounded confused and nostalgic as he explained his Confederate sympathies: "Where else am I to find now anything left of all that constituted the reasons for my Americanism or patriotism? As between the Abolitionists and the Democrats of the North ('who know the right, but yet the wrong pursue'), I regard the latter as the less respectable of the two."[80]

He lived out the war in England, performing small acts of diplomacy for the Confederacy, none of great moment. Denied the involvement he craved, O'Sullivan returned to the act of writing to explain to the unlistening world where the great nationalist of the 1840s stood amidst the rubble of Americanism. Having failed to extinguish Whiggery in the 1830s and 1840s, he now brought all his old Locofoco energy into the fray, identifying the "mad Republican and Abolitionist" party as the source of intrusive government, a new group of Whigs in disguise.[81]

In quick succession, O'Sullivan turned out three tracts from London urging formal recognition of the South and the cessation of hostilities. All were epistolary, addressing Franklin Pierce, Samuel Morse, and Lord Palmerston respectively. The first, entitled *Union, Disunion and Reunion*, shared *Moby-Dick*'s English publisher and also some of that book's conclusions. The "model republic" he had spent his life defending was a pasteboard mask compared to its darker inner workings. The perennial optimist was forced to admit, "with astonishment, grief, shame," that there were "unsuspected defects" in the system, and "some latent germs of evil co-existing with all its great elements of good." O'Sullivan cast about widely trying to find them, criticizing the excesses of partisan intrigue and presidential power, but he was unable to see the central relevance of slavery to the conflict. Instead, he labored to blame the problem on "patronage" and its misuse. By a strange twist of fate, he also criticized the excitement over Manifest Destiny. This argument persuaded no one. In fact, no one paid attention at all. Hurricanes and rocks had "already wrecked the good ship of the State."[82]

The other pamphlets were darker still. The eternal Jacksonian simply could not fathom the course American history had taken, in defiance of his cosmogony. A year later, in *Peace the Sole Chance Now Left for Reunion*, he used an ironic word to argue Lincoln's war signaled the "nullification" of "our whole political theory and system: The attempt to do so is to stultify our own revolution; to blaspheme our very Declaration of Independence; to repudiate all our own history; to cancel our

constitutions State and federal; to sanction all the despotisms, all the alien domina-
tions, of other ages and countries."[83]

In his tortured mind, the South now became the oppressed people fighting foreign domination like the Poles against Russia. He could not grasp that the North,
too, felt it was fighting for the Declaration, defined more broadly than the way he
colored and understood it. He declared "farewell forever to all that constitutes the
essential principle of our boasted Americanism" and resigned himself to supporting
the losing side in the O'Sullivan family tradition.[84]

If O'Sullivan's loyalties were confused, Sanders was an unwavering supporter
of the Confederacy, acting as a Confederate agent in Europe and Canada. In the
summer of 1864, he wrote Tilden, whom he probably knew through O'Sullivan, to
propose a clandestine peace conference at Niagara Falls, but to little avail. When
Abraham Lincoln was assassinated, a twenty-five-thousand-dollar reward was instantly offered for his arrest on the assumption he had something to do with the
murder. He died in 1873, shortly after giving battle one last time in the siege of
Paris, where he had relocated following the war. His prediction that the *Democratic
Review* would last into the twenty-first century was off by 141 years. After he sold his
interest in late 1852, the magazine hobbled along for a few years before expiring, to
no one's great chagrin, in 1859, its energy spent and the democratic principle a
pleasant memory.[85]

The period after the Civil War was even more painful for O'Sullivan, and he
traveled around Europe in fitful desuetude, living in Paris, London, and Lisbon. In
an 1853 debate with Stephen Douglas, the fogyish Lewis Cass had predicted the inevitable anomie youthful nationalism would feel with time: "Young America, as it
passes on in the journey of life, must expect to become Old America itself, and
share in the abuse which that respectable condition is sure to bring it." O'Sullivan
had come to fulfill Hawthorne's dismissive remarks about ambitious youth in his
chapter on Holgrave in *The House of the Seven Gables:*

> The effervescence of youth and passion, and the fresh gloss of the intellect and
> imagination, endow them with a false brilliancy, which makes fools of themselves
> and other people. Like certain chintzes, calicoes, and ginghams, they show fairly
> finely in their first newness, but cannot stand the sun and rain, and assume a very
> sober aspect after washing-day.[86]

Despite the disillusion he must have felt seeing his old friends dominate a cultural scene closed to him, O'Sullivan ultimately returned to New York with his wife
in 1879. One of the few times he appeared in public was to help dedicate the Statue
of Liberty, and it seems he was called upon mainly because no one else could be
found who spoke French properly. There is something bathetic about the image of
O'Sullivan gibbering in a foreign language about liberty to an audience of New
Yorkers who could not understand him, in French or any other tongue. Neglected
by the few who had not already forgotten him, he was effectively "oblivionated," to
use Melville's term.[87]

With little to do in the present, and less to look forward to in the future he had
always cherished, O'Sullivan understandably turned to the past. He became infatuated with spiritualism, the bizarre religion predicated on the idea of ghosts knock-

ing over furniture in dark rooms. In 1885, he wrote a letter to James Russell Lowell, his old contributor, that would appear deranged if it were not so clearly the result of his loneliness. He explained to Lowell that his medium (one of the famous Fox sisters) had transmitted a message to him from Lowell's late wife, and that she was happy in her new location. Among the other spirits he communicated with were those of Narciso Lopez, the king of Portugal, Charles Sumner, Leland Stanford, Jr., and a friend of Julius Caesar's. In his mind, at least, he was surrounded by the important admirers he had always cultivated.[88]

Julian Hawthorne afforded one of the few glimpses of the later O'Sullivan, hinting through his kindly language that his "after-career was not a happy one":

> I saw the dear old gentleman, a generation later, in New York; he had the same clear, untroubled tranquil face as of old; his hair, though gray, was as thick and graceful as ever; his manner was as sweet and attractive; but though, in addition to his other accomplishments, he had become an advanced spiritualist, he had not yet coined into bullion his golden imagination.[89]

Like Melville, several blocks away, the former firebrand was fated to live out his corporeal existence in a grim New York brownstone, almost entirely divorced from the raucous nineteenth-century culture all about him. He traveled to London once to perform genealogical research, a last chance to inquire into the strange family destiny bequeathed to him by his roving ancestors. His last appearance in print completed his reversal of fortune. The October 1894 issue of *The Royalist*, a magazine read by Americans who fancied themselves blue-blooded, contained a long article on the O'Sullivans and their aristocratic heritage. The count of Bearhaven, cited extensively in the article, never mentioned democracy once.[90]

In 1861, the year he realized how little he understood American politics, O'Sullivan recalled his ancestors, writing "a strange fatality has seemed to pursue us, by what sudden end the name is to expire with me, time has yet to show." The "sudden end" came thirty-four years later, after six years of paralysis and declining health. He outlived Melville by four years, passing away in 1895 with none of the fanfare he had so long craved. Although Manifest Destiny was about to be revived, this time in the Philippines and Cuba (finally!), no one remembered its author. An uncomprehending obituary left this ludicrous understatement: "At one time the editor of a political journal, he attached himself to the Democratic party before the war." It added, "He was also well grounded in the dead languages." This was unintentionally accurate, for the democratic rhetoric O'Sullivan had crafted so successfully before the war was ancient history a half-century later, and might as well have been Aramaic. One suspects he would have preferred any sort of violent death, of the kind he had foretold to Hawthorne, to the quiet expiration he was forced to endure in utter seclusion, a very old fogy forgotten by an eternally younger America.[91]

Epilogue

Forever Young

Then as I was getting up to the Closerie des Lilas with the light on my old friend, the statue of Marshal Ney with his sword out and the shadow of the trees on the bronze, and he alone there and nobody behind him and what a fiasco he'd made of Waterloo, I thought that all generations were lost by something and always had been and always would be and I stopped at the Lilas to keep the statue company and drank a cold beer before going home to the flat over the sawmill.

— Ernest Hemingway, *A Moveable Feast*

On May 20, 1994, America's youngish president, Bill Clinton, gave an unheralded speech that included this peroration: "Remember this, my fellow Americans: When our memories exceed our dreams, we have begun to grow old. And it is the destiny of America to remain forever young." This speech, given before UCLA students, was not especially historic. Yet it revealed more clearly than most the familiar touchstones of youth and newness, and the belief that American time somehow exists outside of world time, in defiance of the normal aging process, oblivious to the slow march of history.[1]

What does this impossible belief mean, and what does it tell us about ourselves? What is so wrong with growing old and cherishing memories along with dreams? Certainly, the United States is not "young" in terms of its age as a civilization, or a constituted polity. Whether our origin is dated to 1787, 1776, or an earlier founding moment, we are not nearly as spry as our leaders would have us believe. Nor is this anything to be ashamed of. As Gertrude Stein boasted, somewhat perversely, America is the oldest civilization in the world, since it has been modern the longest.[2]

Equally certainly, the United States holds no monopoly on youthful rhetoric. Many other nations have seen versions of Young America, which stole its name from Young Italy. Mahatma Gandhi exploited the phrase "Young India" against colonial England in much the same way Daniel O'Connell used "Young Ireland," also combining it with journalism. And the phrase "Young Turk," dating from the movement that culminated in the Turkish Republic of 1923, persists in our language to designate someone with overweening ambitions in the O'Sullivan mold.[3]

The leader who probably placed a higher emphasis on youth then anyone this century was not Bill Clinton or John F. Kennedy, but Mao Zedong. The Cultural Revolution was nothing if not a continual exhortation to the youth of China to save their country from its fossilized leaders (except for Chairman Mao, curiously exempted). Mao wrote many passages that might easily have been authored by John O'Sullivan a century earlier. He praised Young China (without using the term) as the vanguard of the Chinese Revolution, because "young people are the most anxious to learn, they are the least conservative in their thinking." He, too, found culture a weapon: "New-democratic culture is national. . . . It belongs to our people and bears our national characteristics." Opposed to "ancient culture" and "feudal dross," Mao urged China's "new culture" to be "democratic and revolutionary," to "go among the masses." Whitman, expecting a very different cultural revolution, had spoken the same language.[4]

In Clinton's defense, he is far from the only American politician to seek out the restorative powers of youth. Particularly since the 1960s, it has been one of the driving themes of electioneering oratory. Kennedy used the trope more successfully than most, drawing an effective contrast between himself and his elderly predecessor. But even Eisenhower's dutiful heir carefully reconceived himself as a "New Nixon" in 1968 (he would define Karen Carpenter as "young America at its best"). What American politician in recent memory has not tried to do the same? Literally thousands of quotations might be culled to show the persistence of our peculiar, unquenchable hope for perpetual youth (a harsher critic might say second childhood). Since Ponce de Leon, the rest of the world has looked to America for inoculation against the normal and natural cycles of aging and death. By the time this book is published, a new generation of politicians will be claiming, yet again, to be a new generation.[5]

The rhetoric of youth is not restricted to liberalism, either, despite O'Sullivan's claim that it was. More accurately, it conjures the promise of "change," another obsession of our politics. To cite a recent example, Newt Gingrich used many of Young America's strategies in *To Renew America*, his quirky declaration of principles. Like O'Sullivan, Gingrich was often opaque about his specific proposals, but displayed ferocious rhetorical energy and a boundless confidence that "history" would prove him right. The Young Americans would certainly agree that "almost once a generation," America needs a "rebirth" to adjust to "new needs and new realities." The "Contract With America," allegedly one of these generational upheavals, joined a tradition dating back to the Revolution. But he also added the contradictory claim: "We are definitely *the first generation in American history* to face such a challenge" (his italics).[6]

The resemblances do not stop here. Gingrich certainly agreed with the *Democratic Review*'s motto, "that government is best which governs least." Like O'Sullivan he relentlessly attacked the "elite culture" that has supplanted "practical, democratic culture." Of course, Gingrich's understanding of cultural elitism was not the same as O'Sullivan's. O'Sullivan distrusted the emerging corporate world and never would have attacked intellectuals with the same rage. He sought a larger idea of America in every sense; a bigger nation, but also a nation big enough to fight poverty and most forms of social injustice. For all its defects, Young America I felt that diverse types of Americans should be included in American cultural politics, not just those conversant in the latest technological wizardry or skilled at economic competition. And the Young Americans approved government support for intellectual activity, judging from Van Buren's support of the *Democratic Review*, Duyckinck's hope for copyright protection, and the magazine's support for arts funding.[7]

Examining the similarities and differences between Gingrich and O'Sullivan, it becomes quite clear that the rhetoric of generational renewal can be applied to just about any cause in American politics. And it can be used to justify either progressive or retrogressive policy, depending on the mood of the audience. The flexible argument goes something like this: New generations need new ideas, in the revolutionary tradition; but they also need to preserve the old values enshrined by the same revolution. Like a reversible raincoat, these contradictory notions can be used to define anything under the sun as an "American" idea. Or as Gingrich stated it more poetically, in a phrasing I am still trying to decipher: "To take the romance out of America is to de-Americanize our own country. To me, America is a romance in which we all partake."[8]

In a nation still struggling to come to terms with the generational struggle of the 1960s, and arguing ferociously about how history ought to be written, it behooves us to look into murky questions like the "romance" of America and its definition from generation to generation. Herman Melville defined this romance quite differently than Gingrich's smiling rhetoric would have us believe. That is probably why Duyckinck was terrified by what he beheld in *Moby-Dick*. The 1840s and 1960s differ more than they resemble each other, but each period witnessed the same strange progress from idealism to apocalypse, linked inextricably to the rise of a new generation that sought to redefine national values. Ironically, each youth movement aged the nation considerably, making clear the limitations as well as the possibilities of democracy. By 1850, as well as 1970, few doubted that an enormous gulf stood between dreams of "America" and the actual United States, an aging nation with problems like any other.

Having grown up in the 1960s, I felt subconsciously intrigued by Young America the first time I stumbled across the name. It was a serendipitous impulse, for the antebellum period is a logical place to look for anyone trying to cast light on the history of generational discontent. Few generations were as excited about the future and their role in shaping it as the young Democrats who came of age under Andrew Jackson. Few were more disappointed. But a final summary of the Young Americans should combine a healthy respect for what they did accomplish with a sober analysis of their shortcomings.

What exactly was Young America? I hope I have clarified a widely misunderstood phenomenon. Young America was several things at almost the same time; a literary clique in the 1840s, a political junto in the early 1850s, and an expansive attitude prevalent afterward. These manifestations were essentially distinct from one another, except for the ubiquitous presence of John O'Sullivan, always straining after novelty and excitement. If nothing else, I hope this study has reestablished the importance of this actor, both central and evanescent, in the cultural politics of the antebellum scene.

With all his complexities, O'Sullivan presents a fascinating figure for analysis and disrupts the notion that history is the simple end-product of an easily discerned causality, the result of irresistible forces marshaling people and events before them. O'Sullivan was chimerical and unpredictable; he changed his opinions significantly between his early and later careers, and he often changed them to suit his audience. Much of his career displays the strikingly powerful effects of human personality, in all of its eccentricity, on events that then assume a life of their own. Despite giving the name to Manifest Destiny, his desultory life illustrates how capricious and illogical historical forces can be, defying human attempts at divination. Forever predicting the "unraveling" of democratic history, by which he meant something natural and orderly, he was shocked at how much history does unravel, disrupting the most carefully conceived plans and theories. Melville wrote Evert Duyckinck that they were "predestinated," but it would be hard to see "destiny" in the strange career of O'Sullivan and Young America, including the coining of Manifest Destiny. Like Ahab's Latin American doubloon, Manifest Destiny meant different things to different people at different times. It might be appropriate, given O'Sullivan's Francophilia, to quote Gustave Flaubert, another witness to 1848: "One doesn't shape one's destiny, one undergoes it."[9]

Did Young America succeed? It depends on the definition of success, of course. Most would argue it was a disaster. The Democratic party imploded, the fragile national coalition fell apart, and 600,000 Americans were killed in the war that followed. Many of the *Democratic Review*'s early contributors ended up disgusted with politics and the rhetoric of nationalism. This is not a very impressive legacy. And there are reasons to belittle Young America. True to its name, it was infantile at times, claiming desired objects as "rights," insisting that the best possible future was foreordained "destiny." This is what Kossuth hinted at when he wrote Mazzini that the Young Americans were "like children." Charles Baudelaire was crueler: "The United States is like a gigantic child. . . . At once young and old, America chatters and gabbles on with an astonishing volubility."[10]

It is easy to single out many areas of myopia in the various Young American agendas. The *Review* writers never showed much sympathy for abolitionism, pathetically wishing the problem of slavery would vanish without extremism or government intervention. While Duyckinck showed some awareness of gender issues, most of the Young Americans were single-mindedly masculine and insisted that "virility" was a crucial component of the American culture they were trying to build. From a modern vantage point, this seems shortsighted, if not downright silly.

An analysis of the first Young America's literary campaign discloses that it lost its momentum after fleeting triumphs in the 1840s and failed abysmally to recognize the achievement it sponsored indirectly: *Moby-Dick*. The second Young America movement, that of Sanders and Douglas, was interesting for its early expression of the now-standard doctrine of American interventionism, and for its acrobatic attempt to defend slavery and European radicalism at the same time. But in the long run, it too was a colossal failure, embarrassing America abroad and ruining the hopes of its own candidates with excess zeal and a belligerent notion of enforced "democracy." It also ridiculed the original Young America, revealing the unbearable strains of nationalism in the decade before the crisis of union.

The strain was most visible in O'Sullivan, who ignored the coming disaster and was utterly undone by it. As Hawthorne noted, O'Sullivan was occasionally "lacking in the moral sense" and seemed to have no idea that slavery undermined the democratic principle in a more fundamental way than high tariffs or intrusive government. His wartime pamphlets defined "Americanism" simply as the concept of government by "consent of the governed," implying the Union war effort was un-American. In so doing, he neglected the Declaration of Independence's other guiding principle, that all men are created equal. This, the heart of true Americanism, was an idea that Young America somehow failed to grasp in its application to people of color.[11]

As early as 1846, Horace Greeley hinted at O'Sullivan's myopia when it came to race and democracy. Greeley admired him in many ways, noting "not many took broader grounds in support of Dorrism than John L. O'Sullivan" and that he championed the underdog in struggle after struggle. But his ambition sometimes compromised his principles:

> The Editor of the News has some of the instincts, and would gladly have the reputation of a Reformer and Philanthropist, if it did not cost too much. Could he serve God and Mammon at once, he would prefer that to serving Mammon alone. But to enjoy influence with and obtain privilege from the present ruling powers at Washington and Albany, is not compatible with an eye steadily fixed on the elevation of the lowly. He is to his party what Macbeth was to the bolder, not baser spirit who lured him through crime to Ruin. At heart an adversary of War, Slavery and all the hoary abuses intwined [*sic*] with them, he has been dragged into advocacy of Texan Annexation with all its incidents and objects, and into a seeming support of the 54'40 bullying with regard to Oregon, well knowing that every day's halting on that ground endangers the peace of the world. . . . Will he not yet remember that 'Democracy' builds monuments for such only of its Editors as have defied its prejudices and sordid policy, and braved the denunciation of its General Committees?[12]

O'Sullivan forgot that final lesson, but not all the Young Americans fared as miserably. Many did speak out against slavery. Parke Godwin was once as ardent as any of them. He ridiculed Europe as "an old man, timid, slow and slightly decrepit," while America was "the eager, untamed, elastic urchin, . . . half-despising the old folks to whom his odd new ways give a world of trouble." In 1855 he posed a difficult question: "What is America, and who are Americans?" He first offered a simple material definition, echoing the annexationists, who "consider America as nothing more than the two or three million square miles of dirt, included between the Granite Hills and the Pacific." But this failed to convey "the real significance and beauty of the terms." He went on to suggest that "America, in our sense of the word, embraces a complex idea." The land mass had existed since time immemorial, but "the true America, a mere chicken still, dates from the last few years of the eighteenth century." Before the Revolution, the colonies were merely "the eggs and embryo of America," but in 1855, the year of *Leaves of Grass*, America was a "fully fledged bird who would shout a cock-a-doodle to the sun."[13]

In other words, America was ideal *and* material, and no amount of land-grabbing would augment the nation's stature without a proper understanding of its underlying moral philosophy. "The real American," according to Godwin, was one who "gives his mind and heart to the grand constituent ideas of the republic . . . no matter whether his corporeal chemistry was first ignited in Kamschatka [*sic*] or the moon." Godwin understood that all the races inhabiting the United States were collectively a part of the true Young America, and he came close to using the phrase melting pot, arguing that from now on "all are mingled in the seething cauldron of our national life." His attack was directed toward the Know Nothings, but it might have also been turned toward O'Sullivan and Sanders, whose extension of physical America neglected these subtle metaphysics.[14]

But perhaps pity is more in order than harsh condescension. Without defending the gaping holes in O'Sullivan's patchwork ideology, I incline to Hawthorne's charitable assessment: "If we had his whole life mapped out before us, I should probably forgive him some things which thy severer sense of right would condemn." To be sure, he had severe limitations, but his bizarre career should not be relegated to the scrapheap because his vision of America's destiny did not unfold according to plan. I hope this book will restore a little of the historical attention he craved. And the other early Young Americans, men like Evert Duyckinck and David Dudley Field, both of whom took an early stand against the extension of slavery, should be given full credit for their many cultural accomplishments.[15]

Despite Young America's periodic moral blindness, it was important for all the reasons O'Sullivan claimed at the outset of the *Democratic Review*. Few intellectual movements have shown so clearly the interpenetration of political and artistic thought, a particular feature of the antebellum era. Not all Young Americans agreed with each other, and many retreated from their original positions, but all felt that American culture, to make its mark in the world, had to come to terms with the unique social system in place here. American literature, art, and law, straining to define themselves, inevitably partook of the democratic feeling of the times, often with an admirable curiosity for new ways of thinking. As the *New York Tribune* wrote, "Young America seeks to discard old forms, explode old notions, tear down all impediments to the onward march of mind and of truth." These are not the worst goals. Many still swear by them.[16]

In my view, O'Sullivan is compelling simply because of where he stood. During the most excruciating period of self-definition in American history, he occupied a vital position dispensing the propaganda of the nation's dominant political party. Although many disagreed with him, finding his exuberance for the "democratic principle" naive, it is important to recognize his achievement. He not only gave voice to the hopes of a rising generation who felt shut out of the political process, but he did it in a way that fused creative expression and political action in unprecedented harmony, vivifying both. Whatever one might say about the failure of Young America, the fact an editor knew and ranged freely with writers and revolutionaries, trading ideas with all of them, merits attention. It fascinates me that O'Sullivan's desk displayed daguerreotypes of Thomas Dorr, Narciso Lopez, and Nathaniel Hawthorne, the taciturn writer we prefer to shroud in the mists of colonial antiquity.

This leads to one of Young America's most concrete achievements, its effect on several of the great creative artists of their time, including Hawthorne, Whitman, and

Melville. All listened to the *Democratic Review*'s pronouncements before ultimately rejecting them to pursue a more complicated vision of reality and national
purpose. When Melville felt the "shock of recognition" at Hawthorne's genius, it
was because he had been trained to find and claim him for "the new, and far better
generation" of modern American writers. In his final flurry of Young Americanism,
Melville wrote about Hawthorne, "The world is as young today, as when it was created." In a sense, he was right, as he also was a year later when he rejected the more
narrow beliefs of Young America in his masterpiece. To quote *Moby-Dick* one last
time:

> There is no steady unretracing progress in this life; we do not advance through
> fixed gradations, and at the last one pause:—through infancy's unconscious spell,
> boyhood's thoughtless faith, adolescence's doubt (the common doom), then scepti-
> cism [sic], then disbelief, resting at last in manhood's pondering repose of If. But
> once gone through, we trace the round again; and are infants, boys, and men, and
> Ifs eternally.[17]

Evert Duyckinck should be given credit for introducing Melville to Hawthorne, and for much more. Young America I helped to establish a modern critical-
literary matrix, using journalistic skills to support publishing and artistic ventures,
and helping creative Americans to develop a sense of their public vocation. With
ceaseless efforts in behalf of the copyright, the Library of American Books, the
American Art-Union, and American jurisprudence, the Young Americans promoted the novel idea that an intellectual and economic infrastructure was necessary to promote and sustain the creativity all Americans were calling for. Despite re-
treating from the antielitist banner they began under, they helped install a fairer
system of cultural distribution, one that has remained essentially intact, with important adjustments every generation or so.

It is logical this activity was centered in New York. As the commercial capital of
the United States from the third decade of the century onward, the city's cultural
brokers insisted on an expansive national outlook, and it was there the battle to define modern American culture was fought. If Young America failed to preserve the
Union, or even its own reputation, it succeeded in rejuvenating American culture
in the 1840s and permanently altered the nation's "politico-literary" map. Afterward,
taste was far less likely to be determined in Boston and Philadelphia. And culture itself was less likely to be defined in Whiggish terms, something created near the top
of society and dispersed sparingly to those trained to appreciate it. Not for the last
time, New York had offered a coarse corrective to America's cultural politics. As
Hawthorne knew, to be American is "a text of deep and varied meaning," far more
complicated than most of his New England acquaintances allowed.[18]

Many of O'Sullivan's and Duyckinck's ideas would echo again. In the early
twentieth century, again in New York, there was a similar rhetorical blast issued
against the guardians of the past. Randolph Bourne (another Columbia graduate)
and Van Wyck Brooks proclaimed themselves the mouthpiece for a revolutionary
"league of youth," "the flying wedge of the young generation," seeking to create
"out of the blind chaos of American society, a fine, free, articulate cultural order."
Like their predecessors, they disliked Boston and punctiliousness, which they de-

fined as one and the same. To revitalize "dusty literary scholarship," they studied history and literature together, and asked that writing display "social purpose" and "vivid high and revolutionary thought."[19]

Point by point, they returned to the catalogue of 1837. Bourne wrote, "The failure of the older generation to recognize a higher ethic, the ethic of democracy, is the cause of all the trouble." His 1920 essay "Trans-National America" repeated O'Sullivan's original Manifest Destiny argument, insisting American culture was not simply Anglo-Saxonism transplanted to a new hemisphere, but something infinitely richer and more complicated. This "super-culture" might even "by some happy chance, determine the future of civilization itself." Bourne and Brooks cited Mazzini's Young Italy and unwittingly repeated the phrase "Young America" to express their generational ambitions. Like O'Sullivan, they looked to a better future, a more tolerant future mingling all the elements of America:

> This strength of coöperation, this feeling that all who are here may have a hand in the destiny of America, will make for a finer spirit of integration than any narrow "Americanism" or forced chauvinism. . . . All our idealisms must be those of future social goals in which all can participate, the good life of personality lived in the environment of the Beloved Community. No mere doubtful triumphs of the past, which redound to the glory of only one of our trans-nationalities, can satisfy us. It must be a future America, on which all can unite, be which pulls us irresistibly toward it, as we understand each other more warmly.[20]

Nor were Bourne and Brooks alone. The Ashcan School, the Lost Generation, the Beat Generation, and the 1960s counterculture all owed something to the linked notions of youth, progress, and "transnational" American culture. All had a strong base in New York City. All issued exciting manifestos, with political currents pulsing near the surface of intellectual arguments. All felt strongly they were replacing a previous generation that had desecrated the national heritage (Hemingway put it well: "Who is calling who a lost generation?"). Any student of these movements might do well to consider Young America as a slightly embarrassing ancestor.[21]

Even today, the ghosts of O'Sullivan and company gambol in the attic of our national memory. "Manifest Destiny" still recurs in one form or another, usually to justify a policy for which there is no clear precedent. Much of the rhetoric of the Cold War amplified thinking from a century earlier, when O'Sullivan argued democracy needed to expand in order to contain its ideological opponent (aristocracy). And within our borders, we still hear a great deal about the "cultural elite" subverting democracy.

Young America is also relevant to the ongoing debate about the role of government in promoting American culture. Many of O'Sullivan's ideas resonated in the politico-cultural symbiosis of the 1930s, on a far grander scale than he would have dared to dream. The Federal Writers Project, the photo-literary documentaries of the era, and the founding of American studies programs all reflected the belief that democracy could be taught through American history and literature. Despite the current climate of disapproval toward the NEA and NEH, conservative theorists have also merged politics and culture in the last half-century. Foreign policy initiatives like the Voice of America and Radio Marti were certainly "politico-literary" in their way, and it makes sense that the Soviet Union cited Young American harangues as evidence of ancient American imperialism. Young America *was* dangerous, as any Cuban or Mexican historian could confirm.

Then there is the future, the borderless place where O'Sullivan was most comfortable. If we take the time to weigh what was good and bad about the intense nationalism of the post-Jacksonian period, we might be better informed the next time we encounter the polarities of Young America I and Young America II: culture versus might; inclusion versus intimidation; compassion versus condescension, and so forth. We might take another small step toward the ancient goal of merging America, the beautiful idea, with America, the often inconvenient fact. We just might discover a Manifest Destiny worthy of our lofty rhetoric.

Some still agree with O'Sullivan's assessment that American culture, as it is disseminated over the world, whispers promises of political freedom to foreign peoples held in feudal dominion by the "old" thinking they have learned. If rock and roll music and Hollywood films do not exactly promote reverence for the Declaration of Independence, it is true they spread American idealism overseas, and a healthy dose of materialism as well. If O'Sullivan were alive today, he would enjoy the relentless din of twentieth-century Young Americanism, as expressed through brilliant cultural triumphs like rollerblades, hair weaves, liposuction, and countless other means of staving off mature adulthood. In fact, he did think about the twentieth century frequently. He loved to calculate how many millions of Americans there would be a hundred years after him, and by a lucky guess, predicted the United States would dominate the world in 1945, a century after Manifest Destiny. Another great rhetorician, Franklin Roosevelt, paid homage to his predecessor when he said "the destiny of American youth is the destiny of America." But just about every president has said something similar.[22]

Surprisingly, O'Sullivan thought he might make it to the White House someday, forgetting that his birth at Gibraltar made him ineligible. In 1842, at the height of his influence, O'Sullivan wrote a fanciful letter to his friend Annie Ward on her eighteenth birthday. Pretending that sixty years had elapsed, he dated the letter 1902 and predicted to her that he had been president twice, as well as "a desperate radical" and a man "who had turned some things topsy turvy." The impossible paradox of these goals lay at the heart of O'Sullivan's failure to achieve either political prominence or true radicalism. But they offer a fascinating insight into his character and the temper of the times. Too far from the American Revolution to remember it, but wishing for a similar upheaval in the republic of letters, he strangely combined nostalgia and futurism, moving inside and outside the established political channels to further his goals, all while touting democracy as the healer of America's and his own contradictions.[23]

O'Sullivan's nemesis and near contemporary, Abraham Lincoln, was luckier in his political fortunes. The former Whig *did* become president twice, and turned things more topsy turvy than he said he would. Although he was far from impartial, having distrusted Young Americanism in most of its manifestations, he left an interesting eulogy of Young America in 1859 that seemed to speak personally to O'Sullivan. Addressing "the unquestioned inventor of Manifest Destiny," a man sympathetic to "spiritual rappings," Lincoln hammered away at Young America's contradictions.

> We have all heard of Young America. He is the most *current* youth of the age. Some think him conceited, and arrogant; but has he not reason to entertain a rather extensive opinion of himself? Is he not the inventor and owner of the *present*, and sole hope of the *future*? . . . He owns a large part of the world, by right of possessing it; and all the rest by right of *wanting* it, and *intending* to have it. . . . He has a great passion—a perfect rage—for the *"new"*; particularly new men for office. . . . He is a great friend of humanity; and his desire for land is not selfish, but merely an impulse to extend the area of freedom. He is very anxious to fight for the liberation of enslaved nations and colonies, provided, always, they *have* land, and have *not* any liking for his interference. As to those who have no land, and would be glad of help from any quarter, he considers they can afford to wait a few hundred years longer. In knowledge he is particularly rich. He knows all that can possibly be known; inclines to believe in spiritual rappings, and is the unquestioned inventor of *"Manifest Destiny."* His horror is for all that is old, particularly "Old Fogy"; and if there be any thing old which he can endure, it is only old whiskey and old tobacco.[24]

Then Lincoln continued, more calmly: "The great difference between Young America and Old Fogy, is the result of *Discoveries, Inventions,* and *Improvements.* These, in turn, are the result of *observation, reflection* and *experiment.*" Recounting a long litany of strides taken by earlier peoples, he argued that ancient history was every bit as volatile and valuable as the present-minded Young Americans thought themselves. But near the end of his speech, he praised the spread of book culture among the people in exactly the same way O'Sullivan or Duyckinck would have in the 1840s. Lincoln exulted the "great mass of men" could finally think for themselves, no longer looking upon "the educated few as superior beings." In Young American language, he revealed his parallel nationalism, using the words *slavery* and *emancipation* in a different sense:

> It is difficult for us, now and here, to conceive how strong this slavery of the mind was; and how long it did, of necessity, take, to break it's [sic] shackles, and to get a habit of freedom of thought, established. It is in this connection, a curious fact that a new country is most favorable—almost necessary—to the immancipation [sic] of thought, and the consequent advancement of civilization and the arts.[25]

Despite the temptation to repeat Lincoln's sarcastic condemnation of Young America, the truth is more complicated than he allowed in 1859, as Manifest Destiny was blossoming into Civil War. Simultaneously admiring and denouncing the Young American imperatives, Lincoln's complex response serves as a helpful guidepost to the modern observer. Perhaps by applying his rule of patience to the study of this impatient, but exceedingly interesting group, we can learn more about the contradictory, combustible era that preceded America's darkest history, as well as its first cultural efflorescence.

Technically, we are no longer a young country, despite the continual recurrence of politicians to a youthful theme grown old. In recent decades, we, like the Young American generation, have experienced all sides of the aging process and have emerged with a chastened sense of youth's ability to transform society. But a nation of Old Fogies can still appreciate the lessons of Young America. Beginning with unlimited hopes for national greatness, finishing cynical and defeated, they witnessed the transformation of a romanticized "America" into an all-too-realistic United States, a country with selfish geopolitical aspirations like any other. The difference between the early, hopeful message of Young America I and the jaded rantings of Young America II revealed good and bad sides of the same rhetorical coin. Many of the original Young Americans would mark the precise moment of the transition as the instant it was asserted America had a Manifest Destiny to overspread the continent through force rather than freedom and imagination.

John O'Sullivan discovered this pretended destiny, and then discovered more slowly the harsher destiny he had also ushered in. How could it be otherwise? No one of his generation had more invested in the outcome, and few paid as high a price for destiny's manifestation. But for all his bombast and backsliding, his early idealism still holds out the possibility of something better for "the Great Nation of Futurity," always just a little bit ahead of the present tense. It is difficult, then as now, to separate "America" from the United States, and one generation from another. Yet it is still exciting to strive for "new history," as O'Sullivan did in 1837, and countless others have done since, knowing they will end up as old history when all is said and done.

Notes

Prologue

1. *Selections from Ralph Waldo Emerson* (ed. Stephen E. Whicher; Boston, 1957), 67.

2. James D. Richardson, ed., *A Compilation of the Messages and Papers of the Presidents, 1789–1902* (n.p., 1907), 3:313; 4:373.

3. John F. Kennedy, *To Turn the Tide* (New York, 1962), 7, 10.

4. I roughly calculated these figures using the 1840 census returns in *Historical Statistics of the United States, Colonial Times to 1970*, 1:16–18.

5. Abraham Lincoln, *Selected Speeches and Writings* (New York, 1992), 20; Stephen B. Oates, *To Purge this Land with Blood: A Biography of John Brown* (New York, 1970), 41–42.

6. For a colorful example of antibank rhetoric, see Robert Rantoul's speech at Worcester on July 4, 1837; *The Memoirs, Speeches and Writings of Robert Rantoul, Jr.* (ed. Luther Hamilton; Boston, 1854), 604.

7. On Mazzini and Young Italy, see Denis Mack Smith, *Mazzini* (New Haven, 1994), 5–12; Marx's letter is in Loyd D. Easton and Kurt H. Guddat, eds., *Writings of the Young Marx on Philosophy and Society* (Garden City, 1967), 40–50.

8. David Walker Howe, *The American Whigs* (New York, 1973), 127; see also Howe, *The Political Culture of American Whigs* (Chicago, 1979).

9. Calvin Colton quoted in David Brion Davis, *Antebellum American Culture: An Interpretive Anthology* (Lexington, Mass., 1979), 197.

10. Walt Whitman, *The Gathering of the Forces* (ed. Cleveland Rogers and John Black; New York, 1920), 2:79.

11. Rantoul, *Memoirs, Speeches and Writings*, 184–185.

12. Nathaniel Hawthorne, *Tales and Sketches* (New York, 1982), 476–477.

13. Julian Hawthorne, *Hawthorne and His Wife* (Boston, 1884), 1:159–160.

14. James R. Mellow, *Nathaniel Hawthorne and His Times* (Boston, 1980), 46.

15. Emory Holloway, ed., *The Uncollected Poetry and Prose of Walt Whitman* (New York, 1932), 1:118. I substituted "spectacles" where Holloway had "spectators," assuming a transcription error.

16. Herman Melville, *Moby-Dick or The Whale* (Chicago, 1988), 117, 158.

17. John William Ward, *Andrew Jackson: Symbol for an Age* (New York, 1953), 1.

18. F. Byrdsall, *The History of The Loco-Foco or Equal Rights Party, Its Movements, Conventions and Proceedings, with Short Characteristic Sketches of Its Prominent Men* (New York, 1842), 17.

19. Theodore Sedgwick, Jr., ed., *A Collection of the Political Writings of William Leggett* (New York, 1840), 2:197, 199, 241–243; the second article was originally published in *The Plaindealer* (March 4, 1837), 209–210. A list of Leggett's writings is in Page S. Procter, Jr., "William Leggett (1801–1839): Journalist and Literator," *The Papers of the Bibliographic Society of America*, 44 (1950), 239–253.

20. *United States Magazine and Democratic Review* 6 (July 1839), 23, 26–27; hereafter

cited as the *Democratic Review*. Unless there is evidence to the contrary, I am assuming un-attributed editorials in the *Democratic Review* to be O'Sullivan's. He admitted as much ("the political editorship was entirely mine") in a letter to Rufus Griswold, September 8, 1842, Griswold Mss., Boston Public Library.

21. Whitman, *The Gathering of the Forces*, 1:218. S. D. Langtree to W. C. Bryant, October 15, 1837; Bryant-Godwin Collection, Mss. Division, New York Public Library. *Democratic Review* 6 (July 1839), 17. On Field, see the *New York Review* 7 (April 1841), 393, 390, 389.

22. Cornelius Mathews to Evert Duyckinck, Duyckinck Collection, Mss. Division, New York Public Library; Cornelius Mathews, *Americanism* (New York, 1845), 15. Duyckinck expressed his desire to write a profile of Leggett in 1844; see Duyckinck to Rufus Griswold, September 3, 1844, Griswold Mss., Boston Public Library. His friends were also excited by Jackson's 1833 tour; see Robert Tomes to Duyckinck, June 5, 1833; Duyckinck Collection, Mss. Division, New York Public Library.

23. Robert V. Remini, *The Life of Andrew Jackson* (New York, 1988), 258.

24. Samuel Gilman Brown, ed., *The Works of Rufus Choate* (Boston, 1862), 1:367; Alexander Everett, *An Address to the Philermenian Society of Brown University, on the Moral Character of the Literature of the Last and Present Century* (Providence, 1837), 52. Everett later contributed to the *Democratic Review*, although he was a Whig throughout his early career. For more on New England and its Whiggish intellectual climate, see Lawrence Buell, *New England Literary Culture: From Revolution through Renaissance* (New York, 1986).

25. Frank Luther Mott, *A History of American Magazines* (Cambridge, 1939), 1:375n; Whitman, *The Gathering of the Forces*, 2:316.

26. Cornelius Mathews, *An Address to the People of the United States in Behalf of the American Copyright Club* (New York, 1843), 9.

27. *Democratic Review* 18 (March 1846), 238–239; (May 1846), 399.

28. *New York Morning News* (July 11, 1845).

29. Siert F. Riepma, in his dissertation, "Young America: A Study in American Nationalism Before the Civil War" (Western Reserve University, 1939), identified approximately eight overlapping variants of Young America, but for my purposes these two groups are the most important. I will discuss other variants later.

30. M. E. Curti, "Young America," *American Historical Review* 32 (October 1926), 34–55; Perry Miller, *The Raven and the Whale: The War of Words and Wits in the Era of Poe and Melville* (New York, 1956). Among the erratic Duyckinck treatments are John Stafford, *The Literary Criticism of "Young America": A Study in the Relationship of Politics and Literature, 1837–50* (Berkeley, 1952), which overstates Duyckinck's politics; and David S. Reynolds, *Beneath the American Renaissance: The Subversive Imagination in the Age of Emerson and Melville* (New York, 1988), which understates them. A more balanced treatment, albeit with minor factual errors, appears in Michael Paul Rogin, *Subversive Genealogy: The Politics and Art of Herman Melville* (New York, 1983). Larzer Ziff confuses the two principal Young Americas in *Literary Democracy: The Declaration of Cultural Independence in America* (New York, 1981). A well-informed chapter on Young America appears in Glenn Wallach, *Obedient Sons: The Discourse of Youth and Generations in American Culture, 1630–1860* (Amherst, 1997).

31. Herman Melville, *The Piazza Tales and Other Prose Pieces, 1839–1860* (ed. Harrison Hayford, Alma A. MacDougall, G. Thomas Tanselle; Evanston, 1987), 361.

32. Whitman, *The Gathering of the Forces*, 1:128.

33. Herman Melville, *Moby-Dick*, 331; *Battle-Pieces and Aspects of the War* (ed. Sidney Kaplan; Amherst, 1972), 21.

34. Lincoln, *Selected Speeches and Writings*, 200.

35. Holloway, *The Uncollected Prose of Walt Whitman*, 2:15–16.

36. Walt Whitman, *Poetry and Prose* (New York, 1982), 393.

37. Mathews, *Americanism*, 14; Hawthorne, *Tales and Sketches*, 758; *The House of the Seven Gables* (ed. Seymour L. Gross; New York, 1967), 81; Horace Traubel, *With Whitman in Camden* (Boston, 1906; rpt. Carbondale, 1982), 1:139.

38. *Sketches of the Speeches and Writings of Michael Walsh* (New York, 1843), 12.

39. *Democratic Review* 8 (November 1840), 430.

40. *New York Review* 7 (October 1840), 430.

41. George Francis Train, *Young America in Wall Street* (New York, 1857), 345.

42. *New-York Historical Society Proceedings, 1845* (New York, 1846), 122; Simms to Duyckinck, June 20, 1845; Duyckinck Collection, Mss. Division, New York Public Library.

43. Melville, "Hawthorne and His Mosses," in *The Piazza Tales*, 252, 247.

44. Herman Melville, *The Collected Poems of Herman Melville* (ed. Howard P. Vincent; Chicago, 1947), 6.

45. *Democratic Review* 6 (December 1839), 504.

46. Melville, *The Piazza Tales*, 248.

47. Ibid., 246.

48. F. O. Matthiessen, *American Renaissance: Art and Expression in the Age of Emerson and Whitman* (New York, 1941), ix, viii.

49. Hawthorne, *Tales and Sketches*, 740.

50. *New York Morning News* (January 25, 1845). I assume this quotation, taken from a review of Rufus Griswold, to be Duyckinck's.

51. *Democratic Review* 30 (March 1852), 210.

1 *The Politics of Culture*

1. "Report from the Secretary of the Treasury, in compliance with a resolution of the Senate of the 26th June last, on the petition of Mary O'Sullivan, widow and executrix of John O'Sullivan, deceased," December 8, 1834, *Senate Documents*, 23rd Congress, 2nd Session, 1834–1835, I, #5, 1. In this as in all matters relating to O'Sullivan, I am indebted to Sheldon Harris, whose unpublished dissertation remains the standard source; see Harris, "The Public Career of John Louis O'Sullivan" (Ph.D. diss., Columbia University, 1958).

2. Van Buren to Cambreleng, July 19 and August 5, 1829; O'Sullivan to Van Buren, March 28, 1845; Van Buren Papers, Library of Congress. The first letter urged Cambreleng to beset the governor and "don't let him leave the City before he consents to employing young O S."

3. Prospectus published in *Washington Globe* (March 13, 1837).

4. O'Sullivan to Rufus Griswold, Sept. 8, 1842; Griswold Collection, Boston Public Library.

5. Julian Hawthorne, *Hawthorne and His Wife* (Boston, 1884), 1:160; *Hawthorne and His Circle* (New York, 1903), 134. Horace Traubel, *With Whitman in Camden*, (Boston, 1906; Carbondale, 1982), 6:379. Mary E. Dewey, ed., *The Life and Letters of Catharine Maria Sedgwick* (New York, 1871), 286–287. The full Howe quotation is in Laura E. Richards and Maud Howe Elliott, *Julia Ward Howe 1819–1910* (Boston, 1916), 2:319–320: "He is a man of fiery temperament, with a slight, boyish figure: has deep blue eyes and dark hair, reminds me of John O'Sullivan in his temperament; is certainly, as Grandpa Ward said of the Red Revolutionists, with whom he dined in the days of the French Revolution, 'very warm.'"

6. Butler to Van Buren, October 14, 1839; Butler Papers, Princeton University Library. Van Buren to Bancroft, April 19, 1845; Bancroft Collection, Massachusetts Historical Society. In 1845, a Tennessee newspaper called him "one of the ablest writers and most accomplished scholars and gentlemen of the times"; see Albert K. Weinberg, *Manifest Destiny: A Study of*

Nationalist Expansionism in American History (Baltimore, 1935; 1963), 111. *The Journal of Benjamin Moran, 1857–1865* (ed. Sarah Agnes Wallace and Frances Elma Gillespie; Chicago, 1948), 1:7.

7. Longfellow to George W. Greene, July 23, 1839, in *The Letters of Henry Wadsworth Longfellow* (ed. Andrew Hilen; Cambridge, 1966), 2:162–163; also in Nathaniel Hawthorne, *The Letters, 1813–1843* (ed. Thomas Woodson, L. Neal Smith, and Norman H. Pearson; Columbus, Ohio, 1984), 56. Dwight Thomas and David K. Jackson, *The Poe Log: A Documentary Life of Edgar Allan Poe, 1809–1849* (Boston, 1987), 387; Thoreau to Emerson, January 24, 1843, *The Correspondence of Thoreau* (ed. Walter Harding and Carl Bode; New York, 1958), 77. Nathaniel Hawthorne to Sophia Hawthorne, Feb. 7, 1856, in Hawthorne, *The Letters, 1853–1856* (eds. Thomas Woodson, James S. Rubino, Neal Smith, Norman Holmes Pearson; Columbus, Ohio), 437–438; Hawthorne, *The English Notebooks* (ed. Randall Stewart; New York, 1962), 95. In a similar vein, John Bigelow, future American minister to France, and a frequent *Review* contributor, called him "a rascal" about money; see John Bigelow, unpub. diary, 1843; Bigelow Collection, Mss. Division, New York Public Library.

8. *Democratic Review* 15 (September 1844), 248. O'Sullivan wrote Dorr in 1853 that he had portraits of Dorr, Hawthorne, and Lopez on his desk; O'Sullivan to Dorr, November 18, 1853, Dorr Papers, Rider Collection, Brown University Library.

9. *Democratic Review* 6 (November 1839), 429.

10. Nathaniel Hawthorne, "The Hall of Fantasy," in *The Pioneer: A Literary Magazine*, February 1843 (ed. Sculley Bradley; facs. ed., New York, 1947), 52. Julius W. Pratt, "Origin of Manifest Destiny," *The American Historical Review* 32 (July 1927), 795–798; and Pratt, "John L. O'Sullivan and Manifest Destiny," *New York History* 14 (July 1933), 213–234.

11. Arthur Schlesinger, Jr., *A Pilgrim's Progress: Orestes A. Brownson* (Boston, 1939, 1966), 156. Frederick Merk, *Manifest Destiny and Mission in American History* (New York, 1963), 34. ("Racial homogeneity of the Anglo-Saxon stock had seemed to him an element of strength in his doctrine.") Reginald Horsman was more sensitive, admitting "he was generally reluctant to criticize all other races as being incapable of improvement"; *Race and Manifest Destiny: The Origins of American Racial Anglo-Saxonism* (Cambridge, 1981), 219.

12. O'Sullivan to George Bancroft, August 24, 1845, Bancroft Collection, Massachusetts Historical Society, January 25, 1845. George Fredrickson paid brief attention to O'Sullivan's wartime activities in *The Inner Civil War: Northern Intellectuals and the Crisis of the Union* (New York, 1965), but this is the exception rather than the rule.

13. Letter from Mrs. J. L. O'Sullivan, June 26, 1892, cited in Thomas Coffin Amory, *Materials for a History of the Family of John Sullivan of Berwick, New England and of the O'Sullivan Family of Ardea, Ireland* (Cambridge, 1893), 73.

14. See Peter Somerville-Large, *From Bantry Bay to Leitrim: A Journey in Search of O'Sullivan Beare* (London, 1980), for information on this forebear. For most genealogical material I am indebted to Harris, "The Public Career of John Louis O'Sullivan," Amory, *Materials for a History of the Family of John Sullivan*, and the manuscripts assembled by Florence Addicks in the Historical Society of Pennsylvania. See also R. T. Nichol, "Some Stray Notes on Cavalier and Jacobite Families in America," *The Royalist* 5 (October 1894), no. 7, 103–107.

15. See the elder O'Sullivan's account of Culloden in Alistair and Henriety Tayler, *1745 and After* (London, 1938). The John Paul Jones incident is described in *The Narrative of Nathaniel Fanning* (New York, 1806), reproduced by William Abbatt, ed., as "extra #21" in *The Magazine of History With Notes and Queries*, "Extra Numbers" 6 (1913), 86. Hawthorne confided this story to his *English Notebooks*, remarking the "horse-whipt" Jones had acted like a "poltroon;" see Hawthorne, *The English Notebooks*, 60.

16. Julian Hawthorne, *Hawthorne and His Circle*, 136. Washington Irving recorded in

his journal attending an elegant dinner with her in Paris in 1825, and when John Bigelow was invited to dine at the O'Sullivans' in December 1843, he wrote, "I am pleased at this for I wish to know his mother for her celebrated style"; see Bigelow, unpub. diary, December 30, 1843, Bigelow Collection, Mss. Division, New York Public Library.

17. See the *Dictionary of American Biography* 14 (New York, 1934), 89; Harris, "The Public Career of John Louis O'Sullivan," 1. The birthdate is confirmed by O'Sullvan's tomb in the Moravian Cemetery, Staten Island, New York. Nathaniel Hawthorne, *The English Notebooks*, 60. The text says "courtship," which I assume to mean "countship."

18. See W. Willshire Riley, *Sequel to Riley's Narrative* (Columbus, Ohio, 1851), 343–366. I am indebted to Robert Allison for this information. Years later, the younger O'Sullivan published a fascinating reminiscence of his Arabian childhood, describing a Poe-like incident in which his ailing mother was presumed dead and on the point of interment when her husband noted faint stirrings of life and revived her. See "Poor Esteer, the Jewess," *Democratic Review* 16 (April 1845), 319–328. Hawthorne noted this incident in his *English Notebooks* (60) as well. Senate Documents, 23rd Congress, 2nd Session, 1834–1835, vol. 3, #65, 3. This source stated the wreck occurred "on the southern coast of this continent," although others have placed it off South America.

19. O'Sullivan attended a Dominican school in Sorèze, France, and also the Westminster School in London; see Florence Addicks, "O'Sullivan Family Notes"; Historical Society of Pennsylvania. On O'Sullivan's Columbia career, see his file in the Columbiana Collection, Columbia University Library. He was occasionally addressed as "esquire," and an 1843 article in the *New York Tribune* described him as a "practised lawyer"; see George Cheever's *Capital Punishment. The Argument of Rev. George B. Cheever in Reply to J. L. O'Sullivan, Esq.* (New York, 1843); the *Tribune* article is cited in Louis P. Masur, *Rites of Execution: Capital Punishment and the Transformation of American Culture, 1776–1865* (New York, 1989), 151.

20. John W. Francis, M.D., *An Address Delivered on the Anniversary of the Philolexian Society of Columbia College, May 15, 1831* (New York, 1831), 14–15. On Leggett, see Lawrence H. White, ed., *Democratick Editorials: Essays in Jacksonian Political Economy by William Leggett* (Indianapolis, 1984).

21. *Senate Documents*, #5, 4; Harris, "The Public Career of John Louis O'Sullivan," 29–39.

22. Obituary of Langtree from the *New York Commercial Advertizer*, September 17, 1842; cited in the *Democratic Review* 11 (November 1842), 446. This obituary says that Langtree was thirty-one when he died of "congestive bilious fever" on September 8, 1842. See also Landon Fuller, "The United States Magazine and Democratic Review, 1837–1859: A Study of its History, Contents and Significance" (Ph.D. diss., University of North Carolina, 1948), 52. Langtree's editorial statement, *Knickerbocker* (April 1834), 320, claimed he was "accountable for all the editorial sins of the *Knickerbocker* for the last twelve months." *Knickerbocker* was spelled *Knickerbacker* in the first several volumes.

23. *Knickerbocker* 2 (July 1833), 4, 7; (December 1833), 486. The Leggett story, titled "The Encounter—A Scene at Sea," appeared in the February 1834 issue.

24. Fuller, "The United States Magazine and Democratic Review," 43n; *Georgetown Metropolitan* (March 3, 1837).

25. *Georgetown Metropolitan* (February 27, 1837).

26. *Democratic Review* 10 (April 1842), 317; *Washington Globe* (March 4, 1837).

27. *American Monthly Magazine* V (new series) (March 1838), 202. Garland to Van Buren, February 4, 1840, Van Buren Papers, Library of Congress. James Curtis, *The Fox at Bay: Martin Van Buren and the Presidency, 1837–1841* (Lexington, 1970), 82, many letters cited. O'Sullivan to Butler, Butler Papers, December 16, 1839, Princeton University Library.

28. O'Sullivan to Rufus Griswold, September 8, 1842, Griswold Collection, Boston Public Library. O'Sullivan to Butler, December 16, 1839, Butler Papers, Princeton University Library. When Butler wrote George Bancroft on May 1, 1838, he put the amount at five hundred dollars (Bancroft Collection, Massachusetts Historical Society).

29. Butler to Bancroft, May 1, 1838, Bancroft Collection, Massachusetts Historical Society.

30. John Spencer Bassett, *Correspondence of Andrew Jackson* (Washington, 1926–35), 5:1, n.d.

31. Jackson to O'Sullivan and Langtree, March 6, 1837; cited in *Washington Globe* (March 13, 1837).

32. O'Sullivan to Rufus Griswold, September 8, 1842, Griswold Collection, Boston Public Library. *Washington Globe* (March 13, 1837).

33. Curtis, *The Fox at Bay*, 82. Charles Francis Adams, ed. *The Memoirs of John Quincy Adams* (Philadelphia, 1876), 9:416.

34. O'Sullivan to Hawthorne, April 19, 1837; in Julian Hawthorne, *Hawthorne and His Wife*, 1:159. Langtree to Bancroft, November 12 and November 19, 1837, Bancroft Collection, Massachusetts Historical Society. O'Sullivan wrote, too, asking that Bancroft merely "magazine-ize" his speeches; O'Sullivan to Bancroft, May 27, 1841, Bancroft Collection, Massachusetts Historical Society.

35. O'Sullivan to Orestes Brownson, August 13, 1837, Brownson Papers University of Notre Dame [microfilm].

36. O'Sullivan to Longfellow, September 1, 1837, Harvard University Library; Longfellow to George W. Greene, July 23, 1839, *The Letters of Henry Wadsworth Longfellow*, 2:162. It is worth noting, however, that Longfellow at least discussed the possibility of writing an article on Anglo-Saxon literature (see O'Sullivan to Longfellow, September 6, 1838, Longfellow Collection, Harvard University Library), and the editor wrote him again in 1841 to solicit his support. Longfellow ended up writing a single poem, "God's Acre," which was published in the December 1841 *Democratic Review*. See *The Letters*, 2:340, 349–352.

37. Rufus Griswold, *The Poets and Poetry of America* (Philadelphia, 1842, 1843), vi; *The Prose Writers of America* (Philadelphia, 1846, 1847), 49.

38. *Western Monthly Review*, 3 (May 1830), 580.

39. Langtree to Bryant, October 15, 1837, Bryant-Godwin Collection, Mss. Division, New York Public Library. *Democratic Review* 1 (October 1837), 1, 13.

40. *Democratic Review* 1 (October 1837), 1–2, , 5, 6, 8–9.

41. Ibid. 1 (October 1837), 9.

42. Ibid. 1 (October 1837), 7.

43. Ibid. 1 (October 1837), 11.

44. Ibid. 8 (September 1840), 361; 6 (September 1839), 216; 3 (November 1838), 262.

45. Ibid. 1 (October 1837), 12–14.

46. Ibid. 11 (August 1842), 196; *New York Morning News* (August 21, 1844). In an interesting article in the *Review* two months later, the literary critic W. A. Jones (an acolyte of Evert Duyckinck's critical school) admired Bancroft as "the historian of the people," particularly because, unlike other historians, he expected future progress to originate in the lower classes; *Democratic Review* 15 (October 1844), 391.

47. Dorr was seen to be extending "the democratic principle" in *Democratic Review* 11 (August 1842), 201. In one of the more bizarre examples of O'Sullivan's political-literary fusion, he composed doggerel with imagery from the Dorr rebellion for a young friend; see O'Sullivan, "Annie's Passport," Beinecke Library, Yale University. *Democratic Review* 11 (August 1842), 198–199.

48. Ibid. 1 (October 1837), 14.

49. The *New York Evening Post* wrote (January 22, 1838), "The number of subscribers, exceeding five thousand, is larger than we have known any similar work to possess at its outset"; Fuller, "The United States Magazine and Democratic Review, 1837–1859," 28. O'Sullivan to Griswold, September 8, 1842, Griswold Mss., Boston Public Library. This view was confirmed in a letter to Van Buren from Benjamin Butler: "The services actually rendered by the Review, in the crisis through which we have just passed, have been of the greatest importance. It was a beacon of light in the darkest hours, and not only pointed out the way to the press throughout the nation, but reflected on the course of your administration, by its high literary and moral tone, a lustre which, I cannot doubt, kept thousands of the educated classes from yielding to the 'hootings of the common enemy'"; B. F. Butler to Van Buren, October 14, 1839; Butler Papers, Princeton University Library.

50. *Boston Quarterly Review* 1 (January 1838), 125. Brownson became a contributor to the *Review* in 1842–43, although he horrified its readership with his growing conservatism; nevertheless, he and O'Sullivan regarded each other highly.

51. *Democratic Review* 1 (January 1838), 217–18, 220.

52. Ibid. 6 (November 1839), 426–428.

53. *American Monthly Magazine* 5 (new series) (March 1838), 212–203. William Marcy to O'Sullivan, February 17, 1839; Marcy Papers, Library of Congress.

54. *Democratic Review* 8 (September 1840), 204–226; 1 (March 1838), 510.

55. Letter from George Sumner to George Greene, November 1840, in "Letters of George Sumner," *Proceedings of the Massachusetts Historical Society* 46 (October 1912–June 1913), 357–362; Fuller, "The United States Magazine and Democratic Review, 1837–1859," 13–14.

56. Sumner, "Letters of George Sumner," 360. Charles Sumner wrote that Judge Story, Nathan Hale, Professor Greenleaf, and "Ticknor" (either William or George) had enjoyed the article, but disapproved of the *Review*. Another Bostonian contributor, Alexander Everett, was "frowned on and persecuted for the very zeal and ability with which he has devoted himself to the republican cause"; see *The Law School Papers of Benjamin F. Butler* (ed. Ronald L. Brown; New York, 1987), 186–197.

57. O'Sullivan to Butler, October 12, 1839 and December 16, 1839; Butler Papers, Princeton University Library. Benjamin F. Butler to Harriet Butler, April 7, 1838, in *The Law School Papers of Benjamin F. Butler*, 160. O'Sullivan explained these difficulties more calmly a few years later; see O'Sullivan to Rufus Griswold, September 8, 1842, Griswold Mss., Boston Public Library.

58. Fuller, "The United States Magazine and Democratic Review, 1837–1859," 55. The early letters between O'Sullivan, Dorr, and Field are in the Dorr Papers, Rider Collection, Brown University Library. Another reason for O'Sullivan's sojourn in the Berkshires may have been his brother Thomas, an "asst. engineer" in Pittsfield, according to a letter he wrote Bancroft, January 17, 1841, Bancroft Collection, Massachusetts Historical Society. Writing Bancroft in 1845, O'Sullivan referred to Sedgwick as "our common friend"; O'Sullivan to Bancroft, August 8, 1845, Bancroft Collection, Massachusetts Historical Society. The Sedgwicks and O'Sullivan socialized frequently in the 1840s; see *The Journal of Richard Henry Dana, Jr.* (ed. Robert F. Lucid; Cambridge, 1968).

59. O'Sullivan to Gilpin, May 24, 1840, cited in Harris, "The Public Career of John Louis O'Sullivan," 92–93; Fuller, "The United States Magazine and Democratic Review, 1837–1859," 54–55; Hawthorne to O'Sullivan, April 20, 1840, in Hawthorne, *The Letters, 1813–1843*, 447–448.

60. *Democratic Review* 10 (February 1842), 118. Merle Curti, in *The American Peace Crusade 1815–1860* (New York, 1965), attributed this article to Samuel Loues. Without mentioning O'Sullivan by name, Curti suggested the contrariety of his straddling two positions

when he wrote (171) that Elihu Burritt's peace appeals were "strikingly in contrast with the rhetorical appeals of Young America to intervene in Old World affairs." O'Sullivan to Van Buren, December 17, 1840, Van Buren Papers, Library of Congress.

61. O'Sullivan to Bancroft, January 17, 1841, Bancroft Collection, Massachusetts Historical Society. The single-mindedness of O'Sullivan's purpose is confirmed in John Bigelow, *William Cullen Bryant* (Boston, 1890), 338. O'Sullivan to Van Buren, November 29, 1841, Van Buren Papers, Library of Congress. *The Letters of William Lloyd Garrison* (ed. Walter M. Merrill; Cambridge, 1973), 3:134. Lydia Maria Child, *Selected Letters, 1817–1880* (ed. Milton Meltzer and Patricia G. Holland; Amherst, 1982), 182. She also referred to capital punishment in *Letters from New York* (1843)

62. O'Sullivan, *Report in Favor of the Abolition of the Punishment of Death by Law* . . . (New York, 1841), 21. See "The Gallows and the Gospel, an Appeal to Clergymen Opposing Themselves to the Abolition of the One, in the Name of the Other," *Democratic Review* 12 (March 1843), 227–236.

63. The Langleys were not just random publishers, but deeply devoted to the Democratic "cause," as indicated by their foreword to the January 1845 *Review*.

64. Kenneth T. Jackson, ed., *The Encyclopedia of New York City* (New Haven, 1995), 923. See also Sean Wilentz, *Chants Democratic: New York City and the Rise of the American Working Class* (New York, 1984), 109–110 (different population figures given, presumably based on different metropolitan definitions). *Democratic Review* 6 (December 1839), 504. On the increase in publishing in New York, see Ronald Zboray, *A Fictive People: Antebellum Economic Development and the American Reading Public* (New York, 1993) 9–11; and Ezra Greenspan, *Walt Whitman and the American Reader* (New York, 1990), 13–38.

65. *Democratic Review* 14 (May 1844), 552.

66. *New York Morning News* (November 27, 1844). The circulation of the *Review* is difficult to pinpoint. A note to the reader in January 1840 claimed 140,000 copies had been distributed, an average of 6,000 per issue. This figure should certainly be taken with a grain of salt, as O'Sullivan had privately estimated the figure at 3,500 to Charles Sumner in 1843 and around 2,000 to Evert Duyckinck in 1845, but even these lower figures compare favorably with rival magazines; O'Sullivan to Charles Sumner, April 12, 1843, Sumner Collection, Harvard University Library; O'Sullivan to Duyckinck, July 6, 1845, Duyckinck Collection, New York Public Library.

67. *New York Tribune* (March 23, 1846).

68. Arthur May Mowry, *The Dorr War: Constitutional Struggle in Rhode Island* (New York, 1970), 170n. For background refer to James C. N. Paul, *Rift in the Democracy* (Philadelphia, 1951), and Arthur M. Schlesinger, Jr., *The Age of Jackson* (New York, 1945, 1989), chapters 32–33. O'Sullivan to Van Buren, December 8, 1843, Van Buren Papers, Library of Congress.

69. O'Sullivan to Van Buren, May 27 and May 28, 1844; Van Buren Papers, Library of Congress. Cass, it should be remembered, had blocked O'Sullivan's appointment to Paris in 1839. O'Sullivan would later consort with these "traitors" in his zeal for Cuba.

70. John Louis O'Sullivan, "Nelson Jarvis Waterbury: A Biographical Sketch" in *The Jarvis Family* (Hartford, 1879). Bigelow diary, June 9, 1844, Bigelow Collection, Mss. Division, New York Public Library. O'Sullivan to Van Buren, October 28, 1844; April 5, 1845, Van Buren Papers, Library of Congress.

71. For more on O'Sullivan's activities in the election, see Sheldon H. Harris, "John Louis O'Sullivan and the Election of 1844 in New York," *New York History* 41 (July 1960), 278–298; John Bigelow Diary (June 20, 1844), Bigelow Collection, Mss. Division, New York Public Library; *New York Morning News* (August 21, 1844). John Bigelow gave Tilden more credit for the paper's founding than he probably deserved in *The Life of Samuel J. Tilden* (New York, 1895), 1:108. The *New York Mirror* (October 22, 1845) called the *News* the "ac-

knowledged organ" of the Young Hickory School, and wrote, "The Morning News is a genteel young Democrat, and represents the ambitious 'centre' of the the Tammany Party, with
the Post and the Globe on the right and the left wings."

72. *New York Morning News* (October 20, 1845); (August 21, 1844); *New York Weekly
News* (November 30, 1844). An almost identical announcment appeared in the *New York
Morning News* (August 21, 1845); very likely Duyckinck was working sporadically throughout
this period.

73. O'Sullivan was hired as an instructor at the Columbia Grammar School in his
junior year (1830), when Duyckinck was a student there, and he was appointed a tutor in
mathematics to Duyckinck's freshman class in 1831. Therefore it is not unreasonable to assume they came into contact while teenagers. The Columbia committee was cited in the
New York Weekly News (March 21, 1846).

74. See Duyckinck's "Capital Punishment" in *Arcturus* 1 (July 1841), 15–22; *Democratic
Review* 11 (December 1842), 666. See also O'Sullivan and Duyckinck's correspondence from
1842 on in the Duyckinck Collection, Mss. Division, New York Public Library. John Bigelow, unpublished diary, November 20, 1844, Bigelow Collection, New York Public Library
(the entry reads, "O'Sullivan B.F. Butler Duyckinck and myself sat together."

75. Harris, "John Louis O'Sullivan and the Election of 1844 in New York," 295. Bigelow
wrote of the *News*, "It was no uncommon thing to hear the success of the Democratic ticket
in 1844 attributed to its agency,"; Bigelow, *Tilden*, 1:109. *New York Morning News* (October
17, 1844); April 19, 1845. It is interesting to note that O'Sullivan was out of the country at the
time the "Manifest Destiny" article ran on December 27, 1845 (see his letter in January 5,
1846, *News*). However, it seems likely he did author the phrase, if only because so many previous editorials used almost identical phraseology.

76. James L. Crouthamel, *Bennett's New York Herald and the Rise of the Popular Press*
(Syracuse, N.Y., 1989), 58.

77. See the *Democratic Reviews* of October 1837, January–April 1838, and January 1839.

78. See the family history composed by Florence Addicks in the Historical Society of
Pennsylvania for more on O'Sullivans in Central America and Cuba.

79. O'Sullivan to Silas Wright, January 25, 1845, Van Buren Papers, Library of Congress. O'Sullivan to Bancroft, August 24, 1845, Bancroft Collection, Massachusetts Historical
Society.

80. O'Sullivan supported William Ladd's peace movement in the *Reviews* of March
1839, February 1842, and March 1842. Merk, *Manifest Destiny and Mission in American History*, 108.

81. *Democratic Review* 5 (January 1839), 29.

82. Ibid. 3 (November 1838), 283; 6 (November 1839), 427. *New York Morning News*
(December 27, 1845); (February 28, 1845); Pratt, "Origin of Manifest Destiny," passim. Abraham Lincoln, *Selected Speeches and Writings* (New York, 1992), 201. William Gilpin, another
famous exponent of the phrase, was the brother of Henry Gilpin, the attorney general who
helped found the *Review*; see Henry Nash Smith, *Virgin Land: The American West as Symbol
and Myth* (Cambridge, 1950, 1978), 37.

83. *Democratic Review* 10 (February 1842), 109. In 1862, criticizing the Union war effort
from England, O'Sullivan wrote, "Independent self-government is a passion in the Anglo-
Celtico-Saxon breast," John L. O'Sullivan, *Union, Disunion and Reunion* (London, 1862),
53. See also the critique of Puritanism in the *New York Morning News* (September 27, 1845).
For a wider discussion of race, see Reginald Horsman, *Race and Manifest Destiny*.

84. Democratic Review 18 (July 1845), 7.

85. See O'Sullivan to Van Buren, March 1, 1845. *Democratic Review* 15 (September
1844), 248.

86. O'Sullivan to Bancroft, May 23, 1845, Bancroft Collection, Massachusetts Historical Society; *Democratic Review* 10 (January 1842), 53.

87. *New York Mirror* (October 22, 1845).

88. *Democratic Review* 15 (September 1844), 248. O'Sullivan to Duyckinck, July 6, 1845; Duyckinck to Charles Eames, August 18, 1845, Duyckinck Collection, Mss. Division, New York Public Library. Bigelow diary, September 7 and December 1845, December 1843, Bigelow Collection, Mss. Division, New York Public Library.

89. O'Sullivan to Van Buren, April 5, 1845 and March 28, 1845, Van Buren Papers, Library of Congress. O'Sullivan to Tilden, June 1, 1845, Tilden Collection, Mss. Division, New York Public Library. Nathaniel Hawthorne to Horatio Bridge, October 7, 1845, in Hawthorne, *The Letters, 1843-1853* (eds. Thomas Woodson, L. Neal Smith, Norman Holmes Pearson; Columbus, Ohio, 1985), 120 121; Harris, "The Public Career of John Louis O'Sullivan" 261–262. Bigelow, unpub. diary, February 6, 1846, Bigelow Collection, Mss. Division, New York Public Library. O'Sullivan's sister was married in November 1845 to Cristobal Madan, the probable source of the intense interest in Cuba that would land O'Sullivan in trouble in the early 1850s. He himself was married on October 21, 1846, to Susan Kearny Rodgers. See Hawthorne, *The Letters, 1843–1853*, 189. John Bigelow described the wedding and O'Sullivan's departure for Cuba in his diary, November 2 and 7, 1846, Bigelow Collection, Mss. Division, New York Public Library. Dorr to O'Sullivan, February 5, 1847, Dorr Mss., Rider Collection, Brown University.

90. Denis Tilden Lynch, *Boss Tweed: The Story of a Grim Generation* (New York, 1927), 140; O'Sullivan to Duyckinck, July 6, 1845, Duyckinck Collection, Mss. Division, New York Public Library. Fuller, "The United States Magazine and Democratic Review, 1837–1859," 84. J. C. Derby, *Fifty Years Among Authors, Books and Publishers* (New York, 1884), 368–376.

91. Randolph Bourne, *History of a Literary Radical and Other Essays* (ed. Van Wyck Brooks; New York 1969), xxv–xxvi.

92. Edward E. Chielens, *American Literary Magazines: The Eighteenth and Nineteenth Centuries* (New York, 1986), 430.

93. *Democratic Review* 6 (September 1839), 211–212; (November 1839), 426; 1 (January 1838), 143; 5 (May 1839), 499; 2 (June 1838), 312, 320; 8 (August 1840), 99; 7 (June 1840), 485; 15 (May 1844), 477; 2 (May 1838), 161; 3 (September 1838), 6–7.

94. Ibid. 13 (July 1843), 96; O'Sullivan to Butler, September 14, 1838, Butler Papers, Princeton University Library. O'Sullivan to Brownson, February 13, 1843, Brownson Papers, University of Notre Dame.

95. Fuller, "The United States Magazine and Democratic Review, 1837–1859," 33.

96. Lee Benson, *The Concept of Jacksonian Democracy: New York as a Test Case* (Princeton, 1961, 1970), 165–185. Van Buren to Gansevoort Melville, March 12, 1844, Van Buren Papers, Library of Congress. O'Sullivan wrote Benjamin Butler of "our common race"; October 12, 1839, Butler Papers, Princeton University Library.

97. *Democratic Review* 5 (March 1839), 304, 307; 1 (October 1837), 14–15.

98. Ibid. 8 (May 1840), 445; 8 (July 1840), 85–87; 6 (November 1839), 430.

99. Ibid. 7 (April-May 1840), 349–442; 7 (January and March 1840), 81–96, 233–241. There were many articles on Louis Napoleon in 1848 as well, for more obvious reasons. The early articles were presumably written by Henry Wikoff, the *Review's* future owner.

100. *New York Morning News* (December 29, 1845); *Democratic Review* 8 (November 1840), 431–474 on Brisbane; 5 (January 1839), 85–91, 7 (June 1840), 529–539, 8 (July 1840), 51–66 on Channing.

101. *Democratic Review* 6 (November 1839), 427; 16 (February 1845), 112. See also Gordon Wood, *The Creation of the American Republic, 1776–1787* (New York, 1969), 100.

102. *Democratic Review* 1, (October 1837), 10–11. O'Sullivan often compared the United

States to a young man; see *New York Morning News* (July 11, 1845; January 5, 1846). O'Sullivan, *Report in Favor of the Abolition of Death by Law . . .* , 126; *New York Morning News* (February 7, 1845); *Democratic Review* 15 (June 1844), 634–635, 637.

103. *Democratic Review* 12 (April 1843), 391.

104. George Forgie, *Patricide in the House Divided: A Psychological Interpretation of Lincoln and His Age* (New York, 1979), especially 104–110. Like most users of the term, Forgie did not really define who constituted "Young America," but he said that spokesmen generally called "for the broadening of majoritarian democracy, for geographic expansion, for the liberation of oppressed peoples, or the self; or for a vital national literature" (104). These, of course, were O'Sullivan's positions. No discussion of the psychology of American filiopietism is complete without Jay Fliegelman's *Prodigals and Pilgrims: The American Revolt Against Patriarchal Authority, 1750–1800* (New York, 1982). Fliegelman wrote of the antebellum generation, "Feelings of filial inferiority contributed to the desire many felt to be free of the demands of filiopietism and to find a stage for their own heroism" (267). *New York Morning News* (July 11, 1845).

105. Michael T. Gilmore, *American Romanticism and the Marketplace* (Chicago, 1985), 24; Ralph Waldo Emerson, *Essays and Lectures* (Joel Porte, ed.; New York, 1983), 226.

106. See John Bigelow, *Retrospections of a Busy Life* (New York, 1909), 1:53–70. For more information about Bigelow, see Margaret Clapp, *Forgotten First Citizen: John Bigelow* (Boston, 1947). Another project he undertook was an "Encyclopedia of American Politics," an ambitious volume that would summarize the nation's achievement in the one intellectual arena for which the United States had earned foreign notice. Despite support from Benjamin Butler, Theodore Sedgwick, and O'Sullivan (who offered to enlist Martin Van Buren to write an article), the project was never completed; see John Bigelow, unpub. diary, December 15, 1844, Bigelow Collection, Mss. Division, New York Public Library; also, Clapp, *Forgotten First Citizen*, 35–36.

107. John Bigelow, unpub. diary, 1843–1844, n.p.; Bigelow Collection, New York Public Library; *Retrospections*, 1:65.

108. *New York Weekly News* (December 14, 1844; June 28, 1845). Miscellaneous O'Sullivan letter, n.d., in Sedgwick Family Papers, Massachusetts Historical Society. See also O'Sullivan's correspondence with Annie Ward in the Yale University Library.

109. Julia Ward Howe, *Reminiscences, 1819–1899* (Boston 1899), 78–79. When Howe, a New Yorker, became enamored of Boston, O'Sullivan teased Charles Sumner about the unfairness of laying claim to one of New York's preeminent "citoyennes": "When you have so many clever women in Boston, it is like plundering the poor man's ewe lamb thus to despoil us of Julia"; see O'Sullivan to Sumner, April 12, 1843, Sumner Collection, Harvard University Library. See also *The Journal of Richard Henry Dana, Jr.*, 1:117–118, 232.

110. *Democratic Review* 9 (September 1841), 269. The *Review* also mentioned "La Jeune Italie" in February 1839 (5:240). Catharine Sedgwick to O'Sullivan, May 5, 1839, Historical Society of Pennsylvania. For more on Young Italy in New York, see Joseph Rossi, *The Image of America in Mazzini's Writings* (Madison, 1954); Rossi posits that Mazzini may have taken the name from a French newspaper called *Jeune France* in 1829 (4). See also Robert Ernst, *Immigrant Life in New York City 1825–1863* (New York, 1979), 123.

111. See Thomas Kite Brown III, *Young Germany's View of Romanticism* (New York, 1941). *Southern Literary Messenger*, 11 (January 1845), 24. I presume this to be Simms, although the piece was unsigned. Benjamin Disraeli, *Coningsby, or the New Generation* (1844; New York, 1961), 434.

112. Sir Charles Gavan Duffy, *Young Ireland* (London, 1880), pp. 290–292, and Denis Gwynn, *Young Ireland and 1848* (Oxford, 1949), 6. See also Richard Davis, *The Young Ireland Movement* (Dublin, 1987). *Democratic Review* 15 (August 1844), 210; Ernst, 123.

113. *Knickerbacker* (July 1833), 7; *American Monthly Magazine*, new series, 1 (May 1836) 453; James Fenimore Cooper, *Home as Found* (New York, 1961), 173.

114. *Boston Quarterly Review* 3 (January 1840), 19. Nicholas Brown, quoted in Chilton Williamson, "The Disenchantment of Thomas Wilson Dorr," *Rhode Island History* (October 1958), 102. The "Young Narragansett" pamphlet is in the Dorr Papers, Rider Collection, Brown University Library. Jon L. Wakelyn, *The Politics of a Literary Man: William Gilmore Simms* (Westport, Conn., 1973), 96, 104, 137; Simms also used the phrase "Young America" on occasion.

115. Siert F. Riepma, "'Young America': A Study in American Nationalism Before the Civil War," 4n; Evans and Walsh are described, 59–64. For more on Evans and the German-Americans, see Sean Wilentz, *Chants Democratic*, 335–354. According to the incomplete holdings of the New York Public Library, Evans and Walsh combined their newspapers on October 12, 1844, and began calling the paper "Young America" on March 29, 1845.

116. *Democratic Review* 14 (February 1844), 156. Emerson's address was delivered February 7, 1844, before the Mercantile Library Association of Boston; some scholars have attributed the movement's name to this speech, but this seems unlikely. There were many *Review* articles on Young Europe, but one series in particular, on the Danish Harro Harring, galvanized readers; the series ran from October to December 1844, and the December issue even reprinted the Young European "Act of Brotherhood" (15:569). See also Bigelow, unpub. diary, June 28, 1844, Bigelow Collection, Mss. Division, New York Public Library; *Democratic Review* 16 (May 1845), 495. For journalistic uses, see Merk, *Manifest Destiny and Mission*, 53–54.

117. Cornelius Mathews, *Americanism* (New York, 1845), 15, 17–18.

118. Ibid., 27, 28, 20,29.

119. See Godwin's note to Evert Duyckinck, ca. 1844, proposing a weekly cultural paper entitled "Young America" that "will be democratic in tendency"; Duyckinck Collection, Mss. Division, New York Public Library. See also Edwin DeLeon, *The Position and Duties of "Young America"* (Columbia, S.C., 1845). DeLeon wrote, "There is a feverish restlessness, a morbid craving after change, pervading every relation of our social system; an impatience of reaping the rewards of regular and steady industry; and speculation in its Protean forms, is the idol before which 'Young America' bows down in worship" (14). For background, see M. E. Curti, "Young America," *American Historical Review* 32 (1926–27), 34–55; David B. Danbom, "The Young America Movement," *Journal of the Illinois State Historical Society* 67 (1974), 294–306.

120. *New York Morning News* (July 11, 1845).

121. Marvin Meyers, *The Jacksonian Persuasion: Politics and Belief* (New York, 1960), 13; Lawrence Kohl, *The Politics of Individualism: Parties and the American Character in the Jacksonian Era* (New York, 1989), 229.

122. *Democratic Review* 1 (October 1837), 9.

123. John R. Wennersten, "Parke Godwin, Utopian Socialism, and the Politics of Anti-slavery," *New-York Historical Society Quarterly* 60 (1976), 123–124.

124. Brownson, "Democracy and Reform," *Boston Quarterly Review* 2 (October 1839), 490.

125. *Democratic Review* 8 (August 1840), 87; 10 (January 1842), 44; Thoreau to Emerson, August 7, 1843, in Walter Harding and Carl Bode, eds., *The Correspondence of Henry David Thoreau* (New York, 1958), 134.

126. George Sumner to George Greene, November 1840, in *Proceedings of the Massachusetts Historical Society*, 46, 357–362.

127. Lynch to Orestes Brownson, January 1, 1843, Brownson Papers, University of Notre Dame.

2 *Democracy and Literature*

1. Prospectus printed in *Washington Globe* (March 13, 1837); *Democratic Review* 15 (September 1844), 248.

2. *Democratic Review* 13 (August 1842), 196.

3. Ibid. 11 (August 1842), 199. *New York Weekly News* (April 11, 1846). O'Sullivan added insult to injury by insinuating the Whigs might take solace in *their* preeminence in the areas of "lying, swearing, praying, boring, shooting, etc." O'Sullivan to Butler, September 14, 1838, Butler Collection, Princeton University Library. See also the satirical poem on this theme, "All the Talents," *Democratic Review* 3 (October 1838), 146–152. Butler to Van Buren, October 14, 1839, Butler Papers, Princeton University Library.

4. O'Sullivan to Lowell, September 9, 1842, Harvard University Library; O'Sullivan to Sumner, April 12, 1843, Harvard University Library.

5. *Democratic Review* 6 (September 1839), 269; (November 1839), 430; (July 1839), 17–28. For Godwin's *Review* contributions, see Godwin to Duyckinck, July 11, 1854, Duyckinck Collection, Mss. Division, New York Public Library, and also Godwin to Rufus Griswold, December 31, 1851; Griswold Collection, Boston Public Library.

6. *Democratic Review* 6 (October 1839), 283-284. According to Godwin's letter to Griswold (*supra*), he authored this article.

7. Ibid. 6 (August 1839), 128. *The Plaindealer* (December 13, 1836), p. 5. On her early contribution, see Mark E. Dewey, ed., *The Life and Letters of Catharine Maria Sedgwick* (New York, 1871), 267. John Pritchard, *Criticism in America* (Norman, 1956), 108. *Democratic Review* 10 (February 1842), 129–140.

8. See Samuel T. Pickard, *Life and Letters of John Greenleaf Whittier* (Boston, 1899), I, 296–301. *Democratic Review* 17 (August 1845), 115–117.

9. Thomas Franklin Currier, *A Bibliography of John Greenleaf Whittier* (Cambridge, 1937), 61, 69, 471. Whittier wrote in the *Review*, "I confess I feel a sympathy for the Irishman," praising the Irish inhabitants of industrial Lowell. See *Democratic Review* 17 (August 1845), 117.

10. O'Sullivan to Whittier, April 6, 1838, Whittier Mss., Harvard University Library. *Democratic Review* 9 (December 1841), 527–528; 12 (May 1843), 475–478. See "Lines Written on Reading Several Pamphlets Published by Clergymen Against the Abolition of the Gallows," *Democratic Review* 11 (October 1842), 374–375; "To the Reformers of England," 12 (January 1843), 15–16. The "kingcraft" reference is in the latter poem.

11. *Democratic Review* 17 (July 1845), 66–68 ; John A. Pollard, *John Greenleaf Whittier: Friend of Man* (Boston, 1949), 308.

12. Emerson to Fuller, February 12, 1843; in *The Letters of Ralph Waldo Emerson* (ed. Ralph L. Rusk; New York, 1939), 3:146–147. The "Field" in question was David Dudley Field, judging from a list in Emerson's journals written around this time that includes "Mr OS" and "DD Field"; see *The Journals of Ralph Waldo Emerson* (ed. Merton M. Sealts, Jr.; Cambridge, 1965), 8:521. Although Margaret Fuller was never much of a contributor, she wrote Elizabeth Peabody in 1839 seeking advice on how to be published there; see *The Letters of Margaret Fuller* (ed. Robert N. Hudspeth; Ithaca, 1983), 91–92.

13. Emerson to Margaret Fuller, February 27, 1843, *Letters*, 3:149; Emerson to Thoreau, September 8, 1843; cited in *Letters*, 3:196–197. The full letter appears in *The Correspondence of Thoreau*, 137–138. See also Emerson's letter to Margaret Fuller announcing his intention to write for O'Sullivan, August 7, 1843, in *Letters*, 3:196–197. *The Journals of Ralph Waldo Emerson*, 8:314.

14. Emerson, *Journals*, 9:413; 10:195. Rhynders was a Tammany Hall politician and Ritchie an editor of the *Richmond Enquirer* and *Washington Union*. Lawrence Sargent Hall, *Hawthorne, Critic of Society* (New Haven, 1944), 102–103.

15. Thoreau to Emerson, January 24, 1843; Thoreau to Helen Thoreau, October 18, 1843; *The Correspondence of Thoreau*, 77, 147. For background information, see Henry David Thoreau, *Reform Papers*, ed. Wendell Glick (Princeton, 1973), 275–279. It is interesting to compare Thoreau's piece with Hawthorne's "Hall of Fantasy," which appeared in Lowell's *Pioneer* in February of the same year and likewise lampoons the idealism of those who would perfect the world. O'Sullivan to Thoreau, July 28, 1843, *The Correspondence of Thoreau*, 130.

16. Thoreau to Emerson, August 7, 1843; Thoreau to Emerson, September 14, 1843; *The Correspondence of Thoreau*, 133–134, 139.

17. Thoreau to Mrs. John Thoreau, October 1, 1843, *The Correspondence of Thoreau*, 141.

18. *Democratic Review* 10 (May 1842), 480. See also James Russell Lowell to George B. Loring, April 20, 1842, *The Letters of James Russell Lowell* (ed. Charles E. Norton; New York, 1893), 1:65, and Landon Fuller, "The United States Magazine and Democratic Review," 166. O'Sullivan to Lowell, September 9, 1842; Lowell Mss., Harvard University Library. *Democratic Review* 11 (October 1842), 431–432. It was in Lowell's magazine, *The Pioneer*, that Hawthorne portrayed O'Sullivan in "The Hall of Fantasy." James Russell Lowell to G. B. Loring, June 15, 1843, *Letters*, 1:70–71. See also O'Sullivan to Lowell, June 22 and August 11, 1843, Lowell Mss., Harvard University Library.

19. Dwight Thomas and David K. Jackson, *The Poe Log: A Documentary Life of Edgar Allan Poe, 1809–1849* (Boston, 1987), 60, 371, 375, 379, 494–495, 587.

20. The "Marginalia" appeared in August and December 1844, April and July 1846. "The Power of Words" in June 1845 and in August 1848, after O'Sullivan's departure, "The Literati of New-York: S. Anna Lewis." Other "Marginalia" pieces appeared later in the *Southern Literary Messenger*. Poe to F. W. Thomas, September 12, 1842, in *The Letters of Edgar Allan Poe*, ed. John Ward Ostrom (Cambridge, 1948), 1:211; and "Our Magazine Literature" in *New World* 6 (March 11, 1943), 302. Joy Bayless hinted Poe may have called O'Sullivan an "ass" as part of a ruse to trick Rufus Griswold into paying him to review Griswold's poetry anthology; see her *Rufus Wilmot Griswold* (Nashville, 1943), 70, 270. Algernon Tassin, *The Magazine in America* (New York, 1916), 143. Poe to Evert Duyckinck, January 30, 1846; *Letters*, 2:312–313.

21. Sidney P. Moss, *Poe's Literary Battles: The Critic in the Context of His Literary Milieu* (Durham, 1963), 168, 179; *Letters*, 1:281.

22. *Democratic Review* 10 (May 1842), 411–435 and (June 1842) 515–540; 9 (December 1841), 597.

23. *The Letters of William Gilmore Simms*, (ed. Mary C. Simms Oliphant, Alfred Taylor Odell, T. C. Duncan Eaves; Columbia, S.C., 1953), 2:122, 142. O'Sullivan to Duyckinck, n.d., Duyckinck Collection, Mss. Division, New York Public Library.

24. *Democratic Review* 21 (October 1847), 300. Other examples of expansionist literature include "A Tale of Texas Life," *Democratic Review* 15 (September 1844), 312–319, or "Life in the Prairie Land," *Democratic Review* 17 (September 1845), 221–231.

25. On the back of a letter O'Sullivan wrote him, Simms wrote, "Author of an excellent report to the New York Legislature on the abolition of punishment of death;" see O'Sullivan to Simms, February 4, 1843, Simms Papers, Manuscripts Collection, Columbia University Library. On Simms's political views, and his participation in "Young Carolina," see Jon L. Wakelyn, *The Politics of a Literary Man: William Gilmore Simms*. On Simms's political portraits, see Duyckinck to Simms, April 2, 1845, Simms Papers, Manuscripts Collection, Columbia University Library.

26. The original works in the *Review* were "The Toll-Gatherer's Day" (October 1837), "Foot-Prints on the Sea-Shore" (January 1838), "Snow-Flakes" (February 1838), "Howe's Masquerade" (May 1838), "Edward Randolph's Portrait" (July 1838), "Biographical Sketch of

Jonathan Cilley" (September 1838), "Chippings with a Chisel" (September 1838), "Lady Eleanore's Mantle" (December 1838), "Old Esther Dudley" (January 1839), "John Ingle-field's Thanksgiving" (published March 1840 under pseudonym "Rev. A. A. Royce"), "The New Adam and Eve" (February 1843), "Egotism; or the Bosom Serpent" (March 1843), "The Procession of Life" (April 1843), "The Celestial Railroad" (May 1843), "Buds and Bird-Voices" (June 1843), "Fire-Worship" (December 1843), "The Christmas Banquet" (January 1844), "The Intelligence Office" (March 1844), "The Artist of the Beautiful" (June 1844), "A Select Party" (July 1844), "A Book of Autographs" (November 1844), "Rappacini's Daughter" (December 1844), and "P's Correspondence" (April 1845). In addition, Hawthorne edited B. F. Browne's "Papers of an Old Dartmoor Prisoner" in seven installments from January to September 1846. In July 1843, he also published a previous work, "The Two Widows."

27. *Democratic Review* 1 (October 1837), 31.

28. O'Sullivan to Henry A. Wise, November 24, 1843, Maine Historical Society.

29. Julian Hawthorne, *Hawthorne and His Wife*, (Boston, 1884), 1:135.

30. Hawthorne to Longfellow, June 4, 1837; cited in Hawthorne, *Twice-Told Tales* (ed. Fredson Bowsers, L. Neal Smith, John Manning, J. Donald Crowley; Columbus, Ohio, 1974), 516.

31. Landon Fuller, "United States Magazine and Democratic Review," 36; see also Moncure Conway, *The Life of Nathaniel Hawthorne* (New York, 1890), 33. These writers believe Elizabeth Peabody was an intermediary, but a letter she wrote in 1885 indicates it was she who sought Hawthorne's mediation to get her work published in the *Review*. See Bruce A. Ronda, ed., *The Letters of Elizabeth Palmer Peabody: American Renaissance Woman* (Middletown, 1984), 420. Julian Hawthorne, *Hawthorne and His Wife*, 1:159–160.

32. Julian Hawthorne, *Hawthorne and His Wife*, 1:173; Julian Hawthorne called her "a creature of unbounded selfishness" (1: 169). Throughout his recounting of this strange episode, Julian Hawthorne referred to O'Sullivan as "Louis"; for a fuller treatment, see Norman Pearson, "Hawthorne's Duel," *Essex Institute Historical Collections*, 94 (1958), 229–242. Nathaniel Hawthorne to O'Sullivan, May 19, 1839, Princeton University Library. See also Hawthorne, *The Letters, 1813–1843* (ed. Thomas Woodson, L. Neal Smith, and Norman H. Pearson; Columbus, Ohio, 1984), 262–263, 278–179, and Fuller, 197. Silsbee's husband to be was Jared Sparks, the future president of Harvard, a man with little interest in cultivating radical literature.

33. A clear summary of the issues behind the duel is in James R. Mellow, *Nathaniel Hawthorne and His Times* (Boston, 1980), 107–111; see also Edwin Haviland Miller, *Salem is My Dwelling Place: A Life of Nathaniel Hawthorne* (Iowa City, 1991), 145–156. Hawthorne, *Hawthorne and His Wife*, 1:174–175.

34. *Democratic Review* 3 (September 1838), 75, 73.

35. O'Sullivan to Henry A. Wise, November 24, 1843, Maine Historical Society.

36. Hawthorne, *Hawthorne and His Circle*, 133–138; Nathaniel Hawthorne, *The Letters, 1813–1843*, 644; Miller, *Salem is My Dwelling Place*, 229.

37. *The Letters of Elizabeth Palmer Peabody*, 420–421; Miller, *Salem is My Dwelling Place*, 123. Hawthorne, *Hawthorne and His Wife*, 1:160–161.

38. Richard Brodhead, *The School of Hawthorne* (New York, 1986), 53–54. F. B. Sanborn, *Hawthorne and His Friends* (Cedar Rapids, 1908), 31.

39. Hawthorne, *The Letters, 1813–1843*, 313, 447; *The Correspondence of Thoreau*, 76–78; Sanborn, *Hawthorne and His Friends*, 31.

40. Hawthorne, *Twice-Told Tales*, 525.

41. Hawthorne, *The Letters, 1813–843*, 617, 677. Hawthorne, *Twice-Told Tales*, 525–526. O'Sullivan to James Munroe, June 12, 1844, Boston Public Library.

42. See Hawthorne to George Hillard (May 14, 1844), *The Letters, 1843–1853*, 35, 41.

Hawthorne, *Twice-Told Tales*, 526. At one point, the disconsolate author wrote, "I wish Heaven would make me rich enough to buy the copies for the purpose of burning them" (525–526).

43. Hawthorne to O'Sullivan, April 19, 1838; *The Letters, 1813–1843*, 272, 668; Hawthorne to Horatio Bridge, March 25, 1843, ibid., 681; *Democratic Review* 16 (April 1845), 377–378.

44. *Democratic Review* 16 (April 1845), 377–378. Hawthorne, *Nathaniel Hawthorne and His Wife*, 284–285. Hawthorne to Duyckinck, April 7, 1845, *The Letters, 1843–1853*, 87.

45. O'Sullivan to Bancroft, April 19, May 10, May 31, June 4, July 11, 1845. Bancroft Collection, Massachusetts Historical Society. O'Sullivan also recommended to Bancroft the consulates at Marseilles, Genoa, and his native Gibraltar (see his letter to Bancroft, March 21, 1845, in Hawthorne, *Hawthorne and His Wife*, 1:284). Bancroft offered instead a clerkship in the new Smithsonian Institution, which was declined. See Hawthorne, *The Letters, 1843–1853*, 85n. Randall Stewart, *Nathaniel Hawthorne: A Biography* (New Haven, 1948), 76. Bancroft had also been Hawthorne's supervisor when he was a weigher and gauger in the Boston Custom House from 1838 to 1840.

46. See Winfield S. Nevins, "Nathaniel Hawthorne's Removal from the Salem Custom House," *Historical Collections of the Essex Institute* 53 (April 1917), 97–132; and Stephen Nissenbaum, "The Firing of Nathaniel Hawthorne," *Historical Collections of the Essex Institute* 114 (April 1978), 57–86. The father, Nathaniel Silsbee, was at this point a former senator, while the son, Nathaniel, Jr., was mayor of Salem. Mayor Silsbee cruelly accused Hawthorne of participation in "general locofoco corruption" (Nevins, "Nathaniel Hawthorne's Removal from the Salem Custom House," 103).

47. *Democratic Review* 16 (April 1845), 345. Nathaniel Hawthorne, *Tales and Sketches* (New York, 1982), 1,021. *The Pioneer: A Literary Magazine*, 52.

48. Hawthorne, *Tales and Sketches*, 896–897, 952; *Mosses from an Old Manse*, 1:35; *Tales and Sketches*, 806, 884, 676.

49. Hawthorne, *The House of the Seven Gables*, 179–182.

50. Hawthorne, *Tales and Sketches*, 746, 757, 759 752, 761–762.

51. Ibid., 800, 805, 798.

52. Ibid., 953, 955, 952.

53. Ibid., 864–865, 881.

54. Hawthorne, *The House of the Seven Gables*, 179–182. Walker Cowen, *Melville's Marginalia* (New York, 1987), 1:596.

55. Nevins, "Nathaniel Hawthorne's Removal from the Salem Custom House," 99, 122, 128. Nissenbaum, "The Firing of Nathaniel Hawthorne," 67. Hawthorne, *The Letters, 1843–1853*, 279–282.

56. In the letter to Hillard, he explained the history of the patronage involving his post, perceptively explaining the ambiguity of a Tyler Democrat's politics; see also his letter to O'Sullivan, April 1, 1853, mentioning various permutations of the Democracy, from Barnburners to Hunkers; *Letters, 1843–1853*, 663. Hawthorne, "The Custom-House," in *The Scarlet Letter* (ed. Sculley Bradley, Richmond Croom Beatty, E. Hudson Long; New York, 1962), 35.

57. B. F. Browne's "Papers of an Old Dartmoor Prisoner," which ran in seven installments in the *Review* from January to September 1846. Nissenbaum, "The Firing of Nathaniel Hawthorne," 78.

58. Hawthorne, *Tales and Sketches*, 740. *Democratic Review* 5 (January 1839), 51.

59. *Democratic Review* 10 (June 1842), 514 (others listed were Bancroft, Bryant, Cass, A. H. Everett, Henry Gilpin, Brownson, B. F. Butler, C. C. Cambreleng, Theodore Sedgwick, Parke Godwin, and Samuel Tilden). *Democratic Review* 11 (August 1842), 199.

60. *Democratic Review* 5 (June 1839), 541 (the writer was presumably Langtree since

O'Sullivan had taken a leave of absence in March due to "impaired health"). *Democratic Review* 8 (September 1843), 268.

61. Floyd Stovall, *The Foreground of Leaves of Grass* (Charlottesville, 1974), 53; Gay Wilson Allen, *The Solitary Singer: A Critical Biography of Walt Whitman* (Chicago, 1955, 1985), 53, 127–130. Emory Holloway, ed., *The Uncollected Prose of Walt Whitman* (New York, 1932), 2:15–16. Joseph Jay Rubin and Charles H. Brown, *Walt Whitman of the New York Aurora: Editor at Twenty-Two* (State College, Pa., 1950), 90. For more on the artisanal Whitman, see M. Wynn Thomas, *The Lunar Light of Whitman's Poetry* (Cambridge, 1987)

62. Whitman's *Democratic Review* pieces included "Death in the School-Room" (August 1841), "Wild Frank's Return" (November 1841), "Bervance; Or, Father and Son" (December 1841), "The Tomb-Blossoms" (January 1842), "The Last of the Sacred Army" (March 1842), "The Child-Ghost; A Story of the Last Loyalist" (May 1842), "A Legend of Life and Love" (July 1842), "The Angel of Tears" (September 1842), "Revenge and Requital: A Tale of a Murderer Escaped" (July-August 1845), and "A Dialogue" (November 1845), which discussed O'Sullivan's pet reform, the capital punishment issue.

63. *Democratic Review* 10 (January 1842), 62. Horace Traubel, *With Whitman in Camden* (Boston, 1906; rpt. Carbondale, 1982), 6:379.

64. Stovall, *The Foreground of Leaves of Grass*, 143, 146, 42. Actually, one of the articles clipped, "America and the Early English Poets," *Democratic Review* 5 (May 1839), 489–498, indicates Whitman was reading the *Review* earlier than Stovall gave him credit for. The list of clippings is in Dr. Richard Maurice Bucke, *Notes and Fragments* (Toronto, 1899; reprint 1972), 193–211. See also *The Gathering of the Forces*, (ed. Cleveland Rogers and John Black; New York, 1920) 1:10n.

65. Betsy Erkkila, *Whitman the Political Poet* (New York, 1989), 20. Stovall, *The Foreground of Leaves of Grass*, 32–34. *The Gathering of the Forces*, 2:6.

66. Whitman, *Uncollected Poetry and Prose*, 1:52; *Poetry and Prose*, 1,079.

67. Whitman wavered at times on capital punishment, but later came out strongly against it; see his editorial of August 26, 1847, in Whitman, *Gathering of the Forces*, 1:113–116. *Democratic Review* 17 (August 1845), 111; (November 1845), 360–364. Whitman moderated his views as he aged, commenting, "I was in early life very bigoted in my anti-slavery, anti-capital punishment, an so on, but I have always had a latent toleration for the people who choose a reactionary course" (Holloway, ed., *The Uncollected Prose of Walt Whitman*, 1:103n; 2:15–16).

68. Whitman, *Gathering of the Forces*, 1:27–28. See his prescient editorial of February 11, 1847, entitled "Abroad," where he predicted the "smothered fires" of France and other European countries would soon "burst forth in one great flame"; *Gathering of the Forces*, 1:29–31. David Reynolds, *Walt Whitman's America: A Cultural Biography* (New York, 1995), 136.

69. Whitman, *Gathering of the Forces*, 166–174, 243–244, 269. Erkkila, *Whitman the Political Poet*, 33.

70. *Democratic Review* 13 (September 1843), 266–279. Whitman, *Gathering of the Forces*, 2:243. Holloway, ed., *The Uncollected Prose of Walt Whitman* 1:163. Stovall, *The Foreground of Leaves of Grass* (Charlottesville, 1974) 53. Like O'Sullivan, Whitman also esteemed the populistic French poet Béranger (Bucke, *Notes and Fragments*, 202).

71. *Democratic Review* 17 (July–August 1845), 66–67, 105-111; Erkkila, *Whitman the Political Poet*, 74; *Democratic Review* 13 (September 1843), 277.

72. Erkkila, *Whitman the Political Poet*, 54, 60.

73. Whitman, *Poetry and Prose*, 1,308, 1,312.

74. Ibid., 1,324–1,325.

75. Whitman's self-review appeared in the *Democratic Review*, 36 (September 1855), 205–212.

76. *Democratic Review* 30 (January 1852), 93. The article on "Fogy Literature" appeared in May 1852. See the April 1850 (26:384) review of *White-Jacket* for early signs the *Review* was tiring of Melville, considering him at the "end of his rope." For Melville's politics, see Hershel Parker, "Melville and Politics: A Scrutiny of the Political Milieux of Herman Melville's Life and Works" (Ph.D. diss., Northwestern University, 1963), and Rogin, *Subversive Genealogy: The Politics and Art of Herman Melville*.

77. Jay Leyda, *The Melville Log: A Documentary Life of Herman Melville* (New York, 1951), 377, 409. See also Merton M. Sealts, Jr., *Melville's Reading: A Check-List of Books Owned and Borrowed* (Madison, 1966), 102. Duyckinck had a nearly complete set of *Democratic Reviews*, and thus Melville might have borrowed any volume. It is also interesting to note Melville (like Whitman) owned books by some of the *Review's* favorite authors, including Pierre Jean de Béranger and Cornelius Mathews. The "Sherman Melville" citation is in 18 (May 1846), 399; the review of *Typee* considered it "most amusing and interesting," slyly describing the book as the story of "a primitive race with whom the intercourse of the author appears to have been on the best possible terms."

78. *Democratic Review* 15 (July 1849), 44–50. For more background on Melville's reception, see Hershel Parker, *Herman Melville: A Biography, 1819–1851* (Baltimore, 1996), 1:411, 550–552, 633–634.

79. John P. Runden, "Columbia Grammar School: An Overlooked Year in the Lives of Gansevoort and Herman Melville," *Melville Society Extracts*, no. 46 (May 1981), 1–3, and "Old School Ties: Melville, the Columbia Grammar School, and the New Yorkers," *Melville Society Extracts*, no. 55 (September 1983), 1–5.

80. Leyda, *The Melville Log*, 83–85; Rogin, *Subversive Genealogy*, 42–76, and Gansevoort Melville diary in *New York Public Library Bulletin*, 79 (December 1965), and 80 (January 1966). It is also striking to compare Gansevoort's predilection for invoking the memory of his Scottish ancestors fighting the English and O'Sullivan's Culloden ancestry.

81. Rogin, *Subversive Genealogy*, 54; John Bigelow, unpub. diary (July 5, 1844), Bigelow Collection, Mss. Division, New York Public Library.

82. The best sources for Gansevoort Melville's political activities are Hershel Parker, "Gansevoort Melville's Role in the Campaign of 1844," *The New-York Historical Society Quarterly* 49 (April 1965), 143–173, and *Herman Melville: A Biography*. Gansevoort's letters to Polk are in Wayne Cutler, ed., *The Correspondence of James K. Polk*, 8 (Knoxville, 1993); a letter of October 3, 1844, says "the Texas question has not been argued before the people on the stump as it should have been, fully, boldly and directly" (145).

83. On Leggett and Melville, see *Arthur Gordon Pym, Benito Cereno, and Related Writings* (ed. John Seelye, Philadelphia, 1967); Leggett's "The Encounter" appeared in the *Knickerbocker* (February 1834) when Langtree was editor; *The Letters of Herman Melville* (ed. Merrell R. Davis and William H. Gilman; New Haven, 1960), 29; *Democratic Review* 18 (March 1846), 238-239. The *Review* mentioned the two brothers together again in August 1847 (21, 120), although Gansevoort was long deceased at that time. On Melville's early puffs in the *News*, see Johannes D. Bergmann, "*The New York Morning News* and *Typee*," *Melville Society Extracts*, no. 31 (September 1977), 1–4. Two recent works effectively describe Melville's relationship with New York City early in his career, Hans Bergmann, *God in the Street: New York Writing from the Penny Press to Melville* (Philadelphia, 1995) and Wyn Kelley, *Melville's City: Literary and Urban Form in Nineteenth-Century New York* (New York, 1996).

84. Leyda, *The Melville Log*, xxviii. The articles, entitled simply, "Flogging in the Navy," appeared in the *Review* in five installments from August to December 1849. *Democratic Review* 19 (December 1846), 453–464. The whaling article was ostensibly a review of J. Ross Browne's *Etchings of a Whaling Cruise*, but exceeded its scope to discuss the entire industry.

Melville, *Moby-Dick*, 117; *Democratic Review* 5 (May 1839), 466. *Democratic Review* 26 (June 1850), 498 ("we think it high time for the President to resume the helm before the ship is stranded"); 27 (July 1850), 16 ("the captain is smoking his pipe"). Alan Heimert treats this issue in "*Moby-Dick* and American Political Symbolism," *American Quarterly* 15 (Winter 1963). He also argues the parallel between "The Town Ho's Story," and the splintering of the Democracy following the Baltimore convention of 1844, "*Moby-Dick* and American Political Symbolism," 529–530. Melville's name appeared in the *Review* in June 1849 (487), when he (along with Duyckinck, Cornelius Mathews, Washington Irving, and other literati) signed a petition denouncing the Astor Place riot, and his brother Allan signed a letter of prominent New York Democrats inviting the Young American Stephen Douglas to give a talk in June 1851 (567).

85. *Democratic Review* 25 (July 1849), 50; 24 (June 1849), 519.

86. Ibid. 28 (April 1851), 291; 25 (December 1849), 570; 26 (May 1850), 413; 28 (March 1851), 259.

87. The *Review*'s notice of *Mardi*, ostensibly by Duyckinck's ally William A. Jones, was notable for its penetrating analysis and the lingering Young American sentiment that "youth, with its pure, deep love, its fervent aspirations, its heavenly visions, is personified" by the novel. See *Democratic Review* 25 (July 1849), 46. Herman Melville, *Mardi: And a Voyage Thither* (Evanston, 1970), 525–526. As Melville was beginning *Moby-Dick*, the *Review* quoted Calhoun's speech about Mexico with strong similarities to the "Fast-Fish" chapter: "Mexico is to us as a *dead body*, and this is the only way that we can cut the cord which binds us to the *corpse*." See the *Democratic Review* 26 (May 1850), 413. Melville wrote, "What at last will Mexico be to the United States? All Loose-Fish" (*Moby-Dick*, 398).

88. Other Langley books included G. T. Poussin, *The Democratic Principle Which Governs the American Union* (translated by Auguste Davezac), and several works of Cornelius Mathews's. See the *New York Morning News* of November 27, 1844. O'Sullivan to Bancroft, April 16, 1844, Bancroft Collection, Massachusetts Historical Society.

89. Henry G. Langley to Rufus W. Griswold, February 3, 1844; Griswold Collection, Boston Public Library. *Democratic Review* 16, 2

90. See Anne Lynch, "Books for the People," *Democratic Review* 12 (June 1843), 603. William Charvat, *The Origins of American Critical Thought, 1810–1835* (Philadelphia, 1936), and Pritchard, *Criticism in America*, passim.

91. *Democratic Review* 1 (February 1838), 319–320. Stafford, *The Literary Criticism of "Young America,"* 42, 47, and passim. Although Stafford overpoliticized Duyckinck, he offered a solid background in the criticism of Young America.

92. *Democratic Review* 15 (August 1844), 161–162; (September 1844), 243, 249.

93. Ibid. 15 (September 1844), 248–249. Jones praised the magazine highly, for understandable reasons: "A first-rate number of the "Democratic," for instance, would have its poems by Bryant, Lowell, and Whittier; its romances by Hawthorne; finished translations of German romance, or light sketches of manners from the French; criticism by Godwin, or Bigelow, or Duyckinck; and politics by Mr. Editor (to which, however, he is by no means restricted, as we have tracked him through the windings of fictitious narrative, the distinctions of a critique, statistical calculations, political argument and enlightened legislation), or Mr. Everett, perhaps his strongest literary vizier" (246).

94. As Benjamin Spencer put it while discussing literary nationalism, "These professions of literary faith in the people thus by no means implied a concurrence in Whitman's desire for an authochtonous utterance of the popular mind," *The Quest for Nationality: An American Literary Campaign* (Syracuse, 1957), 118.

95. *Democratic Review* 15 (September 1844), 249.

96. Ibid. 13 (September 1843), 266.

3 *Young America in Literature*

1. Merrell R. Davis and William Gilman, eds., *The Letters of Herman Melville*, 96. George L. McKay listed the senior Duyckinck as a "bookseller and stationer" in various locales in lower Manhattan from 1793 to 1820 in *A Register of Artists, Engravers Booksellers, Printers & Publishers in New York City, 1633–1820* (New York, 1942). In his otherwise indispensable *The Book in America* (New York, 1939), Helmut Lehmann-Haupt considers father and son to be the same person (102), a small measure of the confusion surrounding Duyckinck's place in literary history. Melville, *Letters*, 96.

2. Jackson's death made the *New York Morning News* on June 17, 1845; on June 18, the *News* announced the publication of the first volume in the Library of American Books.

3. Lewis Mumford, *Herman Melville* (New York, 1929), 79; Melville, *Letters*, 36. William Allen Butler, *Evert Augustus Duyckinck: A Memorial Sketch* (New York, 1879), 3.3. Lewis Mumford, *Herman Melville* (New York, 1929), 79; Melville, *Letters*, 36. William Allen Butler, *Evert Augustus Duyckinck: A Memorial Sketch* (New York, 1879), 3. Duyckinck was proud of his difficult name, boasting it "has fortunately survived the clippings and contractions, not unusual in such cases, for several generations in America"; Duyckinck to A. P. Peabody, February 20, 1854, Historical Society of Pennsylvania.

4. Tetractys manuscript, n.d., filed with Cornelius Mathews correspondence, Duyckinck Collection, Mss. Division, New York Public Library.

5. *The Literary: A Miscellany for the Town*, November 15, 1836, 3, 44, 48. The *Literary* described the Tetractys Club using pseudonyms; Duyckinck was "Dolph Bendernagle." It also contained the first of Young America's many attempts at urban literature, a poem from a series on "Sights in the City." For background, see Arthur Roche, "A Literary Gentleman in New York" (Ph.D. diss., Duke University, 1973), 10.

6. Duyckinck Commonplace Book (Box 27), Duyckinck Collection, Mss. Division, New York Public Library.

7. Tetractys Mss., Mathews Correspondence File, Duyckinck Collection, Mss. Division, New York Public Library. Nathaniel Hawthorne, *The Letters, 1843–1853* (ed. Thomas Woodson, L. Neal Smith, and Norman H. Pearson; Columbus, Ohio, 1984), 671. Hawthorne told Duyckinck ghost stories during this first meeting; see Duyckinck's 1838 Commonplace Book, Duyckinck Collection, Mss. Division, New York Public Library.

8. Cornelius Mathews, "City Sketches: The Ubiquitous Negro," *American Monthly Magazine* 5 (New Series) (January 1838), 54–57; Duyckinck, "The City and the Country," *American Monthly Magazine* 5 (May 1838), 413–416; *Knickerbocker* 16 (July 1840), 29.

9. Duyckinck Diary (1838–1839), Duyckinck Collection, Mss. Division, New York Public Library; Harriet L. P. Rice, *Harmanus Bleecker: Albany Dutchman, 1779–1849* (Albany, 1924), 204.

10. Poe, "The Literati," in *The Complete Works of Edgar Allan Poe,* (New York, 1902), 15:59. Herman Melville, *Mardi: And a Voyage Thither* (Evanston, 1970), 5. *The Letters of James Russell Lowell*, 1:62. *Arcturus* 1:5.

11. See Sidney P. Moss, *Poe's Literary Battles: The Critic in the Context of His Literary Milieu* (Durham, 1963), 3–37, for an informative analysis of the puffing system, and the degree in particular to which Duyckinck and Poe's rivals (i.e., Lewis Gaylord Clark and Longfellow) profited from it.

12. Diary fragments (Volume 5), December 5, December 14, 1842, Duyckinck Collection, Mss. Division, New York Public Library.

13. *Arcturus* praised Rabelais repeatedly; *Arcturus* 3:201–209; 285–292. *New York Review* 7 (1840), 430, 439. Later views of Duyckinck were less populistic. Samuel Osgood wrote, "Although he wished to be up to the times, and did not churlishly reject any elements of the

new order, he was a student of books and a critic of opinions and taste, with little of the dash and muscle that came with the coming push and progress. He also was very much of a recluse, and although bred to the law he was not fond of crowds nor ready in debate, nor telling in ring of voice or play of gesture." See Osgood, *Evert Augustus Duyckinck: His Life, Writings and Influence* (Boston, 1879), 9.

14. *Democratic Review* 17 (September 1845), 217. *Arcturus* 2, 88–93. Auld to George Duyckinck and William A. Butler, Duyckinck Collection, Mss. Division, New York Public Library.

15. Cooper, for example, was taken to task for writing historical romance, "An exhausted vein of writing from which the ore has long disappeared," *Arcturus* 1 (January 1841), 90. Irving, while respected, annoyed the nationalists with comments like this letter to his publisher: "There would be nothing more humiliating to me, than to be mistaken for that loose rabble of writers who are ready to decry everything orderly and established—my feelings go the contrary way"; Paul Johnson, *The Birth of the Modern* (New York, 1991), 59. Hawthorne, *Letters, 1813–1843*, 600. Duyckinck diary (January 13, 1843), Duyckinck Collection, Mss. Division, New York Public Library.

16. Mathews to Duyckinck, circa May 19, 1839, Duyckinck Collection, Mss. Division, New York Public Library. The letter continued: "I therefore regard many questions (perhaps too much so) in a light which falls entirely from the quarter of the sky under which I happened to be born, and I extend my hand rather to my neighbor and countryman, than in the high missionary spirit, to my cosmopolitan brother at the Antipodes or over the sea." Mathews, *The True Aims of Life* (New York, 1839), 23, 37–38.

17. Allen Stein, *Cornelius Mathews* (New York, 1974), 48. Mathews, *The Career of Puffer Hopkins* (New York, 1842, 1970), 39. *Puffer Hopkins* also contains an important early reference to bowling (92).

18. *Southern Literary Messenger* 9 (December 1843), 716.

19. *American Review* 1 (February 1845), 150–151.

20. See, for example, "Literature and Property" by G. A. Sackett, *Arcturus* 1, 109–113. Cornelius Mathews, *An Address to the People of the United States in Behalf of the American Copyright Club* (New York, 1843), 8, 17. For background on the copyright agitation of the late 1830s, see George H. Putnam, *George Palmer Putnam: A Memoir* (New York, 1912), 33; and James J. Barnes, *Authors, Publishers and Politicians: The Quest for an Anglo-American Copyright Agreement, 1815–1854* (Columbus, Ohio 1974). Dickens had come to the United States to help the copyright cause, but more for his own pecuniary reasons than a concern for American literature. Nina Baym rightly says the copyright situation has "not been adequately appreciated" in academic writing on literary nationalism (although she has the Dickens trip as 1846, rather than 1842); see *Novels, Readers and Reviewers; Responses to Fiction in Antebellum America* (Ithaca, 1984), 23.

21. George E. Mize, "The Contributions of Evert A. Duyckinck to the Cultural Development of Nineteenth Century America" (Ph.D. diss., New York University, 1954), 62–63. See also George T. Goodspeed, "The Home Library," *Papers of the Bibliographical Society of America*, 42 (1948), 110–118. Several books were forthcoming when the series was discontinued, including poetry by Simms, W. A. Jones, and others. See the announcement in *Democratic Review* 14 (April 1844), 438. Hawthorne invited Duyckinck to the Old Manse in 1843, the year O'Sullivan went there to recruit writers; Hawthorne, *The Letters, 1813–1843*, 9–10.

22. *Arcturus* 1 (March 1841), 236–243; 3 (January 1842), 160; Mize, "The Contributions of Evert A. Duyckinck to the Cultural Development of Nineteenth Century America," 28, 54. One of the members of the Copyright Club was Edwin DeLeon, the South Carolinian whose speech on Young America in 1845 was credited (incorrectly) by Merle Curti as the birth of the movement.

23. For background, See Ronald J. Zboray, *A Fictive People: Antebellum Economic Development and the American Reading People* (New York, 1993); Lehmann-Haupt, *The Book in America*; Frank Camparato, *Books for the Millions: A History of the Men Whose Methods and Machines Packaged the Printed Word* (Harrisburg, 1971); Baym, *Novels, Readers and Reviewers.* Henry David Thoreau, *Walden* (New York, 1966), 68.

24. Lehmann-Haupt, *The Book in America*, 100. *The Letters of Henry Wadsworth Longfellow*, II, 162.

25. John Paul Pritchard noticed how much this intellectual activity was related to the city's commercial growth; he wrote, "The distinctive flavor of New York literary thinking about the artist . . . tasted strongly of politics and business," *Literary Wise Men of Gotham* (Baton Rouge, 1963), 33. *Reminiscences of Richard Lathers* (ed. Alvan F. Sanborn; New York, 1907), 52. On Duyckinck's dislike for the Harpers, see Goodspeed, "Home Library," 111. On the Harpers' reciprocation, see Ezra Greenspan, "A Publisher's Legacy: The George Palmer Putnam Correspondence," *Princeton University Library Chronicle* 54 (Autumn 1992), 51; Greenspan, "Evert Duyckinck and the History of Wiley and Putnam's Library of American Books, 1845–1847," *American Literature* 64 (December 1992), 678–679. James Harper was elected mayor of New York in 1844, just as Duyckinck was beginning his ambitious literary campaign.

26. Jane Tompkins, *Sensational Designs: The Cultural Work of American Fiction, 1790–1860* (New York, 1985), 17.

27. George Templeton Strong, *The Diary of George Templeton Strong* (ed. Allan Nevins and Milton Halsey Thomas; New York, 1952), 1:310–312. Strong wrote a note "expressing my gratitude, as I conscientiously could for his good intentions—and for nothing else."

28. Poe, *Works*, 15:59.

29. *New York Morning News* (December 27, 1845; July 11, 1845; July 12, 1845). On Duyckinck's closeness to the *Review*, see Duyckinck to Rufus Griswold, September 3, 1844, Boston Public Library. Around this time, Parke Godwin began making noise about a periodical to be called "Young America"; Godwin to Duyckinck, ca. December 1844, Duyckinck Correspondence, Duyckinck Collection, Mss. Division, New York Public Library.

30. *The American Review* 1 (February 1845), 146–147, 150. The name was later changed to *The American Whig Review*.

31. Duyckinck probably began work at the *Review* prior to this date; see Evert Duyckinck to Nathaniel Hawthorne, March 21, 1845, Duyckinck Collection, New York Public Library. He announced his appointment in a letter to William Gilmore Simms, April 2, 1845, Manuscripts Collection, Columbia University Library. W. A. Jones had written on "Criticism in America," for example, in September 1844, praising *Arcturus* to the skies and deriding the "literary toryism" of the *North American Review; Democratic Review* 15 (September 1844), 241–249. Duyckinck lists his friends' contributions in his letter to Simms, April 2, 1845, Columbia University Library. *Democratic Review* 16 (April 1845), 376.

32. Cornelius Mathews, *Americanism* (New York, 1845), 17,14.

33. Ibid., 22–23, 29.

34. Ibid., 28, 27, 22.

35. Ibid., 28–29. Duyckinck diary, November 14, 1838–April 7, 1839, 75, Duyckinck Collection, New York Public Library. Wiley and Putnam had published Mathews's *Appeal to American Authors* in 1842. They also published the *American Review*. Putnam's importance to American literature is just becoming established; see Greenspan, "A Publisher's Legacy," 39–63, and all of "Evert Duyckinck and the History of Wiley and Putnam's Library of American Books, 1845–1847." For background, see also Clarence Gohdes, *American Literature in Nineteenth-Century England* (New York, 1944), 65. Putnam even paid voluntary royalties, though under no obligation to do so; see Lehmann-Haupt, *The Book in America* 105. When

Robert Browning heard of one these payments to Elizabeth Barrett, he praised Wiley and Putnam as "fine fellows, who do a really straightforward and un-American thing." See *The First One Hundred and Fifty Years: A History of John Wiley and Sons, Inc., 1807–1957* (New York, 1957), 33. *New York Weekly News* (January 18, 1845).

36. *Democratic Review* 16 (May 1845), 507–509.

37. The only serious treatment is Greenspan, "Evert Duyckinck and the History of Wiley and Putnam's Library of American Books," 677–693. Kermit Vanderbilt has a chapter on Duyckinck, but only one sentence on the Library in *American Literature and the Academy* (Philadelphia, 1986), 63; Jay Hubbell's *Who Are the Major American Writers?* (Durham, NC, 1972) mentions the Duyckincks' *Cyclopædia*, but not the Library; there is a brief reference in John Tebbel, *Between Covers: The Rise and Transformation of Book Publishing in America* (New York, 1987), 23. The original *Cambridge History of American Literature* did not include a single reference to Evert Duyckinck. *The First One Hundred and Fifty Years*, 16.

38. Duyckinck to Simms, November 29, 1844, Duyckinck Collection, Mss. Division, New York Public Library. Simms was an important literary ally and greatly helped to advance Duyckinck's nationalistic literary schemes in the South. As early as 1843, Mathews had asked Simms's help with a journal that never got off the ground; see Mathews to Simms, January 25, 1844, Manuscripts Division, Columbia University Library. Thoreau, *Walden*, 71, 74.

39. Stafford, *The Literary Criticism of "Young America,"* 24.

40. Greenspan, "A Publisher's Legacy," 50. Circular dated March 1, 1845, Duyckinck Collection, Mss. Division, New York Public Library; *American Review* 1 (May 1845), 521. The article was describing Duyckinck's companion series, the Library of Choice Reading, but the point holds true for both. The *American Review* saw very clearly the importance of canonical selection, even before the vocabulary existed: "Publishers are *school teachers*, and the books they print and circulate, the lessons they teach. We have been amazed at the stupidity of our countrymen on this topic. Give us the exclusive control of the literature of the country, and we could undermine half the churches of the land, and render half the statutes of our courts nugatory."

41. Poe, *Literati*, 58. Mize, "The Contributions of Evert A. Duyckinck to the Cultural Development of Nineteenth Century America," 67. Melville was allowed 12 percent due to *Typee's* success in England and the shrewd machinations of his brother Gansevoort.

42. See Patrick Brancaccio, "'The Black Man's Paradise': Hawthorne's Editing of the *Journal of an African Cruiser*," *New England Quarterly* 53 (March 1980), 23–41. Also, Horatio Bridge, *Personal Recollections of Nathaniel Hawthorne* (New York, 1893), 87–88. See *New York Morning News* (June 18, 1845) for the proud announcement of the Library's inauguration. Roche, "A Literary Gentleman in New York," 170. "Whenever you choose to send me any numbers of your series, I will notice them, for better of worse, in the Democratic paper of this town," Hawthorne to Duyckinck (April 15, 1846), *Letters, 1843–1853*, 153; see also Randall Stewart, "Hawthorne's Contributions to the *Salem Advertiser*," *American Literature* 5 (January 1934), 327–341.

43. Hawthorne to Duyckinck (July 1, 1845), *Letters, 1843–1853*, 106.

44. Emerson to Duyckinck, March 12, 1847, in *The Letters of Ralph Waldo Emerson*, 3:384; Thoreau's letters to Duyckinck are in *The Correspondence of Thoreau*.

45. Duyckinck to Emerson, September 20, 1845; October 2, 1845; October 7, 1845; Duyckinck Collection, Mss. Division, New York Public Library.

46. Duyckinck to Emerson, August 13, 1845; August 27, 1845; September 20, 1845; October 2, 1845; October 7, 1845; Duyckinck Collection, Mss. Division, New York Public Library.

47. Duyckinck to Hawthorne, March 13, 1846, Duyckinck Collection, Mss. Division, New York Public Library.

48. Hawthorne to Duyckinck, July 1, 1845, Hawthorne, *Letters 1843–1853*, 105–106.

Henry T. Tuckerman, from an 1870 article on Hawthorne, cited in Hawthorne, *Letters, 1843–1853*, 170n. Hawthorne had written Tuckerman (June 18, 1846) asking him to review *Mosses* for the New York audience.

49. Duyckinck to Hawthorne, March 21, 1845, Duyckinck Collection, Mss. Division, New York Public Library. Apparently Duyckinck was already working at the *Democratic Review*, although he did not officially become literary editor until April 1845. Putnam was not a Democrat, but he shared many of Young America's hopes. His son's biography pointed out Putnam's friendship with many of the European radicals of the late 1840s, including Mazzini and Louis Blanc. He had also joined a group seeking fair treatment for Ireland in 1838 (see Putnam, *George Palmer Putnam*, 32, 45, 200). At the same time Wiley and Putnam published *The American Review* (1845–52), a moderate Whig competitor with the *Democratic Review*.

50. Kirkland's stories "Love vs. Aristocracy" and "Operative Democracy" fit especially well in the Young America politico-literary calculus; Caroline Kirkland, *Western Clearings* (New York, 1845), 35–56, 168–173. See Whittier's article on "New England Supernaturalism" in the *Democratic Review* 13 (November 1843), 515–516; Hawthorne, *Letters, 1843–1853*, 126, 205; *Democratic Review* 17 (November 1845), 400.

51. Moss, *Poe's Literary Battles*, 46–47, 110, 168. Poe and Duyckinck shared a particular animus toward Lewis Gaylord Clark, the consummate literary insider and editor of the *Knickerbocker*. Clark mistreated each of them within his editorial columns, and this common ground allied them as fellow outsiders. Wiley and Putnam had published *The Narrative of Arthur Gordon Pym* in 1838.

52. *The Letters of Edgar Allan Poe*, 2:332; Sidney P. Moss, *Poe's Major Crisis: His Libel Suit and New York's Literary World* (Durham, 1970), 144–145. Poe, *Complete Works*, 12:247. See Pollin, "*The Living Writers of America*: A Manuscript by Edgar Allan Poe," 166–168.

53. Duyckinck to Hawthorne, March 13, 1846, Duyckinck Collection, Mss. Division, New York Public Library. It is surprising in retrospect to see Duyckinck complaining about Melville's lack of philosophy, since that is precisely the aspect of his thought that most annoyed him in later works such as *Mardi*, *Moby-Dick*, et seq.

54. Moss, *Poe's Literary Battles*, 105. Poe's favorable estimation of Mathews is all the more remarkable given his devastating review of the latter's *Wakondah* in 1842; see the *Complete Works*, 11:25–38.

55. *The Letters of William Gilmore Simms*, 1:438–439. John Bigelow, unpub. diary, October 20, 1844, Bigelow Collection, New York Public Library; Greenspan, "Evert Duyckinck and the History of Wiley and Putnam's Library of American Books, 1845–1847," 688. Simms to Duyckinck, July 16, 1845, Duyckinck Correspondence, Duyckinck Collection, Mss. Division, New York Public Library.

56. Lowell cited in Mumford, *Melville*, 80; Perry Miller, *The Raven and the Whale*, 75. Duyckinck wrote Hawthorne he thought Bridge's "Journal of an African Cruiser" had the rare ability to please both the North and South on the race issue; Duyckinck to Hawthorne, August 13, 1845, Wiley and Putnam Correspondence, Duyckinck Collection, Mss. Division, New York Public Library.

57. William Gilmore Simms, *View and Reviews in American Literature, History and Fiction* (Cambridge, 1962), 9; Margaret Fuller, *Papers on Literature and Art* (London, 1846), 2:124.

58. Duyckinck and Mathews also admired the young Elizabeth Barrett and Duyckinck added her name to the "new generation" in a glowing review. He praised her further for having lauded the "vital sinewy vigor" of Cornelius Mathews's writing. See *American Review* 1 (January 1845), 38-48. Barrett's two volumes of poetry were published in New York in 1844 by H. G. Langley, the publisher of the *Democratic Review*. See also Cornelius Mathews's correspondence with Rufus Griswold (Griswold Collection, Boston Public Library) for more on the Young American campaign to convert her into an ally.

59. Walt Whitman, editorial of July 11, 1846, *The Gathering of the Forces*, (ed. Cleveland Rogers and John Black; New York, 1920), 2:245.

60. Trent Collection, Special Collections, Duke University Library (one of his lists of favorite writers included "E. A. Duyckinck"). See also Floyd Stovall, *The Foreground of Leaves of Grass* (Charlottesville, 1974), 270–271. John Stafford (*The Literary Criticism of "Young America"*) writes that Duyckinck "almost certainly" wrote the article. Perry Miller and Daniel Wells suspect W. A. Jones (see Daniel Arthur Wells, "Evert Duyckinck's *Literary World*, 1847–1853: Its Views and Reviews of American Literature" [Ph.D. diss., Duke University, 1972], 21n). The full list of Whitman's clippings is in Dr. Richard Maurice Bucke, *Notes and Fragments*, (Toronto, 1899; reprint 1972), 193–211. Other clipped articles include Margaret Fuller's "American Literature" (from her *Papers on Literature and Art*) and Duyckinck's scathing review of Rufus Griswold's literary anthology in May 1847. *Democratic Review* 20 (March 1847), 271.

61. Whitman, *Gathering of the Forces*, 2:255–256, 292.

62. Putnam, *George Palmer Putnam*, 153. William Allen Butler, *A Retrospect of Forty Years* (ed. Harriet Allen Butler; New York, 1911), 276. Richard Lathers similarly remembered his undaring personal qualities, including his "constitutional shyness, unctuous and quiet wit, sententious and clever conversation, and slight hesitation in speech. He was in every respect a genial man, and it is said that no one ever saw him affected by ill temper;" see *Reminiscences of Richard Lathers*, 52.

63. *Knickerbocker* 31 (December 1845), 579–580; (November 1845) 453. O'Sullivan to Duyckinck, October 3, 1845; Lowell to Duyckinck, August 1845; Duyckinck Correspondence, Duyckinck Collection, Mss. Division, New York Public Library. Hershel Parker, *Herman Melville*, 1:606. In 1849, another critic blasted the Duyckinck clique as the "you-tickle-me-and-I'll-tickle-you-school"; Hershel Parker, *Herman Melville*, 1:718.

64. *North American Review* 63 (October 1846), 359, 376–377.

65. Mumford, *Melville*, 79. John Bigelow recorded sarcastically the purpose of the *Home-Critic* was "the rendering of justice to American writers, which means the securing of a reputable organ to tickle themselves"; see John Bigelow, unpublished diary, February 3, 1844, Bigelow Collection, Mss. Division, New York Public Library. One of the few precedents as a trade magazine was a short-lived venture started by the Langleys, the *Review's* publishers, in 1843; see Zboray, *A Fictive People*, 21.

66. *Literary World*, April 3, 1847; February 6, 1847.

67. For a fascinating glimpse of Duyckinck's life during his period of unemployment in 1847, see Donald and Kathleen Malone Yannella's transcription of his diary in Joel Myerson, ed., *Studies in the American Renaissance* (Boston, 1978), 207–258.

68. *Literary World* (October 7, 1848), 701.

69. Their friendship began shortly after the death of Melville's older brother Gansevoort in 1846, when Melville was casting about for a new mentor; see in particular his letter to Duyckinck, December 8, 1846, in *The Letters of Herman Melville*, 47–48. Melville to Duyckinck, March 3, 1849, in *The Letters of Herman Melville*, 80.

70. *The Letters of Herman Melville*, 141.

71. Duyckinck to George Duyckinck, March 9–10, 1848, Duyckinck Collection, Mss. Division, New York Public Library; *Literary World* (April 14, 1849), 336–339. As noted in chapter 2, another complimentary review of *Mardi* appeared in the *Democratic Review*, probably written by the Young American W. A. Jones. Melville sent early drafts of *Mardi* to Duyckinck for approval; see Hershel Parker, *Herman Melville*, 1:585.

72. See Gordon Mills, "The Significance of 'Arcturus' in *Mardi*," *American Literature* 14 (May 1942), 159–160. Melville to Duyckinck, February 2, 1850; Leyda, *The Melville Log*, 1:364. On Duyckinck's interest in the European revolutions, see Larry Reynolds, *European Revolutions and the American Literary Renaissance* (New Haven, 1988), 7–12.

73. *The Letters of Herman Melville*, 82, 80.

74. Melville, *White-Jacket*, 150–151.

75. Randall Stewart, "Hawthorne's Contribution to the *Salem Advertiser*" 328; Jay Leyda, *The Melville Log*, 309.

76. Leyda, *The Melville Log*, 377; Melville to Duyckinck, December 12, 1850, *The Letters of Herman Melville*, 118; Melville called Duyckinck "My Beloved" (111).

77. Melville, "Hawthorne and His Mosses," in *The Piazza Tales and Other Prose Pieces*, 247–248; for a more detailed explanation of the complex Melville-Duyckinck relationship, see Perry Miller, *The Raven and the Whale*, 280–291. See also Donald Yannella, "Writing the 'Other Way': Melville, the Duyckinck Crowd, and Literature for the Masses," in John Bryant, ed., *A Companion to Melville Studies* (New York, 1986), 63–81.

78. Melville, "Hawthorne and His Mosses," in *Piazza Tales*, 244–245, 248, 252.

79. Melville's review appeared in the *Literary World* (March 6, 1847), 105–106; the editorial, which I assume to be Duyckinck's, appeared in the *Literary World* (June 19, 1847), 466.

80. Melville, *Moby-Dick*, 3, 6, 112, 117.

81. On Mexico, see *Moby-Dick*, 64, 398.

82. *Literary World* (November 22, 1851); Hawthorne to Duyckinck (Dec. 1, 1851), *Letters, 1843–1853*, 508; *Democratic Review* 30 (January 1852), 93; Evert A. and George L. Duyckinck, *Cyclopædia of American Literature*, 2:673. For more background on Duyckinck's review, see the historical note appended to the Northwestern-Newberry edition of *Moby-Dick*, 690–691, 720–722.

83. *Letters of Herman Melville*, 117, 149. Herman Melville, *Pierre*, (Ed. Harrison Hayford, Hershel Parker, G. Thomas Tanselle, New York, 1971) 13. *Literary World* (August 21, 1852), 119. Mathews had also referred to a "Captain Kidd" style of magazine (one that pirated an author's work) in his forgotten satire *The Career of Puffer Hopkins* (1842), 138.

84. Melville, *Moby-Dick*, vii.

85. Mize, "The Contributions of Evert A. Duyckinck to the Cultural Development of Nineteenth Century America," 53. *The Letters of Herman Melville*, 120. Donald Yannella, "Writing the Other Way," discusses the Holden's request and speculates about "The Fiddler"; Daniel Arthur Wells does the same for "Bartleby" ("Evert Duyckinck's *Literary World*, 1847–1853," 169–179).

86. *Democratic Review* 16 (May 1845), 455; 17 (September 1845), 217. *Reminiscences of Richard Lathers*, 53. Traubel, *With Whitman in Camden* (Boston, 1906; rpt. Carbondale, 1982), 1:139. An amusing anecdote George William Curtis told about Duyckinck's refusal to experiment is recounted in Leyda, *The Melville Log*, 1:409.

87. Watson G. Branch, ed., *Melville: The Critical Heritage* (London, 1974), 228; *Literary World* (March 16, 1850), 271–272. *Literary World* (August 21, 1852), 118.

88. Wells, "Evert Duyckinck's *Literary World*, 1847–1853," 340–344. Parker, *Herman Melville*, 1:588–589. On George Duyckinck, see Reynolds, *European Revolutions and the American Literary Renaissance*, 7–10. Melville, *Moby-Dick*, 152.

89. Joel Headley, *The Great Riots of New York, 1712 to 1873* (New York, 1873). Cornelius Mathews, *Witchcraft* (New York, 1852), 70.

90. Parker, *Herman Melville*, 1:535. Simms to Duyckinck, November 12, 1850, Duyckinck Correspondence, Duyckinck Collection, Mss. Division, New York Public Library.

91. *Literary World* (October 6, 1849), 297; (October 19, 1850), 308.

92. Leyda, *Melville Log*, 420. Derby, *Fifty Years Among Authors, Books and Publishers*, 585. Howard Vincent, *The Trying-Out of Moby-Dick* (Kent State, 1949, 1980), 25 (letter of August 7, 1850).

93. Reynolds, *Beneath the American Renaissance*, 277, 588; Rogin, *Subversive Genealogy*, 73, 327; the pages from Miller cited by Rogin as evidence do not address the question.

94. As early as 1838, Griswold had written to Henry Clay on behalf of a Vermont Whig convention to ascertain his views on slavery; Griswold was also involved with the launching of the Whig *American Review*, and with roughly the same job Duyckinck had at the *Democratic*; see Henry Clay to Griswold, July 28, 1838, and George Colton to Rufus Griswold, August 22, 1844; Griswold Collection, Boston Public Library. Duyckinck to Rufus Griswold, September 3, 1844, Griswold Collection, Boston Public Library. Apparently the project was never completed.

95. *Democratic Review* 11 (August 1842), 178; I assume the review to be O'Sullivan's because of its lukewarm position on the copyright issue, which O'Sullivan did not favor as much as other literary nationalists. Hawthorne also spoofed Griswold in "The Hall of Fantasy": "I saw Mr. Rufus Griswold, with pencil and memorandum-book, busily noting down the names of all the poets and poetesses there, and likewise of some, whom nobody but himself ever suspected of visiting the hall"; see *The Pioneer: A Literary Magazine*, 51. *New York Weekly News* (July 12, 1845).

96. Duyckinck wrote to writers from all regions of the country, while Griswold seemed more comfortable with fellow New Englanders like Horace Greeley, James T. Fields, Henry Raymond, and C. F. Briggs (who called himself "a Yankee like yourself"; Briggs to Griswold, n.d., Griswold Collection, Boston Public Library). It was indeed Briggs who urged Griswold to retaliate so viciously against Duyckinck (Briggs to Griswold, February 13, 1856, Griswold Collection, Boston Public Library). *New York Morning News* (September 19, 1844). And on July 11, 1845, just before Griswold's *Prose Writers* appeared, the *News* had warned "the subject matter of our National Literature must be American," that "we want to see the reflection of vigorous, independent men."

97. Stafford, *The Literary Criticism of "Young America,"* 21, 34; Harry Franco [C. F. Briggs], *The Trippings of Tom Pepper; or, the Results of Romancing* (New York, 1847), 71–72.

98. Joy Bayless, *Rufus Wilmot Griswold: Poe's Literary Executor* (Nashville, 1943), 117, 123.

99. *Literary World*, March 20, 1847. See Mize, "The Contributions of Evert A. Duyckinck to the Cultural Development of Nineteenth Century America," 152–159, for a more elaborate discussion of the Griswold-Duyckinck feud. Amazingly, Griswold added insult to injury by preparing a glorious review of his own book and sending it to Duyckinck for publication in the *Literary World*. Needless to say, it was not printed; Bayless, *Griswold*, 124. Bucke, *Notes and Fragments*, 207 (#433).

100. It should be mentioned that while Griswold was supporting the copyright agitation in print, he was shamelessly pirating English works for profit. As his biographer admits, "Consistency was not one of Griswold's virtues"; Bayless, *Griswold*, 84. Griswold, *The Prose Writers of America*, 16, 544.

101. In a similar vein, Duyckinck had criticized George Putnam's *American Facts* for failing to cite radicals Joel Barlow and Orestes Brownson as important literati, *Democratic Review* 16 (May 1845), 508. Besides the Young Americans, the *Southern Literary Messenger* also deplored Griswold's sectional bias; see Mize, "The Contributions of Evert A. Duyckinck to the Cultural Development of Nineteenth Century America," 155.

102. *Literary World* (January 5, 1850; September 21, 1850); Moss, *Poe's Literary Battles*, 125n. Duyckinck was clearly wounded by the allegation, however, and called Poe a "literary attorney, who pleaded according to his fee." See also Rufus Griswold, *The Cyclopædia of American Literature. A Review* (New York, 1856), 7, 9–10; Bayless, *Griswold*, 197.

103. The argument over the validity of the *Cyclopædia* lasted for years, and in itself ar-

gues against the presumption there was a consensus of genteel critics in the nineteenth century about what constituted the canon. Jane Tompkins, for example, includes Duyckinck with Fields, Lowell, and Whipple in her conception of "a dynastic cultural elite" whose misogynistic aims were served by perpetuating Hawthorne's reputation. Nina Baym, too, inadvertently lumps Duyckinck's crowd with their rivals in her history of antebellum critical responses to fiction. By discussing the reviews offered en masse by the various magazines of the 1840s, it is difficult to get an idea of the important ideological differences separating them. Quoting one sentence from the *Literary World* of 1848, she argues the magazine had adopted an "anti-democratic view," which was not the case at all. Tompkins, *Sensational Designs*, 30; Baym, *Novels, Readers and Reviewers*, 35.

104. Duyckinck diary fragment, January 1-30, 1860, Duyckinck Collection, Mss. Division, New York Public Library.

105. Duyckinck to Simms, February 2, 1869, Simms Papers, Manuscripts Collection, Columbia University Library. In a curious reversal, Duyckinck in 1864 gave a glowing review to a piece of drivel entitled "Young America" by Fitz-Greene Halleck, an aging poet whose aristocratic notions placed him at the antipodes of the Young America position of the 1840s. When the Civil War broke out, Simms also abandoned Young Americanism, writing Duyckinck a decidedly un-Democratic letter: "I know too well that you take no interest in politics. I think this was your error. Your habit in the north is not only to leave everything to majorities, but to suffer to the masses the exclusive keeping of the public soul and conscience"; Simms to Duyckinck, March 15, 1861, Simms Papers, Manuscripts Collection, Columbia University Library.

106. Duyckinck Journal (1875), November 1, 1875, Duyckinck Collection, Mss. Division, New York Public Library. In the same journal, on October 29, he left a eulogy of Wordsworth that was also self-reflexive. Noting Wordsworth had progressed from youthful republicanism to a more conservative position, he wrote, "If the rising sun stirred more strongly the morning air; it was the same beneficent luminary which lent its light and warmth to the atmosphere at its closing hour."

4 Representation without Taxation

1. John K. Howat et al., *Nineteenth-Century America: Paintings and Sculpture* (New York, n.d., n.p. [art work #56]). Twenty-two years later, in July 1858, Powers was still in awe of Jackson, as Nathaniel Hawthorne recorded after a rendezvous with the artist in Florence. The latter summarized the general, appropriately using a sculpting metaphor: "Surely, he was a great man, and his native strength, as well of intellect as of character, compelled every man to be his tool that came within his reach; and the more cunning the individual might be, it served only to make him the sharper tool"; see Schlesinger, *The Age of Jackson*, 42.

2. Recent work touching on genre and social history includes Albert Boime, *The Art of Exclusion: Representing Blacks in the Nineteenth Century* (Washington, 1990); Albert Boime, *The Magisterial Gaze: Manifest Destiny and American Landscape Painting, 1830–1865* (Washington, 1991); Elizabeth Johns, *American Genre Painting: The Politics of Everyday Life* (New Haven, 1991); and David M. Lubin, *Picturing a Nation: Art and Social Change in Nineteenth-Century America* (New Haven, 1994).

3. Alfred Frankenstein, *William Sidney Mount* (New York, 1975), 259.

4. See, for example, *Democratic Review* 3 (September 1838), 56, where art was described as one of the "best friends" of the democratic principle. The early *Knickerbocker* issues under Langtree's editorial supervision had a number of articles on American art, many from the pen of William Dunlap. Henry Gilpin, one of the original backers of the *Review*, had a strong interest in art; see William H. Gerdts, "'The American Discourses': A Survey of

Lectures and Writings in American Art, 1770–1858," *American Art Journal* 15 (1983), no. 3, 72. On O'Sullivan and Henry Inman, see the *Catalogue of Works by the Late Henry Inman with a Biographical Sketch* (New York, 1846).

5. See Waldron Phoenix Belknap, Jr., *American Colonial Painting: Materials for a History* (Cambridge, 1959). Cornelius Mathews, *Americanism* (New York, 1845), 24–25.

6. F. O. Matthiessen, *American Renaissance: Art and Expression in the Age of Emerson and Whitman* (New York, 1941), 51. Emory Holloway, ed., *The Uncollected Poetry and Prose of Walt Whitman* (New York, 1932), 1:236.

7. Alexis de Tocqueville, *Democracy in America* (New York, 1980), 2:51. On the history of patronage in this country, see Lillian B. Miller, *Patrons and Patriotism: The Encouragement of the Fine Arts in the United States, 1790–1860* (Chicago, 1966).

8. Frances Trollope, *Domestic Manners of the Americans* (ed. Donald Smalley; New York, 1949), 345. Mrs. Anna Jameson, *Memoirs and Essays, Illustrative of Art, Literature and Social Morals* (New York, 1846), 100. This work was published by Wiley and Putnam as part of Duyckinck's Library of Choice Reading.

9. James Callow, *Kindred Spirits: Knickerbocker Writers and American Artists, 1807–1855* (Durham, 1967), 6n; see also Neil Harris, *The Artist in American Society: The Formative Years, 1790–1860* (Chicago, 1966), 96–99; Miller, *Patrons and Patriotism*, 90–102. James Callow has the dates slightly different.

10. Ella M. Foshay, *Mr. Reed's Picture Gallery: A Pioneer Collection of American Art* (New York, 1990), 14; Gulian Verplanck, *Discourses and Addresses on Subjects of American History, Arts, and Literature* (New York, 1833), 124, 126. Verplanck foreshadowed the Young Americans in certain areas (he supported the copyright cause and was sympathetic to Jackson in 1828, although he later recanted his Democracy).

11. Ralph Waldo Emerson, *The Complete Essays and Other Writings* (ed. Brooks Atkinson; New York, 1950), 306, 314.

12. Harris, *The Artist in American Society*, 119.

13. See Robert W. Torchia, *John Neagle: Philadelphia Portrait Painter* (Philadelphia, 1989); John I. H. Baur, *John Quidor, 1801–1881* (Brooklyn; n.d.). E. P. Richardson, *A Short History of Painting in America* (New York, 1963), 140.

14. William Dunlap, *History of the Rise and Progress of the Works of Design in the United States* (New York, 1834), 1:451–452. Journal entry of December 29, 1846, cited in Frankenstein, *Mount*, 147.

15. One scholar who has grappled with Mount's politics is Elizabeth Johns, but in my opinion, her 1991 study obfuscated Mount's career by overemphasizing small details within his art and withholding any meaningful statement of a larger social philosophy. Her politicized readings shed interesting light on a neglected topic, but strike me as impressionistic; see *American Genre Painting: The Politics of Everyday Life*. Matthiessen, *American Renaissance*, 598; David S. Reynolds, *Walt Whitman's America: A Cultural Biography* (New York, 1995), 291–295.

16. Bartlett Cowdrey and Hermann Warner Williams, Jr., *William Sidney Mount, 1807–1868: American Genre Painter* (New York, 1944), 1. Hawkins also had claimed the dubious distinction of originating the practice of playing music in a store to ensnare customers; see Frankenstein, *Mount*, 79.

17. Cowdrey and Williams, *William Sidney Mount*, 3. David Cassedy and Gail Shrott, *William Sidney Mount: Annotated Bibliography and Listing of Archival Holdings of the Museums at Stony Brook* (Stony Brook, 1983), 40.

18. See H. Nichols B. Clark, *Francis W. Edmonds: American Master in the Dutch Tradition* (Washington, 1988), 45 and passim; also Clark's article, "A Taste for the Netherlands: The Impact of Seventeenth-Century Dutch and Flemish Genre Painting on American Art,

1800–1860," *American Art Journal* 14 (Spring 1982), 23–38. See also Dennis Berthold's essay, "Melville and Dutch Genre Painting," in Christopher Sten, ed., *Savage Eye: Melville and the Visual Arts* (Kent, Ohio, 1991), 218–245.

19. James Jackson Jarves, *The Art-Idea* (1864; Benjamin Rowland, ed.; Cambridge, 1960), 129-130. Hawthorne wrote of *The House of the Seven Gables*, "Many passages of this book ought to be finished with the minuteness of a Dutch picture, in order to give them their proper effect"; see James T. Fields, *Yesterdays with Authors* (Boston, 1878), 55.

20. Berthold, in Sten, *Savage Eye*, 219–220.

21. Mount was often known as "the American Wilkie" or "the American Teniers"; for more on his influences see Donald Keyes, "The Sources for William Sidney Mount's Earliest Genre Paintings," *The Art Quarterly*, 32 (1969), 258–268; Catherine Hoover, The Influence of David Wilkie's Prints on the Genre Paintings of William Sidney Mount," *The American Art Journal* 12, no. 3 (1981), 4–33. David Cassedy and Gail Shrott, *William Sidney Mount: Works in the Collection of the Museums at Stony Brook* (Stony Brook, 1983), 15. Cowdrey and Williams, *William Sidney Mount*, 5.

22. Cassedy and Shrott, *William Sidney Mount, Works in the Collection*, 19.

23. Frankenstein, *Mount*, 266. Mount's work was ceaselessly described as the most "American" art yet to be created; see, for example, Callow, *Kindred Spirits*, 179.

24. Appropriately, *Bargaining* ended up in the collection of Boss Tweed; Cowdrey and Williams, *William Sidney Mount*, 37. Many other genre painters of the period, including Asher B. Durand and Francis W. Edmonds, painted works that inquired about the intrusion of capitalism into the domestic sphere, but Mount was more prolific on the subject.

25. See Joseph B. Hudson, Jr., "Banks, Politics, Hard Cider and Paint: The Political Origins of William Sidney Mount's Cider Making," *Metropolitan Museum Journal* 10 (1975), 107–118; Stuart P. Feld, "In the Midst of 'High Vintage,'" *Metropolitan Museum of Art Bulletin* 25 (April 1967), 302. Mount's painting *Farmer Husking Corn* may also have been a political allegory, judging from a reference in a book by Mount's patron, Charles A. Davis, comparing corn husking to "the elections"; see Major J. Downing, pseud., *The Letters of J. Downing, Major, Downingville Militia* (New York, 1835), 68n. Finally, Mount listed "A Whig After the Election" as a topic in 1844; Frankenstein, *Mount*, 130.

26. The subject seems to have appeared to him years earlier, for a manuscript fragment from 1844 lists "The Tribune in the Country" as a subject; Frankenstein, *Mount*, 130. An interesting anti-Whig scene Mount listed but apparently never painted was "a Dandy walkin [sic] out with knowledge in his rear; carried by a little black boy—books, etc."; Frankenstein, *Mount*, 174. Barbara Groseclose, "Politics and American Genre Painting of the Nineteenth Century," *Antiques* 120 (1981), 1,214. Another Mount painting that prominently included newspapers was *California News* (1850), also known as *News from the Gold Diggins*.

27. Johns, *American Genre Painting*, 38. Besides his close relationship with Davis, Mount painted a work entitled *Webster Among the People* as part of his aborted series of famous Americans for his "American Portrait Gallery"; see Frankenstein, *Mount*, 153, 204. But unlike Whitman and the *Democratic Review* writers, most of whom moved with Van Buren toward a Free Soil position in the late 1840s, Mount remained adamantly committed to the conservative wing of the Democracy and proudly declared himself a Lewis Cass man in 1848. He reasoned that "every vote given to Van Buren is a Whig vote, which makes the Whigs chuckle prodigiously" (203). He held a particular animus toward the Free Soil Barnburners, whom he called "sore heads" or "Barn Bunkers," since "Bunker is a fish that we manure land with but they *smell* very bad" (204). During the Civil War, Mount had little respect for the Republicans, whom he dismissed as "Lincolnpoops," and he remained committed to his party at his death in 1868.

28. Whitman, *Specimen Days* (Boston, 1971), 6. Reynolds, *Walt Whitman's America*, 291.

29. Mount even tried his hand at composing, authoring a fiddle piece entitled "In the Cars, on the Long Island Railroad" that wordlessly attempted to duplicate the modern American experience of entering a railroad tunnel; Frankenstein, *Mount*, 80, 357–358. Another point linking Mount and Whitman was their common interest in phrenology; Mount owned an 1836 copy of Spurzheim's *Outlines of Phrenology*; see Cassedy and Shrott, *Annotated Bibliography*, 24. Whitman, *Uncollected Poetry and Prose*, 1:104. Whitman particularly disliked formal European music, "with its flourishes, its ridiculous sentimentality, its anti-republican spirit, and its sycophantic influence, tainting the young taste of the republic" (105). Melville, *Moby-Dick*, 174.

30. Whitman, *Specimen Days*, 3; Paul Zweig, *Walt Whitman: The Making of the Poet* (New York, 1984), 123. Whitman was proud of his Dutch ancestry: "A grand race, those Dutch!"; Floyd Stovall, *The Foreground of Leaves of Grass*, (Charlottesville, 1974), 20; he considered it "doubtless the best" influence on him (*Specimen Days*, 11). Holloway, *The Uncollected Poetry and Prose of Walt Whitman*, 1:238. The original article appeared February 1, 1851. *Literary World*, March 9, 1850.

31. See "Pictures," in Whitman, *Leaves of Grass* (ed. Sculley Bradley and Harold W. Blodgett; New York, 1965, 1973), 642–649. Zweig, *Walt Whitman*, 126–127. See also Emory Holloway, *Whitman: An Interpretation in Narrative* (New York, 1926), 86. The excited admiration Whitman felt for foreign artists like Millet who witnessed the 1848 revolutions was part of the same tendency; see Larry Reynolds, *European Revolutions and the American Literary Renaissance* (New Haven, 1988), 128 (Whitman said, "The *Leaves* are really only Millet in another form"); Laura Meixner, "The Best of Democracy . . .", in *Walt Whitman and the Visual Arts* (ed. Geoffrey M. Sill and Roberta K. Tarbell; New Brunswick, 1992), 28–52.

32. Whitman, *Uncollected Poetry and Prose*, 1:246–247. Frankenstein, *Mount*, 241.

33. Cassedy and Shrott, *Works*, 21–22. The invention is credited to John Rand, a New Hampshire inventor about whom little is known, although his invention is credited with having "changed the whole character of painting." See Callow, *Kindred Spirits*, 69–70. Stuart P. Feld, "In the Midst of 'High Vintage,'" 300. John Burroughs had written of Whitman, "His study was out of doors," *Whitman: A Study* (Boston, 1896), 27. Another journal entry, written with quiet determination, stated simply, "There has been enough written on ideality and the grand style of Art, etc., to divert the artist from the true study of natural objects"; John A. Kouwenhoven, *The Arts in American Civilization* (New York, 1948–67), 143. Cassedy and Shrott, *Works*, 51.

34. Like Whitman, his mother came from Quaker stock; his father was a revolutionary veteran and the paymaster of the New York troops in the War of 1812; see Maybelle Mann, *Francis William Edmonds* (Washington, 1975), 7; and Francis William Edmonds, *Autobiography* (versions 1–3), private mss. I am indebted to Maybelle Mann for securing a copy of this manuscript.

35. Dixon Ryan Fox, *The Decline of Aristocracy in the Politics of New York, 1801–1840* (New York, 1919, 1965), 55. A committee to study prisons included the Democratic power brokers O'Sullivan, Edmonds, Theodore Sedgwick, and B. F. Butler; see the *New York Weekly News* (December 14, 1844). O'Sullivan and Judge Edmonds had known each other for years; for O'Sullivan's recommendation, see O'Sullivan to Silas Wright, January 25, 1845, Van Buren Collection, Library of Congress. Samuel Tilden, also from Columbia County, served a clerkship in his office around 1838, inaugurating his long career in the Democracy. Cassedy and Shrott, *Annotated Bibliography*, 23. Discussing the *Democratic Review* circle of anti-capital punishment types in toto, and mentioning Edmonds and Caroline Kirkland by name, the Whig diarist George Templeton Strong considered them part of "that tribe of soft-brained, nerveless sufferers from the lack of moral virility." See *The Diary of George Templeton Strong*, 2:11. Franklin Ellis, *History of Columbia County*, NY (Philadelphia, 1878), 106–107.

36. Clark, *Francis W. Edmonds*, 33, 20–21, 51. His first position was with the Hudson River Bank, an upstate institution whose directors included Van Buren's son Abraham; see *Columbia County at the End of the Century* (Hudson, N.Y., 1900), 1:352. From 1839 to 1855 he was cashier of the Mechanic's Bank, an important Democratic financial institution to which federal funds were shifted after the dismantling of the United States Bank (Bray Hammond, *Banks and Politics in American from the Revolution to the Civil War* [Princeton, 1957], 415). Clark, *Francis W. Edmonds*, 21, 103; *Democratic Review* 28 (June 1851), 567.

37. Clark, *Francis W. Edmonds*, 49. The painting is now lost.

38. Edmonds wrote privately that he hoped the United States would remain agricultural, rather than develop in the urban direction England was moving in; Clark, *Francis W. Edmonds*, 87.

39. References to Putnam, and also to Asher B. Durand abound in Edmonds's unpublished travel diary of 1840–1841; Columbia County Historical Society, Kinderhook, New York. On the trip, see Clark, *Francis W. Edmonds*, 46, 62, 76–8; see also Clark, "A Fresh Look at the Art of Francis W. Edmonds: Dutch Sources and American Meanings," *American Art Journal* 14 (Summer 1982), 73–94.

40. It is conceivable that *The Thirsty Drover* was painted after a poem on drovers by Whittier that had appeared as part of his "Songs of Labor" series earlier in the *Democratic Review*.

41. See Rollo G. Silver, "Whitman in 1850: Three Uncollected Articles," *American Literature* 19 (January 1948), 305.

42. Clark, *Francis W. Edmonds*, 49–50; Johns, *American Genre Painting*, 184–196. Chase Viele, "Four Artists of Mid-Nineteenth Century Buffalo," *New York History* 43, no. 1 (January 1962), 61. Another rendition of "Young America," depicting a young man with a liberty cap, was painted on the ceiling of the Capitol by Constantino Brumidi; see *We, the People: The Story of the United States Capitol* (Washington, 1972), 74–75.

43. Theodore E. Stebbins, Jr., *The Life and Works of Martin Joseph Heade* (New Haven, 1975), 9–11; *A Retrospective Exhibition of the Work of Frederick R. Spencer, 1806–1875* (Utica, 1969), n.p.

44. Christine Anne Hahler, ed., ". . . *illustrated by Darley*" (Wilmington, 1978), 3–6. One of his earliest assignments was Poe's "The Gold Bug," which he illustrated when it originally appeared in 1843 in *The Dollar Newspaper*. See Thomas Bolton, "The Book Illustrations of Felix Octavius Carr Darley," *The Proceedings of the American Antiquarian Society* 41 (April 1951), 137–182. Bolton's article is accompanied by an excellent bibliography, although he and Hahler do not agree on every fact.

45. One of Mathews's early triumphs was arranging to have Dickens's illustrator lend his talents to *The Career of Puffer Hopkins*. Darley illustrated Mathews's short-lived humor magazine, *Yankee Doodle*, later in 1847. Hahler, ed., ". . . *illustrated by Darley*," 5.

46. See Nancy Rash, *The Painting and Politics of George Caleb Bingham* (New Haven, 1991). See *Literary World*, October 23, 1847. Another western Whig painter, David Gilmour Blythe, created magnificent genre paintings around Pittsburgh in the same period; see Bruce Chambers, *The World of David Gilmour Blythe* (Washington, 1980).

47. *Democratic Review* 10 (February 1842), 200. The *Review* also praised two Mount paintings two years later; see *Democratic Review* 14 (April 1844), 438. *Democratic Review* 13 (July 1843), 45–48; Greenough wrote, "There is at present no country where the development and growth of an artist is more free, healthful, and happy than it is in these United States."

48. Ibid. 3 (November 1838), 258, 264.

49. O'Sullivan to Sumner, April 12, 1843, Sumner Collection, Harvard University Library; *Democratic Review* 12 (June 1843), 451–455. Crawford married into the Ward family, and was well known to both O'Sullivan and Sumner. Another article praised the "noble des-

tiny" of "our young painters"; *Democratic Review* 12 (June 1843), 603; Foshay, *Mr. Luman Reed's Picture Gallery,* 49–50. One of the coveted paintings awarded by lottery in 1849 went to a "J. S. O'Sullivan of New York," but there is no O'Sullivan on the membership list of that year (many people signed up at the last minute to go to the lottery). There is a good chance this was J. L. O'Sullivan. When O'Sullivan was minister to Portugal in the 1850s, he attempted to buy a large collection of Spanish Old Masters to send back for the benefit of young American artists; see Neil Harris, *The Artist in American Society,* 378–379; Callow, *Kindred Spirits,* 63n.

50. *Arcturus* 1 (December 1840), 57. *Democratic Review* 15 (September 1844), 249.

51. Mathews, *Americanism,* 25; *Arcturus* 2 (June 1841), 61. *Literary World* February 6, 1847; May 27, 1848; June 5, 1847.

52. Entry for December 30, 1838, Duyckinck Diary, November 14, 1838–April 7, 1839; Duyckinck Collection, Mss. Division, New York Public Library. Duyckinck also owned a William Page portrait of his child and several autographed Cruikshank prints, which Melville may have borrowed from; see *Literary World,* June 5, 1847; and *Moby-Dick* (eds. Luther S. Mansfield and Howard P. Vincent; New York, 1952), 815–816; all other citations to *Moby-Dick* will be to the 1988 Northwestern-Newberry edition.

53. *Democratic Review* 17 (September 1845), 216–217, 213.

54. W. A. Jones, "A Sketch of the Life and Character of William S. Mount," *American Review* 14 (August 1851), 122. The article was reprinted by Jones in his *Characters and Criticisms* (New York, 1857), 257–289. He and Mount corresponded until the end of their lives. Frankenstein, *Mount,* 299 (Mount listed the Jones portrait as an 1854 work; 483).

55. Callow, *Kindred Spirits,* 149–150; Melville, *Pierre,* 276–277.

56. Lillian Miller, *Patrons and Patriotism,* 222.

57. Trumbull's speech of January 28, 1833, quoted in Charles E. Baker's history of the American Art Union, in Mary Bartlett Cowdrey, ed., *American Academy of Fine Arts and American Art-Union: Introduction, 1816–1852* (New York, 1953) 95. For more on the American Academy, see Miller, *Patrons and Patriotism.* Cowdrey, ed., *American Academy of Fine Arts and American Art-Union,* 97.

58. *Yankee Doodle,* October 10, 1845, 5. Diary entry, December 16, 1852; Diary Fragments 1833–1856, Duyckinck Collection, Mss. Division, New York Public Library.

59. Callow, *Kindred Spirits,* 12–29; Mize, "The Contributions of Evert A. Duyckinck to the Cultural Development of Nineteenth Century America," 279; Foshay, *Mr. Luman Reed's Picture Gallery,* 29–30. Foshay suggests that the Sketch Club had a "Democratic allegiance," but this is difficult to determine.

60. Foshay, *Mr. Luman Reed's Picture Gallery,* 37–38.

61. Ibid., 30–31.

62. Ibid., 57.

63. In 1858 the collection became the nucleus of the New-York Historical Society's collection, where it remains to this day; see Foshay, *Mr. Luman Reed's Picture Gallery,* 19–20.

64. Herring and James Longacre had issued the four-volume *National Portrait Gallery of Distinguished Americans* (Philadelphia, 1834); Duyckinck would later edit a book with almost the same title.

65. Among the new members were Francis Edmonds, Charles F. Briggs, and William C. Bryant, soon to be president of the Art-Union. Miller, *Patrons and Patriotism,* 167.

66. *Bulletin of the American Art-Union* (April 1851), 18.

67. Franklin Kelly et al., *Frederic Edwin Church* (Washington, 1989), 190. Warner noted that Church not only profited from exhibitions at the Art Union, but worked in a studio in the Art-Union building at 497 Broadway. For general background, see Rachel N. Klein, "Art and Authority in Antebellum New York City: The Rise and Fall of the American Art-Union," *Journal of American History* 81 (March 1995), 1534–1561.

68. Kouwenhoven, *The Arts in American Civilization*, 138.

69. James Flexner, *That Wilder Image: The Painting of America's Native School from Thomas Cole to Winslow Homer* (New York, 1962, 1970), 54; William H. Griffiths, *The Story of the American Bank Note Company* (New York, 1959), 29; Clark, *Francis W. Edmonds* 37; on Edmonds' early engraving, see his autobiography, versions one and two [mss. in private possession]; *Bulletin of the American Art-Union* (October 1849), 3.

70. F. F. Marbury, in *American Art-Union Transactions for 1845*, 22. Hawthorne, *Mosses from an Old Manse*, 2:91. Similarly, in "Chippings with a Chisel," Hawthorne had written, "The dauber of signs is a painter as well as a Raphael"; *Democratic Review* 3 (September 1838), 19.

71. *Transactions of the Apollo Association for the Year 1840* (New York, 1840), 9; Henry James would parody some of these grandiose expectations in *Roderick Hudson*: "We were the biggest people and we ought to have the biggest conceptions;" Miller, *Patrons and Patriotism*, 214.

72. *Transactions of the Apollo Association, for the Promotion of the Fine Arts in the United States, for the Year 1842* (New York, 1842), 7. Briggs, like his friend James Russell Lowell, enjoyed the company of the Young Americans in the early 1840s, but grew tired of their nationalism by the end of the decade, when he parodied them in *The Trippings of Tom Pepper*.

73. *Transactions . . . 1842*, 135. *Transactions of the American Art-Union, for the Year 1848*, 48.

74. *Transactions of the Apollo Association for the Year 1843* (New York, 1843), 5–6.

75. Ibid., 8, 9, 6; *Transactions of the American Art-Union, for the Promotion of the Fine Arts in the United States, for the Year 1844* (New York, 1844), 6.

76. *Transactions . . . 1844*, 6–7, 10.

77. Cowdrey, ed., *American Academy of Fine Arts and American Art-Union*, 153, 167.

78. *Literary World*, November 25, 1848.

79. Clark, *Francis W. Edmonds* 27. Cowdrey, ed., *American Academy of Fine Arts and American Art-Union: Exhibition Record, 1816–1852* (New York, 1953) 127–128. Cowdrey, ed., *American Academy of Fine Arts and American Art-Union: Introduction, 1816–1852*, 287. *Transactions . . . 1844*, 9.

80. As Mount related in a letter to George Pope Morris, December 3, 1848, the Art-Union tried to "buy pictures at low prices to grind the Artist down." He was also angry because the Art-Union had asked his brother to paint a still life of shell fish, but upon presentation "a Tall, genteel looking Englishman engaged in the office" replied the picture was too "shelly"; Frankenstein, *Mount*, 234, 240, 174. Ironically, this supremely Americanist painter enjoyed an agreeable relationship for several years with the French firm of Goupil, Vibert, and Company, which sponsored the rival International Art Union. The Goupil representative was shrewder in appealing to an artist's natural vanity and liberally sprinkled his letters (addressed to "Monsieur W.S. Mount, peintre célèbre") with effusive compliments like "Three cheers for W. S. Mount!!! the great American Wilkie!!!" (161).

81. From 1838 to 1852, over the entire span of the association's existence, Bingham exhibited frequently, and his *Jolly Flat Boat Men* was the etching distributed to members in 1847. The bulletin praised his "striking nationality of character" and considered, "all these works are thoroughly American in their subjects"; *Bulletin of the American Art-Union* (August 1849), 10. Hahler, ed., ". . . *illustrated by Darley*," 10.

82. *Transactions of the American Art-Union for the Year 1847*, 21–22.

83. *Bulletin of the American Art-Union* (September 1849), 24; the quotation is from the *Southern Quarterly Review*. *Bulletin of the American Art-Union* (December 1851), 138.

84. Membership lists were published by town and state in the annual *Transactions*, and

they offer fascinating evidence of the extent of national interest; members came from each of the states, along with California and a handful of foreign countries. See also *Bulletin of the American Art-Union* 2 (December 1849), 16; Carol Troyen, "Retreat to Arcadia: American Landscape and the American Art-Union," *American Art Journal* 23 (1991), 21–37.

85. Bryant was president of the American Art-Union from 1844 to 1846. All membership information is gleaned from the Art-Union annual *Transactions*. I realize that this information is not completely dependable, because the *Transactions* were often published before the membership lists were finished. Other sympathetic members included Henry Gilpin (1840), Parke Godwin (1841), and various Sedgwicks and Wards. Both Griswold and Clark gave speeches at an opening at the National Academy, as reported in the *Bulletin of the American Art-Union* (April 1851), 32.

86. *Transactions of the American Art-Union, for the Year 1845*, 12. Headley, an occasional minister, not only wrote for Duyckinck's Library of American Books and the *Review*, but was friendly with a number of artists, including Darley; see Duyckinck to Margaret Duyckinck, August 9, 1850, Duyckinck Collection, Mss. Division, New York Public Library.

87. Ibid., 14, 16–17.

88. *Democratic Review* 16 (June 1845), 576–578; 23 (October 1848), 374. There was a poem from the *Review* in the April 1849 *Bulletin of the American Art-Union*, 11:16. It was by William Allen Butler, who was on the Committee of Management with Duyckinck from 1849 to 1851. The Art-Union was mentioned in a play titled "Earning a Living"; *Democratic Review* 25 (August 1849), 167.

89. Bigelow diary, November 20, 1846; December 19, 1846; Bigelow Collection, Mss. Division, New York Public Library. *Spirit of the Times*, February 14, 1846 (Harvard Theater Collection). Duyckinck diary entry from December 18, 1852, Diary Fragments, 1833–1856, Duyckinck Collection, Mss. Division, New York Public Library. The head of the Art-Union in the late 1840s, Prosper Wetmore, was affiliated with the Young Americans of the early 1850s and secured muskets to help the European radicals; see Basil Rauch, *American Interest in Cuba: 1848–1855* (New York, 1948), 214–215.

90. *Arcturus* 1 (December 1840), 57–58; (March 1841), 240.

91. *Literary World*, April 3, 1847; November 25, 1848.

92. Ibid., November 25, 1848. The *Literary World* also engaged in a spirited defense of the Art Union when its business was threatened by the interloping foreigners of the International Art Union; see *Literary World* October 13, 1849; and October 20, 1849. Elsewhere, the magazine mused, "Had it not been for the Art-Union, what masses of its admirers would have limited their artistic experience to the windows of print shops and the mezzotints of the monthly magazines"; *Literary World*, September 1, 1849.

93. Jacques DuMonde (Butler's pseudonym), "The Free Gallery of the American Art Union," (New York, 1849); Duyckinck Collection, Mss. Division, New York Public Library.

94. *Literary World*, November 11, 1848. The friend, James Beekman, had accompanied Duyckinck on his European jaunt in 1838–1839.

95. Johns, *American Genre Painting*, 53, 76, 77.

96. Callow, *Kindred Spirits*, 33. Callow speculated that Duyckinck urged the Art-Union to purchase the works of Christopher Pearse Cranch shortly after receiving a letter from Cranch pleading for help. A list of Committee of Management members is in Cowdrey, ed., *American Academy of Fine Arts and American Art-Union*, 105–107. Diary entry, October 6, 1847, Duyckinck Collection, Mss. Division, New York Public Library. Duyckinck was especially amused when a rival editor, George Colton of the *Whig Review*, began a drunken speech by "thumping an inverted wineglass on the table" and "rivalled an infuriated Dutch windmill in the flourishes of his arms."

97. Matthiessen, *American Renaissance*, 598. Christopher Sten, *Savage Eye*, 225–229.

Melville, "Hawthorne and His Mosses," in *The Piazza Tales*, 249. It has been speculated that Melville created the characters for "The Happy Failure" (1854) after seeing a painting by James Clonney that was hanging at the National Academy in 1847. See John M. J. Gretchko in *Melville Extracts*, No. 86 (September 1991), 9–10. Silver, "Whitman in 1850: Three Uncollected Articles," 305.

98. *Transactions of the American Art-Union for the Year 1849*, 32. Cowdrey, ed., *American Academy of Fine Arts and American Art-Union*, "Introduction," 211 (see also Charles E. Baker's interesting comparison of these statistics to the twentieth century, 216).

99. See E. Maurice Bloch, "The American Art-Union's Downfall," in *New-York Historical Society Quarterly* 37 (1953), 331–359. An entire article was devoted to "The Enemies of the American Art-Union" in the December 1849 *Bulletin*. This righteous morality on the part of Bennett and others was considered high hypocrisy by many. An English diplomat noted, "The disposal of the pictures and engravings by lottery was a fatal objection in the New England States, where gambling in *such* a shape is held in pious horror by a community that unscrupulously risks large stakes in every variety of the desperate game of stock-jobbing, and whose open bettings on the Presidential and other elections is wide-spread and notorious"; Thomas Colley Grattan quoted in Dearinger, 52. Miller, *Patrons and Patriotism*, 171–172.

100. Troyen, "Retreat to Arcadia," 21–37. *Bulletin of the American Art-Union* (May 1849), 9. *Literary World*, March 9, 1850.

101. George Putnam, ed., *The Home Book of the Picturesque* (New York, 1852), 3, 10. Around the same time, Putnam contemplated a book called *The New Art-Union; or Old World Pencils and New World Pens*, that would set the words of American writers to European artworks; see Ezra Greenspan, "A Publisher's Legacy," 62. Miller, *Patrons and Patriotism*, 230.

102. Cowdrey, ed., *American Academy of Fine Arts and American Art-Union*, 201.

103. See Howard Kerr, *Mediums, Spirit-Rappers and Roaring Radicals: Spiritualism in American Literature, 1800–1850* (Urbana, 1972).

104. Frankenstein, *Mount*, 292.

105. There is some question about the keenness of his intellect during these final years; Cowdrey and Williams, *William Sidney Mount*, 8n, 31.

106. Jarves, *The Art-Idea*, 129.

107. Sten, *Savage Eye*, 39.

5 *The Young American Lexicon*

1. Jay Leyda, *The Melville Log: A Documentary Life of Herman Melville* (New York, 1951), 383–386; Luther Stearns Mansfield, "Glimpses of Herman Melville's Life in Pittsfield, 1850–1851," *American Literature* 9 (March 1937), 26–48; James T. Fields, *Yesterdays with Authors* (Boston, 1878), 52–53; Cornelius Mathews, "Several Days in Berkshire," *Literary World*, August 24, August 31, September 7, 1850; Henry Dwight Sedgwick, "Reminiscences of Literary Berkshire, *Century* 50 (August 1895), 552–568; Perry Miller, *The Raven and the Whale: The War of Words and Wits in the Era of Poe and Melville* (New York, 1956) 280–291; Oliver Wendell Holmes, "Astræa: The Balance of Illusion," in *The Complete Works of Oliver Wendell Holmes* (Cambridge Edition, 1872, 1908), 336. For more background, see Hershel Parker, *Herman Melville: A Biography, 1819–1851* (Baltimore, 1996), 1:742–751.

2. Leyda, *Melville Log*, 385.

3. See Robert Ferguson, *Law and Letters in American Culture* (Cambridge, 1984); Brook Thomas, *Cross-Examinations of Law and Literature* (Cambridge, England, 1987); Carl S. Smith, John P. McWilliams, Jr., and Maxwell Bloomfield, *Law and American Literature: A Collection of Essays* (New York, 1983). Herman Melville, *The Confidence-Man* (ed.

Harrison Hayford, Hershel Parker, and G. Thomas Tanselle; Evanston, 1984), 13. Just before his arrival in Stockbridge, Duyckinck had printed a front-page satirical article on "The New York Bar" in the *Literary World* (July 27, 1850), 65.

4. Cornelius Mathews, "Several Days in Berkshire," *Literary World*, August 24, 1850. Mathews wrote, "We meet a tall gentleman in the cars, whom we remember singing the praises of this Berkshire Valley, in a New York omnibus on a hot day, some half a dozen years ago." This describes Field to perfection.

5. *Literary World*, August 31, 1850. Tellingly, Mathews also reported that the climbers had "a glorious sea-feeling" as they started their excursion. Melville, *Moby-Dick*, 449. Mansfield, "Glimpses of Herman Melville's Life in Pittsfield," 30.

6. Mansfield, "Glimpses of Herman Melville's Life in Pittsfield," 31.

7. O'Sullivan had introduced Field to Hawthorne previously (Randall Stewart, *Nathaniel Hawthorne: A Biography* [New Haven, 1948], 106), and he was the key figure whom everyone at the dinner knew in common.

8. *Literary World* (September 7, 1850), 186.

9. David Dudley Field, *The Administration of the Code* (New York, 1852), 5.

10. Perry Miller, *The Life of the Mind in America from the Revolution to the Civil War* (New York, 1965), 241. Alan Heimert, *Religion and the American Mind from the Great Awakening to the Revolution* (Cambridge, 1966), 527–528. Ezra Stiles hoped American jurisprudence would rise to "the highest purity and perfection—especially if hereafter . . . some great law genius, should arise, and, with vast erudition, . . . reduce and digest it all into one great jural system."

11. Field, *Legal Reform: An Address to the Graduating Class of the Law School of the University of Albany* (Albany, 1855), 17. Ironically, when he launched the *Democratic Review* in 1837, O'Sullivan had sworn allegiance to "those universal principles of taste to which we are all alike subject will alone be recognized as the common law;" "Prospectus of Democratic Review," in *Washington Globe* (March 3, 1837).

12. See Morton J. Horwitz, *The Transformation of American Law, 1780–1860* (Cambridge, 1977); William E. Nelson, *Americanization of the Common Law: The Impact of Legal Change on Massachusetts Society, 1760–1830* (Cambridge, 1975); Charles M. Haar, *The Golden Age of American Law* (New York, 1965); Charles Cook, *The American Codification Movement: A Study of Antebellum Legal Reform* (Westport, Conn., 1981) and Perry Miller, ed., *The Legal Mind in America: From Independence to the Civil War* (Garden City, 1962), 111. Alexis de Tocqueville, *Democracy in America*, (New York, 1980), 1:45. Tocqueville, in Haar, *Golden Age of American Law*, 28.

13. See Horwitz, *The Transformation of American Law*, passim; Charles Sellers, *The Market Revolution: Jacksonian America, 1815–1846* (New York, 1991) 51.

14. William B. Hatcher, *Edward Livingston: Jeffersonian Republican and Jacksonian Democrat* (Baton Rouge, 1940), 4. William Livingston had edited the first digest of New York's colonial laws in 1753, and denounced ponderous memorization for making "a young fellow trifle away the bloom of his age"; see Theodore Sedgwick, ed., *A Memoir of the Life of William Livingston* (New York, 1833), 66; Alan Heimert and Andrew Delbanco, *The Puritans in America: A Narrative Anthology* (Cambridge, 1985), 407; Hatcher, *Edward Livingston*, 72–99. *Democratic Review* 9 (July 1841), 7.

15. Edward Livingston, *A System of Penal Laws for the United States of America* (Washington, 1828); *A System of Penal Law for Louisiana* . . . (Philadelphia, 1833). See Hatcher, *Edward Livingston*, 245–288. Clement Eaton, *The Leaven of Democracy* (New York, 1963), 455.

16. See John Bigelow, *William Cullen Bryant* (Boston, 1890), 1:338. *Democratic Review* 16 (February 1845), 109–11. Davezac's contributions to the *Review* include his editing of "Fragments of Unpublished Reminiscences of Edward Livingston," 8 (October 1840),

366–384; "The Conspiracy of Catiline," 9 (August 1841), 144–162; "A Chapter on Gardening," 12 (February 1843), 122–128; and "The Literature of Fiction," 16 (March 1845), 268–282. He also delivered "A Lay Sermon at Sea," published alongside his Livingston fragments in October 1840 (8, 336–345). Horace Traubel, *With Whitman in Camden* (Boston, 1906; rpt. Carbondale, 1982), 5:75–76. Harriet Langdon Pruyn Rice, *Harmanus Bleecker: An Albany Dutchman, 1779–1849* (Albany, 1924), 211. Evert Duyckinck Diary, 1838–1839, Duyckinck Collection, Mss. Division, New York Public Library.

17. *Democratic Review* 8 (November–December 1840), 533.

18. See Perry Miller, *Legal Mind*, 79, 88. Among other reasons for codification excitement, the Code Napoleon had been just been translated and published to great interest; see Cook, *The American Codification Movement*, 71.

19. Cook, *The American Codification Movement*, 185.

20. Emmet was praised by the *Democratic Review* as late as 1852; *Democratic Review* 30 (April 1852), 301–302. William Sampson, *Memoirs of William Sampson, An Irish Exile* (London, 1832).

21. Miller, *Life of the Mind*, 246.

22. William Sampson, *An Anniversary Discourse, Delivered Before the Historical Society of New-York, . . . on the Common Law* (New York, 1824), 7.

23. Ibid., 7, 9. 11, 17.

24. Ibid. 57, 63, 65, 67–68. Field would use the same trope in 1859, comparing the law to "the streams of your own Mississippi Valley" in a speech in Chicago; see Field, *The Magnitude and Importance of Legal Science* (New York, 1859), 13.

25. William Allen Butler, *The Revision of the Statutes of the State of New York and the Revisers* (New York, 1889), 9–10.

26. *Democratic Review* 5 (January 1839), 39. William D. Driscoll, *Benjamin F. Butler: Lawyer and Regency Politician* (New York, 1977; reprint of 1965 Ph.D. diss., Fordham University), 103, 117.

27. See *The Law School Papers of Benjamin F. Butler*. Cornelius Mathews had just graduated (1834) from the university and Samuel Tilden would come there in 1838 to study law while clerking for John Edmonds; for more on Butler see *Democratic Review* 5 (January 1839), 33–48; *National Cyclopedia . . .* (New York, 1907), 5:297. When Jackson died in 1845, Butler gave the New York funeral oration; see Philip Hone, *Diary*, 2:734. Leyda, *Melville Log*, 1:386, 390.

28. Sedgwick's treatise was *The English Practice: A Statement Showing Some of the Evils and Absurdities of the Practice of the English Common Law as Adopted in Several of the United States and Particularly in the State of New York* (New York, 1822). See the *Democratic Review* 7 (February 1840), 129–153, for a profile of both Theodore II and Henry Sedgwick.

29. Miller, *Legal Mind*, 138, 140. Daun Van Ee, *David Dudley Field and the Reconstruction of the Law*, (New York, 1986), 13. On reforms in Massachusetts, see Nelson, *Americanization of the Common Law*.

30. *Democratic Review* 7 (February 1840), 150–151. Sarah Cabot Sedgwick and Christine S. Marquand, *Stockbridge, 1739–1974* (Stockbridge, 1974), 219; Henry Dwight Sedgwick, "Reminiscences of Literary Berkshire," *Century* 50 (August 1895), 557. Bryant's "Reminiscences of Miss Sedgwick," quoted in Mary E. Dewey, ed., *The Life and Letters of Catharine M. Sedgwick* (New York, 1871) 440–442.

31. I have taken the liberty of placing the numeral after this Theodore (1780–1839) to distinguish him from his father (1746–1813) and son (1811–1859) of the same name. He served in the Massachusetts legislature in the 1820s and died in 1839 giving an oration to the Democracy of Pittsfield; see Theodore Sedgwick ["Rusticus"], *Hints for the People* (New York, 1823), 3; *Hints to My Countrymen* (New York, 1826), 64. Sedgwick's many ruminations

on the importance of the book-merchant also offer an interesting reflection of the book trade at a transitional moment. David Dudley Field's brother, Stephen, the Supreme Court justice, considered Sedgwick's *Public and Private Economy* the foundation of his constitutional understanding; see Charles W. McCurdy, "Stephen J. Field and the American Judicial Tradition," in Philip J. Bergan, ed., *The Fields and the Law* (New York, 1986), 6. Henry Dwight Sedgwick, *The English Practice*, p. 4. Another sibling, Charles Sedgwick, wrote Bryant in 1824; "The law is a hag" shrouded in "ugly drapery"; Edward K. Spann, *Ideals and Politics: New York Intellectuals and Liberal Democracy, 1820-1880* (Albany, 1972), 31.

32. Harriet Rice, *Harmanus Bleecker*, 15, 105–106, 201–205. Duyckinck also reported on the activities of Davezac, whom Bleecker had replaced as Van Buren's chargé to the Hague, and whom Duyckinck saw frequently in New York; Rice, *Harmanus Bleecker*, 201–204, 210–211; letters of March 15, 1840 and July 20, 1840.

33. George Wilson Pierson, *Tocqueville in America* (Garden City, 1959), 441. Theodore Sedgwick, *The American Citizen: His True Position, Character and Duties* (New York, 1847). This essay, which was delivered as a lecture at Union College, was published by Wiley and Putnam as they were finishing the Library of American Books.

34. Theodore Sedgwick, *A Statement of Facts in Relation to the Delays and Arrears of Business in the Court of Chancery of the State of New York with Some Suggestions for a Change in its Organization* (New York, 1838). He wrote frequently for Bryant's *Evening Post*, helped secure New York's constitutional convention of 1846, and argued vociferously against Texan annexation (which put him at odds with O'Sullivan). For his later work, see *A Treatise on the Rules Which Govern the Interpretations and Application of Statutory and Constitutional Law* (New York, 1857).

35. Driscoll, *Benjamin F. Butler*, 6. Henry Dwight Sedgwick, "Reminiscences," 552. Sedgwick and Marquand, *Stockbridge*, 106; Butler, *The Revision of the Statutes of the State of New York and the Revisers*, 14; Henry Dwight Sedgwick, "Reminiscences," 552, 567. Edward K. Spann, *Ideals and Politics*, 107.

36. All three of these Democrats were "educated" by the Van Burenites; Edmonds studied under Van Buren directly; Tilden studied under Butler and Edmonds, Bigelow was trained by the Sedgwicks. Edmonds and Bigelow both contributed to codification, Edmonds with a tract in 1848 and Bigelow with articles on law reform in the *Democratic Review*.

37. Edward A. Collier, *A History of Old Kinderhook* (New York, 1914), 429.

38. *Democratic Review* 8 (October 1840), 366–384; 9 (July 1841), 15; 9 (September 1841), 213, 218; 6 (December 1839), 463–472; 20 (March 1848), 199–206.

39. O'Sullivan had helped Charles Anthon teach law at Columbia. This led to a small crisis when he published an article by the young John Bigelow critical of Anthon's classical dictionary; see Bigelow, *Retrospections*, 1:58. As fellow Columbia students, they would have learned constitutional law from the university president, William Alexander Duer, an old Livingston associate and one of Butler's fellow revisers in the 1820s. Duer had practiced with Livingston in both New York and Louisiana; he became a New York Supreme Court judge in 1822, and was president of Columbia from 1829 to 1842.

40. *Democratic Review* 1 (January 1838), 144, 159–160, 162, 171; 6 (November 1839), 427–428.

41. Ibid. 6 (December 1839), 470. Miscellaneous Sedgwick Family Papers, Massachusetts Historical Society. There are random letters from O'Sullivan and his mother to various Sedgwicks dispersed through the collection. See also O'Sullivan to Dorr, July 29, 1836, in which O'Sullivan mentioned a mutual friend from Stockbridge and announced his mother and sister would be traveling there; Mrs. H. Davidson to Dorr, August 3, 1841, mentioned the O'Sullivans and the fact they prefer Stockbridge to Saratoga; Dorr Mss., Rider Collection, Brown University Library.

42. Catharine M. Sedgwick to Mrs. K. S. Minot, *The Life and Letters of Catharine M. Sedgwick*, 286–287. Catharine Maria Sedgwick was one of the first authors he asked to write for the *Review*, and in May 1837, well before the first issue came out, she had already donated an article on the Panic to help him. A letter of May 24, 1837 (167), to her brother Charles Sedgwick read, "I wrote a little article for John O'Sullivan called 'Who and What had not Failed,' which it seemed to me showed a great balance in favor even of the real bankrupts." *New York Herald*, August 22, 1844.

43. Field's correspondence with Dorr dated from 1834, O'Sullivan's from 1835; O'Sullivan mentioned Field frequently in his letters of the 1840s; see Dorr Mss. in the Rider Collection, Brown University Library.

44. Henry M. Field, *The Family of Rev. David D. Field, D.D., of Stockbridge, Mass.* (privately printed, 1860). The works of the senior Field included *History of the Country of Berkshire* (Pittsfield, 1829) and *A History of the Town of Pittsfield* (Hartford, 1844). Henry M. Field, *The Life of David Dudley Field* (New York, 1898), 30; Philip J. Bergan et al., *The Fields and the Law*, 22. Field wrote melodramatically about his early rebellion, "If resistance to college authorities is ever justifiable, it was so then"; "Recollections of My Early Life, No. 2," Field-Musgrave Papers, Special Collections, Duke University Library.

45. Henry M. Field, *Family*, 61, 94–98; Henry M. Field, *Life of David Dudley Field*, 40. The bizarre dénouement of Henry M. Field's presence in Paris in 1848 was his literary revival in Rachel Field's *All This, and Heaven Too* (New York, 1938), a maudlin novel turned into a film by Warner Brothers in 1940. At the end of the film, the Field character, who in real life was a failed minister, marries Bette Davis, extending Young America's life well into the twentieth century. The secret motto of the film, that the United States should intervene to save France, was perfectly consonant with Young American opinion in 1848.

46. Field, "Recollections of My Early Life, No. 2," Field-Musgrave Papers, Special Collections, Duke University Library.

47. Field, Journal (1831–1835), Field-Musgrave Papers, Special Collections, Duke University Library. Van Ee, *David Dudley Field and the Reconstruction of the Law*, 38. Bergan, *The Fields and the Law*, 24; Michael Joseph Hobor, "The Form of the Law: David Dudley Field and the Codification Movement in New York, 1839–1888" (Ph.D. diss., University of Chicago, 1975), 83, 89.

48. Field, Journal of a Visit to Europe, 1836–1837, Field-Musgrave Papers, Special Collections Library, Duke University Library. Henry M. Field, *Life of David Dudley Field*, 43–43; Van Ee, *David Dudley Field and the Reconstruction of the Law*, 14, 18.

49. See the glowing Rantoul portrait in *Democratic Review* 27 (October 1850), 348–363; also Robert Rantoul, Jr., *The Memoirs, Speeches and Writings of Robert Rantoul, Jr.* (ed. Luther Hamilton; Boston, 1854). For more on Rantoul's opposition to capital punishment, see 425–575. Miller, *Legal Mind*, 222–225. Marvin Meyers devoted a chapter to Rantoul in *The Jacksonian Persuasion* and closely examined this speech (229–233). Rantoul was yet another Democrat who eagerly awaited the American future. Beside the three issues above, he defended the right of workers to organize (he won *Commonwealth vs. Hunt* before Lemuel Shaw in 1842) and vociferously supported the Dorr Rebellion. In other words, he argued almost every opinion O'Sullivan did. Emerson, *The Journals*, 5:150. Emerson, *The Complete Essays and Other Writings*, 3.

50. Gulian Verplanck, *Speech When in Committee of the Whole in the Senate of New-York, on the Several Bills and Resolutions for the Amendment of the Law and the Reform of the Judiciary System* (Albany, 1839), 4, 31. David Dudley Field, *Speeches*, 1:222.

51. *Democratic Review* 6 (December 1839), 533. David Dudley Field, *Speeches*, 1:223–226; Henry M. Field, *Family*, 54–55; Henry M. Field, *Life of David Dudley Field*, 46.

52. John L. O'Sullivan, *Report*, 8. Rantoul is cited on p. 9n, and Livingston on p. 127.

53. Henry M. Field, *Family*, 58. David Dudley Field, *Speeches*, 2:213, 215–216.

54. Field, *Speeches*, 2:219.

55. Miller, *Life of the Mind*, 262. *Democratic Review* 12 (February 1843), 155–158; 15 (October 1844), 400–407.

56. O'Sullivan was listed as a new resident member in the *Democratic Review*, 13 (February 1843), 223, just when the *Review* began publishing the Historical Society's proceedings. Other members included William Gilmore Simms, Samuel Tilden, and John W. Edmonds. Homer F. Barnes, *Charles Fenno Hoffman* (New York, 1930), 160–165. *Democratic Review* 16 (May 1845), 492–494; O'Sullivan added in a postscript (520n) that he preferred "America" in spite of the press he gave the issue. The *New York Morning News* contained many articles on Alleghanian themes from April to June 1845, including the announcement that an *Alleghanian Magazine* was in the works (June 21, 1845).

57. Caroline Kirkland, *Western Clearings* (New York, 1845), viii. *New-York Historical Society Proceedings, 1845* (New York, 1846), 227. Simms was a member of the New-York Historical Society despite his residence in South Carolina.

58. *New-York Historical Society Proceedings, 1845*, 117.

59. Mathews never left the theme, writing later books like *The Indian Fairy Book from the Original Legends* (New York, 1869) and *The Enchanted Moccasins* (New York, 1878). Field's relationship to the art scene has never been studied, but it is interesting to note his brother Cyrus, the Atlantic telegraph pioneer, patronized the young Frederic Church. Church's 1847 painting, *View Near Stockbridge*, was performed from a vista that Field later acquired for his home; see Christopher Kent Wilson, "The Landscape of Democracy: Frederic Church's *West Rock, New Haven*," *American Art Journal* 18 (1986, no. 3), 20–39.

60. *New York Morning News*, December 27, 1845. David Dudley Field, *Speeches*, 2:22, 38; Van Ee, *David Dudley Field and the Reconstruction of the Law*, 120–121. For Field on Texas, see Lee Benson, *The Concept of Jacksonian Democracy*, 232, 256.

61. David Dudley Field, *Speeches*, 1:485.

62. Henry M. Field, *Life of David Dudley Field*, 44.

63. In 1841, Dorr wrote that codification was his "favourite plan"; see Marvin E. Gettleman, *The Dorr Rebellion: A Study in American Radicalism, 1833–1849* (New York, 1973), 15n. Field to Dorr, March 16, 1844, Dorr Mss., Rider Collection, Brown University Library.

64. Benjamin F. Butler, *Outline of the Constitutional History of New York* (New York, 1848), 73–74.

65. *Arcturus* 2 (July 1841), 121–122. O'Sullivan was cited on p. 118, and Livingston on p. 116.

66. Bigelow diary, Bigelow Mss., Mss. Division, New York Public Library (his entry on November 25, 1843 treats the constitutional law article). In the final month of O'Sullivan's stewardship, the *Review* published an article on "Prospects of the Legal Profession in America," 18 (January 1846), 26–30, which was found among Whitman's clippings a half-century later. *Democratic Review* 21 (December 1847), 477–478; 22 (June 1848), 529–540; 22 (March 1848), 200, 206. For Field's ambivalence on this point, see Van Ee, *David Dudley Field and the Reconstruction of the Law*, 31.

67. Dorr to Field, September 18, 1852, Dorr Mss., Rider Collection, Brown University Library. David Dudley Field, *The Administration of the Code*, 5.

68. Alison Reppy, ed., *David Dudley Field: Centenary Essays* (New York, 1949), 31.

69. Van Ee, *David Dudley Field and the Reconstruction of the Law*, 41–42.

70. Cook, *The American Codification Movement*, 192.

71. Field, Commonplace Book, Field-Musgrave Papers, Special Collections, Duke University Library. Henry M. Field, *Family*, 55–57; *New York Morning News*, January 17, 1846; Theodore Sedgwick, *The American Citizen* (1847), 29; Butler, *Constitutional History of New York*; John W. Edmonds, *An Address on the Constitution and Codes of Procedure* (New York, 1848). Edmonds critiqued some aspects of the code, including its diminished emphasis on jury duty, but he admired its streamlined language. Field later criticized Edmonds in an 1852 pamphlet, *The Administration of the Code* (10), but they were both from the Van Buren camp of the New York Democracy. For more on the details of the Field Code, see Lawrence M. Friedman, *A History of American Law* (New York, 1973, 1985), 391–411; Reppy, *David Dudley Field*, 9, 31–42.

72. *Democratic Review* 21 (September 1847), 189–202. Flick, *Tilden*, 81. At the Utica convention in June that year, Field read a letter from Van Buren, who was subsequently nominated. Butler, too, participated in the Free Soil agitation (he had a personal memory of the Southern Democracy's treachery in 1844), giving the impression all these reforms were linked, and to be for codification was also to be for Free Soil and Van Buren; O. C. Gardiner, *The Great Issue: or, the Three Presidential Candidates* (New York, 1848), 55–57, 118–137. Gardiner was "the late associate editor of the Democratic Review," and must have known Field through their mutual magazine friends. Butler gave a speech on the history of the Barnburners at the Buffalo Free Soil convention in 1848; see Eric Foner, *Free Soil, Free Labor, Free Men: The Ideology of the Republican Party Before the Civil War* (New York, 1970), 106. On the Roman speech, see *Democratic Review* 22 (October 1850), 87. Field had already attacked "the iron heel" opposing European liberties in the *Democratic Review* (*Speeches*, 2:37), and he sponsored Young Italian speeches in the 1850s; see Joseph Rossi, *The Image of America in Mazzini's Writings* (Madison, 1954), 110. For background on the Free Soil movement, see Edward K. Spann, *Ideals and Politics*, 128–129, 161–173.

73. George Templeton Strong, *Diary*, 2:208 (entry of January 10, 1855). David Dudley Field, *The Lawyer and His Clients* . . . (Springfield, 1871), 1.

74. Field, "Notes for My Autobiography," Field-Musgrave Papers, Special Collections, Duke University Library. Field, *The Lawyer and His Clients*; *Speeches*, 1:488. Stephen N. Subrin, "David Dudley Field and the Field Code: A Historical Analysis of an Earlier Procedural Vision," *Law and History Review* (1988), 314. Bergan, *The Fields and the Law*, 41–43. On Field's unpleasant temperament, see George Martin, *Causes and Conflicts: The Centennial History of the Association of the Bar of the City of New York* (Boston, 1970), 88–91. The old upstate Democratic alliance flickered one last time in 1876 when Field, appointed temporarily to Congress by Boss Tweed, worked tirelessly to secure Samuel Tilden's rights in the disputed election. See Flick, *Tilden*, 228, 357, 388.

75. Friedman, 393, 394, 403; Horwitz, *The Transformation of American Law*, 117. *Harper's Weekly* (November 14, 1874).

76. Dorr to Field, September 18, 1852, Dorr Mss., Rider Collection, Brown University Library.

77. Dorr to Field, December 8, 1849; Dorr to O'Sullivan, August 4, 1849; Dorr Mss., Rider Collection, Brown University Library. The former "People's Champion" was reduced to the "Russian-izing" of ironware (giving the look of Russian craftsmanship to ordinary iron).

78. Field, *Speeches*, 3:239. Van Ee, *David Dudley Field and the Reconstruction of the Law*, 25.

79. Pritchard, *Literary Wise Men of Gotham* (Baton Rouge, 1963), 37. Field, *Speeches*, 2:219. Miller, *Life of the Mind*, 260.

80. David Dudley Field, *A Short Manual of Pleading Under the Code* (Albany, 1856).

81. *Democratic Review* 8 (September 1840), 264–265; 9 (July 1841), 11; (September 1841),

215. Edmonds, *An Address on the Constitution and Codes of Procedure*, 12–17. More recently, Lawrence Friedman has written on the literary quality of the new code, noting it was "tightly worded and skeletal; there was no trace of the elaborate redundancy, the voluptuous heaping on of synonyms so characteristic of Anglo-American statutes. It was, in short, a code in the French sense, not a statute"; see Cook, *The American Codification Movement*, 191.

82. Field, *Speeches*, 490; *Legal Reform*, 20.

83. James Kirke Paulding, *The Merry Tales of the Three Wise Men of Gotham* (New York, 1839), 106, 109, 166–167.

84. Joseph G. Baldwin, *The Flush Times of Alabama and Mississippi* (New York, 1957), 42, 210; Kenneth Lynn, *Mark Twain and Southwestern Humor* (Boston, 1959) 123.

85. Baldwin, *Flush Times of Alabama and Mississippi*, 171. Allen F. Stein, *Cornelius Mathews*, 69–70; it is important also to note that the copyright protection Mathews worked so hard to enact was part of the original plan of the Field Code; Bergan, *The Fields and the Law*, 46; *Literary World*, November 9, 1850. *Democratic Review* 15 (October 1844), 424; 20 (May 1847), 387. Earlier in the decade, Griswold had planned an anthology on "The Bench and Bar in America," apparently never published.

86. See Brook Thomas, *Cross-Examinations of Law and Literature*, for an extensive analysis of Melville and the law.

87. Leyda, *Melville Log*, 635. Bruce A. Harvey, "'Precepts Graven on Every Breast': Melville's *Typee* and the Forms of the Law," *American Quarterly* 45 (September 1993), 394–424. Melville probably also read Field's harangues on Alleghania, if only because they were printed in the same volume of New-York Historical Society Proceedings as an account Schoolcraft wrote of Melville's grandfather's heroics in the defense of Fort Stanwix; see *New-York Historical Society Proceedings*, 1845, 132–158. Melville, *Mardi*, 399; *The Confidence-Man*, 239. Also in *The Confidence-Man*, Melville included a gibe that "accountability is neither to you, nor me, nor the Court of Common Pleas, but to something superior" (191).

88. Melville, *The Piazza Tales*, 14. Leyda, *Melville Log*, 1:160. Gansevoort Melville also knew Benjamin Butler well; see Leyda, *Melville Log*, 194. *Democratic Review* 14 (April 1844), 349.

89. William Sampson, *Is a Whale a Fish? An Accurate Report of the Case of James Maurice against Samuel Judd* . . . (New York, 1819). A sperm whale fighting the krakens is mentioned (36); he discusses the history of the whale as the "royal" fish of England (49), and cites the use of whalebone for the queen's petticoat (68). At the beginning of chapter 90 of *Moby-Dick*, Melville uses the same Bracton that Sampson used on p. 49 of his work.

90. Davezac, "A Lay Sermon at Sea"; *Democratic Review* 8 (October 1840), 339, 344, 338. Melville, *Moby-Dick*, 491.

91. Like Livingston and Sampson, Melville's uncle, Thomas Melvill, Jr., had a deep feeling for French culture, having lived there for years, and Melville always preserved a sense of his Gallic elegance.

92. Melville wrote out a poem about the Berkshires on the back cover of the book; see Leyda, *Melville Log*, 378–379; Merton Sealts, *Melville's Reading*, 60. Melville may also have borrowed the trope of the Virginian in Vermont, which he used in his essay on Hawthorne, from Catharine Sedgwick's *Redwood* (1824); J. E. A. Smith, *The Poet Among the Hills: Oliver Wendell Holmes in Berkshire* (Boston, 1895), 30.

93. Bucke, *Notes and Fragments*, (Toronto, 1899; repr. 1972), 208, 211; see also Floyd Stovall, *The Long Foreground of Leaves of Grass*, 141. Traubel, *Whitman in Camden*, 5:75–76. The anecdote is longer than this quotation indicates.

94. Joseph Jay Rubin and Charles H. Brown, eds., *Walt Whitman of the New York Aurora: Editor at Twenty-Two* (State College, Pa., 1950), 65. Whitman also attended the anti-

capital punishment meetings held by the *Review* insiders, including Davezac, O'Sullivan, Edmonds, Bryant, Hawthorne, and others; see Holloway, *The Uncollected Poetry and Prose of Walt Whitman* (New York, 1932), 2:15–16; 1:136. Whitman, *Complete Poetry and Selected Prose* (ed. James E. Miller, Jr.; Boston, 1959), 7; *Gathering of the Forces*, (ed. Cleveland Rogers and John Black; New York, 1920), 2:137. Field, *Speeches*, 2:218.

95. Miller, *The Legal Mind in America*, 294.

96. Ibid., 295. *Democratic Review* 36 (September 1855), 206.

97. Horwitz, *The Transformation of American Law*, 19. Reppy, *David Dudley Field*, 10, 12. *Democratic Review* 30 (April 1852), 300.

98. Edmonds, *An Address*, 5.

99. Miller, *Life of the Mind*, 259. Field, *A Short History of Pleading Under the Code*, 21–22; *New-York Historical Society Proceedings*, 1845, 122.

100. Foner, *Free Soil, Free Labor, Free Men*, 177. His brother, Stephen J. Field, aggressively promoted entrepreneurial causes during his long tenure on the Supreme Court; see Robert Green McCloskey, *American Conservatism in the Age of Enterprise* (Cambridge, 1951), and Carl Swisher, *Stephen J. Field, Craftsman of the Law* (Washington, 1930).

101. *The Law Papers of Benjamin F. Butler*, 5.

102. Theodore Sedgwick, *Address Before the Alumni Association of Columbia College* (New York, 1858), 11.

103. The *Democratic Review* boasted Butler was descended both from a regicide and Cromwell's sister; 5 (January 1839), 34. Field and Robert Rantoul also grew up with a special fondness for Milton, which may explain some of their later convictions; see Rantoul, *Memoirs*, 3. In 1848, the same year Field promulgated his code, Joel Headley issued *The Life of Oliver Cromwell*, linking the American and Puritan Revolutions: "But for Cromwell's effort and success, it is very doubtful whether the Puritans on this side of the water would have ventured on a contest with the mother-country." *Democratic Review* 23 (October 1848), 334.

104. Field, *Speeches*, 3:352–162, 366–371; Simms was cited on p. 367.

105. Ibid., 2:220.

6 *Young America Redux*

1. Karl Marx, *The Eighteenth Brumaire of Louis Napoleon* (New York, 1963), 15; Marx was sending his articles to Joseph Weydemeyer, who was affiliated with the German radical group Jung Amerika, a distant cousin to the American version; see Siert Riepma, "Young America: A Study in American Nationalism Before the Civil War" (Western Reserve University, 1939), 67–68, for more on the Germans.

2. O'Sullivan to Dorr, January 18, 1846, Dorr Papers, Rider Collection, Brown University Library.

3. O'Sullivan had also profiled Polk in his magazine when he was a congressman; see *Democratic Review* 2 (May 1838), 197–208. O'Sullivan to Van Buren, March 1, 1845, March 28, 1845; Van Buren Papers, Library of Congress; see also Charles Sellers, *James K. Polk, Continentalist, 1843–1846* (Princeton, 1966), 199–200. O'Sullivan to Dorr, November 1, 1846, Dorr Papers, Rider Collection, Brown University Library. For background on the Cuba question, see Basil Rauch, *American Interest in Cuba: 1848–1855*, (New York, 1948), 48–80.

4. Robert E. May, *The Southern Dream of a Caribbean Empire, 1854–1861* (Athens, Ga., 1973, 1989), 7. Amos Aschbach Ettinger, *The Mission to Spain of Pierre Soulé, 1853–1855: A Study in the Cuban Diplomacy of the United States* (New Haven, 1932), 318.

5. O'Sullivan to Buchanan, July 6, 1847, Historical Society of Pennsylvania.

6. Ibid., March 19, 1848.

7. *Polk: The Diary of a President, 1845–1849* (ed. Allan Nevins; London 1929), 321.

Frederick Merk, *The Monroe Doctrine and American Expansionism, 1843–1849* (New York, 1968), 259.

8. *The Correspondence of John C. Calhoun* (ed. J. Franklin Jameson; Washington, 1900), 1,202–1,203. O'Sullivan's letter, dated August 24, 1849, which he wrote from Atlanta on the way to New Orleans, showed contempt for the American neutrality laws and proposed all manner of ways Southerners might "legally" go to Cuba to join the fighting. He also threatened Calhoun that Spain might be so desperate to maintain Cuba they might turn it into another "San Domingo." In other words, O'Sullivan cared little for slavery one way or the other as long as the United States acquired more territory. May, *The Southern Dream of a Caribbean Empire*, 52. One of the chief annexationists was John Quitman, the secessionist governor of Mississippi. O'Sullivan wrote him with great secrecy from New York and Lisbon; see the Quitman Papers, Harvard University Library. See also O'Sullivan to George Cadwalader, October 24, 1849, Historical Society of Pennsylvania; O'Sullivan to Tilden, May 17, 1850, Tilden Collection, Mss. Division, New York Public Library.

9. Rauch, *American Interest in Cuba*, 114, 135, 147, 152; Merk, *Manifest Destiny and Mission* (New York, 1963), 167–168. For more on Lopez, see Charles H. Brown, *Agents of Manifest Destiny: The Lives and Times of the Filibusters* (Chapel Hill, 1980); Herminio Portell Vila, *Narciso Lopez y su Epoca* (Havana, 1930, 1952). May also treats Lopez in *The Southern Dream of a Caribbean Empire*, 25–29. For more on the "Cuban State Trials," see *Democratic Review* 30 (April 1852), 307–319. The expeditions themselves were described in the *Democratic Review* 31 (September–December 1852), 209–224, 352–368, 553–592. See also Sheldon Harris, "The Public Career of John Louis O'Sullivan" (Ph.D. diss., Columbia University, 1958) 275–320.

10. O'Sullivan to Van Buren, May 28, 1844, Van Buren Papers, Library of Congress. Parke Godwin was the most sympathetic, but even he advocated gradual annexation; see "Annexation," in *Political Essays* (New York, 1856), 128–174.

11. *Whittier* (ed. Donald Hall; New York, 1960), 96.

12. *Congressional Globe* 25 (32nd Congress, 1st Session), 302. Landon Fuller confirmed O'Sullivan's presence on the new editorial staff; "The United States Magazine and Democratic Review," 108. Sanders to Caleb Cushing; cited in Robert W. Johannsen, *Stephen A. Douglas* (New York, 1973), 361.

13. See Merle Curti, "George N. Sanders—American Patriot of the Fifties," *South Atlantic Quarterly* 27 (January 1928), 79–87; *The Political Correspondence of the Late George N. Sanders* (New York, 1914); Donald S. Spencer, *Louis Kossuth and Young America: A Study of Sectionalism and Foreign Policy, 1848–1852* (Columbia, Mo., 1977), 116–120; Riepma, "Young America," 74–75. Sanders's grandfather was George Nicholas, a revolutionary colonel who was close to Jefferson and James Wilkinson and had emigrated to Kentucky from Virginia. There he had participated with Wilkinson in land speculation and conspiracies with the Spanish at New Orleans. An anonymously written book entitled *Glimpses of New-York City* (Charleston, 1852) credited Sanders as "the originator of the 'Young America' principles," 72.

14. Curti, "George N. Sanders," 81.

15. Law's shipping lines transported fortune-seekers there (as well as to Havana and New Orleans), and John Weller moved from Ohio to defend Young America as a California senator. Robert W. Johannsen, *The Frontier, the Union and Stephen A. Douglas* (Urbana, Ill., 1989), 295.

16. Other editors included the Irish revolutionaries, T. Devin Reilly and John Savage, and William Corry, a Cincinnati journalist; Landon Fuller, "The United States Magazine and Democratic Review . . . ," Ph.D. diss., University of North Carolina, 1948. 108. Another editor whom Fuller did not identify was Charles Frederick Henningsen, who had fought for republicanism across Europe from Spain to Hungary. *Democratic Review* 30 (January 1852), 1, 5, 12, 51.

17. Ibid. 30 (February 1852), 185; (March 1852), 211.

18. Ibid. 30 (April 1852), 289, 300. I have assumed most of the editorials from 1852 to be Sanders's from their tone and from hints in the Sanders-Douglas correspondence, though some of them could be O'Sullivan's. Sanders would have been pleased to know the yacht *Young America* defended democracy in the 1995 America's Cup (though not very swiftly).

19. Ibid. 30 (April 1852), 376.

20. Ibid. (April 1852), 369.

21. Ibid. (March 1852), 209, 212.

22. Ibid. (January 1852), 93.

23. On Margaret Fuller's revolutionary activities, see Larry Reynolds, *European Revolutions and the American Literary Renaissance* (New Haven, 1988), 54–78; *Democratic Review* 30 (May 1852), 397.

24. *Democratic Review* 30 (May 1852), 93.

25. Ibid. (May 1852), 396, 398, 399. The closest the Sanders *Review* came to literary ambition was the mediocre poem "Young America;" 31 (July 1852), 86–87.

26. *Democratic Review* 30 (January 1852), 1.

27. See Spencer, *Louis Kossuth; The Political Correspondence of the Late Hon. George N. Sanders*, n.p. (Kossuth to Sanders, n.p. (Jan. 27, 1852). Luther S. Mansfield, "Glimpses of Herman Melville's Life in Pittsfield," 48. Reynolds, *European Revolutions and the American Literary Renaissance*, 7–10.

28. Spencer, *Louis Kossuth*, 96–106. Mike Walsh to John Quitman, September 6, 1854; Quitman Papers, Harvard University Library.

29. Rossi, *The Image of America in Mazzini's Writings* (Madison, 1954), 101. Hawthorne, *The Letters, 1853–1856*, (eds. Thomas Woodson, James A. Rubino, L. Neal Smith, Norman Holmes Pearson; Columbus, Ohio, 1987), 230.

30. Parke Godwin, *Political Essays*, 147; *Democratic Review* 30 (March 1852), 214.

31. Ettinger, *Mission to Spain of Pierre Soulé*, 125. Kossuth's anti-Russian sentiments can be read in Rossi, *Image of America in Mazzini's Writings*, 83–84; James Buchanan shrewdly calculated that a Russo-American war would be "the most harmless war ever waged between two powerful nations. Russia would not be mad enough to send troops here and we could not, if we would, send any considerable number of troops to Russia"; see Spencer, *Louis Kossuth and Young America*, 131. James P. Shenton, *Robert P. Walker: A Politician from Jackson to Lincoln* (New York, 1961), xv. A speech Kossuth gave in Salem during his tour painted the Russo-American rivalry in surprisingly modernistic tones; see Rossi, *Image of America in Mazzini's Writings*, 83–84.

32. Ettinger, *The Mission to Spain of Pierre Soulé*, 119. Johannsen, *Stephen A. Douglas*, 346.

33. Roy Franklin Nichols, *The Democratic Machine: 1850–1854* (New York, 1923), 107. *The Letters of Stephen A. Douglas* (ed. Robert W. Johannsen; Urbana, 1961), 228, 233–234, 237.

34. Rauch, *American Interest in Cuba*, 212–213. For more on Law, see *A Sketch of Events in the Life of George Law* (New York, 1855). Law's father was Irish, like O'Sullivan's, although he strangely became prominent in the Know Nothing movement.

35. Johannsen, *Stephen A. Douglas*, 345. Stephen Douglas, *Speech of the Honorable Stephen A. Douglass* [sic], *on the Annexation of Texas: Delivered in the House of Representatives, January 6, 1845*, 7.

36. *Congressional Globe*, 27 (32nd Congress, 2nd Session, Appendix), 173. The debate with Cass is on p. 175. The date of the debate was February 14, 1853.

37. Roy F. Nichols, *The Democratic Machine*, 117. *Democratic Review* 30 (March 1852), 205.

38. Riepma, "Young America," 194. See Curti, "Young America," 38; Ettinger, *Mission to Spain of Pierre Soulé*, 130; Johannsen, *Stephen A. Douglas*, 347. For more on the others, see Reginald Charles McGrane, *William Allen: A Study in Western Democracy* (Columbus, Ohio, 1925); James P. Shenton, *Robert John Walker: A Politician From Jackson to Lincoln* (New York, 1961); Ettinger, *Mission to Spain of Pierre Soulé*; George Fort Milton, *The Eve of Conflict: Stephen A. Douglas and the Needless War* (Boston, 1934), 6. The *Democratic Review* of April 1852 also identified Edward Marshall of California as an important ally.

39. Robert W. Johannsen, "Stephen A. Douglas and the American Mission," in John G. Clark, ed., *The Frontier Challenge: Responses to the Trans-Mississippi West* (Lawrence, Kan., 1971), 115.

40. Ibid., 113–114, 123.

41. James J. Barnes, *Authors, Publishers and Politicians: The Quest for an Anglo-American Copyright Agreement, 1815–1854* (Columbus, Ohio 1974), 199, 214; Milton, *The Eve of Conflict*, 3. Johannsen, "Stephen A. Douglas and the American Mission," 113, 117. Nichols, *The Democratic Machine*, 118.

42. Melville, *Moby-Dick*, 191.

43. Melville, *Moby-Dick*, 194.

44. *Democratic Review* 30 (January 1852), 9, 11, 12; Spencer, *Louis Kossuth and Young America*, 120. Indulging further his penchant for disturbing metaphors, Sanders saw the tiny Douglas as "a second Hercules" coming to "cleanse the Augean stable"; *Democratic Review* 30 (January 1852), 3.

45. Johannsen, ed., *The Letters of Stephen A. Douglas*, 246–247; Milton, *Eve of Conflict*, 88; Johannsen, *Stephen A. Douglas*, 373.

46. Nathaniel Hawthorne, *Life of Franklin Pierce* (1852; New York, 1983), 137 138. *Democratic Review* 31 (September 1852), 277, 278, 279.

47. Edmund Burke to Pierce, June 14, 1852, cited in Curti, "Young America," 45.

48. *Democratic Review* 20 (June 1852), 482, 492; "O K" stood for "ol Kworwrecked, Kooba, Kanada." Pierce was called by rival papers "a discreet representative of Young America"; see Rauch, *American Interest in Cuba*, 225. *Revue des Deux Mondes* 16 (new period), 793–794; Curti, "Young America," 46; Rossi, *The Image of America in Mazzini's Writings*, 93. Charles H. Brown provides helpful background on the activities of the filibusters in the 1852 election; *Agents of Manifest Destiny*, 89–108.

49. Rauch, *American Interest in Cuba*, 220; Rossi, *Image of America in Mazzini's Writings*, 17–30, 105; Riepma, "Young America," 67–68.

50. Rossi, *Image of America in Mazzini's Writings*, 93; Brown, *Agents of Manifest Destiny*, 109–123.

51. Ettinger, *The Mission to Spain of Pierre Soulé*, 163–166, 172–5, 338–339; Rauch, *American Interest in Cuba*, 260; Curti, "Young America, 54; Rossi, *Image of America in Mazzini's Writings*, 95; Roy Franklin Nichols, *Franklin Pierce: Young Hickory of the Granite Hills* (Philadelphia, 1931), 254.

52. Gansevoort Melville's old position, secretary of legation at London, was given to Dan Sickles, another prominent Young American; see Ettinger, *Mission to Spain of Pierre Soulé*, 177. On Sanders's comportment as consul, see Ettinger, *Mission to Spain of Pierre Soulé*, passim; Curti, "George N. Sanders," passim; and Rossi, *Image of America in Mazzini's Writings*, 95–98.

53. Melville, *Moby-Dick*, 121. Curti, "George N. Sanders," 79, 86; Rauch, *American Interest in Cuba*, 283; Ettinger, *Mission to Spain of Pierre Soulé*, 317; Curti, "Young America," 48; Rossi, *Image of America in Mazzini's Writings*, 96.

54. May, *The Southern Dream of a Caribbean Empire*, 41. Ettinger, *Mission to Spain of Pierre Soulé*, 353, 324, 363–364. Rossi, *Image of America in Mazzini's Writings*, 101. O'Sulli-

van claimed to know relatively little of the Ostend activities, see O'Sullivan to Buchanan, November 28, 1854, Historical Society of Pennsylvania.

55. *The Political Correspondence of the Late Hon. George N. Sanders*, n.p. (letter 82, Hugo to Sanders, Oct. 31, 1854). Soulé also secretly visited Hugo; see Ettinger, *Mission to Spain of Pierre Soulé*, 315. *The Political Correspondence of the Late Hon. George N. Sanders*, n. p. (letter 73, Hawthorne to Sanders, May 11, 1854); Hawthorne, *The Letters, 1853–1856*, 283. Hawthorne, *The Letters, 1853–1856*, 142n.

56. Florence Addicks, "O'Sullivan Family Notes," 4:74, Historical Society of Pennsylvania. Leyda, *Melville Log*, 409. O'Sullivan to Dorr, November 18, 1853, Dorr Papers, Rider Collection, Brown University Library.

57. Julian Hawthorne, *Hawthorne and His Circle*, (New York, 1903), 135. Hawthorne, *The Letters, 1853–1856*, 289, 303, 318, 334, 395. He did this favor only from pure friendship, for as he wrote William Ticknor, he had no confidence whatsoever in O'Sullivan's "business-qualifications."

58. Hawthorne, *The Letters, 1853–1856*, 391, 401, 411, 376, 425; Julian Hawthorne, *Hawthorne and His Circle*, 135–138; Julian Hawthorne, *Hawthorne and His Wife*, (Boston, 1884), 2:60–101.

59. Nathaniel Hawthorne, *The Letters, 1857–1864* (eds. Thomas Woodson, James A. Rubino, L. Neal Smith, Norman Holmes Pearson; Columbus, Ohio, 1987), 40; Harris, "The Public Career of John Louis O'Sullivan," 372–379.

60. Hawthorne, *The Letters, 1853–1856*, 256.

61. Ibid., 437–439.

62. Ibid., 572–573; *The Letters of Herman Melville*, 185; Hawthorne, *The Letters, 1843–1853*, 700.

63. Hawthorne, *The Letters, 1857–1864*, 425.

64. Rauch, *American Interest in Cuba*, 227; Ettinger, *Mission to Spain of Pierre Soulé*, 339. Belmont was also the nephew by marriage of John Slidell, the Louisiana politician. For more on these financial Young Americans, see Ivor Bernstein, *The New York City Draft Riots: Their Significance for American Society and Politics in the Age of the Civil War* (New York, 1990), 132–145.

65. Rauch, *American Interest in Cuba*, 219; George Francis Train, *An American Merchant Abroad* (New York, 1857), vi; *Young America in Wall Street* began with a generational statement of support for the young man having "a hard fight in the battle of life, and met with little or no encouragement from the old" (iii). Train quoted in Siert F. Riepma, "Young America," 21.

66. *Democratic Review* 30 (April, 1852), 321, 332. Using a bizarre illustration, Sanders wrote of the Chinese, they were "the vanguard of that great Asiatic commercial army which is to pour hereafter the hoarded wealth of old dotard Custom at the feet of the youthful giant Enterprise," fulfilling "the Grecian myth of the daughter giving suck to the sire." Herman Melville, *Moby-Dick*, 110; E. Daniel Potts and Annette Potts, *Young America and Australian Gold: Americans and the Gold Rush of the 1850s* (St. Lucia, Queensland, Australia, 1974); Train, *An American Merchant Abroad*, passim. See Riepma, "Young America," for more on the various groups under the Young American rubric, including the humor magazines (21n).

67. Curti, "Young America," 41; Rauch, *American Interest in Cuba*, 219–221.

68. Theodore Parker, *Additional Speeches, Addresses, and Occasional Sermons* (Boston, 1855), II, 433. Orestes Brownson, *The Spirit-Rapper* (Boston, 1854), 257; Harold Peterson, *The Man Who Invented Baseball* (New York, 1969), 82. Riepma, "Young America," 24.

69. Mathews, "Song of the Tetractys," Mathews Correspondence File, Duyckinck Collection, Mss. Division, New York Public Library.

70. Theodore Sedgwick, *Address Before the Alumni Association of Columbia College*, 33–34. Robert E. May asserts Sedgwick was in favor of annexing Cuba (*The Southern Dream of a Caribbean Empire*, 180), but this must have conflicted with his antislavery sentiments.

71. Simms to Duyckinck, August 12, 1865, Simms Collection, Columbia University Library.

72. An exception among the Pierce appointees was Dan Sickles, Pierce's secretary of legation at London, who became a Union general. Nathaniel Hawthorne, "Chiefly About War Matters," *The Atlantic* 10 (July 1862), 47n.

73. Melville, *White-Jacket*, 436; *The Piazza Tales and Other Prose Pieces*, 361–362; *The Confidence-Man*, 165. Just as Sanders had tried to supply the European liberals with weapons in 1848 and 1852, O'Sullivan began making armaments at a Spanish copper mine in the late 1850s; see Harris, "The Public Career of John Louis O'Sullivan," 393–395.

74. Melville, *Battle-Pieces and Aspects of the War* (ed. Sidney Kaplan; Amherst, 1972), 260; *Clarel: A Poem and Pilgrimage in the Holy Land* (ed. Harrison Hayford, Alma H. Mac-Dougall, Hershel Parker, and G. Thomas Tanselle; Evanston, 1991), 609; *The Complete Poems of Herman Melville*, 247.

75. John Bigelow, *Retrospections of an Active Life*, 1:279–280.

76. O'Sullivan to Tilden, May 6, 1861, Tilden Collection, Mss. Division, New York Public Library.

77. O'Sullivan to Buchanan, January 10, 1861, Historical Society of Pennsylvania; O'-Sullivan to Tilden, June 25, 1861; June 5, 1861; Tilden Collection, Mss. Division, New York Public Library.

78. O'Sullivan to Tilden, June 5, 1861; June 25, 1861, May 6, 1861; Tilden Collection, Mss. Division, New York Public Library. See also John Bigelow, ed., *Letters and Literary Memorials of Samuel J. Tilden* (New York, 1908), 1:157–162. Years earlier, O'Sullivan had denied the right of a state to secede in the *New York Morning News* (November 29, 1845).

79. O'Sullivan to Tilden, June 25, 1861; August 1, 1861; June 5, 1861; Tilden Collection, Mss. Division, New York Public Library.

80. O'Sullivan to Jefferson Davis, September 5, 1863, Special Collections, Duke University Library.

81. Sheldon Harris, "John L. O'Sullivan Serves the Confederacy," *Civil War History* 10 (September 1964), 286.

82. John L. O'Sullivan, *Union, Disunion and Reunion* (London, 1862), 4–5, 19, 37.

83. John L. O'Sullivan, *Peace the Sole Chance Now Left for Reunion* (London, 1863), 9; he even threw in a gratuitous insult to Nicholas Biddle (17), confirming how anachronistic his mind had become.

84. O'Sullivan, *Peace the Sole Chance*, 10–11; his last pamphlet, *Recognition: Its International Legality, its Justice, and its Policy* (London, 1863), continued to identify the South with the republican struggles; see also George Fredrickson, *The Inner Civil War: Northern Intellectuals and the Crisis of the Union* (New York, 1965), 132–134.

85. Alexander Clarence Flick, *Samuel Jones Tilden: A Study in Political Sagacity* (New York, 1939), 146. It is interesting to note that George Train, the financial Young American, also supported the Parisian radicals in 1870. For more on later manifestations of the *Review*, see Landon Fuller, "The United States Magazine and Democratic Review," 116–139.

86. *Congressional Globe* 27 (32nd Congress, 2nd Session, Appendix), 175.

87. *Lamb's Biographical Dictionary of the United States* (ed. John Howard Brown; Boston, 1903), 6:89.

88. O'Sullivan to James Russell Lowell, February 25, 1885, Lowell Papers, Harvard University Library.

89. Julian Hawthorne, *Hawthorne and His Circle*, 136–137.

90. Rev. R. T. Nichol, "Stray Notes on Cavalier and Jacobite Families in America," *The Royalist* 5, no. 7 (October 1894), 103–107 and insert photograph.

91. O'Sullivan to Dr. P. B. Russell, August 25, 1861; cited in Florence Addicks, "O'Sullivan Family Notes," 3:58, Historical Society of Pennsylvania. *New York Evening Post* (March 26, 1895); Columbiana Collection, Columbia University Library.

Epilogue

1. *Boston Globe* (May 21, 1994), p. 3.

2. Parke Godwin wrote something similar on the theory that America most closely resembled the world of classical antiquity: "Ours is sometimes called the youngest of the nations, and yet in the sense of the adage, that 'the antiquity of time was the youth of the world,' it is the oldest of nations." Godwin, "The Future Republic," Bryant-Godwin Collection, Mss. Division, New York Public Library. Melville expressed the same thought in *Clarel.*

3. "Young India" was both the name of Gandhi's newspaper and an early book; see Mahatma Gandhi, *Young India, 1919–1922* (New York, 1923).

4. Stuart Schram, ed., *The Political Thought of Mao Tse-tung* (New York, 1963, 1969), 356, 357, 359, 360.

5. *New York Times Magazine* (October 6, 1996), 54. The speech in which Kennedy most clearly drew on generational themes was his acceptance speech at the 1960 Democratic convention. Curiously, Che Guevara echoed many of Kennedy's favorite themes in the 1960s (youth, commitment); see in particular "On Being a Communist Youth," in John Gerassi, ed. *Venceremos! The Speeches and Writings of Ernesto Che Guevara* (New York, 1968).

6. Newt Gingrich, *To Renew America* (New York, 1995), 6, 29, 60, 25.

7. Ibid., 56, 34, 33.

8. Ibid., 32. Equally confusing is this remark: "Because we have been so empowered by our dreams and our right to pursue our dreams, we have become a great country filled with good people" (248).

9. Gustave Flaubert, *The Sentimental Education* (trans. Perdita Burlingame, afterword by F. W. Dupee; New York, 1972), 437.

10. Charles Baudelaire, *The Painter of Modern Life* (trans. Jonathan Mayne; New York, 1964), 72, 94.

11. George Fredrickson, *The Inner Civil War: Northern Intellectuals and the Crisis of the Union* (New York, 1965), 132.

12. *New York Tribune* (March 23, 1846).

13. Parke Godwin, "The Future Republic," Bryant-Godwin Collection, Mss. Division, New York Public Library. Godwin, *Political Essays*, 177–179.

14. Parke Godwin, *Political Essays*, (New York, 1856), 177–179, 181; Godwin, "The Future Republic," 33–34; Bryant-Godwin Collection, Mss. Division, New York Public Library.

15. Hawthorne, *The Letters, 1853–1856*, 438.

16. Cited in Riepma, "Young America: A Study in American Nationalism Before the Civil War" (Western Reserve University, 1939), 245.

17. Herman Melville, *The Piazza Tales and Other Prose Pieces* (edited by Harrison Hayford, Alma A. MacDougall and G. Thomas Tanselle; Evanston, 1987), 246, 249; *Moby-Dick* (Evanston, 1988), 492.

18. Hawthorne, *Tales and Sketches* (New York, 1982), 499.

19. Randolph Bourne, *History of a Literary Radical and Other Essays* (ed. Van Wyck Brooks; New York, 1969), xii, 18, 13.

20. Ibid., 292, 118, xvi, xxix, 298–299. Brooks gave the title "Young America" to a section

of his book *Letters and Leadership* (1918), republished in *Three Essays on America* (1934) and *America's Coming of Age* (1958).

21. Ernest Hemingway, *A Moveable Feast*, (New York, 1964), 30.

22. Walter I. Trattner, *From Poor Law to Welfare State: A History of Social Welfare in America* (New York, 1974), 109.

23. O'Sullivan to Annie Ward, November 2, 1842, Yale University Library.

24. Lincoln, *Selected Speeches and Writings*, 200–201.

25. Ibid., 201, 207.

Sources

Note: This is intended as a helpful guide to the principal sources consulted; it is not an exhaustive list of every work cited in the text. Amplified references can be found in the notes.

PRIMARY

Manuscript Collections

Boston Public Library: Griswold Collection, Miscellaneous Correspondence
Brown University Library: Thomas Wilson Dorr Papers (Rider Collection)
Columbia County (NY) Historical Society: Francis Edmonds Diaries
Columbia University Library: Columbiana Collection, William Gilmore Simms Papers
Duke University Library: Field-Musgrave Papers, Trent Collection
Harvard University Library: Henry Wadsworth Longfellow Papers, James Russell Lowell Papers, John Quitman Papers, Charles Sumner Papers, John Greenleaf Whittier Papers
Library of Congress: William Marcy Papers, Franklin Pierce Papers, James Knox Polk Papers, George Sanders Papers, Martin Van Buren Papers
Maine Historical Society: O'Sullivan Correspondence
Massachusetts Historical Society: Bancroft Collection, Sedgwick Collection
New York Public Library: Bryant-Godwin Collection, Bigelow Collection, Duyckinck Collection, Gansevoort-Lansing Collection, Tilden Collection
Princeton University Library: Benjamin F. Butler Papers, Miscellaneous Correspondence
Private Collector: Francis Edmonds Manuscript Autobiographies
University of Notre Dame Library: Orestes Brownson Papers (microfilm)
Yale University Library: Julia Ward Howe Papers, Miscellaneous Correspondence

Published Primary Sources

Adams, John Quincy. *The Memoirs of John Quincy Adams*. Edited by Charles Francis Adams. Philadelphia, 1874–1877.
A Sketch of Events in the Life of George Law. New York, 1855.
Amory, Thomas Coffin. *Materials for a History of the Family of John Sullivan of Berwick, New England and of the O'Sullivan Family of Ardea, Ireland*. Cambridge, Mass., 1893.
Baldwin, Joseph G. *The Flush Times of the Alabama and the Mississippi*. Introduction by William A. Owens. New York, 1957.
Bigelow, John. *Retrospections of a Busy Life*. New York, 1909.

Bridge, Horatio. *Journal of an African Cruiser*. Introduction by Donald H. Simpson. London, 1968.

———. *Personal Recollections of Nathaniel Hawthorne*. New York, 1893.

Briggs, Charles F. ["Harry Franco"] *The Trippings of Tom Pepper; or, the Results of Romancing*. New York, 1847.

Brownson, Orestes. *The Works of Orestes A. Brownson*. Edited by Henry F. Brownson. Detroit, 1882–1887.

Butler, Benjamin F. *The Law School Papers of Benjamin F. Butler*. Edited by Ronald L. Brown. New York, 1987.

———. *Outline of the Constitutional History of New York*. New York, 1848.

Butler, William Allen. *The Revision of the Statutes of the State of New York and the Revisers*. New York, 1889.

Catalogue of Works by the Late Henry Inman with a Biographical Sketch. New York, 1846.

Cheever, George B. *Capital Punishment: The Argument of the Rev. George B. Cheever in Reply to J. L. O'Sullivan, Esq*. New York, 1843.

Congressional Globe. Volume 27, 32nd Congress, 2nd Session, Appendix. Washington, 1853.

Cooper, James Fenimore. *Home as Found*. Introduction by Lewis Leary. New York, 1961.

Dana, Richard Henry, Jr. *The Journal of Richard Henry Dana, Jr*. Edited by Robert F. Lucid. Cambridge, Mass., 1968.

DeLeon, Edwin. *The Position and Duties of "Young America."* Columbia, S.C., 1845.

Derby, J. C. *Fifty Years Among Authors, Books and Publishers*. New York, 1884.

Dewey, Mary E. *The Life and Letters of Catharine Maria Sedgwick*. New York, 1871.

Disraeli, Benjamin. *Coningsby, or the New Generation*. New York, 1961.

Douglas, Stephen A. *The Letters of Stephen A. Douglas*. Edited by Robert W. Johannsen. Urbana, 1961.

———. *Speech of the Honorable Stephen A. Douglass* [sic], *on the Annexation of Texas*. Washington, 1845.

Duyckinck, Evert. *National Portrait Gallery of Eminent Americans*. New York, 1862.

Duyckinck, Evert and George. *The Cyclopædia of American Literature*. New York, 1855–1856.

Dunlap, William. *History of the Rise and Progress of the Works of Design in the United States*. New York, 1834.

Edmonds, John W. *An Address on the Constitution and Codes of Procedure*. New York, 1848.

Ellis, Franklin. *History of Columbia County, New York*. Philadelphia, 1878.

Emerson, Ralph Waldo. *Essays and Lectures*. Edited by Joel Porte. New York, 1983.

———. *The Complete Essays and Other Writings*. Edited by Brooks Atkinson. New York, 1950.

———. *The Journals and Miscellaneous Notebooks of Ralph Waldo Emerson*. Edited by Merton M. Sealts, Jr. Cambridge, Mass., 1960–1982.

———. *The Letters of Ralph Waldo Emerson*. Edited by Ralph L. Rusk. New York, 1939.

Field, David Dudley. *An Address to the Graduating Class of the Law School of the University of Albany*. Albany, N.Y., 1855.

———. *The Administration of the Code*. New York, 1852.

———. *The Lawyer and His Clients* . . . Springfield, Mass., 1871.

———. *The Magnitude and Importance of Legal Science*. New York, 1859.

———. *A Short Manual of Pleading Under the Code*. Albany, N.Y., 1856.

———. *Speeches, Arguments, and Miscellaneous Papers of David Dudley Field*. Edited by A. P. Sprague. New York, 1884.

Field, Henry M. *The Family of Rev. David Dudley Field, D. D., of Stockbridge, Mass*. N.p., 1860.

———. *The Life of David Dudley Field*. New York, 1898.

Fields, James T. *Yesterdays with Authors*. Boston, 1878.

Francis, John W. *An Address Delivered on the Anniversary of the Philolexian Society of Columbia College, May 15, 1831*. New York, 1831.

Fuller, S. Margaret. *Papers on Literature and Art*. London, 1846.

Gardiner, O. C. *The Great Issue: or, the Three Presidential Candidates*. New York, 1848.

Godwin, Parke. *Political Essays*. New York, 1856.

Griswold, Rufus. *The Cyclopædia of American Literature: A Review*. New York, 1856.

———. *Prose Writers of America*. Philadelphia, 1847.

Hawthorne, Julian. *Hawthorne and His Circle*. New York, 1903.

———. *Hawthorne and His Wife*. Boston, 1884.

Hawthorne, Nathaniel. *The English Notebooks*. Edited by Randall Stewart. New York, 1962.

———. *The House of the Seven Gables*. Edited by Seymour L. Gross. New York, 1967.

———. *The Letters, 1813–1843*. Edited by Thomas Woodson, L. Neal Smith, and Norman H. Pearson. Columbus, Ohio 1984.

———. *The Letters, 1843–1853*. Edited by Thomas Woodson, L. Neal Smith, and Norman Holmes Pearson. Columbus, Ohio 1985.

———. *The Letters, 1853–1856*. Edited by Thomas Woodson, James A. Rubino, L. Neal Smith, Norman Holmes Pearson. Columbus, Ohio 1987.

———. *The Letters, 1857–1864*. Edited by Thomas Woodson, James A. Rubino, L. Neal Smith, and Norman Holmes Pearson. Columbus, Ohio 1987.

———. *Life of Franklin Pierce*. Edited by Arthur M. Schlesinger, Jr. New York, 1963.

———. *Mosses from an Old Manse*. Boston, 1875.

———. *The Scarlet Letter*. Edited by Sculley Bradley, Richard Croom Beatty, and E. Hudson Long. New York, 1962.

———. Tales and Sketches. New York, 1982.

———. *Twice-Told Tales*. Edited by Fredson Bowers, L. Neal Smith, John Manning, and J. Donald Crowley. Columbus, 1974.

Holmes, Oliver Wendell. *The Complete Works of Oliver Wendell Holmes*. Cambridge, Mass., 1872, 1908.

The Home Book of the Picturesque. New York, 1852.

Hone, Philip. *The Diary of Philip Hone, 1828–1851*. Edited by Allan Nevins. New York, 1927.

Howe, Julia Ward. *Reminiscences, 1819–1899*. Boston, 1899.

Jackson, Andrew. *Correspondence of Andrew Jackson*. Washington, 1926–1935.

Jameson, Mrs. Anna. *Memoirs and Essays, Illustrative of Art, Literature and Social Morals*. New York, 1846.

Jarves, James Jackson. *The Art-Idea*. Edited by Benjamin Rowland. Cambridge, Mass., 1960.

Jones, W. A. *Characters and Criticisms*. New York, 1857.

Kirkland, Caroline. *Western Clearings*. New York, 1845.

Lathers, Richard. *Reminiscences of Richard Lathers*. Edited by Alvan F. Sanborn. New York, 1907.

Leggett, William. *A Collection of the Writings of William Leggett*. Edited by Theodore Sedgwick. New York, 1840.

———. *Democratick Editorials: Essays in Jacksonian Political Economy*. Edited by Lawrence H. White. Indianapolis, 1984.

Lincoln, Abraham. *Selected Speeches and Writings*. Edited by Don. E. Fehrenbacher. New York, 1992.

Longfellow, Henry. *The Letters of Henry Wadsworth Longfellow*. Edited by Andrew Hilen. Cambridge, Mass., 1966.

———. *Kavanagh: A Tale*. Edited by Jean Downey. New Haven, 1965.

Lowell, James Russell. *The Letters of James Russell Lowell*. Edited by Charles Eliot Norton. New York, 1893.

Mackenzie, William L. *The Life and Times of Martin Van Buren*. Boston, 1846.

Mathews, Cornelius. *Americanism: An Address Delivered June, 1845*. New York, 1845.

——. *An Appeal to American Authors and the American Press, in Behalf of International Copyright*. New York, 1842.

——. *Behemoth: A Legend of the Mound-Builders*. Edited by Donald J. Yanella, Jr. New York, 1970.

——. *The Better Interests of the Country, in Connexion with International Copyright*. New York, 1843.

——. *Big Abel and the Little Manhattan*. Edited by Donald J. Yanella, Jr. New York, 1970.

——. *The Career of Puffer Hopkins*. Edited by Donald J. Yanella, Jr. New York, 1970.

——. *The Motley Book: A Series of Tales and Sketches*. New York, 1838.

——. *A Speech on International Copyright*. New York, 1842.

Melville, Herman. *The Collected Poems of Herman Melville*. Edited by Howard P. Vincent. Chicago, 1947.

——. *The Confidence-Man*. Edited by Harrison Hayford, Hershel Parker, and G. Thomas Tanselle. Evanston, 1984.

——. *Israel Potter*. Edited by Harrison Hayford, Hershel Parker, and G. Thomas Tanselle. Evanston, 1982.

——. *The Letters of Herman Melville*. Edited by Merrell R. Davis and William H. Gilman. New Haven, 1960.

——. *Mardi: And a Voyage Thither*. Edited by Harrison Hayford, Hershel Parker, and G. Thomas Tanselle. Evanston, 1970.

——. *Moby-Dick*. Edited by Luther S. Mansfield and Howard P. Vincent. New York, 1952.

——. *Moby-Dick*. Edited by Harrison Hayford and Hershel Parker. New York, 1967.

——. *Moby-Dick or The Whale*. Edited by Harrison Hayford, Hershel Parker, and G. Thomas Tanselle. Evanston, 1988.

——. *The Piazza Tales and Other Prose Pieces, 1839-1860*. Edited by Harrison Hayford, Alma A. MacDougall, and G. Thomas Tanselle. Evanston, 1987.

——. *Pierre, or The Ambiguities*. Edited by Harrison Hayford, Hershel Parker, and G. Thomas Tanselle. Evanston, 1971.

Melville: The Critical Heritage. Edited by Watson G. Branch. London, 1974.

Moran, Benjamin. *The Journal of Benjamin Moran, 1857–1865*. Edited by Sarah Agnes Wallace and Frances Ellen Gillespie. Chicago, 1948.

New-York Historical Society Proceedings, 1845. New York, 1846.

O'Sullivan, John Louis. *Peace the Sole Chance Now Left for Reunion*. London, 1863.

——. *Recognition: Its International Legality, its Justice and its Policy*. London, 1863.

——. *Report in Favor of the Abolition of the Punishment of Death by Law . . .* New York, 1841.

——. *Union, Disunion and Reunion*. London, 1862.

Parker, Theodore. "The Destination of America" (1848). In *American Literature*, edited by Carl Bode, Leon Howard, and Louis B. Wright. New York, 1966.

Paulding, James Kirke. *The Merry Tales of the Three Wise Men of Gotham*. New York, 1839.

Peabody, Elizabeth. *The Letters of Elizabeth Palmer Peabody: American Renaissance Woman*. Edited by Bruce A. Ronda. Middletown, 1984.

Poe, Edgar Allan. *The Complete Works of Edgar Allan Poe*. Edited by James A. Harrison. New York, 1902.

——. *The Letters of Edgar Allan Poe*. Edited by John Ward Ostrom. Cambridge, Mass., 1948.

Polk, James Knox. *Polk: The Diary of a President, 1845–1849*. Edited by Allan Nevins. London, 1929.

Proceedings of the Massachusetts Historical Society.

Putnam, George Palmer. *American Facts*. London, 1845.

Rantoul, Robert, Jr. *The Memoirs, Speeches and Writings of Robert Rantoul, Jr.* Edited by Luther Hamilton. Boston, 1854.

Sampson, William. *An Anniversary Discourse, Delivered Before the Historical Society of New York . . . on the Common Law*. New York, 1824.

———. *Is a Whale a Fish? An Accurate Report of the Case of James Maurice against Samuel Judd . . .* New York, 1819.

———. *Memoirs of William Sampson, An Irish Exile*. London, 1832.

Sanders, George Nicholas. *The Political Correspondence of the Late George N. Sanders*. New York, 1914.

Sedgwick, Henry. *The English Practice: A Statement Showing Some of the Evils and Absurdities of the Practice of the English Common Law as Adopted in Several of the United States and Particularly in the State of New York*. New York, 1822.

Sedgwick, Theodore [II]. *Hints to My Countrymen*. New York, 1826.

———. *Hints for the People*. New York, 1823.

———. *Public and Private Economy*. New York, 1836–1839.

Sedgwick, Theodore [III]. *An Address Before the Alumni Association of Columbia College*. New York, 1858.

———. *The American Citizen: His True Position, Character and Duties*. New York, 1847.

———. *A Memoir of the Life of William Livingston*. New York, 1833.

———. *A Statement of Facts in Relation to the Delays and Arrears of Business in the Court of Chancery of the State of New York with Some Suggestions for a Change in its Organization*. New York, 1857.

Senate Documents. 23rd Congress, 2nd Session. Washington, 1834–1835.

Simms, William Gilmore. *The Letters of William Gilmore Simms*. Edited by Mary C. Simms Oliphant, Alfred Taylor Odell, and T. C. Duncan Eaves. Columbia, S.C., 1952–1982.

———. *Views and Reviews in American Literature*. Edited by C. Hugh Holman. Cambridge, Mass., 1962.

Smith, J. E. A. *The Poet Among the Hills: Oliver Wendell Holmes in Berkshire*. Boston, 1895.

Strong, George Templeton. *The Diary of George Templeton Strong*. Edited by Allan Nevins and Milton Halsey Thomas. New York, 1952.

Sumner, George. "Letters of George Sumner." *Proceedings of the Massachusetts Historical Society* 46 (October 1912), 357–362.

Thoreau, Henry David. *The Correspondence of Thoreau*. Edited by Walter Harding and Carl Bode. New York, 1958.

———. *Walden and Civil Disobedience*. Edited by Owen Thomas. New York, 1966.

Tilden, Samuel. *Letters and Literary Memorials*. Edited by John Bigelow. New York, 1908.

Tocqueville, Alexis de. *Democracy in America*. Edited by Phillips Bradley. New York, 1980.

Train, George Francis. *An American Merchant Abroad*. New York, 1857.

———. *Young America in Wall Street*. New York, 1857.

Transactions of the American Art-Union for the Year 1845. New York, 1844–1848.

Transactions of the Apollo Association. New York, 1840–1842.

Traubel, Horace. *With Whitman in Camden*. Boston, 1906.

Trollope, Frances. *Domestic Manners of the Americans*. Edited by Donald Smalley. New York, 1949.

Verplanck, Gulian. *Discourses and Addresses on Subjects of American History, Arts and Literature*. New York, 1833.

────. *Speech When in Committee of the Whole in the Senate of New-York on the Several Bills and Resolutions for the Amendment of the Law and the Reform of the Judiciary System.* Albany, N.Y., 1839.

Walsh, Michael. *Sketches of the Speeches and Writings of Michael Walsh.* New York, 1843.

Whitman, Walt. *Complete Poetry and Selected Prose.* Edited by James E. Miller, Jr. Boston, 1959.

────. *The Gathering of the Forces.* Edited by Cleveland Rogers and John Black. New York, 1920.

────. *Leaves of Grass.* Edited by Sculley Bradley and Harold W. Blodgett. New York, 1965, 1973.

────. *Notes and Fragments.* Edited by Richard Maurice Bucke. Toronto, 1899, 1972.

────. *Specimen Days.* Boston, 1971.

────. *The Uncollected Prose of Walt Whitman.* Edited by Emory Holloway. New York, 1932.

────. "Whitman in 1850: Three Uncollected Articles." Edited by Rollo G. Silver. *American Literature* 19 (January 1948), 301–317.

Whittier, John Greenleaf. *Whittier.* Edited by Donald Hall. New York, 1960.

Magazines and Weeklies

American Review
Arcturus
Boston Quarterly Review
Broadway Journal
Brownson's Quarterly Review
Bulletin of the American Art-Union
John-Donkey
Knickerbocker
Literary World
New York Review

North American Review
The Pioneer
Revue des Deux Mondes
Southern Literary Messenger
Spirit of the Times
United States Magazine and Democratic Review
Western Monthly Review
Yankee Doodle
Young America

Newspapers

Georgetown Metropolitan
New York Evening Post
New York Mirror
New York Morning News

New York Tribune
New York Weekly News
Washington Globe

SECONDARY SOURCES

Books and Articles

Allen, Gay Wilson. *The Solitary Singer: A Critical Biography of Walt Whitman.* Chicago, 1955, 1985.

Baker, Jean Harvey. *Affairs of Party: The Political Culture of Northern Democrats in the Mid-Nineteenth Century.* Ithaca, N.Y., 1983.

Barnes, Homer F. *Charles Fenno Hoffman.* New York, 1930.

Barnes, James J. *Authors, Publishers and Politicians: The Quest for an Anglo-American Copyright Agreement, 1815–1854.* Columbus, Ohio, 1974.

Bayless, Joy. *Rufus Wilmot Griswold: Poe's Literary Executor.* Nashville, Tenn., 1943.

Baym, Nina. *Novels, Readers and Reviewers: Responses to Fiction in Antebellum America.* Ithaca, N.Y., 1984.

Belknap, Waldron, Jr. *American Colonial Painting: Materials for a History.* Cambridge, Mass., 1959.

Bender, Thomas. *New York Intellect: A History of Intellectual Life in New York City, from 1750 to the Beginning of Our Own Time.* Baltimore, Md., 1987.

Benson, Lee. *The Concept of Jacksonian Democracy: New York as a Test Case.* Princeton, N.J., 1961, 1970.

Bercovitch, Sacvan. *The Office of the Scarlet Letter.* Baltimore, Md., 1991.

Bergan, Philip, ed. *The Fields and the Law.* New York, 1974.

Bernstein, Ivor. *The New York City Draft Riots: Their Significance for American Society and Politics in the Age of the Civil War.* New York, 1990.

Bigelow, John. *The Life of Samuel J. Tilden.* New York, 1895.

——. *William Cullen Bryant.* Boston, 1890.

Blau, Joseph L., ed. *Social Theories of Jacksonian Democracy.* Indianapolis, Ind., 1954.

Bloch, E. Maurice. "The American Art-Union's Downfall." *New-York Historical Society Quarterly* 37 (1953), 331–359.

Bolton, Thomas. "The Book Illustrations of Felix Octavius Carr Darley." *The Proceedings of the American Antiquarian Society* 41 (April 1951), 137–182.

Brancaccio, Patrick. "Hawthorne's Editing of the *Journal of an African Cruiser.*" *New England Quarterly* 53 (March 1980), 23–41.

Brasher, Thomas L. *Whitman as Editor of the Brooklyn Daily Eagle.* Detroit, Mich., 1970.

Brodhead, Richard. *The School of Hawthorne.* New York, 1986.

Brown, Charles H. *Agents of Manifest Destiny: The Lives and Times of the Filibusters.* Chapel Hill, N.C., 1980.

Brown, Thomas Kite III. *Young Germany's View of Romanticism.* New York, 1941.

Buell, Lawrence. *New England Literary Culture: From Revolution through Renaissance.* Cambridge, UK, 1986, 1989.

Callow, James. *Kindred Spirits: Knickerbocker Writers and American Artists, 1807–1855.* Durham, N.C., 1967.

Cantwell, Robert. *Nathaniel Hawthorne: The American Years.* New York, 1948.

Cassedy, David and Shrott, Gail. *William Sidney Mount: Annotated Bibliography and Listing of Archival Holdings of the Museums at Stony Brook.* Stony Brook, N.Y., 1983.

——. *William Sidney Mount: Works in the Collection of the Museums at Stony Brook.* Stony Brook, N.Y., 1983.

Charvat, William. *The Origins of American Critical Thought, 1810–1835.* Philadelphia, 1936.

Clark, H. Nichols B. "A Fresh Look at the Art of Francis W. Edmonds: Dutch Sources and American Meanings." *American Art Journal* 14 (Summer 1982), 73–94.

——. "A Taste for the Netherlands: The Impact of Seventeenth-Century Dutch and Flemish Genre Painting on American Art, 1800–1860." *American Art Journal* 14 (Spring 1982), 23–38.

——. *Francis W. Edmonds: American Master in the Dutch Tradition.* Washington, D.C., 1988.

Colacurcio, Michael J. *The Province of Piety: Moral History in Hawthorne's Early Tales.* Cambridge, Mass., 1984.

Collier, Edward. *A History of Old Kinderhook.* New York, 1914.

Cook, Charles. *The American Codification Movement: A Study of Antebellum Legal Reform.* Westport, Conn., 1981.

Cowdrey, Bartlett and Williams, Hermann Walker, Jr. *William Sidney Mount, 1807–1868: American Genre Painter.* New York, 1944.

Cowdrey, Mary Bartlett, ed. *American Academy of Fine Arts and American Art-Union: Exhibition Record*. New York, 1953.

——. *American Academy of Fine Arts and American Art-Union: Introduction, 1816–1852*. New York, 1953.

Cowen, Walker. *Melville's Marginalia*. New York, 1987.

Curti, Merle. *The American Peace Crusade, 1815–1860*. New York, 1965.

——. "George N. Sanders—American Patriot of the Fifties." *South Atlantic Quarterly* 27 (January 1928), 79–87.

——. "Young America." *American Historical Review* 32 (October 1926), 34–55.

Curtis, James. *The Fox at Bay: Martin Van Buren and the Presdency, 1837–1841*. Lexington, Ky., 1970.

Danbom, David B. "The Young America Movement." *Journal of the Illinois State Historical Society* 67 (1974), pp. 294–306.

Davis, Merrell R. *Melville's Mardi: A Chartless Voyage*. New Haven, Conn., 1952.

Driscoll, William D. *Benjamin F. Butler: Lawyer and Regency Politician*. New York, 1977.

Eaton, Clement. *The Leaven of Democracy*. New York, 1963.

Erkkila, Betsy. *Whitman the Political Poet*. New York, 1989.

Ettinger, Amos Aschbach. *The Mission to Spain of Pierre Soulé, 1853–1855: A Study in the Cuban Diplomacy of the United States*. New Haven, Conn., 1932.

Ferguson, Robert. *Law and Letters in American Culture*. Cambridge, Mass., 1984.

Flexner, James. *That Wilder Image: The Painting of America's Native School from Thomas Cole to Winslow Homer*. New York, 1962, 1970.

Fliegelman, Jay. *Prodigals and Pilgrims: The American Revolt Against Patriarchal Authority, 1750–1800*. New York, 1982.

Foner, Eric. *Free Soil, Free Labor, Free Men: The Ideology of the Republican Party Before the Civil War*. New York, 1970.

Forgie, George. *Patricide in the House Divided: A Psychological Interpretation of Lincoln and His Age*. New York, 1979.

Foshay, Ella M. *Mr. Reed's Picture Gallery: A Pioneer Collection of American Art*. New York, 1990.

Fox, Dixon Ryan. *The Decline of Aristocracy in the Politics of New York, 1801–1840*. New York, 1919, 1965.

Frankenstein, Alfred. *William Sidney Mount*. New York, 1975.

Fredrickson, George. *The Inner Civil War: Northern Intellectuals and the Crisis of Union*. New York, 1965.

Gilmore, Michael T. *American Romanticism and the Marketplace*. Chicago, 1985.

Graebner, Norman, ed. *Manifest Destiny*. Indianapolis, Ind., 1968.

Greenspan, Ezra. "A Publisher's Legacy: The George Palmer Putnam Correspondence." *Princeton University Library Chronicle* 54 (Autumn 1992), 39–63.

——. "Evert Duyckinck and the History of Wiley and Putnam's Library of American Books, 1845–1847." *American Literature* 64 (December 1992), 677–693

Groseclose, Barbara. "Politics and American Genre Painting of the Nineteenth Century." *Antiques* 120 (1981), 1,210–1,217.

Haar, Charles M. *The Golden Age of American Law*. New York, 1965.

Hahler, Christine Anne. . . . *illustrated by Darley*. Wilmington, Del., 1978.

Hall, Lawrence Sargent. *Hawthorne, Critic of Society*. New Haven, Conn., 1944.

Harris, Neil. *The Artist in American Society: The Formative Years, 1790–1860*. Chicago, 1966.

Harris, Sheldon. "John Louis O'Sullivan and the Election of 1844 in New York." *New York History* 41 (July 1960), 278–298.

——. "John O'Sullivan Serves the Confederacy." *Civil War History* 10 (September 1964), 275–290.

Hatcher, William B. *Edward Livingston: Jeffersonian Republican and Jacksonian Democrat.* Baton Rouge, La., 1940.

Heimert, Alan. "Moby-Dick and American Political Symbolism." *American Quarterly* 15 (Winter 1963), 498–534.

Horsman, Reginald. *Race and Manifest Destiny: The Origins of American Racial Anglo-Saxonism.* Cambridge, Mass., 1981.

Horwitz, Morton. *The Transformation of American Law, 1870–1960.* New York, 1992.

——. *The Transformation of American Law, 1780–1860.* Cambridge, Mass., 1977.

Johannsen, Robert W. *The Frontier, the Union and Stephen A. Douglas.* Urbana, Ill., 1989.

——. *Stephen A. Douglas.* New York, 1973.

——. *To the Halls of the Montezumas: The Mexican War in the American Imagination.* New York, 1985.

Johns, Elizabeth. *American Genre Painting: The Politics of Everyday Life.* New Haven, Conn., 1991.

Kerr, Howard. *Mediums, Spirit-Rappers and Roaring Radicals: Spiritualism in American Literature, 1800–1850.* Urbana, Ill., 1972.

Kohl, Lawrence. *The Politics of Individualism: Parties and the American Character in the Jacksonian Era.* New York, 1989.

Kouwenhoven, John A. *The Arts in American Civilization.* New York, 1948, 1967.

Lehmann-Haupt, Helmut. *The Book in America.* New York, 1939.

Leyda, Jay. *The Melville Log: A Documentary Life of Herman Melville.* New York, 1951.

Mann, Maybelle. *Francis William Edmonds.* Washington, D.C., 1975.

Mansfield, Luther S. "Glimpses of Herman Melville's Life in Pittsfield, 1850–1851." *American Literature* 9 (March 1937), pp. 26–48.

Martin, George. *Causes and Conflicts: The Centennial History of the Association of the Bar of the City of New York.* Boston, 1970.

Marx, Karl. *The Eighteenth Brumaire of Louis Napoleon.* New York, 1963.

Masur, Louis P. *Rites of Execution: Capital Punishment and the Transformation of American Culture, 1776–1865.* New York, 1989.

Matthiessen, F. O. *American Renaissance: Art and Expression in the Age of Emerson and Whitman.* New York, 1941.

May, Robert E. *The Southern Dream of a Caribbean Empire, 1854–1861.* Athens, Ga., 1973, 1989,

McCardell, John. *The Idea of a Southern Nation: Southern Nationalists and Southern Nationalism.* New York, 1979.

Mellow, James R. *Nathaniel Hawthorne in His Times.* Boston, 1980.

Merk, Frederick. *Manifest Destiny and Mission in American History.* New York, 1963.

——. *The Monroe Doctrine and American Expansionism, 1843–1849.* New York, 1968.

Meyers, Marvin. *The Jacksonian Persuasion: Politics and Belief.* New York, 1960.

Miller, Lillian. *Patrons and Patriotism: The Encouragement of the Fine Arts in the United States, 1790–1860.* Chicago, 1966.

Miller, Perry. *The Legal Mind in America: From Independence to the Civil War.* Garden City, N.Y., 1962.

——. *The Life of the Mind in America from the Revolution to the Civil War.* New York, 1965.

——. *The Raven and the Whale: The War of Words and Wits in the Era of Poe and Melville.* New York, 1956.

Milton, George Fort. *The Eve of Conflict: Stephen A. Douglas and the Needless War.* Boston, 1934.

Moss, Sidney. *Poe's Literary Battles: The Critic in the Context of his Literary Milieu.* Durham, N.C., 1963.

———. *Poe's Major Crisis: His Libel Suit and New York's Literary World.* Durham, N.C., 1970.

Mott, Frank Luther. *A History of American Magazines, 1741–1850.* Cambridge, Mass., 1939.

Mowry, Arthur May. *The Dorr War: Constitutional Struggle in Rhode Island.* New York, 1970.

Mumford, Lewis. *Herman Melville.* New York, 1929.

Nelson, William E. *Americanization of the Common Law: The Impact of Legal Change on Massachusetts Society, 1760–1830.* Cambridge, Mass., 1975.

Nevins, Winfield S. "Nathaniel Hawthorne's Removal from the Salem Custom House." *Historical Collections of the Essex Institute* 53 (April 1917), 97–132.

Nichols, Roy Franklin. *The Democratic Machine: 1850–1854.* New York, 1923.

Nissenbaum, Stephen. "The Firing of Nathaniel Hawthorne." *Historical Collections of the Essex Institute* 114 (April 1978), 57–86.

Parker, Hershel. *Herman Melville: A Biography; Volume 1, 1819–1851.* Baltimore, Md., 1996.

Paul, James C. N. *Rift in the Democracy.* Philadelphia, 1951.

Pickard, Samuel T. *Life and Letters of John Greenleaf Whittier.* Boston, 1899.

Pollard, John. *John Greenleaf Whittier: Friend of Man.* Boston, 1949.

Portell Vila, Herminio. *Narciso Lopez y Su Epoca (1848–1850).* Havana, 1952.

Potts, E. Daniel and Annette. *Young America and Australian Gold: Americans and the Gold Rush of the 1850s.* St. Lucia, Australia, 1974.

Pratt, Julius W. "John L. O'Sullivan and Manifest Destiny." *American Historical Review* 32 (July 1927), 795–798.

———. "Origin of Manifest Destiny." *New York History* 14 (July 1933), 213–234.

Pritchard, John Paul. *Criticism in America.* Norman, Okla., 1956.

———. *Literary Wise Men of Gotham.* Baton Rouge, La., 1963.

Putnam, George H. *George Palmer Putnam: A Memoir.* New York, 1912.

Rash, Nancy. *The Painting and Politics of George Caleb Bingham.* New Haven, Conn., 1991.

Rauch, Basil. *American Interest in Cuba: 1848–1855.* New York, 1948.

Reynolds, David S. *Beneath the American Renaissance: The Subversive Imagination in the Age of Emerson and Melville.* New York, 1988.

———. *Walt Whitman's America: A Cultural Biography.* New York, 1995.

Reynolds, Larry. *European Revolutions and the American Literary Renaissance.* New Haven, Conn., 1988.

Rice, Harriet Langdon Pruyn. *Harmanus Bleecker: An Albany Dutchman, 1779–1849.* Albany, N.Y., 1924.

Richards, Laura E. and Elliott, Maud Howe. *Julia Ward Howe, 1819–1910.* Boston, 1916.

Robertson, Priscilla. *Revolutions of 1848: A Social History.* New York, 1952, 1960.

Rogin, Michael Paul. *Fathers and Children: Andrew Jackson and the Subjugation of the American Indian.* New York, 1975.

———. *Subversive Genealogy: The Politics and Art of Herman Melville.* New York, 1983.

Rossi, Joseph. *The Image of America in Mazzini's Writings.* Madison, Wis., 1954.

Rubin, Joseph Jay, and Brown, Charles H. *Walt Whitman of the New York Aurora: Editor at Twenty-Two.* State College, Pa., 1950.

Ruland, Richard. *The Native Muse: Theories of American Literature.* New York, 1972.

Runden, John P. "Columbia Grammar School: An Overlooked Year in the Lives of Gansevoort and Herman Melville." *Melville Society Extracts,* no. 46 (May 1981), 1–3.

——. "Old School Ties: Melville, the Columbia Grammar School and the New Yorkers. *Melville Society Extracts*, no. 55 (September 1983), 1–5.

Sanborn, F. B. *Hawthorne and His Friends*. Cedar Rapids, Iowa, 1908.

Saxton, Alexander. *The Rise and Fall of the White Republic: Class Politics and Mass Culture in Nineteenth Century America*. London, 1990.

Schlesinger, Arthur, Jr. *A Pilgrim's Progress: Orestes A. Brownson*. Boston, 1939, 1966.

——. *The Age of Jackson*. Boston, 1945, 1989.

Sealts, Merton, Jr. *Melville's Reading. A Check-List of Books Owned and Borrowed*. Madison, Wis., 1966.

Sedgwick, Sarah Cabot, and Marquand, Christine S. *Stockbridge, 1739–1974*. Stockbridge, Mass., 1974.

Sellers, Charles. *James K. Polk, Continentalist, 1843–1846*. Princeton, N.J., 1966.

——. *The Market Revolution: Jacksonian America, 1815–1846*. New York, 1991.

Shenton, James P. *Robert P. Walker: A Politician from Jackson to Lincoln*. New York, 1961.

Sill, Geoffrey M., and Tarbell, Roberta K., eds. *Walt Whitman and the Visual Arts*. New Brunswick, N.J., 1992.

Smith, Carl S., McWilliams, John P., Jr., and Bloomfield, Maxwell. *Law and American Literature: A Collection of Essays*. New York, 1983.

Smith, Henry Nash. *Virgin Land: The American West as Symbol and Myth*. Cambridge, Mass., 1950, 1978.

Spann, Edward K. *Ideals and Politics: New York Intellectuals and Liberal Democracy, 1820–1880*. Albany, N.Y., 1972.

——. *The New Metropolis: New York City, 1840–1857*. New York, 1981.

Spencer, Benjamin. *The Quest for Nationality: An American Literary Campaign*. Syracuse, N.Y. 1957.

Spencer, Donald S. *Louis Kossuth and Young America: A Study of Sectionalism and Foreign Policy, 1848–1852*. Columbia, Mo., 1977.

Stafford, John. *The Literary Criticism of "Young America": A Study in the Relationship of Politics and Literature, 1837–1850*. Berkeley, Calif., 1952.

——. "William A. Jones, Democratic Literary Critic." *Huntington Library Quarterly* 12 (May 1849), 289–302.

Stebbins, Theodore. *The Life and Works of Martin Joseph Heade*. New Haven, Conn., 1975.

Stein, Allen F. *Cornelius Mathews*. New York, 1974.

Sten, Christopher, ed. *Savage Eye: Melville and the Visual Arts*. Kent, Ohio, 1991.

Stewart, Randall. *Nathaniel Hawthorne: A Biography*. New Haven, Conn., 1948.

Stott, Richard B. *Workers in the Metropolis: Class, Ethnicity and Youth in Antebellum New York City*. Ithaca, N.Y., 1990.

Stovall, Floyd. *The Foreground of Leaves of Grass*. Charlottesville, Va., 1974.

Taft, Kendall B. *Minor Knickerbockers*. New York, 1947.

Tassin, Algernon. *The Magazine in America*. New York, 1916.

Taylor, William R. *Cavalier and Yankee: The Old South and American National Character*. Cambridge, Mass., 1957, 1979.

Thomas, Brook. *Cross-Examinations of Law and Literature*. Cambridge, England, 1987.

Thomas, Dwight, and Jackson, David K. *The Poe Log: A Documentary Life of Edgar Allan Poe, 1809–1849*. Boston, 1987.

Tompkins, Jane. *Sensational Designs: The Cultural Work of American Fiction, 1790–1860*. New York, 1985.

Troyen, Carol. "Retreat to Arcadia: American Landscape and the American Art-Union." *American Art-Journal* 33 (1991), 21–37.

Van Ee, Daun. *David Dudley Field and the Reconstruction of the Law*. New York, 1986.

Vincent, Howard P. *The Trying-Out of Moby-Dick*. Kent, Ohio, 1949, 1980.

Wakelyn, Jon L. *The Politics of a Literary Man: William Gilmore Simms*. Westport, Conn., 1973.

Wallach, Glenn. *Obedient Sons: The Discourse of Youth and Generations in American Culture, 1630–1860*. Amherst, Mass., 1997.

Weinberg, Albert K. *Manifest Destiny: A Study of Nationalist Expansionism in American History*. Baltimore, Md., 1935, 1963.

Welter, Rush. *The Mind of America, 1820–1860*. New York, 1975.

Wilentz, Sean. *Chants Democratic: New York City and the Rise of the American Working Class*. New York, 1984.

Yanella, Donald. "Writing the 'Other Way': Melville, the Duyckinck Crowd, and Literature for the Masses." *A Companion to Melville Studies*, edited by John Bryant, 63–81. New York, 1986.

Zboray, Ronald J. *A Fictive People: Antebellum Economic Development and the American Reading People*. New York, 1993.

Ziff, Larzer. *Literary Democracy: The Declaration of Cultural Independence in America*. New York, 1981.

Zweig, Paul. *Walt Whitman: The Making of the Poet*. New York, 1984.

Dissertations

Cortissoz, Paul. "The Political Life of Nathaniel Hawthorne." Ph.D. diss., New York University, 1955.

Fuller, Landon. "The United States Magazine and Democratic Review, 1837–1859: A Study of its History, Contents and Significance." Ph.D. diss., University of North Carolina, 1948.

Harris, Sheldon. "The Public Career of John Louis O'Sullivan." Ph.D. diss., Columbia University, 1958.

Hobor, Michael Joseph. "The Form of the Law: David Dudley Field and the Codification Movement in New York, 1839–1888." Ph.D. diss., University of Chicago, 1975.

Mize, George E. "The Contributions of Evert A. Duyckinck to the Cultural Development of Nineteenth Century America." Ph.D. diss., New York University, 1954.

Parker, Hershel. "Melville and Politics: A Scrutiny of the Political Milieux of Herman Melville's Life and Works." Ph.D. diss., Northwestern University, 1963.

Reagan, Daniel W. "The Making of an American Author: Melville and the Idea of a National Literature." Ph.D. diss., University of New Hampshire, 1984.

Riepma, Siert F. "Young America: A Study in American Nationalism Before the Civil War." Ph.D. diss., Western Reserve University, 1939.

Roche, Arthur Murray. "A Literary Gentleman in New York." Ph.D. diss., Duke University, 1973.

Wells, Daniel Arthur. "Evert Duyckinck's *Literary World*, 1847–1853: Its Views and Reviews of American Literature." Ph.D. diss., Duke University, 1972.

Index